J. Q. Adams

GREAT DEBATES IN AMERICAN HISTORY

*From the Debates in the British Parliament on the
Colonial Stamp Act (1764–1765) to the Debates
in Congress at the Close of the Taft
Administration (1912–1913)*

EDITED BY

MARION MILLS MILLER, LITT.D. (PRINCETON)

Editor of "The Life and Works of Abraham Lincoln," etc.

IN FOURTEEN VOLUMES

EACH DEALING WITH A SPECIFIC SUBJECT, AND CONTAINING A SPECIAL INTRODUC-
TION BY A DISTINGUISHED AMERICAN STATESMAN OR PUBLICIST

VOLUME FOUR

SLAVERY FROM 1790 TO 1857

With an Introduction by CHARLES FRANCIS ADAMS, LL.D.
Author of "Lee at Appomattox," etc.

CURRENT LITERATURE PUBLISHING COMPANY
NEW YORK

15744

CONTENTS OF VOLUME FOUR

ILLUSTRATIONS IN VOLUME FOUR

INTRODUCTION

THE DOCTRINE OF EQUALITY AND THE RACE PROBLEM[1]

S O far as the institution of slavery is concerned—in its relations to ownership and property in those of the human species—I have seen no reason whatever to revise or in any way to alter the theories and principles which I entertained when I entered Harvard in 1853, and in the maintenance of which I subsequently bore arms between 1861 and 1865. Economically, socially, and from the point of view of abstract political justice, I hold that the institution of slavery, as it existed in this country prior to the year 1865, was in no respect either desirable or justifiable. That it had its good and even its elevating side, so far at least as the African is concerned, I shall not deny. On the contrary, I see and recognize those features of the institution far more clearly now than I should have said would have been possible in 1853. That the institution in itself, under conditions then existing, tended to the elevation of the less advanced race I frankly admit I did not then think. On the other hand, that it exercised a most pernicious influence upon those of the more advanced race, and especially upon that large majority of the more ad-

[1] Adapted from an address delivered before the University of South Carolina on Founders' Day, January 16, 1913.

vanced race who were not themselves owners of slaves —of that I have become with time even more and more satisfied. The noticeable feature, however, so far as I individually am concerned, has been the entire change of view as respects certain of the fundamental propositions at the base of our whole American political and social edifice brought about by a more careful and intelligent ethnological study. I refer to the political equality of man, and to that race absorption to which I have alluded—that belief that any foreign element introduced into the American social system and body politic would speedily be absorbed therein, and in a brief space thoroughly assimilated. In this all-important respect I do not hesitate to say we theorists and abstractionists of the North, throughout that long antislavery discussion which ended with the 1861 clash of arms, were thoroughly wrong. In utter disregard of fundamental scientific facts, we theoretically believed that all men—no matter what might be the color of their skin or the texture of their hair—were, if placed under exactly similar conditions, in essentials the same. In other words, we indulged in the curious and, as is now admitted, utterly erroneous theory that the African was, so to speak, an Anglo-Saxon, or, if you will, a Yankee, "who had never had a chance,"—a fellow-man who was guilty, as we chose to express it, of a skin not colored like our own. In other words, though carved in ebony, he also was in the image of God.

Following out this theory, under the lead of men to whom scientific analysis and observation were anathema if opposed to accepted cardinal political theories as enunciated in the Declaration of Independence as read by them, the African was not only emancipated, but, so far as the letter of the law, as expressed in an amended Constitution, would establish the fact, the quondam slave was in all respects placed on an equality, political, legal, and moral, with those of the more advanced race.

As one who largely entertained the theoretical views I have expressed, I do not hesitate here to say, as the result of sixty years of more careful study and scientific observation, that the theories then entertained by us were not only fundamentally wrong, but further involved a problem in the presence of which I confess to-day I stand appalled.

It is said, whether truthfully or not, that, when some years ago John Morley, the English writer and thinker, returned to England after a visit to this country, he remarked that the African race question, as now existing in the United States, presented a problem as nearly, to his mind, insoluble as any human problem well could be. I do not care whether Lord Morley made this statement or did not make it. I am prepared, however, to say that, individually, so far as my present judgment goes, it is a correct presentation. To us in the North, the African is a comparatively negligible factor. So far as Massachusetts, for instance, or the city of Boston more especially, is concerned, as a problem it is solving itself. Proportionately the African infusion is there becoming less—never large, it is incomparably less now than it was in the days of my own youth. Thus manifestly a negligible factor, it is also one tending to extinction. Indeed, it would be fairly open to question whether a single Afro-American of unmixed Ethiopian descent could now be found in Boston. That the problem presents itself with a wholly different aspect in Carolina is manifest. The difference too is radical; it goes to the heart of the mystery.

As I have already said, the universal "melting-pot" theory in vogue in my youth was that but seven or, at the most, fourteen years were required to convert the alien immigrant—no matter from what region or of what descent—into an American citizen. The educational influences and social environment were assumed to be not only subtle but all-pervasive and powerful. That this theory was to a large and even dangerous extent erroneous the observation of the last fifty years has proved, and our Massachusetts experience is sadly demonstrating it to-day. It was Oliver Wendell Holmes who, years ago, when asked by an anxious mother at what age the education of a child ought to begin, remarked in reply that it should begin about one hundred and fifty years before the child is born. It has so proved with us;

and the fact is to-day in evidence that this statement of Dr. Holmes should be accepted as an undeniable political aphorism. So far from seven or fourteen years making an American citizen, fully and thoroughly impregnated with American ideals to the exclusion of all others, our experience is that it requires at least three generations to eliminate what may be termed the "hyphen" in citizenship. Not in the first, nor in the second, and hardly in the third, generation, does the immigrant cease to be an Irish-American, or a French-American, or a German-American, or a Slavonic-American, or yet a Dago. Nevertheless, in process of time, those of the Caucasian race do and will become Americans. Ultimately their descendants will be free from the traditions and ideals, so to speak, ground in through centuries passed under other conditions. Not so the Ethiopian. In his case we find ourselves confronted with a situation never contemplated in that era of political dreams and Scriptural science in which our institutions received shape. Stated tersely and in plain language, so far as the African is concerned—the cause and, so to speak, the motive of the great struggle of 1861 to 1865—we recognize the presence in the body politic of a vast alien mass which does not assimilate and which cannot be absorbed. In other words, the melting-pot theory came in sharp contact with an ethnological fact, and the unexpected occurred. The problem of African servitude was solved after a fashion; but in place of it a race issue of most uncompromising character evolved itself.

I am by no means prepared to go the length of an English authority in recently saying that "emancipation on two continents sacrificed the real welfare of the slave and his intrinsic worth as a person to the impatient vanity of an immediate and theatrical triumph."[1] This length, I say, I cannot go; but so far as the present occasion is concerned, with such means of observation as are within my reach, I find the conclusion difficult to resist that the success of the abolitionists in effecting the emancipation of the Afro-American, as unexpected

[1] Bussell's (Dr. F. W.) "Christian Theology and Social Progress." Bampton Lectures, 1905.

and sweeping as it was sudden, has led to phases of the race problem quite unanticipated at least. For instance, as respects segregation. Instead of assimilating, with a tendency to ultimate absorption, the movement in the opposite direction since 1865 is pronounced. It has, moreover, received the final stamp of scientific approval. This implies much; for in the old days of the "peculiar institution" the relations between the two races were far more intimate, kindly, and even absorptive than they now are.

That African slavery, as it existed in the United States anterior to the year 1862, presented a mild form of servitude, as servitude then existed and immemorially had almost everywhere existed, was, moreover, incontrovertibly proven in the course of the Civil War. Before 1862 it was confidently believed that any severe social agitation within, or disturbance from without, would inevitably lead to a Southern servile insurrection. In Europe this result was assumed as of course; and, immediately after it was issued, the Emancipation Proclamation of President Lincoln was denounced in unmeasured terms by the entire London press. Not a voice was raised in its defence. It was regarded as a measure unwarranted in civilized warfare, and a sure and intentional incitement to the horrors which had attended the servile insurrections of Haiti and San Domingo; and, more recently, the unspeakable Sepoy incidents of the Indian mutiny. What actually occurred is now historic. The confident anticipations of our English brethren were, not for the first time, negatived; nor is there any page in our American record more creditable to those concerned than the attitude held by the African during the fierce internecine struggle which prevailed between April, 1861, and April, 1865. In it there is scarcely a trace, if indeed there is any trace at all, of such a condition of affairs as had developed in the Antilles and in Hindustan. The attitude of the African toward his Confederate owner was submissive and kindly. Although the armed and masterful domestic protector was at the front and engaged in deadly, all-absorbing conflict, yet the women and children of the

Southern plantation slept with unbarred doors—free
from apprehension, much more from molestation.

Moreover, during the old days of slavery there was
hardly a child born, of either sex, who grew up in a
Southern household of substantial wealth without holding immediate and most affectionate relations with those
of the other race.   Every typical Southern man had
what he called his "daddy" and his "mammy," his
"uncle," and his "aunty," by him familiarly addressed
as such, and who were to him even closer than are blood
relations to most.   They had cared for him in his cradle;
he followed them to their graves.   Is it needful for me
to ask to what extent such relations still exist?   Of those
born thirty years after emancipation, and therefore
belonging distinctly to a later generation, how many
thus have their kindly, if humble, kin of the African
blood?   I fancy I would be safe in saying not one in
twenty.

Here, then, as the outcome of the first great issue
occupying the thought and exciting the passions of the
period before the Civil War, is a problem wholly unanticipated—a problem which, merely stating, I dismiss.

Charles F. Adams

CHAPTER I

THE SLAVE TRADE

[DEBATES ON EARLY ABOLITIONIST PETITIONS]

Memorial by Quakers Against the Slave Trade: Debate on Its Reference to Committee; in Favor, Thomas Fitzsimons [Pa.], James Madison [Va.], Thomas Hartley [Pa.], Roger Sherman [Conn.]; Opposed, Michael J. Stone [Md.], James Jackson [Ga.], William L. Smith [S. C.], Thomas T. Tucker [S. C.]; Memorial Is Laid on the Table—Memorial by the Pennsylvania Abolition Society Against Slavery: Debate on Its Reference to Committee; in Favor, John Page [Va.], Thomas Scott [Pa.], Madison, Elbridge Gerry [Mass.]; Opposed, Tucker, Ædamus Burke [S. C.], Jackson, Abraham Baldwin [Ga.], Smith—Memorials Are Referred to Committee—Report of Committee—Debate on Its Amendment: Those in Favor of Original Report Indicating Sympathy with Petitioners, Hartley and Elias Boudinot [N. J.]; Those in Favor of Striking Out These Sympathetic Clauses, Alexander White [Va.], Burke, and Smith—Report Is so Amended—The Fugitive Slave Law of 1792: Debate in 1797 on a Petition of Free Negroes Against Its Operation in Their Case; in Favor of the Petition, John Swanwick [Pa.], George Thacher [Mass.], Samuel Sitgreaves [Pa.], Joseph B. Varnum [Mass.]; Opposed, Thomas Blount [N. C.], John Heath [Va.], Madison, Smith, Nathaniel Macon [N. C.]—Speech of John Rutledge, Jr. [S. C.], Against Accepting a Petition of Negroes Against Slavery: ''The South Will Protect Itself''—Petition to Congress by Quakers to Coöperate with Foreign Nations in Suppressing the Slave Trade—Debate in the Senate on the Petition: in Favor, James Burrill [R. I.], Rufus King [N. Y.], David L. Morrill [N. H.]; Opposed, George M. Troup [Ga.], George W. Campbell [Tenn.], James Barbour [Va.]—Later History of the Suppression of the Traffic.

THAT the questions connected with slavery had not been settled by the compromises on the subject in the Constitution [see Chapter xiii, Vol. I] was shown by a petition presented to Congress in its first session, praying for the abolition of the slave trade.

On February 11, 1790, Thomas Fitzsimons [Pa.] presented a petition from the Yearly Meeting in 1789 of

7

Friends (Quakers) in Pennsylvania, New Jersey, Delaware, and western parts of Maryland and Virginia praying:

That Congress might make "a sincere and impartial inquiry whether it be not an essential part of the duty of your exalted station to exert upright endeavors, to the full extent of your power, to remove every obstruction to public righteousness, which the influence or artifice of particular persons, governed by the narrow, mistaken views of self-interest, has occasioned, and whether, notwithstanding such seeming impediments, it be not in reality within your power to exercise justice and mercy, which, if adhered to, we cannot doubt must produce the abolition of the slave trade."

In their preamble the petitioners stated that a similar memorial had been made to Congress in 1783, but that,

" . . . though the Christian rectitude of the concern was by the delegates generally acknowledged, yet, not being vested with the powers of legislation, they declined promoting any public remedy against the gross national iniquity of trafficking in the persons of fellowmen; but divers of the legislative bodies of the different States on this continent have since manifested their sense of the public detestation due to the licentious wickedness of the African trade for slaves, and the inhuman tyranny and blood-guiltiness inseparable from it; the debasing influence whereof most certainly tends to lay waste the virtue and, of course, the happiness of the people."

Mr. John Lawrence also presented an Address from the Society of Friends, in the city of New York, in which they set forth their desire of coöperating with their Southern brethren in their protest against the slave trade.

It was moved to refer the petitions to a committee. This was opposed by James Jackson [Ga.], as diverting the attention of the members from the great question before them to one of "questionable policy," and which Congress could take up without advisers, "because the Constitution expressly mentions all the power they can exercise on the subject."

In the debate which ensued on the subject the leading

speakers in behalf of committing the petitions were James Madison [Va.], Thomas Hartley [Pa.], and Roger Sherman [Conn.]; against committing it, Michael J. Stone [Md.], James Jackson [Ga.], William L. Smith [S. C.], and Thomas T. Tucker [S. C.].

PETITIONS AGAINST SLAVERY

HOUSE OF REPRESENTATIVES, FEBRUARY 11, 1790

MR. MADISON.—I apprehend gentlemen need not be alarmed at any measure it is likely Congress will take, because they will recollect that the Constitution secures to the individual States the right of admitting, if they think proper, the importation of slaves into their own territory for eighteen years yet unexpired; subject, however, to a tax, if Congress is disposed to impose it, of not more than ten dollars on each person. The petition, if I mistake not, speaks of artifices used by self-interested persons to carry on this trade.

If anything is within the Federal authority to restrain such violation of the rights of nations and of mankind, as is supposed to be practiced in some parts of the United States, it will certainly tend to the interest and honor of the community to attempt a remedy, and is a proper subject for our discussion. It may be that foreigners take the advantage of the liberty afforded them by the American trade to employ our shipping in the slave trade between Africa and the West Indies, when they are restrained from employing their own by restrictive laws of their nation. If this is the case, is there any person of humanity that would not wish to prevent them? Another consideration why we should commit the petition is that we may give no ground of alarm by a serious opposition, as if we were about to take measures that were unconstitutional.

MR. STONE feared that, if Congress took any measures indicative of an intention to interfere with the kind of property alluded to, it would sink it in value very considerably, and might be injurious to a great number of the citizens, particularly in the Southern States. He thought the subject was of general concern, and that the petitioners had no more right to interfere with it than any other members of the community. It was an unfortunate circumstance that it was the disposition of religious sects to imagine they understood the rights of human nature better than all the world besides; and that they would, in consequence, be meddling with concerns in which they had nothing to do. As the petition relates to a subject of a general nature, it ought to lie on the table as information. He would never consent to refer petitions, unless the petitioners were exclusively interested. Suppose there was a petition to come before us from a society praying us to be honest in our transactions, or that we should administer the Constitution according to its intent, what would you do with a petition of this kind? Certainly it would remain on your table. He would, however, not have it supposed that the people had not a right to advise and give their opinion upon public measures; but he would not be influenced by that advice or opinion to take up a subject sooner than the convenience of other business would admit.

Mr. HARTLEY thought the memorialists did not deserve to be aspersed for their conduct if influenced by motives of benignity. They solicit the legislature of the Union to prevent, as far as is in their power, the increase of a licentious traffic; nor do they merit censure because their behavior has the appearance of more morality than other people. Congress ought not to refuse to hear the applications of their fellow citizens while those applications contain nothing unconstitutional or offensive.

Mr. JACKSON.—I apprehend, if through the interference of the general Government the slave trade was abolished, it would evince to the people a disposition toward a total emancipation, and they would hold their property in jeopardy. Any extraordinary attention of Congress to this petition may have, in some degree, a similar effect. I would beg to ask those, then, who are desirous of freeing the negroes if they have funds sufficient to pay for them? If they have, they may come forward on that business with some propriety; but, if they have not, they should keep themselves quiet, and not interfere with a business in which they are not interested. They may as well come forward and solicit Congress to interdict the West India trade because it is injurious to the morals of mankind; from thence we import rum, which has a debasing influence upon the consumer. I hope the House will order the petition to lie on the table, in order to prevent an alarm to our Southern brethren.

Mr. SMITH.—If I understood it right on its first reading the petition prays that we should take measures for the abolition of the slave trade. This is desiring an unconstitutional act, because the Constitution secures that trade to the States, independent of congressional restrictions, for a term of twenty-one years. If, therefore, it prays for a violation of constitutional rights, it ought to be rejected as an attempt upon the virtue and patriotism of the House.

MR. SHERMAN observed that the petitioners from New York stated that they had applied to the legislature of that State to prohibit certain practices which they conceived to be improper, and which tended to injure the well-being of the community; that the legislature had considered the application, but had applied no remedy because they supposed that power was exclusively vested in the general Government under the Constitution of the United States; it would, therefore, be proper to commit that petition, in order to ascertain what are the powers of the general Government in the case.

MR. TUCKER.—Congress has no authority, under the Constitution, to do more than lay a duty of ten dollars upon each person imported; and this is a political consideration, not arising from either religion or morality, and is the only principle upon which we can proceed to take it up. But what effect do these men suppose will arise from their exertions? Will a duty of ten dollars diminish the importation? Will the treatment be better than usual? I apprehend not; nay, it may be worse, because an interference with the subject may excite a great degree of restlessness in the minds of those it is intended to serve, and that may be a cause for the masters to use more rigor toward them than they would otherwise exert; so that these men seem to overshoot their object. But if they will endeavor to procure the abolition of the slave trade, let them prefer their petitions to the State legislatures, who alone have the power of forbidding the importation. I believe their applications there would be improper; but if they are anywhere proper it is there. I look upon the address, then, to be ill judged, however good the intention of the framers.

The address was ordered to lie on the table.

On February 12 the Pennsylvania Society for Promoting the Abolition of Slavery, of which Benjamin Franklin was president, presented a memorial, not on the abolition merely of the slave trade but of slavery in general. This declared:

From a persuasion that equal liberty was originally the portion and is still the birthright of all men, and influenced by the strong ties of humanity and the principles of their institution, your memorialists conceive themselves bound to use all justifiable endeavors to loosen the bands of slavery and promote a general enjoyment of the blessings of freedom. Under these impressions they earnestly entreat your serious attention to the subject of slavery; that you will be pleased to countenance the restoration of liberty to those unhappy men who alone in this land of freedom are degraded into perpetual bondage, and who, amid the general joy of surrounding freedom, are groaning in servile subjection; that you will devise means for removing this inconsistency from the character of the American people; that you will promote mercy and justice toward this distressed race, and that you will step to the very verge of the power vested in you for discouraging every species of traffic in the persons of our fellowmen.

Mr. Hartley then called up the memorial presented the day before, from the annual meeting of Friends at Philadelphia, for a second reading; whereupon the same was read a second time and moved to be committed.

In the debate which ensued the leading speakers for commitment were: John Page [Va.], James Madison [Va.], Thomas Scott [Pa.], and Elbridge Gerry [Mass.]; those against commitment were Thomas T. Tucker [S. C.], Ædamus Burke [S. C.], William L. Smith [S. C.], James Jackson [Ga.], and Abraham Baldwin [Ga.].

PETITIONS AGAINST SLAVERY—*Continued*

HOUSE OF REPRESENTATIVES, FEBRUARY 12, 1790

MR. TUCKER was surprised to see another memorial on the same subject, and that signed by a man who ought to have known the Constitution better. He thought it a mischievous attempt as it respected the persons in whose favor it was intended. It would buoy them up with hopes, without a foundation, and as they could not reason on the subject, as more enlightened men would, they might be led to do what they would be punished for, and the owners of them, in their own defence, would be compelled to exercise over them a severity they were not accustomed to. Do these men expect a general emancipation of slaves by law? This would never be submitted to by the Southern States without a civil war. Do they mean to purchase their freedom? He believed their money would fall short of the price.

MR. BURKE saw the disposition of the House, and he feared it would be referred to a committee, maugre all their opposition; but he must insist that it prayed for an unconstitutional measure; did it not desire Congress to interfere and abolish the slave trade, while the Constitution expressly stipulates that Congress shall exercise no such power? He was certain the commitment would sound an alarm and blow the trumpet of sedition in the Southern States.

MR. SCOTT.—I cannot entertain a doubt but the memorial is strictly agreeable to the Constitution; it respects a part of the duty particularly assigned to us by that instrument, and I hope we may be inclined to take it into consideration. We can, at present, lay our hands upon a small duty of ten dollars; I would take this, and if it is all we can do we must be content; but I am sorry that the framers of the Constitution did not go further and enable us to interdict the traffic entirely; for I look upon the slave trade to be one of the most abominable things on earth; and, if there was neither God nor devil, I should oppose it upon the principles of humanity and the law of nature. The petitioners view the subject in a religious light, but I do not stand in need of religious motives to induce me to reprobate the traffic in human flesh; other considerations weigh with me to support the commitment of the memorial, and to support every constitutional measure likely to bring about its total abolition. Perhaps, in our legislative capacity, we can go no further than to impose a duty of ten dollars, but I do not know how far I might go if I was one of the judges of the United States, and those people were to come before me and claim their emancipation; but I am sure I would go as far as I could.

MR. JACKSON differed with the gentleman last up, and supposed the master had a qualified property in his slave. He said the contrary doctrine would go to the destruction of every species of personal service. The gentleman said he did not stand in need of religion to induce him to reprobate slavery, but if he is guided by that evidence upon which the Christian system is founded he will find that religion is not against it. He will see, from Genesis to Revelations, the current setting strong that way. There never was a government on the face of the earth but what permitted slavery. The purest sons of freedom in the Grecian republics, the citizens of Athens and Lacedæmon, all held slaves. On this principle, the nations of Europe are associated; it is the basis of the feudal system. But, suppose all this to have been wrong, let me ask the gentleman if it is good policy to bring forward a business at this moment likely to light up the flame of civil discord; for the people of the Southern States will resist one tyranny as soon as another. The other parts of the continent may bear them down by force of arms, but they will never suffer themselves to be divested of their property without a struggle. The gentleman says if he was a Federal judge he does not know to what length he would go in emancipating these people; but I believe his judgeship would be of short duration in Georgia, perhaps even the existence of such a judge might be in danger.

Mr. Baldwin was sorry the subject had ever been brought before Congress, because it was of a delicate nature as it respected some of the States. Gentlemen who had been present at the formation of this Constitution could not avoid the recollection of the pain and difficulty which the subject caused in that body. The members of the Southern States were so tender upon this point that they had well-nigh broken up without coming to any determination; however, from the extreme desire of preserving the Union and obtaining an efficient Government, they were induced mutually to concede, and the Constitution jealously guarded what they agreed to. If gentlemen look over the footsteps of that body, they will find the greatest degree of caution used to imprint them so as not to be easily eradicated; but the moment we go to jostle on that ground, I fear we shall feel it tremble under our feet. Congress have no power to interfere with the importation of slaves beyond what is given in the ninth section of the first article of the Constitution; everything else is interdicted to them in the strongest terms. If we examine the Constitution we shall find the expressions relative to this subject cautiously expressed and more punctiliously guarded than any other part: "The migration or importation of such persons shall not be prohibited by Congress." But lest this should not have secured the object sufficiently it is declared in the same section "that no capitation or direct tax shall be laid, unless in proportion to the census"; this was intended to prevent Congress from laying any special tax upon negro slaves, as they might, in this way, so burthen the possessors of them as to induce a general emancipation. If we go on to the fifth article we shall find the first and fifth clauses of the ninth section of the first article restrained from being altered before the year 1808.

Gentlemen have said that this petition does not pray for an abolition of the slave trade. I think, sir, it prays for nothing else, and therefore we have no more to do with it than if it prayed us to establish an order of nobility or a national religion.

Mr. W. Smith, of South Carolina, insisted that it was not in the power of the House to grant the prayer of the petition, which went to the total abolishment of the slave trade, and it was therefore unnecessary to commit it. If gentlemen can assign no good reason for the measure, they will not support it when they are told that it will create jealousies and alarm in the Southern States; for I can assure them that there is no point on which they are more jealous and suspicious than on a business with which they think the Government has nothing to do.

When we entered into this confederacy we did it from political, not from moral, motives, and I do not think my constituents want to learn morals from the petitioners; I do not believe they want improvement in their moral system; if they do, they can get it at home.

The gentleman from Georgia has justly stated the jealousy of the Southern States. On entering into this Government they apprehended that the other States, not knowing the necessity the citizens of the Southern States were under to hold this species of property, would, from motives of humanity and benevolence, be led to vote for a general emancipation; and, had they not seen that the Constitution provided against the effect of such a disposition, I may be bold to say they never would have adopted it.

We look upon this measure as an attack upon the palladium of the property of our country; it is therefore our duty to oppose it by every means in our power. Gentlemen should consider that when we entered into a political connection with the other States this property was there; it was acquired under a former government, conformably to the laws and Constitution, therefore anything that will tend to deprive them of that property must be an *ex post facto* law, and, as such, is forbidden by our political compact.

I said the States would never have entered into the confederation unless their property had been guaranteed to them, for such is the state of agriculture in that country that without slaves it must be abandoned. Why will these people, then, make use of arguments to induce the slave to turn his hand against his master? We labor under difficulties enough from the ravages of the late war. A gentleman can hardly come from that country with a servant or two, either to this place [New York] or Philadelphia, but there are persons trying to seduce his servants to leave him; and, when they have done this, the poor wretches are obliged to rob their master in order to obtain a subsistence; all those, therefore, who are concerned in this seduction are accessories to the robbery.

The reproach which they [the abolitionists] cast upon the owners of negro property is the want of humanity. I believe the proprietors have as much humanity as persons in any part of the continent, and are as conspicuous for their good morals as their neighbors. The memorial of the Quakers relates to a matter in which they are no more interested than any other sect, and can only be considered as a piece of advice, which it is not customary to refer to a committee; but if it is supposed to pray for what they think a moral purpose, is that sufficient to induce us to commit it? What may appear a moral virtue in their eyes may not be so in reality. I have heard of a sect of Shaking Quakers, who, I presume, suppose their tenets of a moral tendency. I am informed one of them forbids to intermarry. Now, if these people were to petition Congress to pass a law prohibiting matrimony would gentlemen agree to refer such a petition? I think if they would reject one of that nature as improper they ought also to reject this.

Mr. Page was in favor of the commitment. He lived in a State which had the misfortune of having in her bosom a great number of slaves; he held many of them himself, and was as much interested in the business as any gentleman in South Carolina or Georgia, yet, if he was determined to hold them in eternal bondage he should feel no uneasiness or alarm on account of the present measure, because he should rely upon the virtue of Congress that they would not exercise any unconstitutional authority.

Mr. Madison.—The debate has taken a serious turn, and it will be owing to this alone if an alarm is created; for, had the memorial been treated in the usual way, it would have been considered as a matter of course and a report might have been made so as to have given general satisfaction. If there was the slightest tendency by the commitment to break in upon the Constitution, he would object to it; but he did not see upon what ground such an event was to be apprehended. The petition prayed, in general terms, for the interference of Congress, so far as they were constitutionally authorized: but even if its prayer was, in some degree, unconstitutional, it might be committed. He admitted that Congress is restricted by the Constitution from taking measures to abolish the slave trade; yet there are a variety of ways by which it could countenance the abolition, and regulations might be made in relation to the introduction of them into the new States to be formed out of the Western Territory. He thought the object well worthy of consideration.

Mr. GERRY thought the interference of Congress fully compatible with the Constitution, and could not help lamenting the miseries to which the natives of Africa were exposed by this inhuman commerce. He never contemplated the subject without reflecting what his own feelings would be, in case himself, his children, or friends were placed in the same deplorable circumstances. He then adverted to the flagrant acts of cruelty which are committed in carrying on that traffic; and asked whether it can be supposed that Congress has no power to prevent such abuses? Congress can, agreeably to the Constitution, lay a duty of ten dollars on imported slaves; they may do this immediately. He made a calculation of the value of the slaves in the Southern States, and supposed they may be worth ten millions of dollars. Congress have a right, if they see proper, to make a proposal to the Southern States to purchase the whole of them, and their resources in the Western Territory might furnish them with the means. He did not intend to suggest a measure of this kind; he only instanced these particulars to show that Congress certainly has a right to intermeddle in the business.

The memorials were referred to committee by a vote of 43 to 14.

On March 16 the committee made its report, which was that the Constitution expressly restrained the general Government from prohibiting the importation of slaves until 1808, and, by fair construction, prohibited Congress from interfering before that date with the emancipation of slaves, or the regulation of slaves by the States; the committee trusted, however, that the various legislatures would revise their laws from time to time to ameliorate the condition of the slaves.

The committee went on to declare that Congress had authority to lay a tax not exceeding ten dollars on each slave imported, and to make provision for the humane treatment of the slaves in passage, as well as to prohibit foreigners from fitting out slave ships in a port of the United States. Lastly, they advised that Congress inform the memorialists that, wherever it had jurisdiction in matters concerning slavery, it would be exercised on the principles of "justice, humanity, and good policy."

This report was debated from March 17 to 23, when it was passed, with amendments eliminating the suggestion to the State legislatures that Congress had the power to emancipate slaves after 1808 and the final notice to the memorialists. The vote upon entering on the Journal the original report of the committee, and the amended report, was passed by 29 to 25 votes.

The chief speakers in the debate were, in favor of the original report: Thomas Hartley [Pa.] and Elias Boudinot [N. J.]; against it, Alexander White [Va.], Ædamus Burke and William L. Smith, of South Carolina.

Petitions Against Slavery—*Concluded*

House of Representatives, March 17-23, 1790

Mr. White moved the amendments to the report. Congress had no right to interfere with the States in their regulations of slaves. He did not, however, anticipate the difficulties from a total prohibition which some gentlemen seem to apprehend—and, if Congress had it in their power to interdict this business at the present moment, he did not think the essential interests of the Southern States would suffer. Twenty years ago he supposed the idea he now suggested would have caused universal alarm. Virginia, however, about twelve years since prohibited the importation of negroes from Africa, and the consequences apprehended never were realized; on the contrary, the agriculture of that State was never in a more flourishing situation.

Mr. Hartley reprobated the illiberal treatment which the memorialists had received, and asserted that they were friends to the Constitution, and that on the present occasion they came forward from the most laudable motives, from a wish to promote the happiness of mankind, that their conduct, so far from meriting censure, deserved and would receive the applause of the civilized world.

Mr. Burke animadverted with great freedom on the past and present conduct of the Quakers. He denied that they were the friends of freedom; he said that during the late war they were for bringing this country under a foreign yoke; they descended to the character of spies; they supplied the enemy with provisions; they were guides and conductors to their armies; and whenever the American army came into their neighborhood they found themselves in an enemy's country.

Mr. Burke was proceeding in this strain when he was interrupted by being called to order. A warm altercation ensued.

Mr. Smith.—The memorial from the Quakers contained, in his opinion, a very indecent attack on the character of those States which possess slaves. It reprobates slavery as bringing down reproach on the Southern States, and expatiates on the detestation due to the licentious wickedness of the African trade, and the inhuman tyranny and blood guiltiness inseparable from it. He could not but consider it as calculated to fix a stigma of the blackest nature on the State he had the honor to represent, and to hold its citizens up to public view as men divested of every principle of honor and humanity. Considering it in that light, he felt it incumbent on him not only to refute those atrocious calumnies but to resent the improper language made use of by the memorialists. This application came with the worst grace possible from the Quakers, who professed never to intermeddle in politics but to submit quietly to the laws of the country.

If these were really their sentiments, why did not they abide by them? Why did not they leave that which they call God's work to be managed by himself? Those principles should instruct them to wait with patience and humility for the event of all public measures, and to receive that event as the Divine Will. It was difficult to credit their pretended scruples; because, while they were exclaiming against the Mammon of this world, they were hunting after it with a step steady as time and an appetite keen as the grave.

The memorial from the Pennsylvania Society applied, in express terms, for an emancipation of slaves, and the report of the committee appeared to hold out the idea that Congress might exercise the power of emancipating after the year 1808; for it said that Congress could not emancipate slaves prior to that period. He remarked that either the power of manumission still remained with the several States or it was exclusively vested in Congress; for no one would contend that such a power would be concurrent in the several States and the United States. He then showed that the State governments clearly retained all the rights of sovereignty which they had before the establishment of the Constitution, unless they were exclusively delegated to the United States; and this could only exist where the Constitution granted, in express terms, an exclusive authority to the Union, or where it granted in one instance an authority to the Union and in another prohibited the States from exercising the like authority, or where it granted an authority to the Union to which a similar authority in the States would be repugnant.

He applied these principles to the case in question; and asked whether the Constitution had, in express terms, vested the Congress with the power of manumission? Or whether it restrained the States from exercising that power? Or whether there was any autl.,ity given to the Union with which the exercise of this right by any State would be inconsistent? If these questions were answered in the negative, it followed that Congress had not an exclusive right to the power of manumission. Had it a concurrent right with the States? No gentleman would assert it, because the absurdity was obvious. For a State regulation on the subject might differ from a Federal regulation; in which case one or the other must give way. As the laws of the United States were paramount to those of the individual States, the Federal regulations would abrogate those of the States, consequently the States would thus be divested of a power which it was evident they now had and might exercise whenever they thought proper. But admitting that Congress had authority to manumit the slaves in America, and were disposed to exercise it, would the Southern States acquiesce in such a measure without a struggle? Would the citizens of that country tamely suffer their property to be torn from them? Would even the citizens of the other States which did not possess this property desire to have all the slaves let loose upon them? Would not such a step be injurious even to the slaves themselves? It was well known that they were an indolent people, improvident, averse to labor: when emancipated they would either starve or plunder. Nothing was a stronger proof of the absurdity of emancipation than the fanciful schemes which the friends to the measure had suggested. One was to ship them out of the country and colonize them in some foreign region. This plan admitted that it would be dangerous to retain them within the United States after they were manumitted: but surely it would be inconsistent with humanity to banish these people to a remote country, and to expel them from their native soil, and from places to which they had a local attachment. It would be no less repugnant to the principles of freedom not to allow them to remain here if they desired it. How could they be called freemen if they were, against their consent, to be expelled the country? Thus did the advocates for emancipation acknowledge that the blacks, when liberated, ought not to remain here to stain the blood of the whites by a mixture of the races.

Another plan was to liberate all those who should be born after a certain limited period. Such a scheme would produce this very extraordinary phenomenon, that the mother would be a slave and her child would be free. These young emancipated negroes, by associating with their enslaved parents, would participate in all the debasement which slavery is said to occasion. But, allowing that a practicable scheme of general emancipation could be devised, there can be no doubt that the two races would still remain distinct. It is known from experience that the whites had such an idea of their superiority over the blacks that they never even associated with them; even the warmest friends to the blacks kept them at a distance and rejected all intercourse with them. Could any instance be quoted of their intermarrying? The Quakers asserted that nature had made all men equal and that the difference of color should not place negroes on a worse footing in society than the whites; but had any of them ever married a negro, and would any of them suffer their children to mix their blood with that of a black? They would view with abhorrence such an alliance.

Mr. Smith then read some extracts from Mr. Jefferson's "Notes on Virginia," proving that negroes were by nature an inferior race of beings, and that the whites would always feel a repugnance at mixing their blood with that of the blacks.

Thus that respectable author who was desirous of countenancing emancipation was, on a consideration of the subject, induced candidly to avow that the difficulties appeared insurmountable. The friends to manumission had said that by prohibiting the further importation of slaves and by liberating those born after a certain period a gradual emancipation might take place, and that in process of time the very color would be extinct and there would be none but whites. He was at a loss to learn how that consequence would result. If the blacks did not intermarry with the whites they would remain black to the end of time; for it was not contended that liberating them would whitewash them; if they would intermarry with the whites, then the

white race would be extinct, and the American people would be
all of the mulatto breed. In whatever light, therefore, the subject was viewed the folly of emancipation was manifest. He
trusted these considerations would prevent any further application to Congress on this point, and would so far have weight
with the committee as to cause them to reject the clause altogether, or at least to declare in plain terms that Congress has
no right whatever to manumit the slaves of this country.

The toleration of slavery in the several States was a matter of internal regulation and policy, in which each State had
a right to do as she pleased, and no other State had any right
to intermeddle with her policy or laws. The legislature of
South Carolina had prohibited theatrical representations, deem-
ing them improper; but they did not trouble Congress with an
application to abolish them in New York and Philadelphia.
The Southern citizens might also consider the toleration of
Quakers as an injury to the community because in time of
war they would not defend their country from the enemy, and
in time of peace they were interfering in the concerns of others
and doing everything in their power to excite the slaves in the
Southern States to insurrection; notwithstanding which the
people of those States had not required the assistance of Congress to exterminate the Quakers.

But he could not help observing that this squeamishness was
very extraordinary at this time. The Northern States knew
that the Southern States had slaves before they confederated
with them. If they had such an abhorrence for slavery, why
did they not cast us off and reject our alliance? The truth
was that the best informed part of the citizens of the Northern
States knew that slavery was so ingrafted into the policy of the
Southern States that it could not be eradicated without tearing
up by the roots their happiness, tranquillity, and prosperity;
that, if it were an evil, it was one for which there was no
remedy, and, therefore, like wise men, they acquiesced in it.
We, on the other hand, knew that the Quaker doctrines had
taken such deep root in some of the States that all resistance
to them must be useless: we therefore made a compromise on
both sides, we took each other with our mutual bad habits and
respective evils, for better for worse; the Northern States
adopted us with our slaves and we adopted them with their
Quakers. There was then an implied compact between the
Northern and Southern people that no step should be taken to
injure the property of the latter or to disturb their tranquillity.

The negroes would not be benefited by emancipation; free

negroes never improve in talents, never grow rich, and continue to associate with the people of their own color. This is owing either to the natural aversion the whites entertain toward them, and an opinion of the superiority of their race, or to the natural attachment the blacks have to those of their own color; in either case it proves that they will, after manumission, continue a distinct people and have separate interests. They are an inferior race even to the Indians.

But some persons have been of opinion that if the further importation of slaves could be prohibited there would be a gradual extinction of the species. That would be impossible, because they increase; to occasion an extinction, Congress must prohibit all intercourse between the sexes; this would be an act of humanity they would not thank us for, nor would they be persuaded that it was for their own good; or Congress must, like Herod, order all the children to be put to death as soon as born. If; then, nothing but evil would result from emancipation, under the existing circumstances of the country, why should Congress stir at all in the business, or give any countenance to such dangerous applications? We have been told that the Government ought to manifest a disposition inimical to this practice which the people reprobate. If some citizens, from misinformation and ignorance, have imbibed prejudices against the Southern States, if ill-intentioned authors have related false facts and gross misrepresentations tending to traduce the character of a whole State and to mislead the citizens of other States, is that a sufficient reason why a large territory is to be depopulated, merely to gratify the wish of some misinformed individuals?

This is not an object of general concern, for I have already proved that it does not weaken the Union; but, admit that it did, will the abolition of slavery strengthen South Carolina? It can only be cultivated by slaves; the climate, the nature of the soil, ancient habits, forbid the whites from performing the labor. Experience convinces us of the truth of this. Great Britain made every attempt to settle Georgia by whites alone and failed, and was compelled at length to introduce slaves; after which that State increased very rapidly in opulence and importance. If the slaves are emancipated they will not remain in that country—remove the cultivators of the soil and the whole of the low country, all the fertile rice and indigo swamps, will be deserted and become a wilderness. In a short time the Northern and Eastern States will supply us with their manufactures; if you depopulate the rich low country of South

Carolina and Georgia, you will give us a blow which will immediately recoil on yourselves.

It has been said that the toleration of slavery brings down
reproach on America. It only brings reproach on those who
tolerate it, and we are ready to bear our share. We found

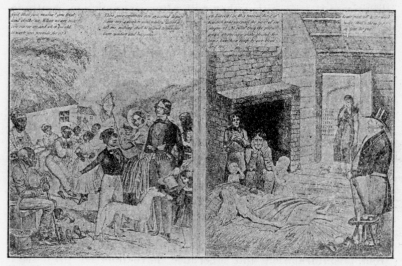

BLACK AND WHITE SLAVES
From the collection of the New York Historical Society

slavery ingrafted in the very policy of the country when we
were born, and we are persuaded of the impolicy of removing
it; if it be a moral evil, it is like many others which exist in all
civilized countries and which the world quietly submits to.

Another objection is that slavery vitiates and debases the
mind of the owner of this sort of property. Where, he asked, is
the proof of this allegation? Do the citizens of the Southern
States exhibit more ferociousness in their manners, more barbarity in their dispositions, than those of the other States?
Are crimes more frequently committed there?

Much had been said of the cruel treatment of slaves in the
Southern States; he denied the fact from experience and accurate information, and believed in his conscience that the slaves
in South Carolina were a happier people than the lower order
of whites in many countries he had visited.

Some have said that slavery is unnecessary: so far from it
that several essential manufactures depend on it. Indigo,
cochineal, and various other dyeing materials which are the produce of the West Indies could be raised only by slaves; the

great staple commodities of the South would be annihilated without the labor of slaves. It is well known that when the African slaves were brought to the coast for sale it was customary to put to death all those who were not sold; the abolition of the slave trade would therefore cause the massacre of the people.

The cruel mode of transportation was another motive to this abolition; but it was to be presumed that the merchants would so far attend to their own interests as to preserve the lives and health of the slaves on the passage. All voyages must be attended with inconveniences, and those from Africa to America not more than others. As to their confinement on board, it was no more than was necessary; the room was full as much as was alloted in ships of war to British seamen. And in cases of disobedience, the captain had a right, for slight offences, to inflict on these sailors corporal punishment without the intervention of a court-martial.

Having thus removed the force of the observations which have been advanced against the toleration of slavery by a misguided and misinformed humanity, I shall only add that I disapprove of the whole of the report; because it either states some power sufficiently expressed in the Constitution which is unnecessary or it sets forth some power which I am clear Congress do not possess.

MR. BOUDINOT said: On resolutions declaring that Congress had not power to prohibit the importation of slaves into any State, or to interfere in their emancipation or internal government, long argument had been used; also much precious time had been spent to prove the lawfulness of the African trade in slaves. This, indeed, was an arduous task, in this day of light and knowledge. Not only the practice of ancient nations and that of all modern Europe had been brought into view, but even the sacred Scriptures had been quoted to justify this iniquitous traffic. It is true that the Egyptians held the Israelites in bondage for four hundred years, and Mr. B. doubted not but much the same arguments as had been used on the present occasion had been urged with great violence by the King of Egypt, whose heart, it is expressly said, had been extremely hardened, to show why he should not consent to let the children of Israel go, who had now become absolutely necessary to him; but gentlemen cannot forget the consequences that followed; they were delivered by a strong hand and stretched out arm, and it ought to be remembered that the Almighty Power that accomplished their deliverance is the same yesterday, to-day, and forever. The New Testament has afforded a number of texts to countenance this doctrine, in the gentleman's opinion. One would have imagined that the uniform tenor of the Gospel that breathes a spirit of love and universal philanthropy to our fellow creatures—that commands our love to our neighbor to be measured by our love to ourselves—that teaches us that whatsoever we would that men should do to us, to do so to them— would have prevented this misapplication. Surely the gentleman overlooked the prophecy of St. Peter, where he foretells that, among other damnable heresies, "through coveteousness shall they, with feigned words, make merchandise of you."

When gentlemen attempt to justify this unnatural traffic, or to prove the lawfulness of slavery, they should advert to the genius of our Government and the principles of the Revolution. By the declaration of Congress, in 1775, setting forth the causes and necessity of taking up arms, they say: "If it was possible for men who exercise their reason to believe that the Divine Author of our existence intended a part of the human race to hold an absolute property in and an unbounded power over others, marked out by His infinite goodness and wisdom as the objects of a legal domination never rightfully resistible, however severe and oppressive, the inhabitants of these colonies might at least require from the Parliament of Great Britain some evidence that this dreadful authority over them had been granted to that body." And, by the Declaration of Independence in 1776, Congress declare: "We hold these truths to be self-evident: that all men are created equal; that they are endowed by their Creator with certain unalienable rights; that among these are life, liberty, and the pursuit of happiness."

This, then, is the language of America in the day of distress. Mr. Chairman, I would not be understood to contend the right of Congress at this time to prohibit the importation of slaves. Whatever might have been the principles of the Revolution or the genius of the Government, by the present Constitution we are clearly and positively restrained till the year 1808, and I am sure that no gentleman in this committee would have the most distant wish to wound this instrument of our connection.

But there is a wide difference between justifying this ungenerous traffic and supporting a claim to property vested at the time of the Constitution and guaranteed thereby. Besides, it would be inhumanity itself to turn these unhappy people loose to murder each other or to perish for want of the necessaries of life. I never was an advocate for so extravagant a conduct.

Many arguments were pointed against the danger of our emancipating these slaves, or even holding up an idea that we had a power so to do, and much time has been taken up to disprove this right in Congress. As no claim of this kind is contended for, and the resolutions already passed expressly contradict it, I shall make no further observations on them.

But the characters of the signers of these memorials are called in question as an argument against the adoption of the resolution on the table. One of these memorials was signed by the society of people called Quakers; the other by Dr. Franklin, as president of a private society in Philadelphia. The indiscriminate abuse that has been thrown out against the Quakers, without distinction, has not comported with the honor or dignity of this House. Not only their characters, but their very names have been called upon, and private anecdotes relating to individuals been mentioned on the floor. With many of the Quakers I have long lived in the habits of friendship, and can testify to the respectability of their characters and the regularity of their lives. Their conduct in the late war has been arraigned, and they have been condemned in the lump. I had the honor of serving the United States at the commencement of the war as commissary-general of prisoners.

Congress not being able to afford them supplies, those unhappy men in this town[1] were reduced to the very depths of distress; without food or raiment, without blankets or firing, they suffered everything that human nature could bear. In this situation many of the Quakers of this city exercised such humanity toward them as did honor to human nature. The miserable prisoner not only felt the happy effects of their exertions in his favor, but participated in their money, their food and clothing. Nay, such were the jealousies created by this conduct, in the British army here, that an armed force entered the house of one of them, seized his books, and, though a man of great property and large commercial dealings, on finding that he had loaned large sums of money to our distressed prisoners, he was turned out of their lines, and with his family was a refugee during the whole of the war afterward, separated from his business and property.

Where is the denomination among us that did not furnish opposers to our glorious Revolution? Were not hundreds of Presbyterians, Episcopalians, and almost of every other denomi-

[1] Congress was in session in New York City.

nation among our enemies? What denominations formed the thousands of new levies that endeavored to deluge our country in blood? On the other hand, were not a Greene and a Mifflin furnished from the Society of the Quakers?

In short, I rejoice to say that our cause was not carried on by fanaticism or religious zeal, but a generous struggle for the rights of human nature. Then why all this abuse of this particular sect, without discrimination? Can any solid argument against the resolution on the table arise from a conduct of this kind? I am at a loss to know what other argument has been used to show the impropriety of the resolution before you. It goes to declare the power of Congress to prohibit foreigners from fitting out vessels in our ports to supply foreigners with slaves from Africa. For my part, I think it a prudent, a humane, and a constitutional resolution. It will render further interference on this subject, perhaps, unnecessary when it is known that the power of Congress extends to remedy the evil. They will hardly venture to risk a voyage that may be ruined before its being finished.

On the whole, sir, I have heard nothing to convince me of the impropriety of the present resolution. I shall therefore vote against striking it out.

It was moved that the sixth article be struck out; but the motion was negatived. The committee of the whole then agreed to the proposition. The seventh article was on motion struck out.

The Fugitive Law

In February, 1792, Congress had passed without debate and, in the House of Representatives with but seven votes in the negative, a Fugitive Law whereby any person "held to labor" in one State or Territory, fleeing to another, might be seized by the one "to whom such labor is due," or his agent, and taken before a Federal judge or local magistrate; and, upon proof of the owner's claim, should be given over by the said authority to the claimant with a certificate warranting the removal of the fugitive to the State or Territory whence he had fled. A person who concealed the fugitive from the claimant, resisted his arrest, or rescued him after arrest would be subject to a fine of $500. The law did not become a subject of discussion in Congress until January 30, 1797, when John Swanwick [Pa.] presented a petition to Congress for certain freedmen of North Carolina against the operation of the law in their case. They averred that the legislature of North Carolina had recently passed an act permitting negroes who had been freed by their masters to be seized and sold back into slavery, in consequence of which act the petitioners had fled to the North, leaving behind them the property which they had accumulated, their gainful occupations, and, in some cases, their families, and were experiencing poverty and distress in their exile, undergoing the while the fear of recapture, a fate which had befallen one of their fellow fugitive freedmen.

The speakers in favor of receiving the petition were John Swanwick and Samuel Sitgreaves of Pennsylvania, George Thacher and Joseph B. Varnum of Massachusetts, and Aaron Kitchell of New Jersey; those opposed to receiving it were Thomas Blount and Nathaniel Macon of North Carolina, James Madison and John Heath of Virginia, and William L. Smith of South Carolina.

Petition of Fugitive Freedmen

House of Representatives, January 30, 1797

Mr. Swanwick said he hoped the petition would be referred to a select committee.

Mr. Blount hoped it would not even be received by the House. Agreeably to a law of the State of North Carolina, he said they were slaves, and could, of course, be seized as such.

Mr. Thacher thought the petition ought to be referred to the Committee on the Fugitive Law. He conceived the gentleman much mistaken in asserting these petitioners to be absolute slaves. They state that they *were* slaves, but their masters manumitted them, and that their manumissions were sanctioned by a law of that State, but that a subsequent law of the same State subjected them to slavery; and, if even there was a law that allowed them to be taken and sold into slavery again, he could not see any propriety in refusing their petition in that House—they certainly are free people. It appeared they were taken under the Fugitive Act, which he thought ought not to affect them; they now came and prayed the House so to model that Fugitive Act as to prevent its affecting persons of their description. He therefore saw great propriety in referring their petition to the committee appointed to amend that act in another part; they could as well consider its relation to the present case. He could not see how there would be a propriety in rejecting their petition; they had an undoubted right to petition the House and to be heard.

Mr. Swanwick was surprised at the gentleman from North Carolina [Mr. Blount] desiring to reject this petition; he could not have thought, nor could he indulge the suspicion now, that the gentleman was so far from acknowledging the rights of man as to prevent any class of men from petitioning. If men were aggrieved, and conceived they have claim to attention, petitioning was their sacred right, and that right should never suffer innovation; whether the House ought to grant was another question.

If the circumstance respecting these people was as they stated, their case was very hard. He animadverted on the atrocity of that reward of ten dollars offered for one of them if taken alive, but that fifty should be given if found dead, and no questions asked. Was not this, he said, encouragement to put a period to that man's existence? Horrid reward! Could gentlemen hear it and not shudder?

Mr. Blount said the gentleman last up was mistaken in calling the petitioners free men; the laws of North Carolina, as he observed before, did not suffer individuals to emancipate their slaves, and he should wish to know what evidence there was to prove these men free, and, except that was proved, the House had no right to attend to the petition.

Mr. Sitgreaves, in answer to the gentleman last up, said he would reverse his question, and ask what evidence he had to prove that these men are not freemen; can he prove they are slaves? Had they not an equal right to be heard with other petitioners?

Mr. Heath was clearly convinced these people were slaves, and therefore hoped their petition would lie on the table. He would remind the gentleman that, if they undertook this business, they would soon have petitions enough of the same kind, and public business would be thereby prevented. It appeared to him to be more within the jurisdiction of the legislature of that State; indeed, the United States had nothing to do with it.

Mr. Madison said he should be sorry to reject any petition whatever in which it became the business of the House to attend; but he thought this case had no claim on their attention. Yet, if it did not come within the purview of the legislative body, he thought it might be suffered to lie on the table. He thought it a judicial case, and could obtain its due in a court of appeal in that State. If they are free by the laws of North Carolina, they ought to apply to those laws and have their privilege established. If they are slaves, the Constitution gives them no hopes of being heard here. A law has been passed to prevent the owners of those slaves emancipating them; it is therefore impossible that any relief can be granted. The petitioners are under the laws of North Carolina, and those laws cannot be the interpreters of the laws of the United States.

MR. SITGREAVES said he was not prepared to deny that this petition is in the situation the gentleman from Virginia [Mr. Madison] states; nor was he prepared to prove that it came under the power of the general Government; but he could see no kind of reason why it should not be sent to a committee who should examine the case and report whether it required legislative interference or whether it was a subject of judicial authority in the country whence the petitioners came. If it should be found to be of a judicial nature, the committee would report so, and the House would honorably refuse it.

MR. W. SMITH said the practice of a former time, in a similar case, was that the petition was sealed up and sent back to the petitioners, not being allowed even to remain on the files of the office. This method, he said, ought to be pursued with respect to the present petition. It was not a matter that claimed the attention of the legislature of the United States. He thought it of such an improper nature as to be surprised any gentleman would present a petition of the kind. These men are slaves, and, he thought, not entitled to attention from that body; to encourage slaves to petition the House would have a tendency to invite continual applications. Indeed, it would tend to spread an alarm throughout the Southern States; it would act as an "entering wedge," whose consequences could not be foreseen. This is a kind of property on which the House has no power to legislate. He hoped it would not be committed at all; it was not a proper subject for legislative attention. He was not of the opinion of some gentlemen that the House were bound to sit on every question recommended to their notice. He thought particular attention ought to be paid to the lateness of the session; if this subject were to be considered, too much time of the House would be devoured which was much wanted on important business.

Mr. Thacher said the gentleman from North Carolina [Mr. Blount] is of the opinion that, these people being slaves, the House ought not to pay attention to their prayer. That the House should not receive a petition without an evidence to prove it was from a free man was quite a new system of conduct which he had never seen the House practice, and hoped he never should see. This was language which opposed the constitutional freedom of every State where the declaration of rights had been made; they all declare that every man is born equally free, and that each has an equal right to petition if aggrieved —this doctrine he never heard objected to.

The gentlemen from Virginia [Mr. Madison and Mr. Heath] had said it was a judicial and not a legislative question; they say the petition proves it, and that it ought not to be attended to. Mr. T. said he saw no proof whatever of the impropriety of the House receiving it. There might be some judicial question growing out of the case; but that was no reason, because it might possibly undergo a judicial course, that the general Government were not to be petitioned.

The gentleman from South Carolina [Mr. Smith] had said "that this was a kind of property on which the House could not legislate"; but he would answer this was a kind of property on which they were bound to legislate. The Fugitive Act could prove this authority; if petitions were not to be received, they would have to legislate in the dark. It appeared plainly that these men were manumitted by their masters; and because a number of men who called themselves legislators should, after they had the actual enjoyment of their liberty, come forward and say that these men should not remain at liberty, and actually authorize their recaptivity, he thought it exceedingly unjust to deprive them of the right of petitioning to have their injuries redressed. These were a set of men on whom the Fugitive Law had no power, and he thought they claimed protection under the power of that House, which always ought to lean toward freedom. Though they could not give freedom to slaves, yet he hoped gentlemen would never refuse to lend their aid to secure freemen in their rights against tyrannical imposition.

Mr. Macon said no man wished to encourage petitions more than himself and no man had considered this subject more. These men could not receive any aid from the general Government, but by application to the State justice would be done. Trials of this kind had very frequently been brought on in all the different courts of that State, and had very often ended in the freedom of slaves; the appeal was fair, and justice was done.

Mr. Varnum said the petitioners stated themselves to be freemen, and he did not see any opposition of force to convince the House they were not; surely it could not be said that color alone should designate them as slaves. He hoped the House would take all possible care that freemen should not be made slaves; to be deprived of liberty was more important than to be deprived of property. He could not think why gentlemen should be against having the fact examined; if it appears that they are slaves, the petition will of course be dismissed, but if it should appear they are free, and receive injury under the Fugitive Act, the United States ought to amend it so that justice should be done.

Mr. Kitchell said that the question was not now whether the petitioners are or are not slaves, but it is on a law of the United States. They assert that this law does act injuriously to them; the question is, therefore, whether a committee shall be appointed to inquire into the improper force of this law on the case of these men; if they are freemen, he said, they ought not to be sent back from the most distant part of the United States to North Carolina, to have justice done them, but .they ought to receive it from the general Government who made the law they complain of.

On the question for receiving the petition being put, —it was negatived—ayes 33, noes 50.

Another petition relative to slavery was presented to the House on January 2, 1800, this time against the Fugitive Law and the slave trade, praying for their repeal. The petitioners were free negroes of Philadelphia, too ignorant to sign their names, affixing their marks instead, and therefore it was evident, said those opposed to receiving the memorial, that white Abolitionists were the real movers in the matter.

This debate is notable because it contains the first threat that the South would secede if the abolition agitation were continued. The maker of the threat was the fiery John Rutledge, Jr., of South Carolina. In his speech he referred to the San Domingo insurrection, which thereafter became a stock illustration of the pro-slavery orators.

The South Will Protect Itself

John Rutledge, Jr., M.C.

Mr. Rutledge thought it a little extraordinary that, when gentlemen from some parts of the Union were positively assured that very serious, nay, dreadful, effects must be the inevitable consequence of their discussion on this subject, they still would persist. He used strong words, he said, because no others would be appropriate. Gentlemen recommended the subject to be calmly argued. Would gentlemen feel calm if measures were taken to destroy most of their property? Would calmness be consistent if entering wedges were prepared to ruin the property of whole estates? Yes, we deem this as an entering wedge to an inevitable loss of our property, if persisted in.

Three emissaries from St. Domingo appeared in the hall of the French Convention, demanding the emancipation of their species from slavery. The convention were told it would operate as an entering wedge that would go to the destruction of property and the loss of one of the finest islands in the world; that it would be murderous in the extreme; that it would open scenes which had never been practiced since the destruction of Carthage; that a whole rich country would be buried in blood; that thousands would instantly be reduced to abject penury; that the first towns in that fine island would be reduced to a heap of ashes. But those gentlemen said no, it cannot be, all our desires originate in philanthropy—we wish to do good! But, sir, we have lived to see these dreadful scenes. These horrid effects have succeeded what was conceived once to be trifling.

Most important consequences may likewise be the result of the present anti-slavery agitation, although gentlemen little apprehend it. There have been Abolition emissaries among us in the Southern States; they have begun their war upon us; an actual organization has commenced; we have had them meeting in their club rooms and debating on that subject, and determinations have been made.

I recollect that gentlemen in France used arguments like the gentleman from Massachusetts [George Thacher]: "We can indemnify these proprietors." But how did they do it, or how can it be done? Not at all. Farther, we were told these things would take place, we need not be alarmed; it was inevitable; that it was reasonable and unavoidable. Sir, it never will take place. There is one alternative which will save us from it, but that alternative I deprecate very much; that is, that we are able to take care of ourselves, and, if driven to it, we will take care of ourselves.

Samuel Goode [Va.] moved:

That the parts of the said petition which invite Congress to legislate upon subjects from which the general Government is precluded by the Constitution have a tendency to create disquiet and jealousy and ought, therefore, to receive no encouragement or countenance from this House.

The motion was adopted by a vote of—yeas 85, nay 1 [Mr. Thacher].

The question of entering into concert with foreign nations for a *humanitarian* purpose was brought forward in the Senate early in the session of 1817-1818 by a petition from the Society of Friends at Baltimore, asking that the Government adopt laws more effectually to prevent the slave trade from being carried on by citizens of the United States under foreign flags (Spanish and Portuguese), and also take measures, in concert with other nations (Great Britain in particular) to secure the entire abolition of the traffic.

Senator James Burrill, Jr., of Rhode Island, moved that the petition be referred to a committee to inquire into the expediency of the legislation and action which it proposed.

He was supported in his motion by Rufus King [N. Y.], David L. Morrill [N. H.]; the motion was opposed by George M. Troup [Ga.], George W. Campbell [Tenn.], and James Barbour [Va.].

The motion was debated on January 2 and 12, 1818, and carried by a vote of 17 to 16.

CONCERT WITH FOREIGN NATIONS TO SUPPRESS SLAVE TRADE

SENATE, JANUARY 2-12, 1818

SENATOR TROUP thought the petition a most extraordinary proposition, and asserted that, according to his apprehension, no measure could be adopted more replete with danger to the

welfare, to the very existence, of this country, than a formal
coalition, for any purposes, with any foreign nation whatever.
It was a policy, a resort to which ought always to be resisted.
He was ready to go as far as anyone in enforcing, within our
own jurisdiction, the abolition of the African slave trade, but
to direct the President to enter into any compact or concert for
this subject with any foreign nation or individuals was a step
he would never consent to. He could not separate from foreign
alliances the idea of foreign politics and foreign wars; and
the proposed measure he should view as the commencement of
a system of foreign connections tending to foreign alliances, to
which Mr. T. expressed great repugnance.

SENATOR BURRILL entirely agreed to the impolicy of foreign
alliances, but he could not view the proposed concert in this
light, nor could he conceive that any such disastrous consequences would follow it as had been anticipated by the gentleman from Georgia. Nor was the principle of the proposed
concert a novelty in this country. By referring to the treaty
of Ghent it would be found that our ministers had either made
or received overtures on this very subject, and a provision was
in consequence inserted in the treaty.[1] The concert had been
considered as indispensable to bring about the entire abolition
of the slave trade; and, Mr. B. said, it had been found impossible to put an entire stop to it without a coöperation among the
nations prohibiting it; for, no matter how many nations prohibit the trade, if one or two are allowed to carry it on, the evil
will still exist.

SENATOR KING said it was the boast of this nation that it
had the reputation of having been the first to begin the abolition of the African slave trade. The example of this country
had excited the emulation of other nations, and all of them
having any connection with this trade, except Spain and Portugal, had come into the measures for its abolition. Those two
had taken time for further consideration, and so long as their
decision was suspended the regulations of other nations would
be inefficient; an entire abolition of the traffic in slaves would
never be effected until all united to suppress it. So long as
Spain or Portugal permitted this trade, and so long as any of
our own people, to their disgrace, continued to pursue it under
those flags, it was necessary to the honor and the interest of
this country to concur in any proper measures for its suppression. He could not perceive, he said, how such a measure
as this motion looked to could lead to any such entangling con-

[1] See Vol. II, page 219.

nection as had been apprehended. What was proposed was an honest and moral concert to put an end to a traffic which is an abomination on the earth.

SENATOR CAMPBELL declared his unwillingness to enter into any compact whatever with any foreign power to regulate our own conduct or to carry our laws into effect. Two nations had thought proper still to permit the trade alluded to. What compact, said Mr. C., are we to form with others to induce these nations to forbid it? Are we to require Spain and Portugal to give up this trade? Are we to unite with France and England to urge them to give it up? And, should they yet refuse, are we to attempt to force them by arms to do so? Are we, he asked, prepared to risk a war for this object? He confessed he could not see to what other result the proposition tended.

SENATOR BURRILL said if the Senate should refuse the inquiry it might give rise to unjust surmises and suspicions as to the sincerity of the Government in passing laws for this purpose, and in entering into the stipulations of the treaty of Ghent. The Senate should be cautious not to give ground for the disgraceful suspicion that they are not sincere and hearty in this cause of suffering humanity. Every gentleman in this House wishes for the entire abolition of this abominable traffic, and this is the general voice of the country. The gentlemen here representing the slaveholding States are as decided as any others on this point, and one of those States (Virginia) was entitled, he believed, to the honor of having been the first State to prohibit it.

SENATOR BARBOUR said America stands in the relation to the rest of the world that Virginia does to America. She took the lead in the humane effort to exterminate this horrible traffic. He rejoiced to see that the great nations of Europe had adopted her precepts, and were imitating her enlightened and philanthropic example. Spain and Portugal constitute the only exception; the former, it is said, with what truth he knew not, has received a pecuniary compensation to abandon the traffic. Should this be true, as he cordially hoped it might be, Portugal will then stand alone. It is reasonably to be anticipated that she will not be able to resist the incumbent load of the civilized world; when their remonstrances are enforced by the united influence of justice, humanity, and philanthropy. Africa, then freed from those disastrous effects which this trade has produced, may, under the benign influence of peace, reason, and religion, indulge a hope that in the fulness of time she may participate in the blessings of civilization, with all its benefi-

cent effects. Nor was he averse to adopting measures in concert with any nation which he believed would be calculated to
hasten the destruction of this trade. For his part, he feared
nothing from an alliance with any nation whose only object
was humanity. No man could more highly appreciate than he
did the soundness of the political maxim inculcated by the
Father of his Country, in his legacy to the American people—
that of avoiding entangling alliances with other nations; yet,
with all his reverence for this wise precept and his determination to pursue its suggestions, he felt no apprehension from the
concert proposed. A concert like the one proposed is in its
character novel; its object is humanity; while alliances denounced by the above wise maxim have for their object dominion and power, to be acquired by the misery of mankind; to
extricate a nation from which is not unfrequently attended
with a violation of honor; or, if executed, it is frequently with
the sacrifice of peace and sometimes with ruin.

In so far, then, as the principal project of the resolution
is concerned, or the means of effecting it, he would go with the
mover; but the part to which he objected was that proposing
that Congress should unite with other nations to produce the
object; this he considered to be improper. Congress can act
only in its legislative capacity; and, by consequence, can enter
into no concert with other nations. That has been assigned to
another branch of the Government. It is through the Executive alone that intercourse and arrangements with other nations
can be effected. Leave it, therefore, where the Constitution has
placed it, without discussing the question how far this body
has a right to advise, in its executive character, the Chief Magistrate upon the propriety of entering into new arrangements
with foreign nations; a question on which there is a difference
of opinion.

SENATOR TROUP said: This word concert, Mr. President,
means something—it means connection, combination, alliance,
for a given object; it means entangling alliance. You propose
a concert with crowned heads! They never concert with themselves, but broils, and quarrels, and wars follow in the train.
History is full of them; and, if entangling connections, sir,
between monarchs, who wield the sword and the purse, who
make peace and war at their will, be fruitful of these mischiefs,
what may we not expect when you enter the lists without the
means of doing what you engage to do?

SENATOR MORRILL said: Coming from New England, where
slavery is unknown, my prejudices may be strong, my views en-

thusiastic; but, sir, allow me to be honest, believe me sincere, permit me to be plain. In New England we believe "all men are born equally free and independent"—thus commences our "Bill of Rights." Whatever their color, powers of mind, property, or rank in society, they are freemen—citizens, not slaves. They have a claim to that freedom in this asylum of liberty.

JOSEPH HEISTER'S CLAIMS TO THE VOTES OF A CHRISTIAN PEOPLE

From the collection of the New York Historical Society

Shall I not desire the termination of slavery? It is a duty, sir, I owe to myself, my country, and my God.

I am in favor of the resolution, sir, because its object comports with the dictates of reason and humanity. Though black, they are human beings, in human shape. That is not their crime, but their misfortune. We then ought to commiserate, not enslave them. Let exertions be made to raise them from their present state of degradation; assist in the mighty work. Every human affection recoils at their bondage. May every benevolent heart beat high for their freedom, and every human arm be extended for their emancipation. It is a cause, sir, in which the world is engaged. As it was commenced by the United States, let them continue their efforts; let Congress say, with all civilized nations, they will joyfully bear a part to accomplish an object so desirable, so humane.

But, sir, I am in favor of the resolution in a political point of view. Carry the great design into effect, and you place those forlorn objects within the reach of political and moral instruction. The basis on which every good government most firmly stands is knowledge and virtue. Diffuse and extend these sacred principles, and you enlarge the basis on which your Government is built; and, in the same proportion, you carry the principles of liberty and the rights of man to those who grope in darkness, and aid in the emancipation of those who are bound in the chains of despotism.

Mr. President, I am in favor of the resolution in a moral point of view. We, sir, are a Christian nation. The Bible is our moral guide. Are not its principles sacred, its precepts salutary, and its commands obligatory? Have not the frowns of indignant Heaven, and the threatenings of Jehovah, rested on nations and cities for their ingratitude to their fellow mortals? Babylon—Babylon the great has fallen! What has brought her down? The scene is viewed in prospect. "The merchants of the earth shall weep and mourn over her." In what did her commerce consist? "In gold, and silver, and precious stones, and pearls, and chariots, and slaves, and the souls of men." Ah, Mr. President, this was the climax of their abominations! They had a traffic in slaves and the souls of men. This brought down the judgments of Heaven. That they may be averted from the world, let the inhuman traffic be abolished to the end of the earth.

In accordance with the report of this and subsequent committees Congress, by the Acts of April 20, 1818, and March 3, 1819, authorized the President to send cruisers to the coast of Africa to stop the slave trade, and by the Act of May 15, 1820, declared the traffic to be piracy. By the Webster-Ashburton treaty of 1842 the Governments of the United States and Great Britain agreed to maintain independent squadrons on the African coast to act in conjunction. However, the slave trade with the United States was not entirely suppressed until the close of the Civil War.

The trade was most active in the years just prior to the war, when the domestic supply of slaves was insufficient to fill the demand for them created by the development of the Southwest. In 1859-60, 85 vessels were fitted out from New York as slavers, and it is estimated that they introduced into the country from 30,000 to 60,000 negroes. During these years the repeal of the laws against the trade was actively urged by many prominent statesmen and newspapers of the South and openly demanded and justified in political conventions, such as the Democratic convention at Charleston, S. C., in 1860 [see Vol. V, chapter vii].

CHAPTER II

THE MISSOURI COMPROMISE

[DEBATE ON THE RESTRICTION OF SLAVERY IN THE TERRITORIES]

Organization of Mississippi Territory—George Thacher [Mass.] Offers
Amendment to Exclude Slavery; It Is Defeated—Missouri Applies for
Admission to the Union—James Tallmadge, Jr. [N. Y.], in the House of
Representatives, Moves to Restrict Slavery in the State—Debate on the
Motion: in Favor, Tallmadge, John W. Taylor [N. Y.], Timothy Fuller
[Mass.], Arthur Livermore [N. H.]; Opposed, Philip P. Barbour [Va.];
Amendment Carried—The Senate Rejects the Tallmadge Amendment and
the Bill Is Lost—Arkansas Territory Organized with Slavery—Senator
Taylor's Proviso Abolishing Slavery North of 36 Degrees and 30 Min-
utes North Latitude; It Is Withdrawn—Debate in Senate on Admission
of Maine and Missouri: in Favor of Restriction of Slavery in Missouri,
Jonathan Roberts [Pa.], Walter Lowrie [Pa.], Rufus King [N. Y.];
Opposed, Freeman Walker [Ga.], Nicholas Van Dyke [Del.], James Bar-
bour [Va.], William Pinkney [Md.]—Proposal of the Missouri Compromise—Debate in the House: Proslavery Speakers, Alexander Smyth
[Va.], Robert W. Reid [Ga.], Benjamin Hardin [Ky.], Louis McLane
[Del.], Philip P. Barbour [Va.], Charles Pinckney [S. C.], John Tyler
[Va.]; Anti-Slavery Speakers, Henry Meigs [N. Y.], John W. Taylor
[N. Y.], Joseph Hemphill [Pa.], John Sergeant [Pa.], William Darling-
ton [Pa.], James Stevens [Ct.]—Missouri Is Admitted Under the Compromise—Debate in Congress on a Clause in the Proposed Constitution
of Missouri Debarring Entrance into the State of Free Negroes—Henry
Clay [Ky.] Secures a Compromise.

THE specific issue under which the slavery question
agitated the country for the greater part of the
period from the formation of the Constitution
under the Civil War was that of restrictions in regard
to slavery in the formation of Territories and the admission into the Union of new States. As has been
related in Volume I [see page 267], the Northwest Territory had been organized in 1787 with the exclusion of
slavery.

On March 23, 1798, the question of the organization

of the Territory of Mississippi (comprising roughly the present States of Alabama and Mississippi) came before the House. A resolution was offered, giving the Territory the government of the Northwest Territory as established by the Ordinance of 1787, with the exception of the prohibition of slavery. George Thacher [Mass.] offered an amendment striking out the excepting clause, and so prohibiting slavery in the Southern Territories as well as in the Northern. The question was put on Mr. Thacher's amendment and negatived, there being only 12 votes in its favor.

Senator Thomas H. Benton remarks of this discussion in his "Debates of Congress" that it "was the first debate on the prohibition of slavery in a Territory which took place under the Federal Constitution, and it is to be observed that the constitutional power of Congress to make the prohibition was not questioned by any speaker. Expedient objections only were urged."

At the close of the War of 1812 the free and slave States were the same in number, nine and nine. In 1816 (under Madison's Administration) Indiana was admitted into the Union as free soil, being a part of the Northwest Territory in which slavery had been prohibited by the Ordinance of 1787. In 1817 Mississippi was formed as a State out of the western part of Mississippi Territory, which had been organized as slave territory. In 1818 Illinois was admitted under the same conditions as Indiana. To preserve the equality of slave and free States the next State should be admitted as slave. When therefore the northern part of Missouri Territory (organized by various Acts of Congress from 1812 onward, out of the Louisiana Purchase, wherein slavery prevailed and was recognized by the treaty with France) applied for admission into the Union, late in 1818, the Southern Congressmen assumed that it would be admitted as slave. They were therefore greatly incensed when James Tallmadge, Jr. [N. Y.], on February 13, 1819, moved an amendment to the bill for its admission declaring all its inhabitants free who should be born after the date of admission, and providing for the gradual emancipation of those now held in bondage.

Mr. Tallmadge's amendment was debated from February 13 to 15, when it was adopted in the Committee of the Whole by a vote of 79 to 67.

The principal speakers in favor of the amendment were, in addition to Mr. Tallmade, John W. Taylor [N. Y.], Timothy Fuller [Mass.], and Arthur Livermore [N. H.]. Philip P. Barbour [Va.] was the only speaker in the negative whose remarks were reported at length.

Henry Clay [Ky.], the Speaker of the House, opposed the amendment, but his arguments must be gleaned from the replies made by his opponents.

Of this debate Senator Benton, in his "Debates of Congress," remarks:

This was the commencement of the great Missouri agitation which was settled by the compromise. No two words have been more confounded of late than these of the restriction and compromise—so much so that some of the eminent speakers of the time have had their speeches against the restriction quoted as being against the compromise—of which they were zealous advocates. Though often confounded, no two measures could be more opposite in their nature and effects. The restriction was to operate upon a State—the compromise on territory. The restriction was to prevent the State of Missouri from admitting slavery—the compromise was to admit slavery there, and to divide the rest of Louisiana about equally between free and slave soil. The restriction came from the North—the compromise from the South. The restriction raised the storm—the compromise allayed it.

Restriction of Slavery in Missouri

House of Representatives, February 13-15, 1819

Mr. Taylor.—Our votes this day will determine whether the high destinies of this region and of these generations shall be fulfilled, or whether we shall defeat them by permitting slavery, with all its baleful consequences, to inherit the land. Let the magnitude of this question plead my apology, while I briefly address a few considerations to the sober judgment of patriots and statesmen.

First. Has Congress power to require of Missouri a constitutional prohibition against the further introduction of slavery as a condition of her admission into the Union?

Second. If the power exist, is it wise to exercise it?

The third section of the fourth article of the Constitution declares that "the Congress shall have power to dispose of and make all needful rules and regulations respecting the territory, or other property, belonging to the United States."

After the formation of a Territory the Congress may admit the State into the Union in pursuance of a power delegated by the same section of the Constitution, in the following words: "New States may be admitted by the Congress into the Union." This grant of power is evidently alternative; its exercise is committed to the sound discretion of Congress; no injustice is done by declining it. But if Congress has the power of altogether refusing to admit new States, much more has it the power of prescribing such conditions of admission as may be judged reasonable. The exercise of this power until now has never been questioned. The act of 1802, under which Ohio was admitted into the Union, prescribed the condition that its constitution should not be repugnant to the ordinance of 1787. The sixth article of that ordinance declares, "there shall be neither slavery nor involuntary servitude in the said territory otherwise than in the punishment of crimes whereof the party shall have been duly convicted." The same condition was imposed by Congress on the people of Indiana and Illinois. These States have all complied with it and framed constitutions excluding slavery. Missouri lies in the same latitude. Its soil, productions, and climate are the same, and the same principles of government should be aplied to it.

But it is said that, by the treaty of 1803, with the French Republic [cession of Louisiana] Congress is restrained from imposing this condition. The third article is quoted as containing the prohibition. It is in the following words: "The inhabitants of the ceded territory shall be incorporated in the Union of the United States, and admitted as soon as possible, according to the principles of the Federal Constitution, to the enjoyment of all the rights, advantages, and immunities of citizens of the United States, and, in the meantime, they shall be maintained and protected in the free enjoyment of their liberty, property, and the religion which they profess." The treaty made no provision for the erection of new States in the ceded territory. That was a question of national policy, properly reserved for the decision of those to whom the constitution had committed the power.

The treaty, therefore, has no operation on the question in debate. Its requirements, however, have been faithfully fulfilled. In 1804 the laws of the United States were extended to that territory. In 1811 a law was passed to enable the people of the Territory of Orleans to form a constitution and State government, and to provide for its admission into the Union. Did Congress then doubt its power to annex conditions to such admission? No, sir, far from it. The government of Orleans had always been administered according to the principles of the civil law. The common law, so highly valued in other parts of our country, was not recognized there. Trial by jury was unknown to the inhabitants. Instead of a privilege, they considered its introduction an odious departure from their ancient administration of justice. Left to themselves, they never would have introduced it. Congress, however, knowing these things, made it a condition of their admission into the Union that trial by jury should be secured to the citizen by a constitutional provision.

Even the language of the Territory was required to be changed as a condition of its admission. French and Spanish were the only languages generally spoken or even understood. But Congress required from them a constitutional provision that their legislative and judicial proceedings should be conducted in the English language. They were not left at liberty to determine this point for themselves. From these facts it appears that Congress, at that day, acted from a conviction that it possessed the power of prescribing the conditions of their admission into the Union.

Gentlemen have said the amendment is in violation of the treaty, because it impairs the property of a master in his slave. Is it then pretended that, notwithstanding the declaration in our bill of rights, "that all men are created equal," one individual can have a vested property not only in the flesh and blood of his fellowman, but also in generations not yet called into existence? Can it be believed that the supreme legislature has no power to provide rules and regulations for ameliorating the condition of future ages? And this, too, when the Constitution itself has vested in Congress full sovereignty, by authorizing the enactment of whatever law it may deem conducive to the welfare of the country. The sovereignty of Congress in relation to the States is limited by specific grants— but in regard to the Territories it is unlimited. Missouri was purchased with our money, and, until incorporated into the family of States, it may be sold for money. Can it then be maintained that, although we have the power to dispose of the whole Territory, we have no right to provide against the further increase of slavery within its limits? That, although we may change the political relations of its free citizens by transferring their country to a foreign power, we cannot provide for the gradual abolition of slavery within its limits, nor establish those civil regulations which naturally flow from self-evident truth? No, sir, it cannot; the practice of nations and the common sense of mankind have long since decided these questions.

Having proved, as I apprehend, our right to legislate in the manner proposed, I proceed to illustrate the propriety of exercising it. And here I might rest satisfied with reminding my opponents of their own declarations on the subject of slavery. How often and how eloquently have they deplored its existence among them? Gentlemen have now an opportunity of putting their principles into practice; if they have tried slavery and found it a curse; if they desire to dissipate the gloom with which it covers their land, I call upon them to exclude it from the Territory in question; plant not its seeds in this uncorrupt soil; let not our children, looking back to the proceedings of this day, say of them, as they have been constrained to speak of their fathers, ''we wish their decision had been different; we regret the existence of this unfortunate population among us; but we found them here: we know not what to do with them; it is our misfortune, we must bear it with patience.''

History will record the decision of this day as exerting its influence for centuries to come over the population of half our continent. If we reject the amendment and suffer this evil, now easily eradicated, to strike its roots so deep in the soil that it can never be removed, shall we not furnish some apology for doubting our sincerity when we deplore its existence—shall we not expose ourselves to the same kind of censure which was pronounced by the Saviour of mankind upon the Scribes and Pharisees, who builded the tombs of the prophets and garnished the sepulchres of the righteous, and said, if they had lived in the days of their fathers, they would not have been partakers with them in the blood of the prophets, while they manifested a spirit which clearly proved them the legitimate descendants of those who killed the prophets, and thus filled up the measure of their fathers' iniquity?

Mr. Chairman, one of the gentlemen from Kentucky [Mr. Clay] has pressed into his service the cause of humanity. He has pathetically urged us to withdraw our amendment and suffer this unfortunate population to be dispersed over the country. He says they will be better fed, clothed, and sheltered, and their whole condition will be greatly improved. Sir, true humanity disowns his invocation. The humanity to which he appeals is base coin; it is counterfeit, it is that humanity which seeks to palliate disease by the application of nostrums, which

CALHOUN CONGRATULATING CLAY ON HIS DEFENCE OF SLAVERY

From the collection of the New York Historical Society

scatter its seeds through the whole system—which saves a finger to-day, but amputates the arm to-morrow. Sir, my heart responds to the call of humanity; I will zealously unite in any practicable means of bettering the condition of this oppressed people. I am ready to appropriate a territory to their use, and to aid them in settling it—but I am not willing, I never will consent, to declare the whole country west of the Mississippi a market overt for human flesh. In vain will you enact severe laws against the importation of slaves if you create for them an additional demand by opening the western world to their employment. While a negro man is bought in Africa for a few gewgaws or a bottle of whisky, and sold at New Orleans for twelve or fifteen hundred dollars, avarice will stimulate to the violation of your laws. Notwithstanding the penalties and confiscations denounced in your statutes and actually enforced on all detected offenders, the slave trade continues. A vigilant execution of the laws may diminish it, but, while you increase the demand and offer so great temptation to the cupidity of unprincipled men, they will encounter every peril in the prosecution of this unhallowed traffic.

It is objected that the amendment is calculated to disfranchise our brethren of the South by discouraging their emigration to the country west of the Mississippi. If it were proposed to discriminate between citizens of the different sections of our Union and allow a Pennsylvanian to hold slaves there while the power was denied to a Virginian, the objection might very properly be made; but when we place all on an equal footing, denying to all what we deny to one, I am unable to discover the injustice or inequality of which honorable gentlemen have thought proper to complain. The description of emigrants may be affected in some measure by the amendment in question. If slavery shall be tolerated, the country will be settled by rich planters, with their slaves; if it shall be rejected, the emigrants will chiefly consist of the poorer and more laborious classes of society. If it be true that the prosperity and happiness of a country ought to constitute the grand object of its legislators, I cannot hesitate for a moment which species of population deserves most to be encouraged by the laws we may pass. Gentlemen, in their zeal to oppose the amendment, appear to have considered but one side of the case. If the rejection of slavery will tend to discourage emigration from the South, will not its admission have the same effect in relation to the North and East? Whence came the people who, with a rapidity never before witnessed, have changed the wilderness between the Ohio and Mississippi into fruitful fields; who have erected there, in a period almost too short for the credibility of future ages, three of the freest and most flourishing States in our Union?

Do you believe that these people will settle in a country where they must take rank with negro slaves? Having neither the ability nor will to hold slaves themselves, they labor cheerfully while labor is honorable; make it disgraceful, they will despise it. You cannot degrade it more effectually than by establishing a system whereby it shall be performed principally by slaves. The business in which they are generally engaged, be it what it may, soon becomes debased in public estimation. It is considered low and unfit for freemen. I cannot better

IV—4

illustrate this truth than by referring to a remark of the honorable gentleman from Kentucky [Mr. Clay]. I have often admired the liberality of his sentiments. He is governed by no vulgar prejudices; yet with what abhorrence did he speak of the performance, by your wives and daughters, of those domestic offices which he was pleased to call servile! What comparison did he make between the "black slaves" of Kentucky and the "white slaves" of the North; and how instantly did he strike a balance in favor of the condition of the former! If such opinions and expressions, even in the ardor of debate, can fall from that honorable gentleman, what ideas do you suppose are entertained of laboring men by the majority of slaveholders? Whom of that class have they ever called to fill stations of any considerable responsibility? When have we seen a Representative on this floor, from that section of our Union, who was not a slaveholder? I appeal to gentlemen whether the selection of a laboring man, however well educated, would not be considered an extraordinary event?

An argument has been urged by a gentleman from Virginia [Mr. Barbour] against the proposed amendment connected with our revenues. He said that by prohibiting the further introduction of slaves into the proposed State we should reduce the price and diminish the sales of our public lands. In my opinion, the effect would be precisely the reverse. True it is that lands for cultivation have sold higher in Alabama than in Illinois, but this is owing not to the rejection of slavery in the one and its admission into the other, but to the different staples they are capable of producing. The advanced price of cotton has created in the market a demand for lands suited to its cultivation and enhanced their value far beyond any former precedent. But, to test the truth of the position, we must ascertain the relative value of land in adjoining States, the one allowing and the other rejecting slavery, where the climate, soil, productions, and advantages of market are similar. Pennsylvania and Maryland furnish fair specimens of comparison in all these respects. But here the result is in direct opposition to the conjecture of the gentleman from Virginia. Land on the Pennsylvania side of the line, where the power of holding slaves does not exist, uniformly sells at a higher price than lands of equal quality on the Maryland side, where the power is in full exercise. It, therefore, is probable that the further introduction of slavery into Missouri, far from increasing, would actually diminish the value of our public lands. But, should the fact be otherwise, I entreat gentlemen to consider whether it become the high character of an American Congress to barter the present happiness and future safety of unborn millions for a few pieces of pelf, for a few cents on an acre of land. For myself, I would no sooner contaminate the national treasury with such ill-gotten gold than I would tarnish the fame of our national ships by directing their employment in the African slave trade.

If I agreed in opinion with the gentleman from Georgia [Mr. Cobb] that this amendment does not present an insurmountable barrier against the further introduction of slavery; that Missouri, after becoming a State, may call a convention and change this feature of her constitution—even then I should consider the amendment scarcely less important than if it were a fundamental and unalterable compact. On this subject we have experience, and the result has justified the best hopes of our country. Slavery was excluded from the Territories north of the Ohio. Our power over their municipal regulations has since been withdrawn; they have taken the government into their own hands. But who has not seen the moral effect produced on the inhabitants by the ordinance of 1787? It is as permanent as the soil over which it was established. The exclusion of slavery from all these States is now more effectually insured by public sentiment than by their constitutional prohibitions. Require the government of Missouri to commence right, and the same moral effect will then be produced. No convention of the people will ever permit the future introduction of slaves. Let their political institutions be established in wisdom, and I shall confidently trust in the good sense of the people to direct them hereafter. But, be the event as it may, I at least shall have the satisfaction of reflecting that, if the misfortune of slavery shall be entailed upon this country, everything in my power will have been done to prevent it.

MR. FULLER.—The Constitution expressly makes a republican form of government in the several States a fundamental principle, to be preserved under the sacred guarantee of the National Legislature. [Art. 4, Sec. 4.] Now, sir, the amendment proposed by the gentleman from New York [Mr. Tallmadge] merely requires that slavery shall be prohibited in Missouri. Does this imply anything more than that its constitution shall be republican? The existence of slavery in any State is so far a departure from republican principles. The Declaration of Independence, penned by the illustrious statesman then and at this time a citizen of a State which admits slavery, defines the principle on which our national and State constitutions are all professedly founded. The second paragraph of that instrument begins thus: "We hold these truths to be self-evident—that all men are created equal—that they are endowed by their Creator with certain inalienable rights—that among these are life, liberty, and the pursuit of happiness." Since, then, it cannot be denied that slaves are men, it follows that they are in a purely republican government both free, and are entitled to liberty and the pursuit of happiness.

Mr. Fuller was here interrupted by several gentlemen, who thought it improper to question in debate the republican character of the slaveholding States, which had also a tendency, as one gentleman [Mr. Colston of Virginia] said, to deprive those States of the right to hold slaves as property, and he adverted to the probability that there might be slaves in the gallery listening to the debate.

Mr. F. assured the gentleman that nothing was further from his thoughts than to question on that floor the right of Virginia and other States which held slaves when the Constitution was established to continue to hold them. With that subject the national legislature could not interfere, and ought not to attempt it. Sir, it is my wish to allay, not to excite, local animosities; but I shall never refrain from advancing such arguments in debate as my duty requires, nor do I believe that the reading of our Declaration of Independence, or a discussion of republican principles on any occasion, can endanger the rights or merit the disapprobation of any portion of the Union.

The honorable Speaker cites the first clause in the second section of the fourth article: "The citizens of each State shall be entitled to all the privileges and immunities of citizens of the several States," which he thinks would be violated by the condition proposed in the constitution of Missouri. To keep slaves —to make one portion of the population the property of another—hardly deserves to be called a privilege, since what is gained by the masters must be lost by the slaves. But, independently of this consideration, I think the observations already offered to the committee, showing that holding the black population in servitude is an exception to the general principles of the Constitution, and cannot be allowed to extend beyond the fair import of the terms by which that exception is provided, are a sufficient answer to the objection. The speaker proceeds in the same train of reasoning, and asks, if Congress can require one condition, how many more can be required, and where these conditions will end? With regard to a republican constitution, Congress are obliged to require that condition, and that is enough for the present question; but I contend, further, that Congress has a right, at their discretion, to require any other reasonable condition. Several others were required of Ohio, Indiana, Illinois, and Mississippi. The State of Louisiana, which was a part of the territory ceded to us at the same time with Missouri, was required to provide in her constitution for trials by jury, the writ of habeas corpus, the principles of civil and religious liberty, with several others peculiar to that State. These certainly are, none of them, more indispensable ingredients in a republican form of government than the equality of privileges of all the population; yet these have not been denied to be reasonable and warranted by the national Constitution in the admission of new States.

One gentleman, however, has contended against the amendment because it abridges the rights of the slave-holding States to transport their slaves to the new States for sale or otherwise. This argument is attempted to be enforced in various ways, and particularly by the clause in the Constitution last cited. It admits, however, of a very clear answer by recurring to the ninth section of article first, which provides that "the migration or importation of such persons as any of the States then existing shall admit shall not be prohibited by Congress till 1808." This clearly implies that the *migration* and importation may be prohibited *after* that year. The importation has been prohibited, but the migration has not hitherto been restrained; Congress, however, may restrain it when it may be judged expedient. Hitherto it has not been found necessary for Congress to prohibit migration or transportation from State to State. But now it becomes the right and duty of Congress to guard against the further extension of the intolerable evil and the crying enormity of slavery.

The expediency of this measure is very apparent. The opening of an extensive slave market will tempt the cupidity of those who otherwise perhaps might gradually emancipate their slaves. We have heard much, Mr. Chairman, of the Colonization Society,[1] an institution which is the favorite of the humane gentlemen in the slave-holding States. They have long been lamenting the miseries of slavery and earnestly seeking for a remedy compatible with their own safety and the happiness of their slaves. At last the great desideratum is found—a colony in Africa for the emancipated blacks. How will the generous in-

---

[1] See the following chapter.

tentions of these humane persons be frustrated if the price of slaves is to be doubled by a new and boundless market! Instead of emancipation of the slaves, it is much to be feared that unprincipled wretches will be found kidnapping those who are already free, and transporting and selling the hapless victims into hopeless bondage. Sir, I really hope that Congress will not contribute to discountenance and render abortive the generous and philanthropic views of this most worthy and laudable society.

Mr. Barbour.—Our power in relation to this subject is derived from the first clause of the third section of the fourth article of the Constitution, which is in these words: "New States may be admitted, by the Congress, into this Union." Now, sir, although, by the next succeeding clause of the same section, "Congress has the power to make all needful rules and regulations respecting the territory of the United States"; and although, therefore, while the proposed State continued a part of our territory, upon the footing of a territorial government, it would have been competent for us, under the power expressly given, to make needful rules and regulations—to have established the principle now proposed; yet the question assumes a totally different aspect when that principle is intended to apply to a State. This term State has a fixed and determinate meaning; in itself it imports the existence of a political community free and independent, and entitled to exercise all the rights of sovereignty of every description whatever. As it stands in the Constitution, it is to be defined with some limitation upon that principle of construction which has reference to the subject-matter. The extent of the limitation, according to this rule, is obviously this, that it shall enjoy all those rights of sovereignty which belong to the original States which composed the Federal family, and into a union with which it is to be admitted. Now, sir, although the original States are shorn of many of their beams of sovereignty—such, for example, as that of declaring war, of regulating commerce, etc.; yet we know that, even by an express amendment to the Constitution, all powers not expressly delegated are reserved to the States respectively; and of course the power in question of deciding whether slavery shall or shall not exist.

Gentlemen had said that slavery was prohibited in many of the original States. Does not the House, said Mr. B., at the first glance, perceive the answer to this remark? It is an argument from fact to principle, and in this its utter fallacy consists. It is true that slavery does not exist in many of the original States; but why does it not? Because they themselves, in the exercise of their legislative power, have willed that it shall be so. But, though it does not now exist, it is competent for them, by a law of their own enactment, to authorize it—to call it into existence whenever they shall think fit.

Sir, how different would be the situation of Missouri if the proposed amendment be adopted. The State would obviously labor under this disadvantage in relation to the other States; that, whereas the older free States might introduce slavery, Missouri could not, unless, indeed, another opinion, which has been advanced, is correct, that Missouri might forthwith change its constitution, and get rid of the difficulty. If that be the case, sir, as has been justly remarked, we were doing worse than nothing to legislate upon the subject.

But, said he, if we pursue this reasoning still further, and follow it up to all the consequences to which it will lead, we shall be more forcibly struck with its impropriety. If we have a right to go one step in relation to new States, beyond the footing upon which the original States stand; if we have a right to shear them of one beam more of sovereignty, we have the same right to take from them any other attribute of sovereign power.

Again, if we had the power to say that their constitution should provide that there should not be slavery, we had the same power over the converse of the proposition, and to require them to provide that there should be slavery; he believed this latter principle would not be contended for.

It is said that the like prohibition has been enacted as it respects the States northwest of the River Ohio. In the first place, the House would recollect that an ordinance was passed by the old Congress, at a period anterior to the present Constitution, ordaining that as a fundamental article in relation to all the Northwest Territory, and therefore the precedent, if it would otherwise have any weight, failed in its application. But, he said, he did not hesitate to express it as his decided opinion that the ordinance which he had just mentioned was utterly void, and, consequently, that those States might introduce slavery among them, if they so willed, because the territory which composes them originally belonged to Virginia. She had conquered it by her arms; she ceded it to the United States upon the express condition that it should be formed into States as free, sovereign, and independent as the other States. The prohibition of slavery was ordained by the Continental Congress, after the cession had been made, which would unquestionably render those States less sovereign than the original States of the Federal Union.

But it has been said that we imposed conditions on the admission of the State of Louisiana into the Union. What were those conditions? That civil and religious liberty should be established, and the trial by jury secured. It cannot be necessary to remind the House that these several provisions attached also to the original States, by the most explicit declaration to that effect, in the first, fifth, and seventh amendments to the Constitution of the United States.

Our business is to create a political community of a particular character, as prescribed by the constitution; to itself it will belong to regulate its interior concerns, and, among others, to decide whether it will or will not admit involuntary servitude.

In respect to the justice of the measure, he would beg leave to submit some remarks to the House. Although the slaves in the South were held as property, although certainly degraded in the scale of society by reason of their servitude, we felt for them those sympathies which bind one man to another, though that other may be our inferior. Such were the feelings of the Southern people toward their slaves that nothing scarcely but the necessity of the master would induce him to sell a faithful slave. If the master emigrated, he would carry his slaves with him, not only for the various reasons which he had already stated, but because, going into a wilderness, where much labor was necessary to clear the country, they were, on that account, peculiarly necessary. Under these circumstances a prohibition of the importation of slaves would, in almost every instance, be tantamount to a prohibition of the emigration of the Southern people to the State of Missouri. He asked whether it could be just to adopt such a regulation as would open an illimitable tract of the most fertile land to the northern part of the United States, and, in effect, entirely shut out the whole Southern people? If it were correct in relation to Missouri, it would be equally so as to the whole tract of country lying west of the Mississippi. He hoped, from this view of the subject, the House would be struck with its monstrous injustice.

Again, he would ask if it can be good policy to perpetuate fixed boundaries, either natural or artificial, between the slaveholding and non-slaveholding States? He had thought that the great object of our Federal compact was union. The surest possible mode of securing our political union, next to promoting the common defence and general welfare, is to give, as far as possible, every facility to the intercourse between the different sections of this extensive Republic; that, by the attrition which will be the result of that intercourse, the asperities of our mutual prejudices and jealousies may be rubbed off; and, in short, that we may be knit together by a sympathy of feelings, by a community of habits and manners which ought to bind us together as brothers of the same great political family. Already is the Northern part of our country, together with that north-west of the river Ohio, divided from us by those distinguishing names of slaveholding and non-slaveholding. Let us not make the Mississippi another great natural boundary for the purpose of perpetuating the same distinctions and dividing our country into castes. Gentlemen mistake when they suppose that, if slaves be permitted to be carried to Missouri, the Northern people will not emigrate to that State. Look at the fact in the Southern States; the Northern hive is continually pouring forth its swarms of emigrants, and many of them, especially of the mercantile class, alight and settle among us; they soon become familiar with our habits and modes of life, prosper in an eminent degree, far beyond our own people, and, indeed, he hesitated not to say, were entirely satisfied and happy, although they were in a slaveholding State. Gentlemen equally mistake when they suppose that their countrymen of the North, who are obliged to labor, would be degraded to a level with the slaves. Sir, our experience proves the contrary. We, too, have some of our citizens who are unable to purchase slaves, and who, therefore, till the ground with their own hands. But, sir, notwithstanding this, they have all that erectness of character which belongs to them as freemen, conscious of their political and civil rights; and he who should dare to treat them with disrespect, because fortune had not poured as much wealth into their laps as into his, would draw down upon him the execration of all good men.

Another effect of this amendment would be, in an essential degree, to affect the value of the countless millions of public lands beyond the Mississippi. He said he had already endeavored to show that it would obstruct the emigration from the Southern States. Precisely in proportion as it produced this effect, it would, of course, lessen the number of purchasers, and diminish the competition.

MR. LIVERMORE spoke as follows: I propose to show what slavery is, and to mention a few of the many evils which follow in its train; and I hope to evince that we are not bound to tolerate the existence of so disgraceful a state of things beyond its present extent, and that it would be impolitic and very unjust to let it spread over the whole face of our Western territory. Slavery in the United States is the condition of man subjected to the will of a master who can make any disposition of him short of taking away his life. In those States where it is tolerated, laws are enacted making it penal to instruct slaves in the art of reading, and they are not permitted to attend public worship or to hear the Gospel preached. Thus the light of science and of religion is utterly excluded from the mind, that the body may be more easily bowed down to servitude. The bodies of slaves may, with impunity, be prostituted to any purpose and deformed in any manner by their owners. The sympathies of nature in slaves are disregarded; mothers and children are sold and separated; the children wring their little hands and expire in agonies of grief, while the bereft mothers commit suicide in despair. How long will the desire of wealth render us blind to the sin of holding both the bodies and souls of our fellow-men in chains! But, sir, I am admonished of the Constitution, and told that we cannot emancipate slaves. I know we may not infringe that instrument, and therefore do not propose to emancipate slaves. The proposition before us goes only to prevent our citizens from making slaves of such as have a right to freedom. In the present slaveholding States let slavery continue, for our boasted Constitution connives at it; but do not, for the sake of cotton and tobacco, let it be told to future ages that, while pretending to love liberty, we have purchased an extensive country to disgrace it with the foulest reproach of nations. Our Constitution requires no such thing of us. The ends for which that supreme law was made are succinctly stated in its preface. They are, first, to form a more perfect union and insure domestic tranquillity. Will slavery effect this? Can we, sir, by mingling bond with free, black spirits with white, like Shakespeare's witches in Macbeth, form a more perfect union and insure domestic tranquillity? Secondly, to establish justice. Is justice to be established by subjecting half mankind to the will of the other half? Justice, sir, is blind to colors, and weighs in equal scales the rights of all men, whether white or black. Thirdly, to provide for the common defence and secure the blessings of liberty. Does slavery add anything to the common defence? Sir, the strength of a republic is in the arm of freedom. But, above all things, do the blessings of liberty consist in slavery? If there is any sincerity in our profession that slavery is an ill, tolerated only from necessity, let us not, while we feel that ill, shun the cure which consists only in an honest avowal that liberty and equal rights are the end and aim of all our institutions, and that to tolerate slavery beyond the narrowest limits prescribed for it by the Constitution is a perversion of them all.

Slavery, sir, I repeat, is not established by our Constitution; but a part of the States are indulged in the commission of a sin from which they could not at once be restrained, and which they would not consent to abandon. But, sir, if we could, by any process of reasoning, be brought to believe it justifiable to hold others to involuntary servitude, policy forbids that we should increase it. Even the present slaveholding States have an interest, I think, in limiting the extent of involuntary servitude; for, should slaves become much more numerous, and, conscious of their strength, draw the sword against their masters, it will be to the free States that the masters must resort for an efficient power to suppress servile insurrection.

An opportunity is now presented, if not to diminish, at least to prevent, the growth of a sin which sits heavy on the soul of every one of us. By embracing this opportunity we may retrieve the national character, and, in some degree, our own. But if we suffer it to pass unimproved, let us at least be consistent, and declare that our Constitution was made to impose slavery, and not to establish liberty. Let us no longer tell idle tales about the gradual abolition of slavery; away with colonization societies if their design is only to rid us of free blacks and turbulent slaves; have done also with Bible societies whose views are extended to Africa and the East Indies, while they overlook the deplorable condition of their sable brethren within our own borders; make no more laws to prohibit the importation of slaves, for the world must see that the object of such laws is alone to prevent the glutting of a prodigious market for the flesh and blood of man, which we are about to establish in the West, and to enhance the price of sturdy wretches, reared like black cattle and horses for sale on our own plantations.

On the following day (February 16) the amendment of Mr. Tallmadge was altered in character, divided into two sections, and then passed; the first section, prohibiting the further introduction of slavery, by a vote of 87 to 76, and the second, emancipating at the age of 25 all slaves born in the State after its admission into the Union, by a vote of 82 to 78.

The House then passed the bill to admit Missouri into the Union.

The bill was sent to the Senate on February 17, 1819.

This body, on February 27, struck out, by a vote of 31 to 7, the clause relating to children of the slaves, and, by a vote of 22 to 16, that relating to further introduction of slavery into the State. The House refused to accept these amendments by a vote of 78 to 66, and, the Senate adhering to its action, the bill was lost and Missouri remained a Territory.

ORGANIZATION OF ARKANSAS TERRITORY

February 17, 1819, the House, in Committee of the Whole, began the discussion of the bill to organize the southern part of Missouri Territory into the Territory of Arkansas. The debate was wide and long continued, covering most of the ground of the preceding discussion, but differing in part, as the present proposition was to impose a condition on a territorial government and not on a State. Louis McLane [Del.] suggested that a line should be fixed north of which slavery hereafter should not be permitted in admitting new States into the Union.

On February 19 the House voted, 89 to 87, to strike out the clause liberating, at the age of 25, slaves born in the Territory, and, 90 to 86, to strike out the clause prohibiting the introduction of slavery into the Territory. The Senate, on March 1, concurred in the bill and the Territory was thus organized as slave.

Upon the passage of the bill in the House Mr. John W. Taylor [N. Y.], after stating that he thought it important that some line should be designated beyond which slavery should not be permitted, etc., moved the following amendment as an additional section to the bill:

"That neither slavery nor involuntary servitude shall hereafter be introduced into any part of the Territories of the United States lying north of 36 degrees and 30 minutes of north latitude."[1]

---

[1] This proposed line, while exempting Arkansas from the restriction, would have included the State of Missouri in it, as it followed the latitude of 36° 30′ through its whole course in the Louisiana Purchase.

The amendment, meeting opposition, was withdrawn by the mover for introduction at a more favorable occasion.

Before the meeting of the next Congress the legislatures of many of the Northern States, including Delaware, passed resolutions endorsing the Tallmadge proviso. In many cases the vote was unanimous, showing that old party lines had been wiped out by this new and portentous issue. For the first time in American politics the North and the South stood solidly arrayed against each other.

Congress met on December 6, 1819. Alabama was admitted as a slave State on December 14. Missouri again demanded admission. The district of Maine, in Massachusetts, separated by New Hampshire from the rest of the State and differing from it in politics, being Republican, while the "Old Bay State" almost alone in the Union remained Federalist, also applied for admission as a separate State. On January 3, 1820, the House of Representatives passed the bill, and it went up to the Senate, where a determined effort was made by the pro-slavery majority (which included three Northern Senators) to block its passage except on condition that Missouri, with a constitution permitting slavery, was also admitted. Accordingly, after a hard-fought fight with the minority, lasting a month, the majority on February 16, 1820, passed a bill (23 votes to 21) admitting Maine, but with a "rider" admitting Missouri without restriction as to slavery.

Senator Jesse B. Thomas [Ill.] then proposed a compromise in the Missouri section of the bill, which was in effect the restriction proposed in the House the preceding session by John W. Taylor [N. Y.], with Missouri excepted from its application. This was adopted by the Senate on February 17 by a vote of 34 to 10, the extreme pro-slavery men voting in the negative.

In the meantime the House, beginning on January 24, 1820, had been debating the Missouri bill with great fervor. The Tallmadge amendment (restricting slavery) of the last session had been reintroduced, as well as the Thomas compromise.

On February 28, by a vote of 97 to 76, the House disagreed to the changes made in its Maine bill by the Senate. The Senate refused to recede from its amendments, and a joint conference committee was appointed by both chambers. On March 2 this committee reported that the Senate should recede from its union of the Maine and Missouri bills, that the House should give up the Tallmadge proviso, and that both chambers should unite in admitting Missouri with the Thomas amendment (the compromise).

The Tallmadge amendment was then struck out in the House by a vote of 90 to 87; the Thomas amendment was passed by a vote of 134 to 42, and a proviso was concurred in to secure the return of fugitive slaves from every part of the Louisiana Purchase. Similar action was taken by the Senate, and the bill went to the President, who, after conferring with his Cabinet as to the constitutionality of the Thomas amendment and receiving a unanimous opinion in the affirmative, signed the Missouri bill on March 6, 1820. The President had already (on March 3, 1820) signed the act admitting Maine.

In the Senate debate the chief speakers whose speeches were reported were: in favor of the restriction of slavery, Jonathan Roberts [Pa.] and Walter Lowrie [Pa.], Rufus King [N. Y.]; opposed, Freeman Walker [Ga.], Nicholas Van Dyke [Del.], James Barbour [Va.], and William Pinkney [Md.].

THE ADMISSION OF MISSOURI

SENATE, JANUARY 13-FEBRUARY 16, 1820

SENATOR ROBERTS.—I am willing to consider Missouri as an inchoate State; no one will more gladly see her admitted into the Union; but I wish to see the page of her constitution irradiated with the fundamental principles of civil and religious liberty—to see her become a party to that covenant round which the patriots of '76 pledged their lives, their fortunes, and their sacred honor. The committee have attached the admission of Missouri to the bill for admitting Maine, under the pretext of congeniality. How insufficient the pretence! What ludicrous incongruity do the two propositions present! You are not acting on a section of two or three lines; as to Maine, it is her constitution you are ratifying. What do you find on the front of it? "Article 1, section 1: All men are born free and equal, and are free to worship God in their own way." Here is a substantial pledge to the good old faith. To her we may say, Come, sister, take your place in our constellation; the luster of your countenance will brighten the American galaxy. But do not urge us to admit Missouri, under a pretence of congeniality—with the visage of a savage, deformed with the hideous cicatrices of barbaric pride—with her features marred as if the finger of Lucifer had been drawn across them.

Senator Walker discussed the constitutional phase of the question.

The gentlemen who rely upon the 9th section of the 1st article of the Constitution contend that the power impliedly acknowledged to reside in Congress to prohibit the migration of slaves is sufficiently extensive to authorize the interdiction of carrying slaves from one State to another of this Union, or from the States to the Territories belonging to the United States; and that Congress may well regulate the intercourse between the States and Territories, in this regard, and totally prohibit the "migration" of slaves.

The construction which I am disposed to give to this section is—that the word "importation," as its appropriate meaning would indicate, looks abroad and was intended to embrace slaves brought into this country from Africa and elsewhere by water. The word "migration" was intended to embrace such as should be brought into the United States by land, from the contiguous territory belonging to foreign powers. For it would have been idle and vain to have prohibited the "importation" or the bringing of slaves directly into our ports—while there should be no interdiction of "migration" from the territory of foreign powers immediately adjoining the territory of the United States, and it must be recollected that, at the time of the adoption of the Federal Constitution, this country was bordered in different directions by territory belonging to other nations. By giving this construction you satisfy the full meaning of both words.[1]

[1] This clause in the Constitution forms a part of the staple in every speech on the Missouri question, being quoted for opposite purposes by the two sides to the question—by one side, the phrases "migration" and "importation" being held to be synonymous and applicable to slaves within the United States, and their removal from one State to another; by the other side being held as words of different import, and applicable both to

MR. LOWRIE.—In the Constitution it is provided that "the migration or importation of such persons as any of the States now existing shall think proper to admit shall not be prohibited by the Congress prior to the year 1808," etc. In this debate it seems generally to be admitted, by gentlemen on the opposite side, that these two words are not synonymous; but what their meaning is they are not so well agreed. One gentleman tells us it was intended to prevent slaves from being brought in by land; another gentleman says it was intended to restrain Congress from interfering with emigration from Europe.

These constructions cannot both be right. I shall give you no construction of my own, but refer to the authority of James Madison and James Wilson, who were both members of the Constitutional Convention, and who gave their construction to these words, long before this question was agitated. Mr. Madison observes that to say this clause was intended to prevent emigration does not deserve an answer. And Judge Wilson says expressly it was intended to place the new States under the control of Congress as to the introduction of slaves.

It is further said that the Louisiana treaty guarantees their property to all the inhabitants of Missouri, and that this property embraces slaves. The inhabitants then there were the parties we admit to this treaty; and, whatever may have been their rights or their property, they are not touched by this amendment. But farther proof is still wanted, because it is denied that the word *property*, in this treaty, means slaves. Here I

slaves and free persons, brought or coming from abroad. "Migration" implied voluntary action—importation, involuntary. The puzzle in the clause came from the use of both words, and from the necessity as well as the impossibility of finding a consistent meaning for each one. The care of the Constitution, in the use of language, was known. Far from using an equivocal phrase, it would not use two of the same import where one was enough; yet here was an exception—a departure from that laudable care; and, according to Mr. Madison, it was done on purpose, and for the ease of scrupulous consciences. Mr. Madison, in his letter of November, 1819, to Mr. Robert Walsh, thus accounts for it: "Some of the States had scruples about admitting the term 'slaves' into the instrument; hence the descriptive phrase, 'migration, or importation of persons'; the term migration allowing those who were scrupulous of acknowledging expressly a property in human beings to view *imported* persons as a species of emigrants, while others might apply the term to foreign malefactors sent or coming into the country. It is possible, though not recollected, that some might have had an eye to the case of freed blacks as well as malefactors." So that this phrase, "migration," which gave so much trouble to our Congress, and excited such alarming apprehension in one-half of the Union, was only a mode of getting a unanimous vote for the same thing, to wit: the non-importation of Africans for slaves after a certain day.—*Thomas H. Benton in "Debates of Congress."*

ask no rule of construction that is foreign to the subject. Apply to the writers on the law of nations; let them pass upon these words; try them by the principles of the Constitution; submit them to the test of reason; there all speak the same language; they tell you that *slaves* and *property* are not convertible terms. In the history of our Government, we have a case fully in point: When Virginia ceded the Northwestern Territory to Congress, it was on condition that it should become a member of the Federal Union, and have the same rights, sovereignty, freedom, and independence, as the other States. This language is as strong as that of the treaty with France; neither can it be denied that, at the time Virginia made this cession, there were in this territory a number of inhabitants professing to be her citizens and owning slaves.

Congress, with the knowledge of these facts, and the deed of cession before them, passed the ordinance of 1787, by which slavery was banished from this fair portion of our territory.

Humanity to the slaves themselves, it is said, requires the rejection of this amendment. How is the matter of fact on this point? Every gentleman here knows the situation of slaves in the South—the husband is in one family, the wife in another, the children in another. In removing, no respect to these relations can be paid—all must be disregarded; the husband and the wife must part, to meet no more; the father is dragged away, and the mother and the children left, or they are taken and he by force is compelled to stay behind; or, if he escapes after them, he is pursued, bound, and brought back. This, sir, is not fancy; these scenes, but a few months ago, I witnessed in person, among emigrants going to this said Missouri. Our humanity may be called sickly, but it gives no sanction to scenes like these.

Gentlemen have endeavored to prove that, by opening the extensive regions of the West to the introduction of slaves, nothing is thereby done to spread slavery; that, whether they are admitted west of the Mississippi or not, the number remains the same. I presume, sir, that every gentleman here has paid some attention to the principle which governs the population of the human race. It is capable of demonstration that the population increases faster than the means of subsistence; the one increases in a geometrical, the other in an arithmetical, progression. In every nation the population presses more or less against the means of subsistence, and from its very nature must continue to do so until the end of time.[1]

[1] The doctrine of the Rev. Thomas Robert Malthus.

IV—5

Apply these principles to the case before us, and what becomes of the gentleman's argument? Seventy years ago the penetrating mind of Dr. Franklin discovered this principle. Go, says he, to Africa, and see if you can discover the gap from whence the negroes have come, that have blackened half America, the West Indies, and many other places! The spring of population will always keep the number full. A market extended as the forests of your Western regions is thus opened for the sale of human flesh. Every inducement which avarice or the insatiable love of gain could desire is held out to the slaveholder to increase the number of his slaves. Under such inducements this class of population will increase with a rapidity heretofore unknown. Even at the rate of increase from 1800 to 1810, in a single century there will be upward of twenty-seven millions of slaves in the United States. This single fact, founded as it is on arithmetical certainty, is sufficiently alarming; but, sir, it points you to a very different policy from the one contended for by the honorable members on the other side.

SENATOR VAN DYKE.—Sir, it must be admitted by every statesman that this Constitution never was designed to have jurisdiction over the domestic concerns of the people in the several States. No, sir, these are wisely left exclusively to the State sovereignties, as their natural guardians. The proposed amendment, if adopted, will regulate, by an irrevocable provision in a statute, one of the domestic relations of the people of the State of Missouri. If Congress can regulate one, why not all of these domestic relations? Even the contract of marriage and the period of release from guardianship may become the subject of discussion in some future Congress, on the admission of some future State. If such a power exists, who shall stay its hand or prescribe its limits?

SENATOR BARBOUR.—The gentleman from Pennsylvania asks shall we suffer Missouri to come into the Union with the savage mark of slavery on her countenance? I appeal to that gentleman to know whether this be language to address to an American Senate, composed equally of members from States precisely in the condition that Missouri would be in, were she to tolerate slavery. Are these sentiments calculated to cherish that harmony and affection so essential to any beneficial results from our Union? But, sir, I will not imitate this course, and I will strive to repress the feeling which such remarks are calculated to awaken.

Gentlemen assure us that they do not mean to touch slavery in the old States. What kind of ethics is this that is bounded by latitude and longitude, which is inoperative on the left, but is omnipotent on the right bank of a river? Such a doctrine is well calculated to excite our solicitude; for, although the gentlemen who now hold it are sincere in their declarations, and mean to content themselves with a triumph in this controversy, what security have we that others will not apply the doctrine to the South generally?

Let it not be supposed that in the abstract I am advocating slavery. Like all other human things, it is mixed with good and evil—the latter, no doubt, preponderating. Whether slavery was ordained by God himself in a particular revelation to his chosen people, or whether it be merely permitted as a part of that moral evil which seems to be the inevitable portion of man, are questions I will not approach; I leave them to the casuists and the divines. It is sufficient for us, as statesmen, to know that it has existed from the earliest ages of the world, and that to us has been assigned such a portion as, in reference to their number and the various considerations resulting from a change of their condition, no remedy, even plausible, has been suggested, though wisdom and benevolence united have unceasingly brooded over the subject.

However dark and inscrutable may be the ways of heaven, who is he that arrogantly presumes to arraign them? The same mighty power that planted the greater and the lesser luminary in the heavens permits on earth the bondsman and the free. To that Providence, as men and Christians, let us bow. If it be consistent with his will, in the fulness of time, to break the fetter of the slave, he will raise up some Moses to be their deliverer. To him commission will be given to lead them up out of the land of bondage. At his approach, seas will subside and mountains disappear. When the revelation shall be made, and the jubilee of emancipation be proclaimed, philanthropy will lift its voice to swell the joyful note, which, sweeping the continent and the isles of the new world, and resounding through the old, shall cause the oppressor to let go his prey, the dungeon to surrender its victim, and give emancipation to the slave. Till then let us draw consolation from the reflection that, however incomprehensible this dispensation may be to us, it is a link in that great concatenation which is permitted by omnipotent power and goodness, and must issue in universal good.

Senator Rufus King of New York followed with a speech which was not reported. Its arguments can, however, be inferred from the succeeding speech of

Senator William Pinkney of Maryland. These two were the giants of the contest.

SENATOR PINKNEY.—Mr. President, the sentiments of the gentleman from New York [Senator King], if not borrowed from, are identical with, the worst visions of the political philosophy of France when all the elements of discord and misrule were let loose upon that devoted nation. I mean "the infinite perfectibility of man and his institutions," and the resolution of everything into a state of nature.

Sir, it is not an occasion like this, although connected, as contrary to all reasonable expectation it has been, with these fearful and disorganizing theories, which would make our estimates, whether fanciful or sound, of natural law, the measure of civil rights and political sovereignty in the social state, that can harm the Union. It must indeed be a mighty storm that can push from its moorings this sacred bark of the common safety. I will continue to cherish the belief, in defiance of the deadly speculations which, invoking the name of God to aid their faculties for mischief, strike at all establishments, that the union of these States is formed to bear up against far greater shocks than, through all vicissitudes, it is ever likely to encounter.

Sir, it is avowed that, while Maine is to be ushered into the Union with every possible demonstration of studious reverence on our part, and on hers with colors flying, and all the other graceful accompaniments of honorable triumph, the more infantine and feeble Missouri is to be repelled with harshness, and forbidden to come at all unless with the iron collar of servitude about her neck, instead of the civic crown of republican freedom upon her brows, and is to be doomed forever to leading strings unless she will exchange those leading strings for shackles.

I am told that you have the power to establish this odious and revolting distinction, and I am referred for the proofs of that power to various parts of the Constitution, but principally to that part of it which authorizes the admission of new States into the Union.

I think I may assume that if such a power be anything but nominal it is much more than adequate to the present object; that it is a power of vast expansion, to which human sagacity can assign no reasonable limits; that is a capacious reservoir of authority, from which you may take, in all time to come, as occasion may serve, the means of oppression as well as of benefaction.

Wm Pinkney

I shall not, I am sure, be told that I exaggerate this power. No man can contradict me when I say that, if you have this power, you may squeeze down a new-born sovereign State to the size of a pigmy, and then, taking it between finger and thumb, stick it into some niche of the Union, and still continue, by way of mockery, to call it a State in the sense of the Constitution. You may reduce it to a thing of skin and bone, and then place the ominous skeleton beside the ruddy and healthful members of the Union, that it may have leisure to mourn the lamentable difference between itself and its companions, to brood over its disastrous promotion, and to seek, in justifiable discontent, an opportunity for separation, and insurrection and rebellion. What may you not do by dexterity and perseverance with this terrific power? You may give to a new State, in the form of terms which it cannot refuse, a statute book of a thousand volumes, providing not for ordinary cases only, but even for possibilities; you may lay the yoke, no matter whether light or heavy, upon the necks of the latest posterity; you may send this searching power into every hamlet for centuries to come, by laws enacted in the spirit of prophecy, and regulating all those dear relations of domestic concern which belong to local legislation, and which even local legislation touches with a delicate and sparing hand. This is the first inroad. But will it be the last? This provision is but a pioneer for others of a more desolating aspect. It is that fatal bridge of which Milton speaks,[1] and when once firmly built, what shall hinder you to pass it when you please for the purpose of plundering power after power, at the expense of new States, as you will still continue to call them, and raising up prospective codes, irrevocable and immortal, which shall leave to those States the empty shadows of domestic sovereignty, and convert them into petty pageants, in themselves contemptible, but rendered infinitely more so by the contrast of their humble faculties with the proud and admitted pretensions of those who, having doomed them to the inferiority of vassals, have condescended to take them into their society and under their protection?

"New States *may* be admitted by the Congress into this Union." It is objected that the word "may" imports power, not obligation—a right to decide—a discretion to grant or refuse.

To this it might be answered that *power* is *duty*, on many occasions. But let it be conceded that it is discretionary. What

---

[1] Over the Hellespont, across which Xerxes passed "the liberties of Greece to yoke."

consequence follows? A power to refuse, in a case like this, does not necessarily involve a power to exact terms. You must look to the *result*, which is the declared object of the power. Whether you will arrive at it or not may depend on your will; but you cannot compromise with the result intended and professed.

What, then, is the professed result? To admit a State into this Union.

What is that Union? A confederation of States equal in sovereignty, capable of everything which the Constitution does not forbid, or authorize Congress to forbid. It is an equal Union between parties equally sovereign. They were sovereign, independently of the Union. The object of the Union was common protection for the exercise of already existing sovereignty. The parties gave up a portion of that sovereignty to insure the remainder. As far as they gave it up by the common compact they have ceased to be sovereign. The Union provides the means of defending the residue, and it is into that Union that a new State is to come. By acceding to it the new State is placed on the same footing with the original States. It accedes for the same purpose; that is, protection for its unsurrendered sovereignty. If it comes in shorn of its beams—crippled and disparaged beyond the original States—it is not into the original Union that it comes. For it is a different sort of Union. The first was Union *inter pares;* this is a Union between *disparates,* between giants and a dwarf, between power and feebleness, between full proportioned sovereignties and a miserable image of power—a thing which that very Union has shrunk and shriveled from its just size, instead of preserving it in its true dimensions.

It is into "this Union"—that is, the Union of the Federal Constitution—that you are to admit or refuse to admit. You can admit into no other. You cannot make the Union, as to the new State, what it is not as to the old; for then it is not *this Union* that you open for the entrance of a new party. If you make it enter into a new and additional compact, is it any longer the same Union?

If I am told that, by the bill relative to Missouri, you do not legislate upon a New State, I answer that you do; and I answer, further, that it is immaterial whether you do or not. But it is upon Missouri, as a State, that your terms and conditions are to act. Until Missouri is a State, the terms and conditions are nothing. You legislate in the shape of terms and conditions prospectively; and you so legislate upon it that when it comes into the Union it is bound by a contract degrading and diminishing its sovereignty, and is to be stripped of rights which the original parties to the Union did not consent to abandon, and which that Union (so far as depends upon it) takes under its protection and guaranty.

It is said that the word *may* necessarily implies the right of prescribing the terms of admission.

Give to that word all the force you please, what does it import? That Congress is not *bound* to admit a new State into this Union. Be it so for argument's sake. Does it follow that when you consent to admit into this Union a new State you can make it less in sovereign power than the original parties to that Union; that you can make the Union as to it what it is not as to them; that you can fashion it to your liking by compelling it to purchase admission into a Union by sacrificing a portion of that power which it is the sole purpose of the Union to maintain in all the plenitude which the Union itself does not impair? Does it follow that you can force upon it an additional compact not found in the compact of Union; that you can make it come into the Union less a State, in regard to sovereign power, than its fellows in that Union; that you can cripple its legislative competency (beyond the constitution which is the pact of Union, to which you make it a party as if it had been originally a party to it) by what you choose to call a *condition*, but which, whatever it may be called, brings the new government into the Union under new obligations to it, and with disparaged power to be protected by it?

I may be told, perhaps, that the restriction, in this case, is the act of Missouri itself; that your law is nothing without its consent, and derives its efficacy from that alone.

No State or Territory, in order to become a State, can alienate or surrender any portion of its sovereignty. It is under an incapacity to disqualify itself for all the purposes of government left to it in the Constitution, by stripping itself of attributes which arise from the natural equality of States, and which the Constitution recognizes, not only because it does not deny them, but presumes them to remain as they exist by the law of nature and nations. Inequality in the sovereignty of States is unnatural, and repugnant to all the principles of that law. Hence we find it laid down by the text writers on public law that "Nature has established a perfect equality of rights between independent nations"; and that, "whatever the quality of a free sovereign nation gives to one it gives to another."[1]

[1] Vattel, *Droit des Gens,* liv. 2, c. 3, s. 36.

The Constitution of the United States proceeds upon the truth of this doctrine. It takes the States as its finds them, *free and sovereign alike by nature.* It receives from them portions of their power for the general good, and provides for the exercise of it by organized political bodies. It diminishes the individual sovereignty of each, and transfers what it subtracts to the Government which it creates; it takes from all alike, and leaves them relatively to each other equal in sovereign power.

One of the most signal errors with which the argument on the other side has abounded is this of considering the proposed restriction as if leveled at the introduction or establishment of slavery. And hence the vehement declamation which, among other things, has informed us that slavery originated in fraud or violence.

That slavery, like many other human institutions, originated in fraud or violence may be conceded; but, however it originated, it is established among us, and no man seeks a further establishment of it by new importations of freemen to be converted into slaves.

It can be nothing to the purpose of this argument, therefore, as the gentlemen themselves have shaped it, to inquire what was the origin of slavery. What is it now, and who are they that endeavor to innovate upon what it now is (the advocates of this restriction who desire change by unconstitutional means, or its opponents who desire to leave the whole matter to local regulation?) are the only questions worthy of attention.

Sir, if we too closely look to the rise and progress of long-sanctioned establishments and unquestioned rights, we may discover other subjects than that of slavery with which fraud and violence may claim a fearful connection, and over which it may be our interest to throw the mantle of oblivion. What was the settlement of our ancestors in this country but an invasion of the rights of the barbarians who inhabited it? That settlement, with slight exceptions, was effected by the slaughter of those who did no more than defend their native land against the intruders of Europe, or by unequal compacts and purchases, in which feebleness and ignorance had to deal with power and cunning. The savages who once built their huts where this proud capitol,[1] rising from its recent ashes, exemplifies the sovereignty of the American people, were swept away by the injustice of our fathers, and their domain usurped by force, or obtained by artifices yet more criminal. Our continent was full of those aboriginal inhabitants. Where are they or their de-

[1] The new capitol was first occupied during this session.

scendants? Either "with years beyond the flood," or driven back by the swelling tide of our population from the borders of the Atlantic to the deserts of the West. You follow still the miserable remnants, and make *contracts* with them that seal their ruin. You purchase their lands, of which they know not the value, in order that you may sell them to advantage, increase your treasure, and enlarge your empire. Yet further; you pursue as they retire; and they must continue to retire until the Pacific shall stay their retreat, and compel them to pass away as a dream. Will you recur to those scenes of various iniquity for any other purpose than to regret and lament them? Will you pry into them with a view to shake and impair your rights of property and dominion?

If it is incompetent to sovereign power to continue slavery in Missouri, in respect of slaves who may yet be carried thither, show me the power that can continue it in respect of slaves who are there already. Missouri is out of the old limits of the Union, and beyond those limits, it is said, we can give no countenance to slavery, if we can countenance or tolerate it anywhere. It is plain that there can be no slaves beyond the Mississippi at this moment but in virtue of some power to make or keep them so. What sort of power was it that has made or kept them so? Sovereign power it could not be, according to the honorable gentlemen from Pennsylvania and New Hampshire [Messrs. Roberts, Lowrie, and Morrill], and if sovereign power is unequal to such a purpose, less than sovereign power is yet more unequal to it. The laws of Spain and France could do nothing; the laws of the territorial government of Missouri could do nothing toward such a result, if it be a result which no laws, in other words, no sovereignty, could accomplish. The treaty of 1803 could do no more in this view than the laws of France, or Spain, or the territorial government of Missouri. A treaty is an act of sovereign power, taking the shape of a compact between the parties to it; and that which sovereign power cannot reach at all it cannot reach by a treaty. Those who are now held in bondage, therefore, in Missouri, and their issue are entitled to be free, if there be any truth in the doctrine of the honorable gentlemen; and if the proposed restriction leaves all such in slavery it thus discredits the very foundation on which it reposes. To be inconsistent is the fate of false principles; but this inconsistency is the more to be remarked, since it cannot be referred to mere considerations of policy, without admitting that such considerations may be preferred, without a crime, to what is deemed a paramount and indispensable duty.

The gentlemen can scarcely be sincere believers in their own principle. They have apprehensions, which they endeavor to conceal, that Missouri, as a State, will have the power to continue slavery within its limits; and, if they will not be offended, I will venture to compare them, in this particular, with the duelist in Sheridan's comedy of "The Rivals," who, affecting to have no fear whatever of his adversary, is, nevertheless, careful to admonish Sir Lucius to hold him fast.

Let us take it for granted, however, that they are in earnest in their doctrine, and that it is very necessary to impose what they prove to be an unnecessary restraint: how do they support that doctrine?

The honorable gentleman on the other side [Mr. King] has told us, as a proof of his great position, that man cannot enslave his fellow man, in which is implied that all laws upholding slavery are absolute nullities; that the nations of antiquity, as well as of modern times, have concurred in laying down that position as incontrovertible.

He refers us, in the first place, to the Roman law, in which he finds it laid down as a maxim: *Jure naturali omnes homines ab initio liberi nascebantur.*[1] From the manner in which this maxim was pressed upon us, it would not readily have been conjectured that the honorable gentleman who used it had borrowed it from a slaveholding empire, and still less from a book of the Institutes of Justinian, which treats of slavery, and justifies and regulates it. Had he given us the context, we should have had the modifications of which the abstract doctrine was, in the judgment of the Roman law, susceptible. We should have had an explanation of the competency of that law, to convert, whether justly or unjustly, freedom into servitude, and to maintain the right of a master to the service and obedience of his slave.

The honorable gentleman might also have gone to Greece for a similar maxim and a similar commentary, speculative and practical.

He next refers us to Magna Charta. I am somewhat familiar with Magna Charta, and I am confident that it contains no such maxim as the honorable gentleman thinks he has discovered in it. The great charter was extorted from John, and his feeble son and successor, by haughty slaveholding barons, who thought only of themselves and the commons of England (then inconsiderable), whom they wished to enlist in their efforts against the Crown. There is not in it a single word which

---

[1] "By natural right all men from the beginning were born free."

condemns civil slavery. Freemen only are the objects of its protecting care. *"Nullus liber homo"* is its phraseology. The serfs who were chained to the soil, the villeins regardant and in gross were left as it found them. All England was then full of slaves, whose posterity would by law remain slaves as with us, except only that the issue followed the condition of the father instead of the mother. The rule was *"Partus sequitur patrem."* [1] —a rule more favorable undoubtedly, from the very precariousness of its application, to the gradual extinction of slavery, than ours, which has been drawn from the Roman law, and is of sure and unavoidable effect.

Of the Declaration of our Independence, which has also been quoted in support of the perilous doctrines now urged upon us, I need not now speak at large. The self-evident truths announced in the Declaration of Independence are not truths at all, if taken literally; and the practical conclusions contained in the same passage of that declaration prove that they were never designed to be so received.

The Articles of Confederation contain nothing on the subject, while the actual Constitution recognizes the legal existence of slavery by various provisions. The power of prohibiting the slave trade is involved in that of regulating commerce, but this is coupled with an express inhibition to the exercise of it for twenty years. How, then, can that Constitution which expressly permits the importation of slaves authorize the national government to set on foot a crusade against slavery?

The clause respecting fugitive slaves is affirmative and active in its effects. It is a direct sanction and positive protection of the right of the master to the services of his slave, as derived under the local laws of the States. The phraseology in which it is wrapped up still leaves the intention clear, and the words, "persons held to service or labor in one State under the laws thereof," have always been interpreted to extend to the case of slaves, in the various acts of Congress which have been passed to give efficacy to the provision, and in the judicial application of those laws. So also in the clause prescribing the ratio of representation—the phrase, "three-fifths of all other persons," is equivalent to *slaves*, or it means nothing. And yet we are told that those who are acting under a Constitution which sanctions the existence of slavery in those States which choose to tolerate it are at liberty to hold that no law can sanction its existence!

---

[1] "The offspring follows [the condition of] the father." In Roman law, *ventrem*, the womb, is substituted for *patrem*.

We are informed that there is a clause in the Constitution
which declares that Congress shall guarantee to every State a
republican form of government; that slavery and such a form
of government are incompatible; and, finally, as a conclusion
from these premises, that Congress not only have a *right*, but
are *bound* to exclude slavery from a new State. Here, again,
sir, there is an edifying inconsistency between the argument and
the measure which it professes to vindicate. By the argument,
it is maintained that Missouri cannot have a republican form of
government and at the same time tolerate negro slavery. By
the measure it is admitted that Missouri may tolerate slavery, as
to persons already in bondage there, and be nevertheless fit to be
received into the Union. What sort of Constitutional mandate
is this, which can thus be made to bend, and truckle, and compromise, as if it were a simple rule of expediency that might
admit of exceptions upon motives of countervailing expediency?
There can be no such pliancy in the peremptory provisions of
the Constitution. They cannot be obeyed by moieties and violated in the same ratio. They must be followed out to their full
extent, or treated with that decent neglect which has at least
the merit of forbearing to render contumacy obtrusive by an
ostentatious display of the very duty which we in part abandon.
If the Decalogue could be observed in this casuistical manner,
we might be grievous sinners, and yet be liable to no reproach.
We might persist in all our habitual irregularities, and still be
spotless. We might, for example, continue to covet our neighbors' goods, provided they were the same neighbors whose goods
we had before coveted, and so of all the other commandments.

The debates in the House of Representatives on the
various phases of the Missouri bill extended from
January 26 to March 2, 1820. In these the speakers
were clearly aligned as pro-slavery or anti-slavery in
sentiment, the two classes with few exceptions hailing
the one from the North, the other from the South.
The chief pro-slavery speakers were: Alexander
Smyth [Va.], Robert W. Reid [Ga.], Benjamin Hardin
[Ky.], Louis McLane [Del.], Philip P. Barbour [Va.],
Charles Pinckney [S. C.] and John Tyler [Va.]; the
leading anti-slavery speakers were: Henry Meigs
[N. Y.], John W. Taylor [N. Y.], Joseph Hemphill
[Pa.], John Sergeant [Pa.], William Darlington [Pa.]
and James Stevens [Conn.].

Henry Clay, as Speaker of the House, did not take a prominent part in the debate nor was he called on to vote upon the measure. "It was afterwards," says Senator Benton, "when the constitution formed by Missouri was resisted on account of the free negro and mulatto clause, and which revived the original question with all its portentous consequences, that Mr. Clay took the lead which earned for him the title of Pacificator."

The debate in the House centered around the Taylor compromise proviso.

THE MISSOURI COMPROMISE

HOUSE OF REPRESENTATIVES, JANUARY 26-MARCH 2, 1820

On January 26 Mr. Meigs introduced a resolution devoting the public lands to the colonization of freedmen. He said:

There is a wonderful singularity in the present controversy, which destroys all confidence in the weight and value of that process of mind which we so proudly dignify with the title of reasoning. Sir, I never yet knew that reason and logic were to be found on this side or that of a parallel of latitude or longitude. What is the fact in this case? Why, sir, the parallel of latitude of 39 degrees almost precisely marks the division between the reason and argument of the North and South. That line of demarcation separates the slaveholding from the non-slaveholding States. On the south side of that line we find the climate and soil adapted to slaves, and there are the slaves; on the north side of that line we discover that the soil and climate require no slaves, and, therefore, few or no slaves are found. What, sir! is it possible, then, that one-half of us can be rationally and argumentatively on one side of the parallel of latitude, and the other half of us upon the other? I did believe that the truths of philosophy, that reason, that the Principia of Newton were the same in every latitude, in every climate, and on every soil of this globe.

Reason divided by parallels of latitude! Why, sir, it is easy for prejudice and malevolence, by aid of ingenuity, to erect an eternal, impenetrable wall of brass between the North and South, at the latitude of thirty-nine degrees! But, in the view of reason, there is no other line between them than that celestial arc of thirty-nine degrees which offers no barrier to the march of liberal and rational men.

Sir, we have been now for a long time occupied in this debate, misspending our time and the public money. I feel well assured that the body of the people will judge our conduct rightly. They will soon ask us what is the controversy about? Did you, from motives of policy and regard for the welfare of the whites, propose to remove the growing black race from this country? No. Did you, actuated by humane considerations for the unfortunate slaves, propose to redeem them from their bondage and restore them to liberty and the land of their fathers? No. What then? Did you propose to draw such lines of restriction around the slave population as would ere long starve them out, and so prevent their becoming dangerous to the whites? If you did, remember that such is the increasing kindness of the slaveholders, so ameliorated the condition of the slave, that not one slave, not one child less will be born, and not one can die by starvation. Sir, the truth is that nothing has yet been proposed beneficial either to the white or black race in all this long-drawn debate. Give me leave to say, sir, that this consideration induced me to introduce the resolution which now lies upon the table, devoting the public lands to the emancipation and colonization of the unfortunate slaves. If we want some object upon which to exhaust our enthusiasm, here is one worth it all. Not the subjugation of a people, but the redemption of a nation.

Mr. Taylor moved to amend the bill by inserting a clause restricting slavery with a proviso for the return of fugitive slaves.

He supported his amendment with the argument that the power of holding slaves was not a Federal right.

Congress, within its sovereignty, has constantly endeavored to prevent the extension of slavery, and has maintained the doctrine "that all men are born equally free," but has disclaimed, and continues to disclaim, any right to enforce this doctrine upon State sovereignties.

Mr. Smyth opposed this view. He said:

The right to own slaves being acknowledged and secured by the Constitution, can you proscribe what the Constitution guarantees? Can you touch a right reserved to the States or the people? You cannot.

If you possessed power to legislate concerning slavery, the adoption of the proposition on your table, which goes to emancipate all children of slaves hereafter born in Missouri, would be a direct violation of the Constitution, which provides that "no person shall be deprived of property without due process of law; nor shall private property be taken for public use without just compensation." And, if you cannot take away that which is in existence, you cannot take away that which will come into existence hereafter. If you cannot take away the land, you cannot take the future crops; and if you cannot take the slaves, you cannot take their issue, who, by the laws of slavery, will be also slaves. You cannot force the people to give up their property. You cannot force a portion of the people to emancipate their slaves.

It has been said that the Constitution vests in Congress a power to make all needful regulations respecting the territory of the United States; and this power, it is supposed, authorizes us to exclude slaves from the territories of the United States, and also to demand from any of those territories about to become States a stipulation for the exclusion of slaves. The clause obviously relates to the territory belonging to the United States as property only. It speaks not of the jurisdiction. A power to dispose of and make all needful regulations respecting the property of the United States is very different from a power to legislate over the persons and property of the people. When the property of the United States is sold and conveyed, it ceases to be an object of the power to make regulations respecting it.

By treaty we are bound to admit Missouri into the Union; to allow her a representation for her slaves; to guarantee to her a republican form of government (that is, a government by and for the people themselves, not a government imposed on them, nor a patrimonial government) ; and to leave her all power not delegated by the Constitution to the United States, nor prohibited by it to the States. Treaties are in part the supreme law of the land and paramount to the constitution of any State; yet you propose to violate the treaty with France by the means of a State constitution, which is of inferior obligation to a treaty.

Every State is interested that every other State shall preserve its rights. The States should possess the same rights, so that the invasion of the rights of one should be the invasion of the rights of all. You will unite in opposition ten of the States; you will form local parties, the most dangerous of all parties; you will unite the State governments, defending State rights, to the people, defending their property to the amount of five hundred millions. Louisiana, being equally interested in the construction of the treaty, must make common cause with Missouri, and the other slaveholding States may make common cause with them.

If you let the people of Missouri alone to exercise the right of self-government, as it is exercised by the people of the other States, perhaps they may of themselves exclude slavery. If such is their sovereign will and pleasure, be it so. Let the will of the people be done. But if you attempt to force your own will upon them, perhaps they may know and duly appreciate their rights. Then they will not give up the sacred right of self-government. The people who have not a right to legislate for themselves are not free. They do not enjoy a republican form of government. It would be an event to be lamented if any portion of this free people should give up their constitutional rights.

Mr. Reid acknowledged that slavery was "an unnatural state; a dark cloud which obscures half the luster of our free institutions," but he claimed that it was "a fixed evil which we can only alleviate." The welfare of both whites and blacks forbade emancipation.

Can we incorporate them [the blacks] with us, and make them and us one people? The prejudices of the North and of the South rise up in equal strength against such a measure; and even those who clamor most loudly for the sublime doctrines of your Declaration of Independence, who shout in your ears, "all men are by nature equal!" would turn with abhorrence and disgust from a parti-colored progeny! Shall we then be blamed for a state of things to which we are obliged to submit? Would it be fair; would it be manly; would it be generous; would it be just, to offer contumely and contempt to the unfortunate man who wears a cancer in his bosom, because he will not submit to cautery at the hazard of his existence? For my own part, surrounded by slavery from my cradle to the present moment, I yet

> "Hate the touch of servile hands;
> I loathe the slaves who cringe around:"

and I would hail that day as the most glorious in its dawning which should behold, with safety to themselves and our citizens, the black population of the United States placed upon the high eminence of equal rights, and clothed in the privileges and immunities of American citizens! But this is a dream of philanthropy which can never be fulfilled; and whoever shall act in this country upon such wild theories shall cease to be a benefactor and become a destroyer of the human family.

Mr. Reid then argued that slavery should be admitted into the Territories in order to lessen the evil by scattering it.

Slaves, divided among many masters, will enjoy greater privileges and comforts than those who, cooped within a narrow sphere and under few owners, will be doomed to drag a long, heavy, and clanking chain through the space of their existence. Danger from insurrection will diminish. Confidence will grow between the master and his servant. The one will no longer be considered as a mere beast of burden, the other as a remorseless despot void of feeling and commiseration. In proportion as few slaves are possessed by the same individual will he look with less reluctance to the prospect of their ultimate liberation. Emancipations will become common, and who knows but that the Great Being, to whose mercies all men have an equal claim, may, in the fulness of his time, work a miracle in behalf of the trampled rights of human nature?

On February 4 Mr. Hardin said that the South in this controversy was contending not for victory, but for its political existence.

We have already surrendered to the non-slaveholding States all that region of the American empire between the great rivers Ohio and Mississippi; and if you tear from us that immense country west of the Mississippi, we may at once surrender at discretion, crouch at the feet of our adversaries, and beg mercy of our proud and haughty victors.

Mr. Hardin then suggested that what was essentially the Missouri Compromise be adopted.

Mr. Hemphill discussed the Ordinance of 1787 in its relation to the subject under discussion. He denied

IV—6

that it was, as charged, "the production of usurped power." The States having relinquished power over the Northwest Territory, Congress had been compelled to organize a government there. It had the power to restrict slavery, and, believing it right to do so, had restricted it. When the Territory was divided into States the people endorsed the restriction.

The Constitutional Convention validated the acts of the Congress under the Confederation, including the Ordinance of 1787.

Could the present question in any shape have been proposed to the convention, I appeal to the candor of the committee if, in their opinion, it would have been sustained for a moment by the patriots of that early day? Slavery in the old States could not be extinguished, but, as to States that were to grow up out of the Constitution, it never was intended that they should be inconsistent with the solemn professions made to the world.

Mr. Hemphill argued that the situations of Missouri and of the Northwest Territory were identical with respect to the fact that both regions were "common funds" of the nation. Therefore there was no more injustice in forbidding slaveholders to take their slaves into Missouri than in debarring them from so entering Ohio, Indiana, or Illinois. Let them take their favorite negroes with them as free persons, and the generous act would be repaid by a life-long attachment to them of the grateful servants.

Mr. Hemphill opposed any compromise on the subject. With clear prescience he said:

Under the circumstances, it will be impossible to compromise a question of this character. A compromise usually has for its basis mutual concessions, which are equally obligatory; but, if we should pass a law excluding slavery from the remaining territory, where would be the security that another Congress would not repeal it? It will be but an ordinary act of legislation, and whenever there shall be an application for a new State we shall be met with the same constitutional objections that now exist. It is, in fact, yielding all for which we have been contending, and, if we once give up the ship, slavery will be tolerated in the State of Missouri and we can never after remove it.

It is true that a compromise was made on the subject of slavery at the adoption of the Constitution, but it was one of an obligatory nature, and it arose out of circumstances that could not be controlled. The Constitution was necessary to save us from domestic discord and foreign ambition; we were then in our infancy; but, now our national strength bids defiance to any nation, where, I ask, is the necessity of deceiving ourselves or our constituents by this mere pretence of a compromise?

The gentlemen on the other side tell us that, if the restriction is carried, the Union will be dissolved. I have a more exalted opinion of the patriotism of the South; they will never cause American blood to be spilled, unless for reasons that would justify them in the eyes of the world; and, in the language of Mr. Jefferson, "the Almighty has no attribute that would side with them in such a cause as this would be." Has it come to this, that the extension of slavery is to be considered as one of the pillars of our liberty? This, indeed, would be a political paradox.

Mr. McLane denied that the Declaration of Independence referred to slaves.

The Declaration was the act of open resistance on the part of the white freemen of the colonies against the pretensions of the mother country to govern them without their consent; to assert their inalienable right of self-government, and to alter or abolish it whenever it should be necessary to affect their safety and happiness. It was the resistance of freemen to the assumption of a power on the part of Great Britain, precisely similar to that which we are now endeavoring to impose upon the people of Missouri. It expressly asserts the principles that "all just powers of government are derived from the consent of the governed; and the right of the people to alter or abolish and institute it anew, as to them shall seem most likely to affect their safety and happiness." I do not deny that the principles of the Declaration of Independence are those of the Constitution; on the contrary, I admit that they are those upon which all our institutions repose; they are those upon which the people of Missouri claim the right to make their own constitution, and resist the imposition of any species of government deriving its powers from any other source. But I contend that it never designed to assume or assert any principle whatsoever in regard to the slave population of the United States, and therefore that it cannot be used in this debate, either as declaratory of their rights or explanatory of the principles of the Constitution and Government in their behalf. It is unreasonable to assert the contrary, when everyone knows that, while the freemen of this country were openly resisting the usurpations of the British Crown, they did not relax in the slightest degree their hold upon the negro slave; and to him it was a matter of entire unconcern who should govern his master, as in all conditions his master would continue to govern him.

I do not advocate the consistency of all this: I take things as I find them under our form of government; though when we throw our eye toward St. Domingo, and reflect upon the scenes which ensued—the heedless enthusiasm which characterized the French Revolution—we cannot fail to admire the cautious wisdom of our ancestors in not hazarding the great object of their struggle by suddenly letting loose their unfortunate, though degraded, slave population. Besides, sir, the principles of the Declaration of Independence would not be satisfied by merely loosening the shackles of the slaves; they would assert not only the rights of a freeman but an equality of those rights, civil and political. And where is the State in the Union in which the emancipated negro has been admitted to the enjoyment of equal rights with the white population? I know of none.

Mr. McLane then replied to the argument that Congress could restrict slavery in a new State because of its constitutional power to make "all needful rules and regulations respecting the territory or other property belonging to the United States."

This clause, he said, was designed to relate to *revenue*. Nevertheless he admitted it was a plenary grant, *but only so long as the regions affected remained in a state of territorial dependence.*

The instant we authorize a Territory to form its constitution to enter the Union, its territorial disabilities and the power of Congress over it crumble together in the dust.

He also denied that the power to restrict slavery in a new State could be derived from the interstate commerce clause of the Constitution. The prevention in the clause of the migration or importation of certain persons until 1808 related to *foreign* immigrants only.

The word "migration" cannot apply to the forcible or involuntary removal of a slave from any state, foreign or domestic. It is the voluntary act of a free agent; and a slave has no such will, and is no such agent. It is no exercise of a right when the unhappy slave is taken by his owner from place to place—he obeys a hard fate which he cannot control, and he can with no more propriety be said to migrate than the exile who is driven from his family and home into involuntary banishment.

Mr. McLane, as a conclusion of his reasoning, argued for restriction of slavery in a territory, but none when it entered the Union. This was a practical solution of the problem, since the applicant for statehood having no slaves in its borders would naturally, of its own desire, restrict slavery in forming its constitution.

Mr. Sergeant spoke against compromise as forbidden by the principles of both sides of the controversy. For his part he would never agree to the admission of Missouri with slavery. Slavery once introduced there, the hope of extinguishing it by emancipation was destroyed. The reduction in the value of slaves was the only inducement that would ever effect the abolition of the evil institution.

Mr. Barbour repeated his former claim that the Ordinance of 1787 was a usurpation. On this point he quoted an extract from "The Federalist," No. 38, affirming that the acts of the "Old Congress" were "without the least color of constitutional authority." In his "Debates of Congress" Thomas H. Benton gives the following note on this point:

The phrase "constitutional authority," as here used by Mr. Madison (who was the author of this number), could not apply to the Constitution of the United States, as the ordinance was made before that instrument. It could refer only to the Articles of Confederation, which gave the fundamental law to the Old Congress, and was, in fact, its Constitution; and which, cer-

tainly, gave to the Congress none of the powers exercised in
the enactment of the ordinance; nor was it supposed to grant
such powers at the time.

Answering the contention that slavery, being a question adjusted in the Constitution by compromise, was a
matter between only the original thirteen States who
formed the Constitution, he said:

There were other subjects besides slavery adjusted by compromise; I will mention the most prominent one—that of an
equal representation in the Senate. This is incontestably proven
by the circumstance that, in the clause providing for amendments, it is declared that the Constitution shall not even be so
amended as to deprive any State of its equal suffrage in the
Senate without its own consent; this is the only provision which
is forever put beyond the reach of amendment, in the ordinary
mode. Now, sir, this was emphatically the work of a compromise in a vital part of the Constitution; the principle of
gentlemen, if true, would lead to the conclusion that the new
States were not entitled to the benefit of this provision, because
they were not parties to the compromise; yet no gentleman will
maintain this position; and, if he will not, he must give up the
other upon the subject of slavery.

But, say, gentlemen, the powers which the Constitution does
not give us we can get from the several States by compact.
They say that both the United States and the State of Missouri
are competent to make a contract; and that, if the one party
make a proposition, and the other accept it, this is obligatory on
them both. Even if this principle were true, an abundant answer is furnished by an argument which I believe has been already urged, and which I shall therefore only state, without
pursuing it; it is that, by the treaty, which was a compact prior
in point of time, and paramount in point of obligation, the
people of Missouri have acquired certain rights, that therefore
it is not competent for you, merely because you are the stronger,
to say that you will not comply with its stipulations unless
they will agree to another compact, the effect of which will be
to deprive them of one of the rights which it gave them.

Gentlemen say that slavery is a moral wrong, and as such
cannot be the subject of sovereignty; I answer that it is essential to sovereignty, and the highest act of its exercise to decide
what is embraced within its limits, and that the very act of one
government attempting to decide this question for another is a

glaring violation of the sovereignty of that other; I answer further that sovereignty, in relation to the internal concerns of a State, has no limits but the discretion and moral sense of the State itself, unless it relate to a subject the power over which has been specially delegated, and it has been the purpose of my whole argument to prove that this has not been so delegated. Suppose that a state, like ancient Sparta, should by its laws even sanction the barbarous practice of putting its Helots to death; suppose that it was so lost to the moral sense as to permit the most enormous crimes against the laws of morality or religion to escape with impunity; have we the power to interfere in these matters of municipal legislation, unless it be in relation to a subject over which the Constitution gives us power? I must be pardoned for repeating that we have no more than one of the governments of Europe.

The next clause from which the right to impose this restriction is derived is that which gives us power to make all needful rules and regulations respecting the territory of the United States. I beg leave to remind the committee that, as it respects the now Territory of Missouri, we have, by one of our own regulations, given it a legislative body; that we have extended to that body the whole power of legislation, subject only to the limitation that their laws shall not be inconsistent with the Constitution and laws of the United States; a limitation to which every State in the Union is equally subject: the question of slavery is one of a legislative character; it therefore already belongs to them to decide it by our own grant. Let me ask gentlemen can a grant of political power be revoked at the will of those who grant it? Would it not excite some surprise in this hall to talk of revoking a common charter of incorporation such as that of the Bank of the United States, unless for some cause of forfeiture of that charter? Whatever is our power over the Territories, it is acknowledged that it coexists with the territorial condition, and that when that ceases the power over them, as such, ceases also. It is acknowledged that we could not impose this condition after the State is admitted; and yet it is contended that it may be done just before its admission, by virtue of a territorial power which must necessarily exist at the moment when the admission takes place; in a word, it is argued that, by virtue of a power confessedly temporary, we can impose a condition in its character perpetual if we so will. I cannot show the glaring impropriety of this position in so palpable a mode as by likening it to a case of municipal law. Let us put the case of guardian and ward. A guardian has power to make leases of his ward's land, during his minority, and to expire with it; the moment after his ward reaches majority he has no power over the estate; and yet, sir, upon the principle now contended for, he might enter into a contract the day before the minority ceased which would bind the ward and his heirs forever. If such a proposition as this were stated in the judicial hall, in another part of this Capitol, the gentleman would be told that it could not even be received for discussion.

The gentleman from Pennsylvania [Mr. Hemphill] asked can a man have a vested interest in an unborn human being? And he answered, no. If this be the doctrine, sir, though that gentleman did not apply it, and I believe did not intend to apply it to the old States, I repeat again that it proclaims universal emancipation, after failure of the present generation of slaves. Sir, it is of no importance that the present Congress do not apply it; we are but actors who fret our busy hour upon the stage and then pass away; others will come to act their parts, and these principles may then be put into practical execution in their utmost extent. I will not detain the committee to prove that a property in the parent implies property in the progeny. The maxim, *"Partus sequitur ventrem,"* is as old as the civil law; it is founded upon the immutable principle that wherever I have property in the capital stock I have the same property in its products. He who owns the land owns all the fruit which it produces. If, then, you may admit my property in the parent, you cannot deny it in the child. If, indeed, you deny my right to a vested interest in an unborn human being, you may, perhaps, go one step further and deny the same interest in those who now exist. The argument is as strong in one case as the other. Assume but this principle, and then you need not wait for futurity to do this great work of emancipation. No, sir, you may say at once to every bondman in the United States you are free.

I look upon the Union of these States as the ark of our political safety; if that be lost, we may bid farewell, a long farewell, to all our pleasing hopes and fond anticipations of future greatness and glory. They will be as the illusions of a deceitful dream. But, while I deprecate disunion as the most tremendous evil, I cannot shut my eyes against the light of experience; I cannot turn a deaf ear to the warning voice of history; from these we learn that harmony is the spirit which can alone animate and sustain a confederate republic. While this spirit exists, it is displayed in acts of legislation reciprocally beneficent to every member of the confederacy, and these be-

come new ligaments to bind them together in the bonds of
brotherhood; this spirit is not all at once extinguished, nor are
the bonds of union suddenly burst asunder; but when, instead
of this beneficent spirit of legislation which I have described, a
different course prevails, this spirit of harmony gives way successively to jealousy, distrust, and, finally, discord; let but this
last spring up among us, you may consider the days of the
Republic as numbered, and that it is fast hastening to its dissolution.

When that sad catastrophe shall befall us this noble confederacy which, in its undivided state, could stand against a
world in arms, will be broken, if not into its constituent parts,
into some minor confederacies, the victims of foreign intrigue
and of their own border hatred. Where, then, will be your
commerce which covers every sea? Where your army and
navy, the means of your defence, the instruments of your glory?
They will be remembered only to make the contrast with your
then situation more painful. What will become, then, of this
boundless tract of Western land, the subject of the present contest, which has poured and would continue to pour such rich
streams of wealth into your treasury? It may become the
theater on which the title to itself may be decided, not by
congressional debate, not by construction of treaties or constitutions, but by that force which always begins where constitutions end. I conjure you, then, beware lest by this measure
you excite the discontent of one-half of the Union, by legislating injuriously to them upon a subject in which they have so
deep a stake of interest and you have none in point of property;
take care that you do not awaken the painful reflection that the
federal arm is strong only to destroy.

Charles Pinckney, who had taken a prominent part
in the Constitutional Convention [see Vol. I, chapters x
and xii], spoke with authority upon the intention of that
convention in regard to points which had become subjects of contention in the present debate.

He denied that the North had made a concession to
the South in including three-fifths of slave population
in the basis of representation in the House of Representatives. Instead, the concession was from the South.

In our first national compact, the Confederation, in which
the equality of vote was preserved, the first squeamishness was

shown on the subject of not using or even alluding to the word slavery, or making it a part of our political machinery. In this compact the value of the lands and improvements was made the rule for apportioning the public burdens and taxes. But the Northern States, who are always much more alive to their interests than the Southern, found that their squeamishness was inconsistent with their interest; and, as usual, made the latter prevail. They found it was paying too dear for their qualms to keep their hand from the slaves any longer. At their instance, and on their motion, as will appear by a reference to the Journals of the Old Congress, the rule was changed, and apportionment was based on population, including the whites and three-fifths of other descriptions. This rule was retained by the Constitutional Convention.

Mr. Pinckney then explained the expectation of the convention in regard to Federal revenue, saying that it was assumed that this would come from direct taxation. Instead, however, Congress early adopted indirect taxation in the form of tariffs and excises, which has resulted in the benefit of the North and the injury of the South. The exports of the States from Maine to Pennsylvania now annually amounted to $18,000,000; those of the other States to $32,000,000, enabling an almost double importation of foreign products on which duties were assessed.

And here let me ask from whence do these exports arise? By whose hands are they made? I answer, entirely by the slaves; and yet these valuable inhabitants, without whom your very Government could not go on, and the labor of two or three of whom in the Southern States is more valuable to it than the labor of five of their inhabitants in the Eastern States, the States owning and possessing them are denied a representation here but for three-fifths, while the whole of the comparatively unproductive inhabitants of the Northern and Eastern States are fully represented here. Is it just—is this equal? And yet they have the modesty to complain of the representation as unjust and unequal; and that they have not the return made them they expected, by taxing the slaves, and making them bear a proportion of the public burdens. Some writers on political economy are of opinion that the representation of a State ought always to be equally founded on population and taxation. It is my duty to believe that these are the true criterions; for my own State (South Carolina) having, in her House of Representatives, 124 members, 62 of them are apportioned by the white population and 62 on taxation; thus representing the contributions of our citizens in every way, whether arising from services or taxes.

Mr. Pinckney then discussed the "migration" clause in the Constitution.

The reasons for restraining the power to prevent migration hither for twenty years were, to the best of my recollection, these: That, as at this time, we had immense and almost immeasurable territory, peopled by not more than two millions and a half of inhabitants, it was of very great consequence to encourage the emigration of able, skilful, and industrious Europeans.

It was maintained that the safest mode would be to pursue the course for twenty years, and not, before that period, put it at all into the power of Congress to shut it; that, by that time, the Union would be so settled and our population would be so much increased we could proceed on our own stock, without further accession of foreigners; that, as Congress were to be prohibited from stopping the importation of slaves to settle the Southern States, as no obstacle was to be thrown in the way of their increase and settlement for that period, let it be so with the Northern and Eastern, to which, particularly New York and Philadelphia, it was expected most of the emigrants would go from Europe: and it so happened, for, previous to the year 1808, more than double as many Europeans emigrated to these States as Africans were imported into the Southern States.

Having thus, I trust, proved clearly that you have no right to adopt this inhibition of slavery, but are forbidden to do so by the Constitution, as well as by the treaty, I ought perhaps to stop here; but there are some other points which I ought not to pass unnoticed. One of these is the ordinance of July, 1787, passed by the Old Congress, at the period of the sitting of the convention in Philadelphia, for forming the Constitution, by which that body (the Old Congress) undertook to form a code for the future settlement, government, and admission into the Union of all the territory northwest of the River Ohio ceded by Virginia to the United States in 1785. On this subject I beg leave to remark that, by the Confederation of the United States, the Old Congress had no power whatever but that of admitting new States, provided nine States assented. This ordinance, therefore, in prescribing the forms of government, as they respected legislative, executive, and judiciary powers, in establishing bills of rights, and the times and terms of their admission into the Union, and inhibiting servitude therein, is chargeable with ingratitude and usurpation. It is chargeable with ingratitude when we reflect that the cession of the great tract of country—this rising empire of freemen—was gratuitously, and with noble disinterestedness and patriotism, made by Virginia, that the passing of an ordinance which contained a provision which could not but go to prevent the admission of Virginians there, as they could not move there with their slaves, was a most ungracious and ungrateful return to that State for her liberality, and could not but meet with the disapprobation of this nation.

Let us, sir, recollect the circumstances the Old Congress were in at the time they passed this ordinance: they had dwindled almost to nothing; the convention had been then three months in session; it was universally known a constitution was in its essentials agreed to; and the public were daily expecting (what soon happened) the promulgation of a new form of government for the Union. I ask, sir, was it under these circumstances proper for a feeble, dwindled body, that had wholly lost the confidence of the nation, and which was then waiting its supercession by the people—a feeble, inefficient body, in which only seven or eight States were represented, the whole of which consisted of but seventeen or eighteen men—a number smaller than your large committees; a body literally in the very agonies of political death;—was it, sir, even decent in them (not to say lawful or constitutional) to have passed an ordinance of such importance?

Mr. Darlington replied to the argument of Mr. Reid that slavery, admittedly a poison, should be diluted by dispersion throughout the territories.

Rather would he call slavery a contagious disease in the body politic. Like smallpox, it ought to be confined in the smallest possible limits. The Congress of 1787 introduced a sort of political vaccination into the constitutions of Ohio, Indiana, and Illinois, which effectually secured those States from the evil; and I am also for extending the same salutary process to our infant sister, Missouri. And why? Is it to injure her? Is it to mutilate or disfigure her? No, sir, it is to secure her health and to preserve her beauty!

Replying to the argument that all citizens of the United States had common rights in the Territories, and therefore that Congress could not prevent slaveholders going there with their property, he said that it was admitted that Missouri could exclude slavery. What then became of the common right?

My inference, therefore, is that the right to carry slaves into a new State or Territory is not a Federal right, but a local one.

Mr. Tyler delivered a speech of great argumentative force and rhetorical beauty.

Tell me not of implied and doubtful powers; against them I weigh the very nature of our Government and the spirit of our institutions. They are founded on the great principle that man is capable of self-government; that he requires no foreign aid in regulating his domestic concerns. Our Revolution was founded on this principle; England denied to us the right to legislate, except by her special authority; nay, she proclaimed the very principle which you now proclaim as applicable to Missouri—the right to bind you by her own system of legislation. To this the American spirit did not bow. It went forth to the battle, in the majesty of its strength, and achieved the victory of our independence. But, sir, the principle which we are called on to adopt goes, by a sightless distance, further than England ever dared to go. Her acts of legislation were fleeting and ephemeral; liable at all times to repeal; but we are to legislate, not only for the present day but for all ages to come. This restriction, if adopted, is unalterable and interminable in its duration. No succeeding generation have any power over it. It constitutes the very essence of the political existence of Missouri. It is the condition precedent, and must, through all future time, attach to the estate.

Gentlemen have exultingly read to us the Declaration of Independence. From it they have gathered that which, as an abstract truth, I am not disposed to deny: "that all men are, by nature, equally free, sovereign, and independent." Can this proposition admit of application to a state of society? Does not its fallacy meet you in every walk of life? Distinctions will exist. Virtue and vice, wealth and poverty, industry and idleness constitute so many barriers, which human power cannot break down, and which will ever prevent us from carrying into operation, *in extenso,* this great principle. Take this principle and preach it up to the monarchs of the world; will they descend from their lofty eminences or raise mankind to a level with themselves? No, sir, the principle, although lovely and beautiful, cannot obliterate those distinctions in society which society itself engenders and gives birth to. Liberty and equality are captivating sounds; but they often captivate to destroy. England had her Jack Cades and levelers. Look, I pray you, to revolutionary France. These were the principles of that day. Mark the consequences! Murder and rapine stalked over the land, and the guillotine, the work, too, of a philanthropist of that day, was the sad monument of this fallacy. Liberty and equality were proclaimed by Robespierre and his associates at the very moment when these men were enriching the fields of France with the blood of her citizens. Nor was the doctrine confined to political institutions, but, advancing with a daring step, it fought even with the Creator and mocked at the immutable truth of religion.

Turn your eyes also to South America. The throne of the Incas was washed from under them by the tide which flowed in from Spain. The native of the forest was deprived of his freedom and made to toil for his new master. Then, too, sprung up a philanthropist, who claimed for the Indian an equal rank in creation with the inhabitants of Spain. His claim was admitted, and Africa mourned over the mistake, and her deepest curses may still be uttered against the memory of Las Casas.

But, Mr. Chairman, although I do not believe that this principle of equality can be applied to man *in extenso,* yet I love it, and admire it as an abstract truth, and will carry it into operation whensoever I can; and, sir, I call on gentlemen to lend me their aid in the present instance. If we cannot raise the black man up to the level of the white—and that we have not the constitutional power to do so none here have denied—let us raise, at least, the white man up to this level. Extend an equality of rights to the people of Missouri. Place them upon a footing with the people of New York, Connecticut, and of the other States. They have the right to alter, to amend, to abolish their constitutions. You say to the people of New York, alter your constitution as you see fit in all its parts. Will you say in the same breath to the people of Missouri, you shall not exercise this right in regard to your constitution? Is this your boasted equality? If it be, sir, "I will have none of it." It is base coin, and will not pass current.

This is said, too, to be a parental care for Missouri. I am pleased with plain and simple illustrations: would a father act in the way in which you propose to act? His child has attained the age of twenty-one; by the laws of society that child is entitled to an equality of rights with himself; and what would you think of the parent who should say to the child: "Sir, you are now a man, but you shall not exercise the rights of a man, *except upon conditions*"? Would the child submit? Would a kind parent hold such language?

Missouri is now full grown; this, your offspring, has attained full age; attempt no longer to trammel her; let her set up for herself, and, although you may advise her, do not attempt to force her. Sir, she will not and ought not to submit to force; she would disgrace her parent stock if she did so. The proud Roman spirit which inhabits every portion of this country spurns control. Would you humble this spirit if you could? If you would, you cannot do it; but, if you could, your country would have no cause to thank you for so doing.

What will be the consequences if you persist in this measure? A sectional feeling is already generated; a geographic line is drawn. Tell me not of that policy which shall divide the people of this country by local feelings and prejudices. This is the bane of a republic—it is the rock which ought to be most cautiously avoided—sir, it is the greatest of all dangers to the union of these States. Take not my poor word for it. Nay, disregard the admonitions of him who has so often been called the Father of his Country. Forget the valedictory address of Washington. But can you, or will you, close your eyes to the lights of experience? United Greece stood up successfully against the mighty power of Xerxes; and the fall of Leonidas was but the precursor of the glory achieved at Marathon and Platæa. But Sparta wished to domineer over Athens, and their intestine feuds opened the channel to that flood of vandalism which deluged Greece and obliterated all trace of freedom. Such, too, was the fate of the Achaian League. I beseech gentlemen then to pause, lest they produce a similar division of sentiment in this happy land.

Let us avoid a question like the present. Gentlemen on the opposite side may yield without dishonor. They pursue but a scheme of policy; we are differently situated; we cannot, without violation of our oaths, support this measure. We believe in our consciences that the Constitution confers on us no such power. For myself, I cannot and will not yield one inch of ground. Let me, then, adjure our brethren from the North to

come and sit down once more by our side. I call on them to
heal the differences which this measure has produced. Your
course is palpable and plain. You have two roads before you;
take this, and all is harmony and peace; over that hang doubts
and fears. I invoke the Genius of the Constitution to cover
and protect us against the evils which threaten us. What if
you impose the restriction, and Missouri, instead of submitting,
shall form herself into a community and demand admittance,
or sever from the Union? Will you then retract? How much
more honorable to do it now! Or do you mean to persist in
your object at all hazards, and, if she prove refractory, reduce
her to submission? Do you believe that Southern bayonets
will ever be plunged in Southern hearts?

When the compromise measure was presented to
the House by the conference committee Mr. Stevens
spoke as follows:

I have listened with pain to the very long, protracted debate that has been had on this unfortunate question. I call it
unfortunate, sir, because it has drawn forth the worst passions of man in the course of the discussion.

If the deadliest enemy this country has, or ever had, could
dictate language the most likely to destroy your glory, prosperity, and happiness, would it not be precisely what has been
so profusely used in this debate—sectional vaunting? Indeed,
sir, there is no view of this unhappy division of our country
but must be sickening to the patriot and in direct violation of
the dictates of wisdom, and the last, though not least, important
advice of the Father and Friend of his Country. He forbids
the use of the words Northern and Southern, Atlantic and Western, as descriptive of the various parts of your country.

But, sir, we have now arrived at a point at which every
gentleman agrees something must be done. A precipice lies
before us at which perdition is inevitable. Gentlemen on both
sides of this question, and in both Houses, indoors and out of
doors, have evinced a determination that augurs ill of the high
destinies of this country! And who does not tremble for the
consequences?

I wish not to be misunderstood, sir. I don't pretend to
say that in just five calendar months your Union will be at an
end; your Constitution destroyed; your proud trophies, won in
the most valiant combat, profaned; glories of half a century,
gained by yourselves and your departed friends, and unequaled

in the history of any country or people on the face of the earth, made the sport of an envying world; and all this in a sacrilegious contest, at the end of which no wise man would give a pea-straw for his choice on which side to be found, as the victors would have lost all and the vanquished have nothing left to excite envy.

But, sir, I do say, and, for the verity of the remark, cite the lamentable history of our own time, that the result of a failure to compromise at this time, in the way now proposed, or in some other way satisfactory to both, would be to create ruthless hatred, irradicable jealousy, and a total forgetfulness of the ardor of patriotism, to which, as it has heretofore existed, we owe, under Providence, more solid national glory and social happiness than ever before were possessed by any people, nation, kindred, or tongue under Heaven.

In accordance with the act of Congress Missouri adopted a constitution and presented it to Congress for ratification. This contained a clause by which the State legislature was obliged to pass laws against the entry of free colored persons into the State. The Northern Senators and Representatives objected to this clause as an infringement upon the national Constitution, which declares (Art. IV, sec. 2) that "the citizens of each State shall be entitled to all privileges and immunities of citizens in the several States."

After a spirited debate of several weeks in both chambers of the national legislature, at the end of which the Missouri constitution remained unratified, Henry Clay, the Speaker of the House, proposed a conference of committees from the Senate and House which brought forward a compromise measure, allowing the admission of the State provided that the legislature should pass an act declaring that it would never exclude any citizen of another State from the privileges and immunities to which he is entitled under the Constitution of the United States. The measure was adopted by Congress on February 28, 1821, and approved by the President on March 2. The legislature complied with this condition demanded of it and the State was admitted, thus putting an end to the portentous struggle of two years and one-half duration.

CHAPTER III

The Right of Petition

[DEBATES ON THE RECEPTION OF PETITIONS FOR ABOLITION OF
SLAVERY IN THE DISTRICT OF COLUMBIA]

The Colonization Society—It Requests Aid of the Government—Debate in
the Senate on the Request: in Favor, Ezekiel Chambers [Md.]; Opposed,
Robert Y. Hayne [S. C.]; Memorial Laid on the Table—The American
Anti-Slavery Society Is Formed—Agitation Is Directed Against Slavery
in the District of Columbia—Petition Against It Is Introduced and Sup-
ported by Representative Charles Miner [Pa.]—Plan of Southern Con-
gressmen to "Gag" Such Petitions—Debate on a Resolution in the
House of Representatives to Lay on the Table All Anti-Slavery Peti-
tions: in Favor, Leonard Jarvis [Me.], Henry L. Pinckney [S. C.],
Franklin Pierce [N. H.], Waddy Thompson [S. C.]; Opposed, John
Quincy Adams [Mass.], Francis Granger [N. Y.]; Motion Is Carried,
Henry A. Wise [Va.] Refusing to Vote on Constitutional Grounds—
Caleb Cushing [Mass.] and Mr. Adams Present Anti-Slavery Petitions
Which Are Laid on the Table—Mr. Adams Questions the Chair About the
Admissibility of a Petition He Holds from Slaves—Dixon H. Lewis
[Ala.], Seconded by Seaton Grantland [Ga.] Moves to Censure Mr.
Adams for Violating the Dignity of the House—Various Modifications
of the Motion by John M. Patton [Va.], Mr. Thompson, and George C.
Dromgoole [Va.]—Motion Is Negatived After Debate, in Which These
Movers, and Julius C. Alford [Ga.], Francis W. Pickens [S. C.], Mr.
Pinckney and Richard French [Ky.] Defend Resolution, and Mr. Adams,
Churchill C. Cambreleng [N. Y.], and Mr. Cushing Oppose It—President
Jackson Recommends Legislation to Prevent Circulation in the Mails
of Abolition Publications—Senator Thomas H. Benton [Mo.] Submits
a Specimen of an "Incendiary" Cartoon—Bill Introduced in Senate
by Special Committee to Penalize Postmasters Accepting Such Mail—
Minority Report of John C. Calhoun [S. C.] on the Subject: "Abolition
and Disunion"—John P. King [Ga.], of the Majority, Opposes the Report—Reply by Calhoun: "Slavery Paramount to Federal Laws"—Reply to Calhoun by Daniel Webster [Mass]: "Freedom of the Mails"—
Bill Is Lost—President Martin Van Buren's Position on Abolition—
William Slade [Vt.] Makes an Abolition Speech in the House—Hopkins
Halsey [Ga.] and R. Barnwell Rhett [S. C.] Call on Southern Repre-

sentatives to Withdraw for Conference—Rhett Proposes Secession; It is
Negatived by the Conference, and a Proposal of a "Gag Law" by John
M. Patton [Va.] Is Endorsed; It is Adopted by the House.

T HE question of the abolition of slavery in places
where it already prevailed by law in distinction
to the *restriction* of the institution to its existing
legal limits began to be systematically agitated soon
after the Missouri Compromise.

The leader in this movement was Benjamin Lundy,
editor of *The Genius of Universal Emancipation.* In
1829 he was joined by William Lloyd Garrison, who
afterwards (January 1, 1831) established *The Liberator.*

Lundy and other men who became prominent in the
abolition movement, such as James G. Birney and Gerrit
Smith, had originally been members of the Colonization Society, and to understand the progress of the anti-
slavery movement it will be well at this point to discuss
briefly the origin and character of the less radical
organization.

As early as 1801 President Jefferson and James
Madison, then Governor of Virginia, had considerable
correspondence on the subject of colonizing free negroes
out of the country as a step forward in solving the
slavery question. A number of philanthropists early
in the century also began to agitate the project, and in
1816 a Colonization Society was organized in Princeton,
N. J. A few years afterwards it was reorganized at
Washington, D. C., as the "National Colonization
Society." Bushrod Washington, a nephew of George
Washington, and an Associate-Justice of the Supreme
Court, was made its president, and *The African Reposi-
tory* was established as its organ.

The society grew rapidly, and by 1827 it had branches
in almost every State, and was supported by distinguished people of every political complexion, including
James Madison and Henry Clay, as well as Benjamin
Lundy and other abolitionists.

In 1821 a region on the east coast of Africa at Cape
Mesurado was purchased and named Liberia, its chief
town being called Monrovia for President Monroe. On

February 7, 1827, the society, through Senator Ezekiel Chambers [Md.], presented a memorial to the Senate asking Government aid to send free negroes to Liberia. The memorial was opposed by Senator Robert Y. Hayne [S. C.]. It was laid on the table.

GOVERNMENT AID TO COLONIZE NEGROES

SENATE, FEBRUARY 7-9, 1827

SENATOR CHAMBERS.—I know no question not immediately involving the very existence of the Government which ought to excite so deeply the anxious reflection of every patriot. That part of the population of the States which it is the object of the society to remove is a degraded, miserable race of beings. They are not, cannot be, citizens of your country—they do not add to your physical energies—they do not effect the legitimate object of any one appropriate class of a well-organized community—they are anything but a laboring class. It were well did they only present a negative character, but your free blacks exert the most deleterious influence. The corrupting poison of their example and their habits has infected our slaves and made them indolent and immoral.

You are advised by intelligent and discreet men whose lives have been devoted to the consideration of this subject that the plan now proposed will probably remove, certainly lessen, these evils. You are advised that the means of accomplishing the plan are in the power and under the legal control of Congress. If authority be required to sanction such opinions, you have it in the deliberate and formal decisions of the legislatures of a large proportion of the States of this Union—States in which slavery is allowed, and States in which it is not allowed. The States of Virginia, Maryland, Kentucky, and Tennessee have each made a legislative declaration of their views upon this subject. Georgia has so far expressed an opinion, in that she has directed the captive Africans, who, by former laws of Congress, were placed at the disposal of the State, to be delivered to this Colonization Society to be sent to Africa.

SENATOR HAYNE.—The gentleman from Maryland has vindicated the object of the society. He insists that it is not the wish or intention of the society to interfere with or in any way disturb the policy of the Southern States. So say the society. But, sir, facts speak stronger than professions. And what are the facts? Are not the members and agents of this society everywhere (even while disclaiming all such intentions) making proclamations that the end of their scheme is universal emancipation? Have we not heard their orators, at their meetings here, openly held under the eyes of Congress, asking whether, when all the free people of color are transported, we are to stop there; and answering their question by the avowal that the great work will be but then begun? Sir, let any man examine the whole scope and tendency of the reports and speeches made to this society, nay, of this very manifesto, published by their authority, and he must be dull of apprehension if he does not perceive that the spirit which lurks beneath their fair professions is hostile to the peace and best interests of the Southern States; and not the less so because it comes clothed in the garb of friendship and with professions of peace and good will. Besides, sir, does not every Southern man know that, wherever the Colonization Society has invaded our country, a spirit of hostility to our institutions has instantly sprung up?

Passing over the indirect evils of this society, what would be the direct tendency and effect of the adoption of its policy by the Federal Government? The national funds are to be appropriated for the purpose of transporting such slaves as their owners may consent to emancipate for that purpose. If this be taken up as a national object; if we have the power and the inclination, and should resolve to appropriate the public money to this object, of course we would be at liberty to offer any temptation we please to induce the owners of slaves to consent. It is useless to disguise the truth—if this policy should ever be adopted by this Government, the members of the society will go directly into the market as the purchasers of our slaves, for the purpose of emancipation and transportation. Now, I will ask gentlemen to contemplate dispassionately the effect that is to be produced on the Southern States, by this Government being notoriously in the market, with its treasury of $20,000,000 or $30,000,000, as the purchasers of our slaves for the purpose of emancipation. Can you touch this mass of a now contented, happy, and useful class of beings without disquieting their minds, creating dissatisfaction, destroying their usefulness, and bringing ruin on the whole community? Much has been already done to destroy the confidence and impair the mutual affection which have hitherto so happily subsisted between the master and his slave; but adopt this policy and they will be destroyed forever. Besides, sir, once bring this Government into the market as purchasers and they will fix their own terms. Once admit the principle, and, in its application, it must inevitably lead to divesting us of our property on such terms as Congress may choose to prescribe; the insidious movements of colonization and abolition societies, the distribution of political tracts, and a few incendiary resolutions introduced into Congress and the State legislatures (events which have, in part, occurred even in our own time) will reduce the value of our property to any standard this Government chooses to prescribe. So it has been in the West Indies, and so it will be here. I am informed by a gentleman who has lived many years in the West Indies that, by the perpetual agitation of this question in Great Britain, in and out of Parliament, lands in that country have been reduced to less than half their value; and slaves to ten pounds per head; and should the British Government choose to purchase them it will be the easiest thing in nature so to shake the public confidence in that species of property as to reduce their value to nothing.

In this view of the subject, can any man be so blind as not to see and feel the dangerous tendency of the measures recommended to us by this society? Sir, the truth cannot be disguised—it must be told. The only safety of the Southern States is to be found in the want of power on the part of the Federal Government to touch the subject at all. Thank God, the Constitution gives them no power to engage in the work of colonization, or to interfere with our institutions, either for good or for evil. This is the very "Ark of the Covenant," in which alone we will find safety.

In December, 1833, the American Anti-Slavery Society was formed in Philadelphia, with Beriah Green as president and Lewis Tappan and John G. Whittier as secretaries.

SLAVERY IN THE DISTRICT OF COLUMBIA

The first attempts to secure the abolition of slavery were directed upon the District of Columbia as the point of easiest attack, since Congress had sole power over the "Federal District," limited only by conditions of the grants of the territory from Maryland and Virginia, and by the general restrictions of its powers in the Constitution.

During the session of 1828-29 a petition was presented to Congress signed by over 1,000 citizens of the

District praying for a gradual emancipation of slavery therein, owing to the great abuses which had arisen in regard to the treatment of the slaves; it was referred to a committee which failed to report it.

Early in the next session (on January 6, 1829) the subject was again brought before the House by Charles Miner [Pa.]. He offered a preamble and resolution; the preamble stated at length such abuses in the District growing out of slavery as the kidnapping of free negroes, use of public prisons for the domestic slave trade, etc., and the resolution declared that a committee be appointed to investigate these abuses and to inquire into "the expediency of providing by law for the gradual abolition of slavery within the District in such manner that the interests of no individual shall be injured thereby."

On January 9 the preamble was separated from the resolutions and the whole was voted upon in sections, the preamble being negatived by a vote of 141 to 37, the first resolution adopted by 120 to 29, and the second resolution adopted by 114 to 66. Nothing, however, came of the inquiry thereby ordered.

On January 13, 1836, Leonard Jarvis [Mo.] moved in the House that "the subject of the abolition of slavery in the District of Columbia ought not to be entertained by Congress," and that petitions to this effect "ought to be laid upon the table without being referred or printed." On February 8 Henry L. Pinckney [S. C.] moved that a special committee be appointed to consider the petitions, Mr. Jarvis's resolution and all others dealing with the subject, "with instructions to report that Congress possesses no constitutional authority to interfere in any way with the institution of slavery in any of the States," and ought not to interfere in case of the District of Columbia. This was passed by an overwhelming vote, Henry A. Wise [Va.] refusing to vote, saying:

I refuse to vote at all upon such a proposition; because to affirm any proposition by declaratory resolution is to admit it needs affirmation; and because Congress has no constitutional power either to affirm or deny any proposition whatever in relation to slavery in the States.

On May 18, 1836, Mr. Pinckney presented the report of the committee. It was a very exhaustive one, occupying an hour and a half in reading. It concluded with the resolutions it had been instructed to present, together with the Jarvis resolution, expanded so as to prohibit all consideration of resolutions, as well as petitions, on the subject of slavery. After considerable debate the resolutions were adopted: the first, declaring Congress had no constitutional authority to interfere with slavery in the States, by 182 votes to 9; the second, that it ought not so to interfere in the District of Columbia, by 132 votes to 45; and the third, that consideration be refused petitions and resolutions on the subject of slavery, by 117 votes to 68. When the name of John Quincy Adams was called on the third resolution the ex-President rose and, refusing to vote, said: "I hold the resolution to be a direct violation of the Constitution of the United States, the rules of this House, and the rights of my constituents." Mr. Adams resumed his seat amid loud cries of "order" from all parts of the hall.

In the debate on the motion the speakers in behalf of the right of petition were ex-President Adams and Francis Granger [N. Y.], and those in opposition in greater or less degree were Franklin Pierce [N. H.], Waddy Thompson, Jr. [S. C.], and Henry L. Pinckney [S. C.].

The Gag Law

House of Representatives, December 16, 1835-February 12, 1836

Mr. Pierce.—This was not the last memorial of the same character which would be sent here. It was perfectly apparent that the question must be met now, or at some future time, fully and explicitly, and such an expression of this House given as could leave no possible room to doubt as to the opinions and sentiments entertained by its members. He, indeed, considered the overwhelming vote of the House the other day, laying a memorial of similar tenor, and, he believed, the same in terms, upon the table, as fixing upon it the stamp of reprobation. He supposed that all sections of the country would be satisfied with that expression; but gentlemen seemed now to consider the vote as equivocal and evasive. He was unwilling that any imputation should rest upon the North, in consequence of the misguided and fanatical zeal of a few—comparatively very few—who, however honest might have been their purposes, he believed had done incalculable mischief, and whose movements he knew received no more sanction among the great mass of the people of the North than they did at the South. For one, he, while he would be the last to infringe upon any of the sacred reserved rights of the people, was prepared to stamp with disapprobation, in the most express and unequivocal terms, the whole movement upon this subject.

MR. ADAMS.—I am perfectly satisfied that the true and only method of keeping this subject out of discussion is to refer all petitions of this kind to the Committee on the District of Columbia, or some other committee of the House, to receive their report, and to accept it unanimously. This does equal justice to all parties in the country; it avoids the discussion of this agitating question on the one hand and, on the other, it pays a due respect to the right of the constituent to petition.

From the moment that these petitions are referred to the Committee on the District of Columbia, they go to the family vault "of all the Capulets," and you will never hear of them afterward.

But if you are to lay these petitions on the table, if you come to the resolution that this House will not receive any more petitions, what will be the consequence? In a large portion of this country every individual member who votes with you will be left at home at the next election, and some one will be sent who is not prepared to lay these petitions on the table.

What will be the next consequence? Sir, you will have discussion; and, to my regret I say it, discussion has been called for and challenged upon this floor. It has been challenged. And what will the discussion amount to? A discussion upon the merits of slavery. Sir, on such a discussion every speech made by a representative from the north of Mason and Dixon's line, in this House, will be an incendiary pamphlet, and what will you do with them? The speeches of my colleagues, probably of myself, will be incendiary; because, if discussion is thrust upon us, I doubt not I might make a speech as incendiary as any pamphlet upon which such torrents of denunciation have here been poured. If I were capable of the craven and recreant spirit of shrinking from expressing, not probably so much my own sentiments as those of my constituents, I should go home to their scorn, and they would send here a man who would represent them more faithfully.

Well, sir, what becomes of these incendiary pamphlets, the speeches in this House, if they go to the public? What will be done with them by the public press? The newspapers report these speeches; every speech is circulated through your whole country; and how can you arrest it? Will you introduce a resolution that members of this House shall not speak a word in derogation of the sublime merits of slavery? You must have a resolution of this kind, to follow the one laid upon your table this morning—a resolution that no member of this House shall dare to utter an incendiary sentiment? And what is that incendiary sentiment? Why, it is, in substance, the contents of these pamphlets. Well, sir, you begin with suppressing the right of petition; you must next suppress the right of speech in this House; for you must offer a resolution that every member who dares to express a sentiment of this kind shall be expelled, or that the speeches shall not go forth to the public—shall not be circulated. What will be the consequence then? You suppress the right of petition; you suppress the freedom of speech; the freedom of the press and the freedom of religion; for, in the minds of many worthy, honest, and honorable men—fanatics, if you please so to call them—this is a religious question, in which they act under what they believe to be a sense of duty to their God; and, however erroneous may be their conclusions, it is not for me, nor for this House, to judge them. Therefore, sir, in deference to what has been heretofore the usage of this House, in deference to the respect which is due to the right of petition, and the respect which is due to the right of freedom of speech, freedom of the press, and freedom of religion, I hope that this petition will be left where it has been placed by the House, in the possession of the Committee on the District of Columbia, and that we shall hear no more about it.

MR. THOMPSON.—As to discussing this subject before any human tribunal, I will not. I will not condescend to vindicate to this House or elsewhere this or any other of our domestic institutions. It is no affair of yours; you have no right to touch it, still less to demand a reason of us for its continuance. The gentleman from New Hampshire, Mr. Pierce—and I must say that his voice sounded in my ear as the voice of a friend—

said that we of the South could not know the state of things
at the North; that in his district there was not one abolitionist
in five hundred. If I did not know it before, I do now, sir,
because he has said so. Let me say, in my turn, that he does
not know the state of feeling at the South; and I do, with a
full knowledge of all my responsibilities, declare that, in my
opinion, nothing will satisfy the excited, the almost frenzied,
South but an indignant rejection of these petitions; such a rejection as will, at the same time that it respects the right of
petitioning, express the predetermination, the foregone conclusion, of the House on the subject—a rejection, sir, that will
satisfy the South and serve as an indignant rebuke to the
fanatics of the North. But we are told that such a course,
while it would satisfy the South, would offend the people of the
North. How so, sir? I had thought that it was the South
that was interfered with, the South that was injured, that it
was the South that was to be satisfied. Who is it at the North
that we are to conciliate? The fanatics? Fanatics, did I say,
sir? Never before was so vile a band dignified with that name.
They are murderers, foul murderers, accessories before the fact,
and they know it, of murder, robbery, rape, infanticide. Sir,
this question must be settled; if I may so speak, it must be
killed; a just regard to the rights and feelings of the South, to
the peace and harmony of this great Republic, the permanency
of our institutions, demand it; in short, sir, every consideration
which can address itself to a patriot demands it. Yes, sir, in
the presence of the armed monarchies of Europe, with all the
powerful elements both on this and the other side of the Atlantic, already in incipient commotion, already rumbling in
their deep crater, he is wilfully blind who does not see that
the time is not distant when union, concert, all the patriotism,
all the virtue, all the wisdom of our whole country will be
demanded. Shall we, sir, continue to stir this most prolific source
of discord, aye, of hatred, or shall we settle it, and forever?

MR. GRANGER.—Sir, who are these petitioners? They are
persons who, looking to the letter of the Constitution of their
country, and finding there that Congress has the right of exclusive legislation for this district, and not looking beyond that,
to the grants of session by the States of Virginia and Maryland,
to see under what reservations those grants were made and accepted, and without stopping to ask the still more important
question whether the residents of the District of Columbia require any interference, suppose that Congress have the right to
legislate upon this subject. Starting upon this abstract propo-

sition, they have supposed they had a right to appear at the bar of this House, and to ask that the seat of Government of a free nation should be inhabited by those only who are free.

Such, sir, is the condition of these petitioners; and I can never consent that they should be designated as murderers, or that their names should be mingled with those of the abolitionists.

Mr. PINCKNEY considered the question settled. The Government had made a solemn covenant upon this subject with the slaveholding States; Congress might violate the Constitution; it could not, would not, violate the public faith. It was bound hand and foot. The South had nothing now to fear, except from those who are determined to continue the agitation of slavery for the purpose of excitement. Abolitionism has attained its height. It has begun to go down, and will soon disappear entirely, if we do not fan the flame ourselves and will only allow our friends in the non-slaveholding States to fight the fanatics in their own way, and not trammel them in their operations by mixing up extraneous and unnecessary questions with the subject of abolition.

CENSURE OF JOHN QUINCY ADAMS

HOUSE OF REPRESENTATIVES, FEBRUARY 6-9, 1837

During the next session of Congress, on February 6, 1837, Caleb Cushing [Mass.] presented in the House various petitions from ''ladies'' of his State praying for the abolition of slavery in the District of Columbia. These were received and laid on the table, without debate or commitment, under the resolution of the House. John Quincy Adams [Mass.] then rose and said that he presented a petition from nine ''ladies'' or women (which term he used became afterwards a subject of dispute) of Fredericksburg, Va. He would not name them, he said:

''Because, from the disposition which at present prevailed in the country, he did not know what might happen to them if he did name them. It was not a petition for the abolition of slavery in the District of Columbia, but it was a petition praying Congress to put a stop to the slave trade in the District of

JOHNNY Q. [ADAMS] INTRODUCING HAYTIAN AMBASSADOR TO LADIES OF NEW ENGLAND

Columbia. Whether it was genuine or not, it was not for him to determine.''

The petition was ordered to lie on the table, under the resolution.

MR. ADAMS said he held in his hand a paper on which, before it was presented, he desired to have the decision of the Speaker, James K. Polk [of Tennessee]. It was a petition from twenty-two persons, declaring themselves to be slaves. He wished to know whether the Speaker considered such a petition as coming within the order of the House.

The Speaker said he could not tell until he had the contents of the petition in his possession.

MR. ADAMS said that if the paper was sent to the clerk's table it would be in possession of the House, and if sent to the Speaker he would see what were its contents. He [Mr. A.] wished to do nothing except in submission to the rules of the House.

The Speaker said that it was the first time in the recollection of the Chair that persons not free had presented a petition to this House. The Chair wished to take the sense of the House, which he had a right to do.

DIXON H. LEWIS [Ala.] believed that the House should punish severely such an infraction of its decorum and its rules; and he called on the members from the slaveholding States to come forward now and demand from the House the punishment of the gentleman from Massachusetts.

SEATON GRANTLAND [Ga.] would second the motion, and go all lengths in support of it.

MR. LEWIS said that, if the House would inflict no punishment for such flagrant violations of its dignity as this, it would be better for the representatives from the slaveholding States to go home at once.

JULIUS C. ALFORD [Ga.] said that, if the gentleman from Massachusetts should present this petition, that moment he [Mr. Alford] should move, as an act of justice to the South, which he in part represented, and which he conceived had been treated with indignity, that it be taken from the House and burned; and he hoped that every man who was a friend to the Constitution would support him. There must be an end to this constant attempt to raise excitement, or the Union could not exist much longer. The moment any man should disgrace the Government under which he lived by presenting a petition from slaves praying for emancipation, he hoped that petition would, by order of the House, be committed to the flames.

JOHN M. PATTON [Va.] moved to suspend the rule to enable him to submit a motion to take from the table, to be hereafter disposed of as the House may decide, the paper already presented by the gentleman from Massachusetts, and which had been laid on the table under the resolution of the House; he alluded to the paper presented as a petition from nine ladies of Fredericksburg. He [Mr. P.] would state in his place, and on his responsibility, that the name of no lady was attached to that paper. He did not believe there was a single one of them of decent respectability. He believed the signatures to be genuine, and he recognized only one name which he had known before, and that was the name of a free mulatto woman of the worst fame and reputation. He therefore moved that the paper which had been received and laid on the table should be taken from the table and returned to the gentleman from Massachusetts.

Waddy Thompson [S. C.], moved as an amendment to the motion of the honorable gentleman from Virginia [Mr. Patton] the following resolution:

Resolved, That the honorable John Quincy Adams, by the attempt just made by him to introduce a petition purporting on its face to be from slaves, has been guilty of a gross disrespect to this House, and that he be instantly brought to the bar to receive the severe censure of the Speaker.

He said: The gentleman from Massachusetts offered to present a petition from slaves, and so purporting to be on its face, in open and wilful violation of what he knew to be the rules of this House, and insulting to a large portion of its members. Does the gentleman, even in the latitude which he gives to the right of petition, think that it includes slaves? If he does not, he has wilfully violated the rules of the House and the feelings of its members. Does that gentleman know that there are laws in all the slave States, and here, for the punishment of those who excite insurrection? I can tell him that there are such things as grand juries; and if, sir, the juries of this District have, as I doubt not they have, proper intelligence and spirit, he may yet be made amenable to another tribunal, and we may yet see an incendiary brought to condign punishment.

MR. LEWIS offered the following amendment, which he suggested to his friend from South Carolina [Mr. Thompson] to accept as a modification:

Resolved, That John Quincy Adams, a member from the State of Massachusetts, by his attempt to introduce into this House a petition from slaves, for the abolition of slavery in the District of Columbia, committed an outrage on the rights and feelings of a large portion of the people of this Union; a flagrant contempt on the dignity of this House; and, by extending to slaves a privilege only belonging to freemen, directly invites the slave population to insurrection; and that the said member be forthwith called to the bar of the House, and be censured by the Speaker.

Mr. Thompson accepted the modification.

Mr. Adams then rose and said: Gentlemen are really consuming the time of the House in such a manner that I think the obligation rests upon me to ask them to modify their resolution. It may be as severe as they propose; but I ask them to change the matter of fact a little, so that when I come to the bar I may not, in one single word, put an end to their resolution.

I did not present the petition. I said I had a paper purporting to be a petition from slaves. I asked the Speaker whether he considered such a paper as included within the general order of the House, that all petitions, memorials, resolutions, and papers, relating in any way, or to any extent whatever, to the subject of slavery should be laid on the table. I intended to take the decision of the Speaker before I went one step toward presenting or offering to present that petition.

If the House should choose to read the petition, I can state to them they would find it something very much the reverse of that which the resolution states it to be; and if the gentleman from Alabama [Mr. Lewis] still shall choose to bring me to the bar of the House, he must amend his resolution in a very important particular; for he probably may have to put into it that my crime has been for attempting to introduce the petition of slaves that slavery should not be abolished.

Mr. Thompson was sorry to see the air of levity which it is attempted to throw over this matter. Is it a light thing, for the amusement of others, to irritate, almost to madness, the whole delegation from the slave States? It is intimated that the petition does not pray for the abolition of slavery, but a very different object. It makes not the slightest difference; it is the attempt to introduce a petition from slaves for any object; as insolent if it be for one purpose as for another.

Mr. T. then further modified his resolution by substituting the three following resolutions:

1. *Resolved,* That the honorable John Q. Adams, by an effort to present a petition from slaves, has committed a gross contempt of this House.

2. *Resolved,* That the member from Massachusetts above named, by creating the impression and leaving the House under such impression, that

the said petition was for the abolition of slavery, when he knew that it was
not, has trifled with the House.

3. *Resolved*, That the honorable John Q. Adams receive the censure of
the House for his conduct referred to in the preceding resolutions.

FRANCIS W. PICKENS [S. C.] said that presenting the petition was in itself admission that Mr. Adams had communi-
cation with slaves, and was evidence, in law, of collusion. It
broke down the principle that the slave could be known only
through his master. For this he was indictable, under statute,
for aiding and abetting insurrection; and for such conduct is
he not amenable to the censure of this House? The privilege
of speech protected a member from being questioned before any
other tribunal, but does not exempt him from being questioned
before this House.

CHURCHILL C. CAMBRELENG [N. Y.] observed: When the
honorable member from Alabama [Mr. Lewis] presented his
resolution he felt that, great as the sacrifice was to bring to
the bar of this House one who had occupied the highest station
on earth, as President of the United States, yet it ought to be
made. But now, after having heard the explanation of the honorable gentleman [Mr. Adams], he viewed the subject altogether in a different light. It appeared to him that that gentleman [Mr. Adams] had been hoaxed by some young men in
Fredericksburg. The contents of the petition were known in
this House before the gentleman from Massachusetts announced
them. It was manifestly designed to make him appear ridiculous
by presenting a petition praying for his own expulsion. It came
from a slaveholding quarter, and was no doubt designed to
insult him for presenting so frequently abolition petitions.

HENRY L. PINCKNEY [S. C.].—It seems, then, that the petition
which the gentleman offered to present is not a petition in point
of fact; that it is nothing more than a quiz, or a hoax, which
has been played off upon the gentleman himself; and that,
probably, in retaliation for the joke practiced on himself, he
determined to carry it still further by playing it off upon the
House. But whether the petition was genuine or not; whether
it prayed for the abolition of slavery or the expulsion of the
gentleman himself; and whether the gentleman was in jest or
earnest, his conduct was unquestionably reprehensible, and such
as ought to be visited with the severest censure of the House.
If the petition was genuine, it was an indignity to the House
to have offered to present it, purporting, as it did, to come
from slaves. Does not the gentleman know that the right of
petition only attaches to the free white people of the Union,

and that slaves can be heard in a legislative body only through the agency of their owners? But if the petition was a hoax, then the conduct of the gentleman was still more unjustifiable. It was adding insult to injury. The gentleman, if such is his disposition, may enjoy this joke, and enjoy this scene; but farces of this kind neither suit the humor of the slaveholding States nor comport with the character and dignity of the legislature of the nation.

GEORGE C. DROMGOOLE [Va.] said he preferred action on a question of this character rather than debate, and he had risen only for the purpose of requesting the gentleman from South Carolina [Mr. Thompson] to accept a modification he would send to the clerk's table.

The modification was read, as follows:

1. *Resolved,* That the honorable John Quincy Adams, a member of this House, by stating in his place that he had in his possession a paper purporting to be a petition from slaves, and inquiring if it came within the meaning of a resolution heretofore adopted (as preliminary to its presentation), has given color to the idea that slaves have the right of petition, and of his readiness to be their organ; and that for the same he deserves the censure of this House.

2. *Resolved,* That the aforesaid John Q. Adams receive a censure from the Speaker, in the presence of the House of Representatives.

MR. THOMPSON accepted the above as a substitute for his own resolutions.

MR. ALFORD.—Mr. Speaker, the member from Massachusetts would screen himself from the censure of this House because he has not sent his petition from slaves to your table. Sir, he has sent the petition from the free negroes of Fredericksburg, and that is as wrong and insulting to us as if it were from slaves. The Constitution of these United States no more allows the one than the other, and both are equally insulting.

Sir, there seems to be some difference of opinion among our friends here as to what course we ought to pursue in this awful crisis of our beloved country. Some of our friends, as patriotic as any, have urged, in this debate, that we ought not to sit here and submit to this outrageous course of things; that, if it does not cease, we should go home. No, sir; no, sir; this must not be; we will neither submit nor retire. If they prosecute this measure in this House by attempts at legislating us out of our rights, we will resist it here by legislative acts as long as we can; and if at last they prove too strong for us, and succeed in passing unconstitutional laws, to rob us of our property, to murder our wives and children, still we will not submit; they must change the Constitution before they can bind us by any laws of abolition; this they never can do if the South is true to itself. And true we shall be, I hope in God, to our Constitution, our wives, our children, and our country. If still they pursue us to the last, and attempt to do by force what they never can do by law, we will not be found wanting; we will not desert this Capitol nor this country. This is the Old Dominion; this land is ours as well as theirs; it was ceded by Virginia and Maryland, where slavery is tolerated by law. Shall we leave it, then, to the dominion of force, and that, too, inflicted by the unhallowed arm of the wild and worse than savage fanatic? No, never!

Let me tell gentlemen it is a firm and unconquerable resolution never to surrender one jot or tittle of our constitutional rights upon this subject. We have a common interest in this Government, a common title in this capital; it bears the name of the immortal Washington, and he was a Southern man. Shall we, then, ever surrender the one or desert the other? No, never! Never until this fair city is a field of Waterloo and this beautiful Potomac a river of blood.

CALEB CUSHING [Mass.].—Gentlemen talk to us of these our great fundamental rights—as the freedom of speech, of opinion, of petition—as if they were derived from the Constitution of the United States. I scout such a doctrine. If there were a drop in my veins that did not rebel against the sentiment, it would be bastard blood. Sir, I claim to be descended from the king-killing Roundheads of the reign of Charles the First; through a race of men not unremembered in peace or war; never backward in the struggles of liberty; a family upon the head of a member of which the first price of blood was set by Great Britain, in revenge for his early devotion to the cause of independence. I venerate their character and their principles. I am ready to do as they did—to abandon all the advantages of country, home, fortune, station—to fly to some Western wilderness—and to live upon a handful of parched corn and a cup of cold water, with God's blessing on honest independence—sooner than surrender one jot or tittle of those great principles of liberty which I have sucked in with my mother's milk. I disdain to hold these rights by any parchment title. The people of the Commonwealth of Massachusetts, the people of every State of this Union, came into it in the full possession and fruition of all these rights. We did not constitute this Government as the means of acquiring new rights, but for the protection of old ones, which nature had conferred upon us; which the

Constitution rightly regards as preëxisting rights; and as to
which all the Constitution does is to provide that these rights
neither you nor any power on earth shall alter, abrogate, or
abridge. They are rights of Heaven's own giving. We hold
them by the supreme tenure of revolution. We hold them
by the dread arbitrament of battle. We hold them by
the concession of a higher and broader charter than all
the constitutions in the land—the free donation of the eternal God, when he made us to be men. These, the cardinal
principles of human freedom, he has implanted in us and placed
them before and behind and around us for our guard and guidance, like the cloud by day and the pillar of fire by night which
led the Israelites through the desert. It is a liberty, native,
inborn, original, underived, imprescriptible; and acknowledged
in the Constitution itself, as preëminently before and above the
Constitution.

Now, in their denunciations of the North, it is these, the
very primordial rights of the universal people of the United
States, that gentlemen from the South assail. They strike at
the freedom of opinion, of the press, and of speech, out of doors
—and the rights of petition and debate in this House.

It seems to be imputed as a crime, to a portion of the inhabitants of the non-slaveholding States, that they entertain
sentiments condemned by a majority of this nation. But can it
be a crime? I appeal once again to that portion of the members from the South who are foremost in this debate—I mean
the gentleman from South Carolina [Mr. Thompson] and his
friends—who on certain subjects differ in opinion with a great
majority of their countrymen; and I ask them whether they
stand prepared to abide by and sustain the doctrine that opinions unacceptable to the majority are a moral or political
crime? Will they apply to themselves the rule of judgment
which they urge so vehemently against the people of the North?
Will they deliberately sanction such an odious doctrine? I
know they cannot. They must perceive that it is impossible
by any act of the will to control the conclusions of the mind. It
is our duty, in all the contingencies of life, to weigh well the
facts and the reasonings upon which our judgments are to be
formed; to apply to every question a conscientious desire to
arrive at the truth; to spare no means to inform ourselves
rightly as to the matters which the mind is to judge. But the
result is not a thing within the scope of the will. And it is
monstrous, therefore, to bring opinions to the bar of legal censure. It is a violation of the interior sanctuary of a man's own

soul. It is the very acme of tyranny. The arbitrary power to condemn and punish opinion is that which gave birth to the Protestant Reformation, and which has rendered the Inquisition a byword of odium and reproach. It is that self-same thing from which our fathers fled—the Puritans, the Catholics, the Quakers, the Huguenots—when they left their native Europe to found an asylum for conscience in this New World. It is that which has nerved the arm and edged the sword in every contest of liberty which lightens along the history of civilized man.

Sir, I put it to gentlemen, in all directness and sincerity, do they suppose that angry attacks on the freedom of opinion, of speech, of the press, of petition, of debate are likely to check the spread in the United States of that disapprobation of slavery which is but another form, conversely considered, of the love of liberty? Do they deem it possible to smother the opinions and stifle the petitions of the free men of the United States? Ay, and of the free women too? For I confess it seems to me a strange idea to uphold, in this enlightened age, that woman, refined, educated, intellectual woman, is to have no opinion or no right to express that opinion. Do gentlemen soberly think their cause can be strengthened in the country by bringing to the bar of the House for contempt, by subjecting to censure, by expelling a representative of one of the free States, because he may have given color to the idea that slaves can petition Congress?

RICHARD FRENCH [Ky]. said: The honorable gentleman from Massachusetts [Mr. Cushing] contended that the right of petition was a natural right, derived from our Creator; and, being a natural right, so derived, belonged to all human beings. If that gentleman meant that all men have the natural right to supplicate the Deity, he is right. If he meant that all men, while in a state of nature, had the right to petition their fellow-beings for what they wanted, he is right. If he meant that all men, in their personal relations and intercourse, have the same right now, he is right. But if he meant that all men have the right to petition the Government, I think he is wrong.

Sir, there was a time when civil government did not exist; and how can a man be said to have a natural right to petition a political being who had no voice in its creation—who is neither party nor privy to the body politic?

That gentleman was pleased also to favor us with what he termed the abstract opinions of the abolitionists—opinions which, as he said, they honestly and conscientiously entertained. And what are those opinions? That slavery is, in the abstract, a social, moral, and political evil. I will not, Mr. Speaker, debate the question whether slavery be or be not, in the abstract, a social, moral, or political evil, but I refer to what the honorable gentleman said to prove what are the grievances of the abolitionists and what their objects. Slavery, according to his *exposé* of their views, is their grievance—universal emancipation, then, must be their object.

If they prevail in that object, through the action of Congress, what becomes of the rights of the slave States, as guaranteed to them by the Constitution? What becomes of the Government? Sir, it is plain that the end of these things, if successful, terminates in the overthrow of the Government.

MR. PATTON then moved the following amendment of the motion before the House:

Resolved, That any member who shall hereafter present to the House any petition from the slaves in this Union ought to be considered as regardless of the feelings of the House, the rights of the Southern States, and unfriendly to the Union.

Resolved, That the honorable John Q. Adams having solemnly disclaimed all design of doing anything disrespectful to the House, in the inquiry he made of the Speaker, as to the petition purporting to be from slaves, and having avowed his intention not to offer to present the petition to the House, was of opinion that it ought not to be presented—therefore, all further proceedings in regard to his conduct do now cease.

MR. THOMPSON accepted.

MR. ADAMS.—Petition, sir, is a right belonging to every human creature, which does not depend upon the condition of the petitioner, and which cannot be denied to man in any condition. This, sir, is the principle involved in the inquiry put by me to the Chair—a principle more than recognized by the Constitution, which has declared that this right shall suffer no abridgment, no limitation whatever! If you now abolish this principle, this first and humblest right given from God to every human being, a limitation will next be put to the right of petitioning, in the fullest extent to which party madness might hereafter be inclined to carry it. If the House shall decide that the paper I possess comes under the order of the House of the 18th of January, I will present the petition, and in doing so shall be doing my duty—a duty of the highest importance to my country, to humanity, and to human nature. What, sir? Will you put the right of petitioning, of craving for help and mercy and protection, on the footing of political privileges? It is an idea which has not even been entertained by the utmost extreme of human despotism; no despot, of any age or clime, has ever denied this humble privilege to the poorest or the meanest of human creatures. If this House decides that it will not receive petitions from slaves, under any circumstances, it will cause the name of this country to be enrolled among the first of barbarous nations. A petition is a supplication; and supplication for what? For relief from those who have the power to give relief, and who are placed in a situation to attend to the cry of distress. That would be a sad day, sir, in my opinion, when a vote should pass this House that would not receive a petition from slaves! What would it lead to? When the principle is once begun of limiting the right of petition, where would it stop? Gentlemen have objected to the petition immediately preceding that which I presented because it came from colored people! from color! That, sir, is giving color to an idea with a witness![1] The honorable gentleman makes it a crime because I presented a petition which he affirms to be from colored women, which women were of infamous character, as the honorable gentleman says, prostitutes, I think the gentleman said.

MR. PATTON explained. He did not say they were prostitutes; the objection he made was that the petition came from free mulattoes in the South; he did not object on the ground of opposition to the right of petition, but because he considered that the House ought to refuse to open its doors to applications from the Southern slaves. As to the infamous character of the women in question he mentioned that, not as if he deemed it a reason for refusing the right to petition, but because he wished to wipe away the stain from the ladies of Fredericksburg, as these women had been called "ladies of Fredericksburg" by the honorable gentleman [Mr. Adams]. He was sure that no ladies from Fredericksburg had sent such a petition to this House.

MR. ADAMS continued: He was not certain that he called them ladies or whether the petition itself had not stated that they were ladies. Whenever he presented petitions from ladies he was not in the habit of using that term for their designation; the word "woman" was an expression much dearer to his heart than that of "lady." But to return to the idea he was about to enforce. He thought the honorable gentleman had said that they were infamous; but the proposition which he would ever maintain was that the sacred right of petition, of begging for mercy, as it did not depend upon condition, so also it did not

---

[1] One of the resolutions presented to the House charges Mr. Adams with giving color to the idea, etc.

depend upon character; it was a right which could not be denied to the poorest, the humblest, and the most wretched; and, moreover, it was a right which could not be refused to the most vile, the most abandoned, or most infamous. He did not, however, know that they were in the present case infamous, but he thought that was the word used in debate by the honorable gentleman, and that it was so reported in the *National Intelligencer.*

Mr. Patton again explained. He had not said that he knew those women.

MR. ADAMS continued: He was glad to hear the honorable gentleman disclaim any knowledge of them; for he had been going to ask, if they were infamous women, then who was it that had made them infamous? Not, he believed, their own color, but their masters; and he had heard it said, in proof of this fact, and he was inclined to believe it was the case, that there existed great resemblances in the South between the progeny of the colored people and the white men who claimed the possession of them. Thus, perhaps, the charge of being infamous might be retorted upon those who made it, as originating from themselves.

[Great agitation in the House.]

If you once admit the principle that the right of petition is limited, and will not apply to slaves, the next thing will be to limit it still further, by extending the limitation to free colored people; and, after this, the next limitation will be to the question of the character of the petitioners; then the next limitation will be to inquire on what side of political parties are the petitioners; and then, sir, from one side all petitions will be perfectly good and receivable, but on the other side all the petitions will be from people of bad character, according to the representations of any member who may say he does not know who they are; they will be all infamous, sir, who are on the wrong side. This will be the case. To this state will things come if the right of petition shall be limited by peculiar distinctions, and shall be made to rest on such grounds as these which have been relied upon in this debate.

I do not propose, sir, to go through all the speeches which fell upon me so thickly, which came down, pouncing upon me like so many eagles upon a dove, calling me infamous, with other harsh expressions; nay, from one quarter of the House I heard cries, "Expel him! Expel him!" All of these, sir, remind me of what Dame Quickly says: "Oh! day and night, but these are bitter words." But, sir, I was to be found guilty, sir, for permitting the House to believe as true a thing which there had not been one word uttered by me authorizing them even to infer, much less to believe.

I did not get up soon enough to set all these gentlemen right, to show them the best way to censure me, and prevent them from running wild in the manner they had done, bringing forward resolutions in such rapid succession, but all of them, unfortunately for the movers, contrary to facts. I beg the honorable gentlemen [Messrs. Lewis and Thompson] to remember that in offering this resolution to the House, inflicting censure upon one who has never, in all his parliamentary career, given offence to them, they went a little beyond the bounds of that course of conduct which is due from one gentleman of this House to another; and I would only give them one word of friendly admonition that, when in future they may wish to censure me, they would first be careful to pay more attention to facts.

If the law of South Carolina is a good argument to the gentleman from South Carolina [Mr. Thompson], and if a member of that legislature is made amenable for words spoken in debate, not only to the legislature but also to the grand and petit juries—if that, sir, is the law of South Carolina, I thank God I am not a citizen of South Carolina! [Great agitation.]

Such a sentiment, sir, uttered in this House, such a threat held out to the representatives of this nation, when it shall come before the world in the report of this debate, cannot fail to excite contempt and amazement; and it will be a matter of no less surprise that, when utterance was given to such a sentiment, it was not immediately rebuked by the Speaker. What, sir! We, the representatives of the nation, are all of us subject to the grand jury of the District of Columbia for words here spoken? We from the Northern and Eastern States are liable, sir, to be indicted as felons and incendiaries for presenting petitions not exactly agreeable to some members from the South? Is that the tenure on which we hold our seats? If it is, I wish the House may pass the resolution that whoever hereafter proposes to hand up a petition from slaves is an enemy to the Union.

If, when the gentleman [Mr. Thompson], instead of coming at once to a solution of that question, brought forward his resolution of censure against me—sir, if he thought to frighten me from my purpose—if that, sir, was his object, he mistook his

man! I am not to be intimidated by the gentleman from South
Carolina [Mr. Thompson], nor by all the grand juries in the
universe. The right by which every member of this House
holds his seat here is of the deepest and utmost importance to
the whole nation; and I trust this debate will be read by every
portion of the country, and that, among other astonishing things
in this debate, the astonishing threat of the gentleman will not
be unnoticed. We have heard, sir, of the great superiority of
Anglo-Saxon blood. What, sir! is there a drop of that blood
flowing in the veins of any man who will subscribe to such a
political doctrine as this? How little does such a person understand of the true principles of freedom in relation to the powers
of a legislative assembly! I would ask every member of this
House what would have been the issue if, in the British House
of Commons, one member of Parliament should tell another
member that, for what he had said or done in Parliament, he
should be made amenable to the grand jury of the city of West-
minister? Sir, it would be too ridiculous for indignation; it
would excite one universal shout of laughter; it would from
thenceforth render him who had uttered the menace

> "Sacred to ridicule his whole life long,
> And the sad burden of some merry song."

It is not possible for me to make my defence in any system
or order. What defence can be made against this new crime of
giving color to ideas? But, I beg to say, I should deem it to be
the heaviest calamity which has ever befallen me in the course
of a life checkered with many vicissitudes if a vote of censure
from this House should pass upon my name or upon any action
of mine in this House. And now, when I thus speak, am I
treating with contempt this House? Have I ever done so? Has
not the honor of this House been among the first and dearest
sentiments of my heart? I have reverenced this House as the
representatives of the whole people of this Union. I have further felt that sentiment which is called the *esprit de corps.* I
appeal to this House if I have not been the first to come forward and defend its honor and dignity on more than one occasion. And now am I to be brought to the bar for a contempt
of this House, for doing that which was done in the most re-
spectful manner which it was possible to devise? For asking a
question of the Speaker; consulting him first upon the admissibility of a petition by the rules of the House? If I am deserving censure for making this inquiry of the Speaker, your
Speaker, who made the inquiry of the House, is much more

deserving of censure. But if a majority of this House shall be found to pass censure on me, be it so; and if I have an enemy, let him know that he has triumphed; for a worse calamity could not befall me on earth.

Here I will say that I am not conscious of having given the least particle of offence to the House, nor of having done anything which I would not do over again. My conduct was dictated by a sense of duty, and in the same persuasion of what was my duty I remain still unshaken. But, sir, among other things alleged as reasons for censuring me, it has been said I have trifled with the House. I have already disclaimed, and again I not only disclaim any such intention but I deny that any man in this House has ever had cause to believe that I ever trifled with the House. I never was more serious in any moment of my life; therefore, I am unwilling that a resolution should pass containing the declaration that the House ceased all further action on the subject because I made disclaimers. I renounce all advantages on the ground of my having made a disclaimer. While I totally disclaim any intention of trifling with the House, while I totally disclaim any purpose of offending or provoking any of the members of this House, while I totally disclaim any contemptuous course or any violation of the rules and orders of the House, sir, at the same time, I disclaim not any particle of what I have done; not a single word of what I have said do I unsay; nay, I am ready to do and to say the same again to-morrow.

The question was then taken on the first resolution and decided in the negative—yeas 92, nays 105.

The question was then taken on the second resolution, and passed in the negative—yeas 21, nays 137.

Mr. Adams fulfilled his promise in overflowing measure by presenting hundreds of abolition petitions to Congress, only to see them all subjected to the formal process of tabling or reference to the oblivion of a committee room.

During the debates in the Senate on the anti-slavery petitions frequent reference was made by the Southern Senators to "incendiary" publications and pictures sent South through the mails by Northern abolitionists, which, it was claimed, were calculated to excite the slaves to revolt, and, like the insurgent negroes of San Domingo, massacre the white owners and their wives and children. Thomas H. Benton [Mo.], in a speech upon the subject, exhibited one of these pictures in the Senate chamber. As described by him it represented "a large and spreading Tree of Liberty, beneath whose ample shade a slave owner was at one time luxuriously reposing, with slaves fanning him; at another, carried forth in a palanquin, to view the half-naked laborers in the cotton field, whom drivers, with whips, were scourging to the task."

President Jackson, in his message at the beginning of the session, had already brought the subject of these publications to the attention of Congress, and suggested that the Federal legislature should enact such measures as would prevent the Postoffice Department, "which is designed to foster an amicable intercourse and correspondence between all the members of the Confederacy" from "being used as an instrument of an opposite character."

On motion of John C. Calhoun [S. C.] the Senate appointed a special committee consisting of three Southerners and two Northerners, of which he was made chairman, to report on the matter. The committee brought in a bill subjecting to penalties any postmaster who should knowingly put in the mail any publication or picture touching on the subject of slavery to go into any State or Territory where such prints were forbidden by its laws.

The bill was accompanied by a voluminous report of a *minority* of the committee, which was evidently framed by Senator Calhoun. Parts of this report occasioned much controversy, the chief issues being (1) its presentation of the "compact" theory of the United States Government, which, if accepted, would justify the South Carolina "Nullifiers" for their actions,[1] and (2) its assumption that the internal peace of the slave States was in imminent danger from the actions of the Abolitionists, and therefore that it was the right of these States to demand that the free States suppress the abolition agitation at its sources within their borders.

[1] See Volume V, chapters i and ii.

ABOLITION AND DISUNION

MINORITY REPORT OF SENATOR CALHOUN ON SUPPRESSING ANTI-SLAVERY AGITATION

He who regards slavery in those States simply under the relation of master and slave, important as that relation is, viewed merely as a question of property to the slaveholding section of the Union, has a very imperfect conception of the institution and the impossibility of abolishing it without disasters unexampled in the history of the world. To understand its nature and importance fully, it must be borne in mind that slavery, as it exists in the Southern States, involves not only the relation of master and slave but also the social and political relations of two races of nearly equal numbers, from different quarters of the globe, and the most opposite of all others in every particular that distinguishes one race of men from another. Emancipation would destroy these relations—would divest the masters of their property, and subvert the relation, social and political, that has existed between the races from almost the first settlement of the Southern States. It is not the intention of the committee to dwell on the pecuniary aspect of this vital subject, the vast amount of property involved, equal at least to $950,000,000; the ruin of families and individuals; the impoverishment and prostration of an entire section of the Union, and the fatal blow that would be given to the productions of the great agricultural staples, on which the commerce, the navigation, the manufactures, and the revenue of the country almost entirely depend. As great as these disasters would be, they are nothing compared to what must follow the subversion of the existing relation between the two races, to which the committee will confine their remarks. Under this relation the two races have long lived in peace and prosperity, and if not disturbed would long continue so to live. While the European race has rapidly increased in wealth and numbers, and at the same time has maintained an equality, at least morally and intellectually, with their brethren of the non-slaveholding States, the African race has multiplied with not less rapidity, accompanied by great improvement physically and intellectually, and the enjoyment of a degree of comfort with which the laboring class in few countries can compare, and confessedly greatly superior to what the free people of the same race possess in the non-slaveholding States. It may, indeed, be safely asserted that there is no example in history in which a savage people, such as their ancestors were when brought into the country, have ever advanced in the same period so rapidly in numbers and improvement.

To destroy the existing relations would be to destroy this prosperity and to place the two races in a state of conflict which must end in the expulsion or extirpation of one or the other. No other can be substituted, compatible with their peace or security. The difficulty is in the diversity of the races. So strongly drawn is the line between the two, in consequence of it, and so strengthened by the force of habit and education, that it is impossible for them to exist together in the same community, where their numbers are so nearly equal as in the slaveholding States, under any other relation than that which now exists. Social and political equality between them is impossible. No power on earth can overcome the difficulty. The causes resisting lie too deep in the principles of our nature to be surmounted. But, without such equality, to change the present condition of the African race, were it possible, would be but to change the form of slavery. It would make them the slaves of the community instead of the slaves of individuals, with less responsibility and interest in their welfare on the part of the community than is felt by their present masters; while it would destroy the security and independence of the European race if the African should be permitted to continue in their changed condition within the limits of those States. They would look to the other States for support and protection, and would become, virtually, their allies and dependents; and would thus place in the hands of those States the most effectual instrument to destroy the influence and control the destiny of the rest of the Union. It is against this relation between the two races that the blind and criminal zeal of the abolitionists is directed— a relation that now preserves in quiet and security more than 6,500,000 of human beings, and which cannot be destroyed without destroying the peace and prosperity of nearly half the States of the Union, and involving their entire population in a deadly conflict that must terminate either in the expulsion or extirpation of those who are the object of the misguided and false humanity of those who claim to be their friends. He must be blind indeed who does not perceive that the subversion of a relation which must be followed with such disastrous consequences can only be effected by convulsions that would devastate the country, burst asunder the bonds of Union, and ingulf in a sea of blood the institutions of the country. It is madness to suppose that the slaveholding States would quietly submit to be sacrificed. Every consideration—interest, duty, and humanity, the love of country, the sense of wrong, hatred of oppressors and treacherous and faithless confederates, and finally despair—would impel them to the most daring and desperate resistance in defence of property, family, country, liberty, and existence. But, wicked and cruel as is the end aimed at, it is fully equaled by the criminality of the means by which it is proposed to be accomplished. These, as has been stated, consist in organized societies and a powerful press, directed mainly with a view to excite the bitterest animosity and hatred of the people of the non-slaveholding States against the citizens and institutions of the slaveholding States. It is easy to see to what disastrous results such means must tend. Passing over the more obvious effects, their tendency to excite to insurrection and servile war, with all its horrors, and the necessity which such tendency must impose on the slaveholding States to resort to the most rigid discipline and severe police, to the great injury of the present condition of the slaves, there remains another, threatening incalculable mischief to the country. The inevitable tendency of the means to which the abolitionists have resorted to effect their object must, if persisted in, end in completely alienating the two great sections of the Union. The incessant action of hundreds of societies and a vast printing establishment throwing out daily thousands of artful and inflammatory publications, must make, in time, a deep impression on the section of the Union where they freely circulate, and are mainly designed to have effect. The well-informed and thoughtful may hold them in contempt, but the young, the inexperienced, the ignorant and thoughtless will receive the poison. In process of time, when the number of proselytes is sufficiently multiplied, the artful and profligate, who are ever on the watch to seize on any means, however wicked and dangerous, will unite with the fanatics and make their movements the basis of a powerful political party that will seek advancement by diffusing, as widely as possible, hatred against the slaveholding States. But, as hatred begets hatred, and animosity animosity, these feelings would become reciprocal, till every vestige of attachment would cease to exist between the two sections, when the Union and the Constitution, the offspring of mutual affection and confidence, would forever perish. Such is the danger to which the movements of the abolitionists expose the country. If the force of the obligation is in proportion to the magnitude of the danger, stronger cannot be imposed than is at present on the States within whose limits the danger originates, to arrest its further progress—a duty they owe, not only to the States whose institutions are assailed, but to the Union and Constitution, as has been shown, and, it may be added, to themselves.

John P. King of Georgia, spokesman of the majority of the committee, said that positions had been assumed and principles insisted upon by Mr. Calhoun which were not only inconsistent with the bill reported, but, he thought, inconsistent with the "existence of the Union itself, and which, if established and carried into practice, must hastily end in its dissolution."

In reply to Senator King Senator Calhoun said:

SLAVERY PARAMOUNT TO FEDERAL LAWS

SENATOR CALHOUN

The legislatures of the South, backed by the voice their constituents expressed through innumerable meetings, have called upon the non-slaveholding States to repress the movements made within the jurisdiction of those States against their peace and security. Not a step has been taken; not a law has been passed, or even proposed. Nor have we been less disappointed as to the proceedings of Congress. Believing that the general Government has no right or authority over the subject of slavery, we had just grounds to hope Congress would refuse all jurisdiction in reference to it, in whatever form it might be presented. The very opposite course has been pursued. Abolition petitions have not only been received in both Houses, but received on the most obnoxious and dangerous of all grounds—that we are bound to receive them; that is, to take jurisdiction of the question of slavery whenever the abolitionists may think proper to petition for its abolition, either here or in the States. Thus far, then, we of the slaveholding States have been grievously disappointed. One question still remains to be decided that is presented by this bill. To refuse to pass this bill would be virtually to coöperate with the abolitionists—would be to make the officers and agents of the postoffice department in effect their agents and abettors in the circulation of their incendiary publications in violation of the laws of the States. It is your unquestionable duty, as I have demonstrably proved, to abstain from their violation; and, by refusing or neglecting to discharge that duty, you would clearly enlist, in the existing controversy, on the side of the abolitionists against the Southern States. Should such be your decision, by refusing to pass this bill, I shall say to the people of the South, look to yourselves— you have nothing to hope from others. But I must tell the Senate, be your decision what it may, the South will never abandon the principles of this bill. If you refuse coöperation with our laws, and conflict should ensue between your and our law, the Southern States will never yield to the superiority of yours. We have a remedy in our hands, which, in such events, we shall not fail to apply. We have high authority for asserting that, in such cases, "State interposition is the rightful remedy"—a doctrine first announced by Jefferson— adopted by the patriotic and Republican State of Kentucky by a solemn resolution in 1798, and finally carried out into successful practice on a recent occasion, ever to be remembered, by the gallant State which I, in part, have the honor to represent. Let it be fixed, let it be riveted in every Southern mind, that the laws of the slaveholding States for the protection of their domestic institutions are paramount to the laws of the general Government in regulation of commerce and the mail, and that the latter must yield to the former in the event of conflict; and that, if the Government should refuse to yield, the States have a right to interpose, and we are safe. With these principles, nothing but concert would be wanting to bid defiance to the movements of the abolitionists, whether at home or abroad, and to place our domestic institutions, and with them, our security and peace, under our own protection, and beyond the reach of danger.

FREEDOM OF THE MAILS

SENATOR WEBSTER

SENATOR DANIEL WEBSTER opposed the bill because of its vagueness and obscurity in not sufficiently defining what were the publications the circulation of which it intended to prohibit. It is impossible to say what publications might not be prohibited from circulation. No matter what is the publication, whether for or against slavery, if it touches the subject in any shape or form, it will fall under the prohibition. Even the Constitution of the United States might be prohibited, and the person who is clothed with the power to judge in this delicate matter is one of the deputy postmasters, who, notwithstanding the difficulties with which he is encompassed in coming to a correct decision, must decide correctly, under pain of being removed from office. It would be necessary also for the deputy postmasters referred to in this bill to make themselves acquainted with all the various laws passed by the States touching the subject of slavery, and to decide on them, no matter how variant they might be with each other. The bill conflicts with that provision in the Constitution which prohibits Congress from passing any law to abridge the freedom of speech or of the press. What is the liberty of the press? It is the liberty of printing as well as the liberty of publishing, in all the ordinary modes of publication; and is not the circulation of papers through the mails an ordinary mode of publication? I am afraid that we are in some danger of taking a step in this matter that we may hereafter have cause to regret, by its being contended that whatever in this bill applies to publications touching slavery applies to other publications that the States might think proper to prohibit, and Congress might, under this example, be called upon to pass laws to suppress the circulation of political, religious, or any other description of publications which produced excitement in the States. Is this bill in accordance with the general force and temper of the Constitution and its amendments? It is not in accordance with that provision of the instrument under which the freedom of speech and of the press was secured. Whatever laws the State legislatures might pass on the subject, Congress is restrained from legislating in any manner whatever, with regard to the press. It will be admitted that, if a newspaper come directed to me, I have a property in it; and how could any man, then, take that property and burn it without due form of law? And I do not know how this newspaper could be pronounced an unlawful publication without a legal trial. The right of an individual in his papers is secured to him in every free country in the world. In England, it is expressly provided that the papers of the subject shall be free from all unreasonable searches and seizures—language to be found in our Constitution. This principle established in England, so essential to liberty, has been followed out in France, where the right of printing and publishing is secured in the fullest extent, the individual publishing being amenable to the laws for what he publishes, and every man prints and publishes what he pleases, at his peril.

The bill was finally rejected by a vote of 25 to 19, 6 votes of the majority being from slave States.

In a tie vote on one of the preliminary stages Martin Van Buren [N. Y.], Vice-President of the United States and President of the Senate, had given his casting vote in favor of the bill. In his inaugural address as President, March 4, 1837, Mr. Van Buren referred to his position on the abolition question as follows:

Perceiving, before my election, the deep interest this subject was beginning to excite, I believed it a solemn duty fully to make known my sentiments in regard to it; and now, when every motive for misrepresentation has passed away, I trust that they will be candidly weighed and understood. At least they will be my standard of conduct in the path before me. I then declared that, if the desire of those of my countrymen who were favorable to my election was gratified, "I must go into the presidential chair the inflexible and uncompromising opponent of every attempt, on the part of Congress, to abolish slavery in the District of Columbia, against the wishes of the slaveholding States; and also with a determination equally decided to resist the slightest interference with it in the States where it exists." I submitted also to my fellow-citizens, with fullness and frankness, the reasons which led me to this determination. The result authorizes me to believe that they have been approved, and are confided in, by a majority of the people of the United States, including those whom they most immediately affect. It now only remains to add that no bill conflicting with these views can ever receive my constitutional sanction.

On December 20, 1837, William Slade [Vt.] presented in the House two memorials on the abolition of slavery in the District of Columbia. He had entered into a general denunciation of slavery when Henry A. Wise [Va.] called him to order for speaking beside the question. The Speaker, John White [Ky.], asked Mr. Slade to confine his remarks to the subject. Mr. Slade continued, quoting from the Declaration of Independence.

Thereupon Hopkins Halsey [Ga.] and R. Barnwell Rhett [S. C.] called upon the delegations of their respective States to withdraw from the House to the room of the Committee on the District of Columbia.

The Southern Representatives met in the committee room and Mr. Rhett brought forward two resolutions: (1) that, the Constitution having failed to protect the South in the peaceable possession and enjoyment of

their rights and peculiar institutions, it was expedient
that the Union be dissolved, and (2) that a committee
of two members from each State be appointed to report
upon the best means of peaceably dissolving it. It was
intended to present these in Congress, where, though
certain to be tabled, they would serve to voice the protest of the South against the abolition agitation.

Mr. Rhett's propositions were negatived by the conference, and one by John M. Patton [Va.] was adopted,
to the effect that all petitions, etc., on slavery be laid
on the table without being *read* or *debated*. Upon the
next day Mr. Patton read the resolution for the information of the members and asked leave to submit
it. John Quincy Adams [Mass.] objected, whereupon
Mr. Patton moved for a suspension of the rules in order
to submit the resolution. To carry this motion a two-
thirds majority was necessary, and this was obtained
on the vote, 135 yeas to 60 nays. The resolution was
then submitted, and Mr. Patton, to shut off debate,
moved the "previous question." Mr. Adams rose to
speak when his voice was drowned by cries of "Order!"
from over the House. The question (requiring only a
majority) was carried against a minority vote of 74,
and the gag law was thereby extended to forbid petitions on slavery even to be read in the House.

CHAPTER IV

THE WILMOT PROVISO

[DEBATES ON THE PROHIBITION OF SLAVERY IN THE TERRITORIES]

David Wilmot [Pa.] Introduces in the House, as an Amendment to Bill
Appropriating Money to Buy Mexican Territory, the Proviso That Sla-
very Shall Be Excluded from the Purchase—Senator Lewis Cass [Mich.]
Advances Doctrine of "Popular Sovereignty"—Debate: in Favor, Mr.
Wilmot, Timothy Jenkins [N. Y.], Joshua R. Giddings [O.]; Opposed,
William H. Brockenbrough [Fla.]—John C. Calhoun [S. C.] In-
troduces in Senate Resolutions Denying the Right of Congress to Pro-
hibit Slavery in the Territories; His Argument on the Resolutions—
Reply by Thomas H. Benton [Mo.]—Resolutions of Daniel Webster
[Mass.] Against Prosecuting the Mexican War for Territorial Aggran-
dizement—Senator Benton's Commentary on the Calhoun Resolutions—
Cession by Mexico to United States of California and New Mexico—
Bill to Organize These Territories and Oregon, Leaving Slavery to Be
Settled by the Supreme Court—Debate in the Senate: in Favor, John
M. Clayton [Del.], John H. Clarke [R. I.], Sidney Breese [Ill.], Samuel
S. Phelps [Vt.], Joseph R. Underwood [Ky.], Andrew P. Butler [S. C.],
Henry S. Foote [Miss.], Alfred Iverson [Ga.], Reverdy Johnson [Md.];
Opposed, Jacob W. Miller [N. J.], Thomas Fitzgerald [Mich.]; Thomas
Corwin [O.], George E. Badger [N. C.], John A. Dix. [N. Y.]—Bill Is
Passed in the Senate, but Tabled in the House on Motion of Alexander
H. Stephens [Ga.]; Stephens's Argument—House Organizes Oregon Ter-
ritory Without Slavery—Free Soil Party Declares Against Slavery in All
the Territories—Debate in the Senate on the Oregon Bill: Pro-Slavery
Speakers, James M. Mason [Va.], Senator Butler, Senator Calhoun, John
Bell [Tenn.], General Samuel Houston [Tex.]; Anti-Slavery Speakers,
William L. Dayton (N. J.], Senator Webster, John M. Niles [Ct.]—
Bill Is Passed—President Polk on "Popular Sovereignty"—President
Polk Recommends a Compromise on the Question of Slavery in the Territories Acquired from Mexico—The House Adopts the Wilmot Proviso
in Organizing the Territories—California Applies for Admission to the
Union—Senator Stephen A. Douglas [Ill.] Reports Bill for Its Admission with Implicit Recognition of the Principle of "Popular Sovereignty"—Senator Robert M. T. Hunter [Va.] Presents and Supports
a Protest of the Virginia Legislature Against the Wilmot Proviso and

133

Abolition of Slavery or the Slave Trade in the District of Columbia—
Isaac P. Walker [Wis.] Moves in the Senate to Extend the Constitution
Over the Territories: Debate on the Subject Between Daniel Webster
[Mass.] and John C. Calhoun [S. C.]; Senator Walker's Motion Modi-
fied by John M. Berrien [Ga.], and Passed—Contest for Speaker of the
House of Representatives: Howell Cobb [Ga.] Elected—Threats of Dis-
union Made by Richard K. Meade [Va.], Robert Toombs [Ga.], Alexan-
der H. Stephens [Ga.], William F. Colcock [S. C.], Thomas L. Clingman
[N. C.].

O N August 8, 1846, a bill was introduced in the
House to appropriate $2,000,000 for defraying
extraordinary expenses which might be incurred
in the intercourse between the United States and foreign
nations (*i. e.*, in connection with the Mexican War) to
be applied by the President. To this David Wilmot,
a Democrat from Pennsylvania, offered as an amendment a proviso which had been drafted by Judge H. R.
Brinckerhoff [O.] : that, if any part of the appropriation were to be used to purchase Mexican territory,
"neither slavery nor involuntary servitude shall ever exist in any part of said territory except for crime, whereof
the party shall first be duly convicted." The amendment was adopted by a vote of 83 to 64, and the bill as
amended was passed by a vote of 85 to 79. The bill,
with, of course, the proviso, failed to come to a vote in
the Senate owing to the closing of the session.

During the recess of Congress the legislatures of
every Northern State from New Hampshire to Ohio
inclusive, and also Delaware, approved the proviso, both
parties voting in its favor. It was expected that at
the next session it would pass both Houses.

Early in this session (December 24, 1847), therefore,
Senator Lewis Cass [Mich.], in order to defeat the
proviso, enunciated a new doctrine in a letter to Alfred
O. P. Nicholson, a Representative from Tennessee, saying that the principle of the Wilmot Proviso "should be
kept out of the national legislature, and left to the people
of the Confederacy in their respective local governments." This became known as the doctrine of "popular sovereignty." It was eagerly accepted by the
Southern Democrats and pro-slavery Democrats in the

North, such as Stephen A. Douglas [Ill.], and they read anti-slavery Democrats, such as Wilmot, out of the party.

A bill appropriating $3,000,000 with the proviso was introduced in both Houses. It passed in the House on February 15 (115 yeas to 106 nays) with the proviso, but the proviso was stricken out in the Senate on March 1, and in this form the bill was accepted by the House on March 3, 115 yeas to 81 nays.

In the debates in the House leading speakers in behalf of the proviso were Wilmot, Timothy Jenkins [N. Y.], and Joshua R. Giddings [O.]. William H. Brockenbrough [Fla.] was the principal speaker in opposition.

THE WILMOT PROVISO

HOUSE OF REPRESENTATIVES, FEBRUARY 8-MARCH 3, 1847

MR. WILMOT.—Sir, it will be recollected by all present that, at the last session of this Congress, an amendment was moved to a bill of a similar character by me, in the form of a proviso, by which slavery should be forever excluded from any territory that might be subsequently acquired by the United States from the Republic of Mexico.

Sir, permit me to say that upon that occasion that proviso was sustained by a very decided majority of this House. Nay, sir, more; it was sustained, if I mistake not, by a majority of the Republican party on this floor. And I am prepared to show, I think, that the entire South were then willing to acquiesce in what appeared to be, and, so far as the action of this House is concerned, in what was, the legislation, will, and declaration of this Union on the subject. It passed in this House. Sir, there were no threats of disunion sounded in our ears. It passed here, and it went to the Senate, and it was the judgment of the public, and of many men well informed, that, had it not been defeated there for the want of time, it would have passed that body and become the established law of the land.

Sir, the friends of this Administration, of whom I am one, did not then charge upon me, did not throw the whole burden upon me, nor upon those who acted with me, of having, by the introduction and support of that proviso at an untimely period of the question, defeated a measure especially necessary for the establishment of peace between this country and Mexico.

Yes! no anathemas were fulminated against me then. I was not then denounced as an abolitionist. And there was then no cry that the Union was to be severed in consequence of the proviso. But I fear that the hesitation and the warning of Northern men on this question have induced the South to assume a bolder attitude. Why, sir, in God's name, should the Union be dissolved for this? What do we ask in this matter? We ask but sheer justice and right. Sir, we ask the neutrality of this Government on this question of slavery. I have stood up at home and fought, time and again, against the abolitionists of the North. I stand by every compromise of the Constitution. I adhere to its letter and its spirit. And I would never invade one single right of the South. So far from it am I that I stand ready, at all times and upon all occasions, as do nearly the entire North, to sustain the institutions of the South as they exist, with our money and with our blood, when that day comes, as many—many Southern men—fear it may come. When that day comes, sir, the North stands with them. We go for every compromise of the Constitution.

But, sir, this is another question—entirely another question. We ask that this Government preserve the integrity of free territory against the aggressions of slavery—against its wrongful usurpations. Sir, I was in favor of the annexation of Texas. I supported it with the whole influence which I possessed, and I was willing to take Texas in as she was. I sought not to change the character of her institutions. Texas was a slave country, and, although it was held out to us, that two slave and two free States might be made out of it, yet the whole of Texas was given up to slavery, every inch. We voted for the annexation of Texas. The Democracy of the North was for it, to a man. We are for it now—firmly for it. Sir, we are fighting this war for Texas, and for the South. But, we are told, California is ours. And all we ask in the North is that the character of its territory be preserved. It is free, and it is part of the established law of nations, and all public law, that, when it shall come into this Union, all laws there existing, not inconsistent with its new allegiance, will remain in force. This fundamental law, which prohibits slavery in California, will be in force; this fundamental law, which prohibits slavery in New Mexico, will be in force. Shall the South invade it? Shall the South make this Government an instrument for the violation of its neutrality, and for the establishment of slavery in these territories, in defiance of law? That is the question. There is no question of abolition here, sir. It is a question whether the South shall be permitted, by aggression, by invasion of right, by subduing free territory and planting slavery upon it, to wrest this territory to the accomplishment of its own sectional purposes and schemes? That is the question. And shall we of the North submit to it? Must me yield this? It is not, sir, in the spirit of the compact; it is not, sir, in the Constitution.

MR. JENKINS denounced the war as a presidential war, and a war of conquest, and would vote for the "Wilmot Proviso" as the most effectual means, if carried, of bringing it to a speedy termination. The object of the Administration was to acquire new territory to make it slave territory, and if this prohibition of slavery were imposed by Congress, their warlike spirit would quickly subside.

MR. BROCKENBROUGH said, upon the subject of the "Wilmot Proviso," unlike many gentlemen from the South, he had no fears for the institution of slavery, or for the dissolution of the Union; not from any wilful blindness, but because, after calm reflection, it appeared to him that whenever the governments of this country, either State or Federal, had undertaken to legislate in advance of public opinion, and prescribe rules for public opinion, their enactments were but a dead letter on the statute book. Any legislation at this time, declaring that lands which may hereafter be acquired by the United States shall be occupied by one portion of the country to the exclusion of the other, would be perfectly futile and ineffectual. From the beginning of the Government down to the present day, the North and the South had been advancing with giant and equal stride toward the West, and no arbitrary line could restrain the advances of the institutions of either. The Missouri compromise line had only been acquiesced in by the South because north of that line slavery could not go, from the nature of the case, so as to be for the interest of the people.

But granting that the principles of the amendment could be enforced (in case it were adopted), Mr. B. presented a picture of the blighting influences it would entail upon the South, resulting finally in the extermination of the entire white race in that section; a consequence disastrous in the extreme to the North and all sections of our country.

On the other hand, if this institution were allowed to take its natural course, and to spread southward and westward, by diffusion it would lose its strength, and in the course of a century, he prophesied, its very existence itself. It was already beginning to ebb in the Southern States, he asserted, and white labor and industry were coming in to take the place of those of the slave.

MR. GIDDINGS said that the country was at a crisis. Congress was to decide whether or not the blood and treasure poured out on American soil were for the purpose of establishing slavery upon territory hitherto consecrated to freedom. Gentlemen from the South solemnly warn us that, if we persist in our determination to exclude slavery from the acquired territory, the Union will be dissolved. For his part he preferred to see it rent into a thousand fragments rather than have his country disgraced and its moral purity sacrificed by the prosecution of a war for the extension of human bondage.

He welcomed the issue. It had to be met; there would be no compromise between slavery and freedom, any more than between crime and virtue.

He referred at length to the united opposition of Northern men of all parties against prosecuting the war to extend slavery, and predicted that the Administration which was responsible for this policy would be repudiated at the next election.

When we next assemble here the Whigs will probably constitute a majority of this body. Will they, by their votes, increase our national debt, by continuing our conquests in Mexico? Will they send more of our fellow-citizens there to be sacrificed to this Moloch of slavery? If so, they, too, will suffer the penalty due to such crimes, and in turn will be driven from power.[1]

After an extended reply to the argument that there could rightly be any property in man, Mr. Giddings concluded his speech as follows:

Our political horizon is overcast; "clouds and darkness are round about us"; impenetrable darkness shuts the future from our view. Foreign war and internal strife, animosities and heart-burnings, indicate that this nation is doomed to suffer the just penalty incurred by the oppression, outrage, and crime which we have perpetrated upon our fellow men. If God deals out to offending nations retributive justice, we cannot escape His displeasure. Yet, when the just penalty of our transgressions shall have been visited upon us; when thousands more of our brethren shall have fallen victims to this unholy war,

---

[1] The Democrats were defeated the following year. The Whigs took up the war, and carried it on, and were again driven from power, precisely according to this prophecy.

and tens of thousands more, widows and orphans, shall weep and mourn under bereavement; when the immorality brought upon our nation, by this war, shall have tortured the hearts of hundreds of thousands of mothers and wives and daughters, and the righteous punishment for our transgressions shall have been meted out to us; our rulers, our legislators, will acknowledge that *"righteousness alone exalteth a nation,"* while *"sin is a reproach to any people."*

On February 19, 1847, John C. Calhoun [S. C.] introduced in the Senate resolutions on the subject of slavery in the Territories. In the way of introduction he gave statistics showing that the balance of power was shifting in favor of the free States, and that, unless *all* the territory about to be acquired from Mexico, including that above the line of the Missouri compromise, were to be left free to introduce slavery, "the Government would be overwhelmingly in the hands of the non-slaveholding States." Thomas H. Benton [Mo.] and Daniel Webster [Mass.] opposed the resolutions.

"Let Us Be Done with Compromises!"

Senator Calhoun

Sir, if this state of things is to go on; if this determination, so solemnly made, is to be persisted in—where shall we stand, as far as this Federal Government of ours is concerned? We shall be at the entire mercy of the non-slaveholding States. Can we look to their justice and regard for our interests? Now, I ask, can we rely on that? Ought we to trust our safety and prosperity to their mercy and sense of justice? These are the solemn questions which I put to this and the other side of the chamber.

Sir, what is the entire amount of this policy that there shall be no further addition to the slaveholding States? I will not say that it is designed. I will not say from what cause it originated. I will not say whether blind fanaticism on one side, whether a hostile feeling to slavery entertained by many not fanatical on the other, has produced it; or whether it has been the work of men who, looking to political power, have considered the agitation of this question as the most effectual mode of obtaining the spoils of this Government. I look to the fact itself. It is a policy now openly avowed as one to be persisted in. It is a scheme, Mr. President, which aims to monopolize the powers of this Government, and to obtain sole possession of its territories.

Now, I ask, is there any remedy? Does the Constitution afford any remedy? And, if not, is there any hope? These, Mr. President, are solemn questions—not only to us, but, let me say to gentlemen from the non-slaveholding States, to them. Sir, the day that the balance between the two sections of the country—the slaveholding States and the non-slaveholding States—is destroyed, is a day that will not be far removed from political revolution, anarchy, civil war, and widespread disaster. The balance of this system is in the slaveholding States. They are the conservative portion—always have been the conservative portion—always will be the conservative portion, and with a due balance on their part may, for generations to come, uphold this glorious Union of ours. But if this scheme should be carried out—if we are to be reduced to a handful—if we are to become a mere ball to play the presidential game with—to count something in the Baltimore caucus—if this is to be the result—woe, woe, I say, to this Union!

How, then, do we stand in reference to this territorial question—this public domain of ours? Why, sir, what is it? It is the common property of the States of this Union. They are called "the Territories of the United States." And what are the "United States" but the States united? Sir, these Territories are the property of the States united; held jointly for their common use. And is it consistent with justice, is it consistent with equality, that any portion of the partners, outnumbering another portion, shall oust them of this common property of theirs—shall pass any law which shall proscribe the citizens of other portions of the Union from emigrating with their property to the Territories of the United States? Would that be consistent, can it be consistent with the idea of a common property, held jointly for the common benefit of all? Would it be so considered in private life? Would it not be considered the most flagrant outrage in the world, one which any court of equity would restrain by injunction—which any court of law in the world would overrule?

Mr. President, not only is that proposition grossly inconsistent with the Constitution, but the other, which undertakes to say that no State shall be admitted into this Union which shall not prohibit by its constitution the existence of slaves, is equally a great outrage against the Constitution of the United States. Sir, I hold it to be a fundamental principle of our political system that the people have a right to establish what government they may think proper for themselves; that every State about to become a member of this Union has a right to form its own government as it pleases; and that, in order to be admitted, there is but one qualification, and that is that the government shall be republican. Now, sir, it is proposed, from a vague, indefinite, erroneous, and most dangerous conception of private individual liberty, to overrule this great common liberty which the people have of framing their own constitution! Sir, the right of self-government on the part of individuals is not near so easily to be established by any course of reasoning as the right of a community or State to self-government. And yet, sir, there are men of such delicate feeling on the subject of liberty—men who cannot possibly bear what they call slavery in one section of the country—(although it was not so much slavery as an institution indispensable for the good of both races)—men so squeamish on this point that they are ready to strike down the higher right of a community to govern themselves in order to maintain the absolute right of individuals in every possible condition to govern themselves!

Mr. President, the resolutions that I intend to offer present, in general terms, these great truths. It is due to the States which we represent that there should be a fair expression of what is the sense of this body. Upon that expression much depends. It is the only stand which we can make under the Constitution. It is the only position we can take that will uphold us with anything like independence—which will give us any chance at all to maintain an equality in this Union, on those great principles to which I have referred. Overrule these principles, and we are nothing! Preserve them, and we will ever be a respectable portion of the Union.

Sir, here let me say a word as to the compromise line. I have always considered it as a great error—highly injurious to the South, because it surrendered, for mere temporary purposes, those high principles of the Constitution upon which I think we ought to stand. I am against any compromise line.

I see my way in the Constitution. I cannot in a compromise. A compromise is but an act of Congress. It may be overruled at any time. It gives us no security. But the Constitution is stable. It is a rock. On it we can stand. It is a firm and stable ground, on which we can better stand in opposition to fanaticism than on the shifting sands of compromise.

Let us be done with compromises. Let us go back and stand upon the Constitution!

Well, sir, what if the decision of this body shall deny to us this high constitutional right, not the less clear because deduced from the whole body of the instrument and the nature of the subject to which it relates? What, then, is the question? I will not undertake to decide. It is a question for our constituents—the slaveholding States. A solemn and a great question. If the decision should be adverse, I trust and do believe that they will take under solemn consideration what they ought to do. I give no advice. It would be hazardous and dangerous for me to do so. But I may speak as an individual member of that section of the Union. There I drew my first breath. There are all my hopes. There are my family and connections. I am a planter—a cotton planter. I am a Southern man and a slaveholder; a kind and a merciful one, I trust—and none the worse for being a slaveholder. I say, for one, I would rather meet any extremity upon earth than give up one inch of our equality—one inch of what belongs to us as members of this great republic. What! acknowledge inferiority! The surrender of life is nothing to sinking down into acknowledgment of inferiority.

I have examined this subject largely—widely. I think I see the future if we do not stand up as we ought. In my humble opinion, in that case, the condition of Ireland is prosperous and happy—the condition of Hindustan is prosperous and happy—the condition of Jamaica is prosperous and happy, to what the Southern States will be if they should not now stand up manfully in defence of their rights.

Mr. President, I desire that the resolutions which I now send to the table be read.

The resolutions were read as follows:

Resolved, That the Territories of the United States belong to the several States composing this Union, and are held by them as their joint and common property.

Resolved, That Congress, as the joint agent and representative of the States of this Union, has no right to make any law, or do any act whatsoever, that shall directly, or by its effects, make any discrimination between the States of this Union, by which any of them shall be deprived of its full and equal right in any Territory of the United States, acquired or to be acquired.

Resolved, That the enactment of any law which should directly, or by its effects, deprive the citizens of any of the States of this Union from emigrating, with their property, into any of the Territories of the United States, will make such discrimination, and would, therefore, be a violation of the Constitution, and the rights of the States from which such citizens emigrated, and in derogation of that perfect equality which belongs to them as members of this Union, and would tend directly to subvert the Union itself.

Resolved, That it is a fundamental principle in our political creed that a people, in forming a constitution, have the unconditional right to form and adopt the government which they may think best calculated to secure their liberty, prosperity, and happiness; and that, in conformity thereto, no other condition is imposed by the Federal Constitution on a State, in order to be admitted into this Union, except that its constitution shall be republican; and that the imposition of any other by Congress would not only be in violation of the Constitution, but in direct conflict with the principle on which our political system rests.

SENATOR BENTON.—Mr. President, there is something yet to be done to give effect to the ten regiment bill, and other important measures require our attention. Now, if anybody thinks that I am going to lay aside the necessary business of the session to vote on such a string of abstractions, he is greatly mistaken.

SENATOR CALHOUN.—The Senator says he cannot take up abstractions. The Constitution is an abstraction. Propriety is an abstraction. All the great rules of life are abstractions. The Declaration of Independence was made on an abstraction; and when I hear a man declare that he is against abstract truth in a case of this kind I am prepared to know what his course will be! I certainly supposed that the Senator from Missouri, the representative of a slaveholding State, would have supported these resolutions. I moved them in good faith, under a solemn conviction of what was due to those whom I represent, and due the whole South and the whole Union. I have as little desire as any Senator to obstruct public business. All I want is a decision, and a decision before the three million bill is decided.

SENATOR BENTON.—The Senator from South Carolina says he calculated on my support. He is mistaken. He knows very well from my whole course in public life that I never would leave public business to take up firebrands to set the world on fire.

SENATOR CALHOUN.—The Senator does not at all comprehend me. I expressed a hope that he would be found ready to support the principles presented in my resolutions.

SENATOR BENTON.—I shall be found in the right place. I am on the side of my country and the Union.

SENATOR WEBSTER observed that, should the resolutions of the Senator from South Carolina be taken up, he (Mr. Webster) should follow the example thus set him, and call up his own as follows:

Resolved, That the war now existing with Mexico ought not to be prosecuted for the acquisition of territory to form new States to be adopted into the Union.

Resolved, That it ought to be signified to the Government of Mexico, that the Government of the United States does not desire to dismember the Republic of Mexico, and is ready to treat with the Government of that republic for peace, for a liberal adjustment of boundaries, and for just indemnities due by either Government to the citizens of the other.

Mr. Calhoun never called for the consideration of his resolutions, consequently Mr. Webster never called up his, nor was any further notice of either taken in the Senate.

In his "Thirty Years' View" (1856) Senator Benton thus comments on Calhoun's resolutions:

THE FIREBRAND RESOLUTIONS OF SENATOR CALHOUN

SENATOR BENTON

The resolutions were sent out to all the slave States, and adopted by some of them; and there commenced the great slavery agitation, founded upon the dogma of *"no power in Congress to legislate upon slavery in the territories,"* which has led to the abrogation of the Missouri compromise line—which has filled the Union with distraction—and which is threatening to bring all Federal legislation, and all Federal elections, to a mere sectional struggle, in which one-half of the States is to be arrayed against the other. The resolves were evidently introduced for the mere purpose of carrying a question to the slave States on which they could be formed into a unit against the free States; and they answered that purpose as well on rejection by the Senate as with it; and were accordingly used in conformity to their design without any such rejection, which —it cannot be repeated too often—could in no way have decided the constitutional question which they presented.

These were new resolutions—the first of their kind in the (almost) sixty years' existence of the Federal Government— contrary to its practice during that time—contrary to Mr. Calhoun's slavery resolutions of 1838—contrary to his early and long support of the Missouri compromise—and contrary to the reënactment of that line by the authors of the Texas annexation law. That reënactment had taken place only two years before, and was in the very words of the anti-slavery ordinance of '87, and of the Missouri compromise prohibition of 1820, and was voted for by the whole body of the annexationists, and was not only conceived and supported by Mr. Calhoun, then Secretary of State, but carried into effect by him in the dispatch of that messenger to Texas in the expiring moments of his power.

The words of the reënactment were: *"And in such State or States as shall be formed out of said territory north of the said Missouri compromise line, slavery or involuntary servitude (except for crime) shall be prohibited."* This clause reëstablished that compromise line in all that long extent of it which was ceded to Spain by the treaty of 1819, which became Texan by her separation from Mexico, and which became slave soil under her laws and constitution. So that, up to the third day of March, in the year 1845—not quite two years before the date of these resolutions—Mr. Calhoun, by authentic acts, and the two Houses of Congress, by recorded votes, and President Tyler, by his approving signature, acknowledged the power of Congress to prohibit slavery in a territory! and not only acknowledged the power, but exerted it! and actually prohibited slavery in a long slip of country, enough to make a "State or States," where it then legally existed.

These resolutions of 1847, called firebrand at the time, were further characterized as nullification a few days afterwards, when Mr. Benton said of them, that, *"as Sylla saw in the young Cæsar many Mariuses, so did he see in them many nullifications."*

On July 13, 1848, after the treaty of peace with Mexico the Senate elected a committee to frame a bill for the territorial governments of Oregon, California, and New Mexico. John M. Clayton [Del.] was chairman of the committee.

On July 18 this committee reported its bill—the provisions of which will transpire in the course of the debate which thereupon ensued.

The chief speakers in favor of the bill were Clayton, John H. Clarke [R. I.], Sydney Breese [Ill.], Samuel S. Phelps [Vt.], Edward A. Hannegan [Ind.], Andrew P. Butler [S. C.], Henry S. Foote [Miss.], Alfred Iverson [Ga.], and Reverdy Johnson [Md.]; and the chief speakers who opposed it were Jacob W. Miller [N. J.], Thomas Fitzgerald [Mich.], Thomas Corwin [O.], Joseph R. Underwood [Ky.], George E. Badger [N. C.], and John A. Dix [N. Y.].

IV—10

TERRITORIAL ORGANIZATION OF OREGON, CALIFORNIA AND NEW MEXICO

SENATE, JULY 18, 1848

SENATOR CLAYTON said that he felt it due, in justice to each and every one of his colleagues, to say that, amid all their long conferences and laborious discussions on the various topics necessarily considered by them, the most conciliatory spirit had been evinced by them, each endeavoring to maintain the honor and interest, not merely of his own section of country, but that of the whole nation, and each endeavoring to yield so much as he felt could be properly and honorably conceded, without the sacrifice of what was essentially due to his own constituents, and the people of all the States. After a full interchange of views, a vote was taken on a proposition moved by the Senator from Missouri [David R. Atchison], "that the spirit of the Missouri compromise be adopted to govern the settlement of all the Territories of the United States." On this question the committee divided, five for and three against the motion. As the condition of the territory was now said to be different from that to which that compromise applied in 1820, a motion was made by the Senator from Kentucky [Mr. Underwood] to amend that proposition, by providing that "all the territory in New Mexico and California, south of the parallel of 36° 30', shall be placed on the same footing in all respects as to slavery that existed in Louisiana while it was a Territory." On this question the committee divided, four for the motion and four against it.

At this stage of the proceedings all compromise appeared to be impossible. But the committee proceeded afterwards to consider a proposition to endeavor to adjust the great question, at least so far as to enable Congress to extend the laws over and provide for the administration of justice in the territories, leaving for the present the settlement of it to the laws of population, or the adaptation of soil, climate, and all circumstances to the various kinds of labor. While it was admitted on all sides that by far the greatest portion of the Territories was properly adapted to free labor, and would necessarily be free soil forever, yet it was also with equal unanimity conceded that there was a portion of it where free labor never could be introduced, owing to the climate and the peculiar productions of that portion. It was thought that if Oregon, which no one imagines can ever be slaveholding, could be

organized as the people of that Territory desired, by the temporary adoption of their present laws interdicting or prohibiting slavery till the territorial legislature proposed to be
organized, by a popular vote, under the bill referred to us,
could enact some law on the subject, most of the objections
would be obviated, without any sacrifice of principle by those
who urged them, and that, after thus disposing of the question,
so far as relates to Oregon, the Territories of California and
New Mexico could be organized in the same bill by the appointment of a governor, secretary, and judges, to compose, according to the old precedents, a temporary legislature for each of
these Territories, but without the power to legislate on the subject of slavery, thus placing that question beyond the power
of the territorial legislature, and resting the right to introduce or prohibit slavery in these two Territories on the Constitution, as the same should be expounded by the judges, with a
right of appeal to the Supreme Court of the United States.
It was thought that by this means Congress would avoid the
decision of this distracting question, leaving it to be settled by
the silent operation of the Constitution itself; and that, in case
Congress should refuse to touch the subject, the country would
be slaveholding only where, by the laws of nature, slave labor
was effective and free labor could not maintain itself. On the
other hand, in case Congress should hereafter choose to adopt
the compromise line of 36° 30′ (north of which, I suppose, it is
not expected that slave labor can be introduced), or any other
rule of settlement, it will be free to act as to its wisdom and
patriotism shall seem fit.

After many conflicts of opinion these views thus generally
expressed were substantially agreed upon with great unanimity.

Senator Clayton continued:

I do not expect, sir, that this or any other proposition which
the wit of man can possibly suggest will prevent agitation on
this subject, which is now daily spreading through the country,
and, I fear, dividing it into geographical parties. If the Missouri compromise of 36° 30′ should be adopted, the agitators
would immediately raise the standard of repeal and agitate as
fiercely as ever. They will agitate after the passage of any bill.
But this bill resolves the whole question between the North and
South into a constitutional and a judicial question. It asks
of men of all sections only to stand by the Constitution, and
suffer that to settle the difference by its own tranquil operation.
If the Constitution settles the question either way, let those who
rail at the decision vent their indignation against their ancestors

who adopted it. We offer no bill to introduce slavery by congressional enactment into any free territory. If, as the South contends, the Constitution gives the right to carry their slaves there, they will maintain that right. If, as the North contends, the Constitution confers no such right, they will vindicate their claim. It is the honest opinion of a large majority of the committee that by the passage of this bill the safety of the Union will be placed beyond the reach of agitation, and that the question, and the only question, which now threatens to endanger it may be, not immediately, but ultimately, put at rest forever.

SENATOR CLARKE stated that the bill now reported received the sanction of six out of the eight members of the committee, two of the members (of whom he was one) objecting to it. His views and the views of his State (Rhode Island) were decidedly against the introduction of slavery into a free State, and against the extension of slavery to any territory which we may have acquired by conquest. He intended to move again in the Senate the amendment which he had unsuccessfully proposed in committee. As far as he understood the opinion of the committee, it was that the Territory of Oregon was in every sense a free Territory. On looking over the bill, he found that this principle did not seem to be sufficiently carried out in the construction of the bill. He stated that it was his intention to move an amendment to the sixth section of the bill; the closing paragraph is: "All the laws passed by the legislative assembly shall be submitted to the Congress of the United States, and, if disapproved, shall be null and of no effect." To this he moved to add a proviso, that no law on the subject of slavery shall be in force until it shall have received the approval of Congress.

It was urged in committee that, on the Territories of California and New Mexico coming into the possession of the United States, every owner of a slave would have a right to bring his property into the Territories. To this it was objected that, this being a constitutional question, it should be referred to the supreme court of the Territory, with an appeal to the Supreme Court of the United States. To this effect he also proposed to submit an amendment.

SENATOR MILLER referred to the debate which had already taken place, on the power of Congress to abolish slavery, in which it was strenuously denied by the Senators from the Southern States; yet, in this bill there was an assumption of the power, in the clause prohibiting the passage of any law which abolishes slavery. Believing in this power, he was not opposed to its exercise, but he was opposed to its admission for the benefit of one part of the Union, and not of the other. He had prepared an amendment providing that the laws now in existence in the Territories shall continue in force. As to the inhibition of the territorial legislatures in Mexico to pass any laws respecting slavery, what did it mean but a prohibition of the passing of any laws abolishing slavery? Slavery would then, of course, go to California and New Mexico, as there is no law there to prevent it. If a person takes his slave there, and his property is taken, and he appeals to the Supreme Court, the court will probably decide that, as Congress has passed no law prohibiting slavery there, slavery may exist there. And while the question remains undecided, the slave will stand on the same footing with his master—under the protection of the Constitution—and strife and bloodshed may ensue. He alluded to the difficulty which would stand in the way of any slave who desired to bring his case, by a writ of habeas corpus, before a judicial tribunal for decision; he illustrated this by the case of the agent of the State of Massachusetts, Mr. Samuel Hoar, who was sent to Charleston, South Carolina, for the purpose of testing the constitutionality of the law where he could have no lawyer to aid him, and was himself imprisoned, and then compelled to leave the State.

SENATOR BREESE.—If the Senator from New Jersey will allow me, I will ask him if the question of servitude could not be brought before the Supreme Court of the United States, very readily, by an action, by the slave, of assault and battery and false imprisonment? Such a suit would bring up the question fairly, and without the intervention of a jury. The person claimed as a slave brings his action, and there never has been found any difficulty in obtaining the aid of counsel, even in slave States, for such purpose. The master pleads to the action that true it is he holds the plaintiff in his custody, as he has a right to do, for he is his slave. The slave replies, setting forth the fact that California, on its cession to the United States, was free; that slavery did not exist there, and that it is not recognized by the Constitution of the United States or any act of Congress; and that by virtue of that Constitution he is free. The defendant demurs, and the question of law arising thereon is decided by the court, and, if the decision be *against* the slave, the Supreme Court of the United States have jurisdiction under the 25th section of the Judiciary Act of 1789, because a decision has been pronounced against a right claimed under the Constitution. [Menard *vs.* Aspasia, in 5th Peters' Rep.]

SENATOR MILLER resumed. He was willing to vote for a bill which prohibited slavery in any Territory which was free at the time of the passage of the bill. If slavery existed in a Territory at the time of its acquisition by the United States, he would leave it to the people to determine whether it should continue. He would not vote for its abolition there. He had not voted against the continuance of slavery when Texas was admitted into the Union, because it had previously been in existence there. For whose benefit should we now extend slavery in California and New Mexico, where it has already been abolished? Great Britain had introduced slavery in this country, and what was the general tone of public opinion on this subject? Was it not termed a curse which had been entailed on us by Great Britain? And shall we extend this curse to the Territories over which we extend our protection?

The South asserted that it had a greater interest in the question than the North. This he denied. He denied that the South had any exclusive privilege to carry her slaves to the Territories for sale. The North had an equal right to enjoy the profit of such a traffic, and had therefore as great an interest in the question as the South. Slavery does not exist now on the Pacific, and by his vote it should never be permitted there.

The proper way to settle the question was by the legislative authority. The people would not rebel against the law, and he was not disposed to surrender the power of Congress over the subject.

SENATOR PHELPS.—What was the condition in which California and New Mexico have come under our care? Slavery has been abolished there. Such is the state in which we receive them. By the laws of nations, the laws of all conquered countries remain until changed by the conqueror. If these laws are to be retained, there is an express law containing a prohibition of slavery, and this will continue until we shall change it. He insisted that there was nothing in the bill to warrant the belief that it could ever carry slavery into these territories. If there was cowardice in the bill, he had no fear on the subject. He would rather attach the term to the weathercock of popular impulse, to him who fears to do a wise act, lest he should offend some transient caprice. If there were any to whom responsibility should attach, it was to those who voted for the annexation of Texas, out of which grew the Mexican war. The Senator from Connecticut [Mr. Niles] had given the casting vote on the question of the annexation of Texas, and he was responsible for all the difficulties which had grown out of it. That Senator had thrown the most offensive epithets on this bill and its originators, and he was bound to come forward and aid in a compromise. If the old coat and jacket of anyone are to be stuffed with straw and burnt in effigy, they should be those of the Senator from Connecticut rather than mine.

SENATOR FITZGERALD had strong objections to parts of the bill, yet if he thought it would produce harmony and peace he would vote for it, although it would be his last act, and he should thereafter be plunged in disgrace. But he feared, from what he had heard, that its friends were doomed to disappointment. There was a political storm raging in the North, the effects of which no one could foresee. It threatened to come upon us like a whirlwind, and who can tell where it may be stayed? He alone was responsible for his own acts. He would give another reason why he voted against the raising of the committee. He was not in very good humor at that time, because he had heard imputations thrown on Northern States, and, among others, upon the State represented by him, on the subject of fugitive slaves.

Senator Corwin said that it was fitting that slavery should follow conquest—the law in both cases is simply the law of force. Slavery had its origin in capture.

As in the case of *lands* acquired by conquest, long possession and continued acquiescence (in the judgments of men) ripen the claim into legal right, so, in the case of legal slavery, the *captive*, originally held only by force, in time, by the law of men, and by the judgment of men, becomes *property!!* And we are told by the Senator from Virginia [Mr. Mason] that the posterity of such become property only through the magical influence of these words, Roman words: *"Partus sequitur ventrem"*—"The child follows the condition of its mother." Admirable—philosophical—rational—Christian maxim!!! If the mother be captured in war, it seems then the will of a just God, "whose tender mercies are over all his works," that her offspring to the remotest time shall be doomed to slavery. What sublime morality, what lovely justice combine to sanctify this article in that new decalogue of freedom which we say it is our destiny to give to the world! All over the world the air is vocal with the shouts of men made free. Every gale that floats across the Atlantic comes freighted with the death-groans of a king; every vessel that touches your shores bears with her tidings that the captives of the Old World are at last becoming free—that they are seeking, through blood and slaughter —blindly and madly, it may be—but nevertheless resolutely— deliverance from the fetters that have held them in bondage. What does it all mean? It means that they have been redeemed from *political* servitude; and in God's name I ask, if it be a boon to mankind to be free from political servitude, must it not be accepted as a matter of some gratulation that they have been relieved from personal servitude—absolute subjection to the arbitrary power of others?

According to the doctrine preached in these halls—in free America—instead of sending shouts of gratulation across the water to these people, we should send to them groans and commiseration for their folly, calling on them to beware how they take this business into their own hands—informing them that universal liberty is a curse; that, as one man is born with a right to govern an empire, he and his posterity must continue to exercise that power, because in this case it is not exactly *partus sequitur ventrem,* but *partus sequitur patrem*—that is all the difference. The crown follows the father! Under your law the chain follows the mother!

Senator Corwin then reverted to the American Revolution.

The men of 1776 did not believe that one man was born "booted and spurred" to ride another. And, if, as they said, no man was born to *rule* another, did it not follow that no man could rightfully be born to *serve* another? Sir, in those days, Virginia and Virginia's sons, Washington and Jefferson, had as little respect for that maxim, *partus sequitur ventrem,* as for that other cognate dogma, "Kings are born to rule."

Mr. President, these men, when they spoke of slavery and its extension, did not get up some hybrid sort of "compromise" and consult some supreme court. They declared slavery an evil, a wrong, a prejudice to free colonies, a social mischief, and a political evil; and, if these were denied, they replied, "These truths are self-evident." And from the judgments of men they appealed to no earthly court; they took an appeal "to the Supreme Judge of the World." When I am asked to extend to this new empire of ours, now in its infancy, an institution which they pronounced an evil to all communities; when I refuse to agree with some here whose judgments I revere, and whose motives I know to be pure, I can only say I stand where our fathers stood of old, I am sustained in my position by the

men who founded the first system of rational liberty on earth.
I ask any Southern man, if there were not a slave on this continent, would you send your ships to Africa and bring them
here? If you would not bring them from the shores of Africa
—buying them with some imagined *"partus sequitur ventrem"*
branded on them somewhere—how can you prove to me that it
would be right to transfer them from Maryland or Virginia,
three thousand miles, to the shores of the Pacific? If slavery
were a curse to you in the beginning, but struck its roots so
deep into your social and municipal system, as was then said,
that it could not be eradicated entirely, how is it that you
call upon me, as a matter of conscience and duty, to transfer
this curse to an area of square miles greatly exceeding that
of the thirteen States when the Confederation was formed?
Is it true that I am obliged to receive into my family a man
with the smallpox or the leprosy, that they may be infected?
But the gentleman from Virginia has said that it must be done.
Why? Because it is compassion to the slave. He can not be
nurtured in Virginia; your lands are worn out. Sir, that statement sounded ominous in my ears. It gave rise to some reflection. Why are your lands worn out? Are the lands of Pennsylvania worn out? Are those of Connecticut worn out? Is
not Massachusetts more productive to-day than when the foot
of the white man was first impressed upon her soil? Your lands
are worn out, because the slave has turned pale the land
wherever he has set down his black foot! It is slave labor that
has done all this. And must we then extend to these Territories
that which produces sterility wherever it is found, till barren
desolation shall cover the whole land? If you can call upon me,
as a matter of compassion, to send the slave to California or
Oregon, you can call upon me by the same sacred obligation
to receive him into Ohio as a slave, and I would be just as
much bound, as a citizen of Ohio, to say that the Constitution
should be so construed as to admit slaves there, because they
have made the land in Virginia barren, and they and their
masters were perishing, till Ohio had also become a wilderness.

It is a sad commentary upon the perfection of human
reason that, with but a very few exceptions, all eminent lawyers
on this floor from the South have argued that you have no right
to prohibit the introduction of slavery into Oregon, California,
and New Mexico; while, on the other hand, there is not a man
in the free States, learned or unlearned, clerical or lay, who
has any pretensions to legal knowledge, but believes in his
conscience that you have a right to prohibit slavery. Is not

that a curious commentary upon that wonderful thing called human reason?

SENATOR UNDERWOOD.—It is regulated by a line!

SENATOR CORWIN.—Yes, by 36° 30', and what is black on one side of the line is white on the other, turning to jet black again when restored to its original locality. How is that? Can I have confidence in the Supreme Court of the United States, when my confidence fails in Senators around me?

I recollect very well when we did not stop to inquire how the Supreme Court had decided or ordained. It had decided, with John Marshall at its head—a man whose lightest conjectures upon the subject of constitutional law have always had with me as much weight as the well-considered opinion of almost any other man---that Congress had power to establish just such a bank as you had;[1] but with what infinite scorn did Democratic gentlemen—Jackson Democrats as they chose to be called—curl their lips when referred to that decision of the Supreme Court. Then the cry was, "We are judges for ourselves; we make no law unless we have the power to enact it." Now, however, the doctrine is that here is one only tribunal competent to put the matter at rest forever.

Senator Corwin criticized the impracticability and injustice of the method of getting a decision of the Supreme Court as laid down in the bill. To test the law a man must go to California with his slaves. "I do not know how it may be in other parts of the world," said Senator Corwin, "but in the State of Ohio we do not travel three thousand miles to get justice."

Sir, this bill seems to me a rich and rare legislative curiosity. It does not enact "a law," which I had supposed the usual function of legislation. No, sir; it only enacts "a law-suit." So we virtually enact that, when the Supreme Court say we *can* make law, *then* we *have* made it!

In the meantime, said the Senator, while the case is under consideration in the Supreme Court, slavery will have taken root and appeal will be made by the advocates of slavery against interference with vested property interests.

The greatest absurdity in the bill, however, was that,

[1] See Vol. XIII, chapter iv.

as in all cases before the Supreme Court, the appellant must give bond to twice the value of the property in dispute; in this case a negro must give bonds to twice the value of himself!

Under this complexity of legal quibbling and litigation, it is expected that the negro will stand before the bar and contend with his master, and, coming on to Washington, will prosecute his appeal two years before the Supreme Court, enjoying the opportunity of visiting his old friends about Baltimore!

SENATOR UNDERWOOD regarded it as our true policy to let slavery alone. Climate and population are continuing to drive slavery further and further to the South, to the latitude where free labor could not flourish. He read a number of extracts from a pamphlet in his hands, showing that in the first stage after the introduction of slavery the increase of slaves is great; in the second stage, the white population increases in an equal ratio with the slaves; and, in the third stage, the slave race diminishes rapidly.

SENATOR BUTLER said the discussion had worn a calm and temperate character until yesterday, when the Senator from Ohio [Mr. Corwin] poured forth from his full mind arguments and statements which had forever banished from his breast the hope of a successful termination of the efforts at compromise.

If it was a question how much the non-slaveholding States had gained from the labor of the slaveholding States, the figures of rhetoric would soon give way before the figures of arithmetic. If the forefathers of the South, when they gave their consent to the Constitution, had supposed that they were giving to the North authority for the unlimited expansion of their political power, while they were imposing on the South the Procrustean process, by which she was always to be clipped and kept within narrow fetters, would they have ever given their consent to the instrument?

He commented severely on the course of the Eastern States in refusing to give up the fugitive slaves from the South.

He was not disposed to indulge in declamation. He had admired the oratory of the Senator from Ohio, which he characterized as equally beautiful and *ad captandum*,[1] but he charged that the love of power was at the bottom of it. He ridiculed the moral tone of the Senator's speech, and related an anecdote of a party of clergymen at a religious revival, who were called to dine on venison, when, after the blessing had been asked,

[1] "Playing to the galleries."

one whispered to the clergyman that Pequod had killed the deer on Sunday. What was to be done? The minister told his brethren that the venison had been killed on Sunday. Could they eat it? Why, you have asked a blessing, I believe! Yes. Well, then, that will partly consecrate the venison; so we may eat the meat, and then give Pequod thirty-nine lashes. This was morality! and such was the morality of the North in its treatment of the South.

SENATOR FOOTE feared that the decision of the Supreme Bench, as that court is now constituted, would be against the South. And then, said he, where are we? He laid it down that the Northern men were the shrewdest men in the Union. He had traveled over every part of the Union to the Rio Grande, and had found Yankees everywhere; and he had never found one who was not anxious to own a slave. And they were the most rigid of masters—they were masters indeed. As soon as a Yankee could command four hundred dollars he laid it out in a slave, because in a cotton-growing country he knew that a slave was the most valuable property he could possess. He admired the Yankees very much. He had never desired to hang them all. And if he had, as had been charged against him, ever used such an expression in the heat of the moment, he would now retract it. He was perfectly satisfied that the Yankees would never vote for the abolition of slavery if they could gain any profit by continuing it.

SENATOR IVERSON spoke on the general subject of slavery, alleging the insecurity of trusting to Northern compromises, contending that both the Whig candidates [1] were unsound on this question, and arguing the hopelessness of the cause of the South in the event of their success.

Senator Johnson defended the Supreme Court against the charges of the Senator from Ohio [Mr. Corwin].

While statesmen, politicians, were found differing on a subject, the Supreme Court was unanimous. On the question of the constitutionality of the United States Bank, while Congress was deciding one way, the court was unanimously the other way. The members of the Supreme Court were not politicians. They were born in a different atmosphere, and they addressed themselves to different hearers. Politicians wre always differing and disputing—one taking this side of a question, and another

[1] General Zachary Taylor [La.] and Millard Fillmore [N. Y.].

taking an opposite view, all equally honest. How desirable, then, in a case of such importance as this, to call in a third party, rather than that we should be driven to despair—above all, to bloodshed.

He was not the advocate of slavery itself; he never had been so. He would rejoice to see the institution at an end, and it was with sincere regret he admitted that it was the agitation which had been stirred up in the North which had alone prevented the friends of freedom from emancipating the slaves in Maryland. He alluded to Connecticut, from which State the compromise was opposed as having scarcely become a free State, and to Ohio, where free negroes were treated as slaves.[1]

The Senator from Ohio had complained that California was three thousand miles from Washington, and no slave could find means to employ a lawyer to carry up his case. He would reply to this that there could not be found in the whole Southern bar a lawyer who would not gratuitously give his services to a black man, to free him from slavery, where there was a reasonable ground for the application. He also referred to the readiness of judges to decide in favor of the slave. And he believed that, if this bill should pass, there would be always found at the Southern bar members who would be ready to sue out the freedom of slaves who were entitled to it. The question whether a slave owner is entitled to carry his slaves into the territory will be decided on the first appeal, and that will decide the matter in every future case which can arise. The question rises above party and sectional considerations. It assumes the character and dignity and importance of a national one.

SENATOR BADGER regarded this bill as a complete surrender of the rights of the South. Among the powers granted to Congress by the Constitution, he included that of governing the territory ceded to the nation. That power included either the introduction or the abolition of slavery in the territories ceded to us. The power of acquiring territory has been sustained by the decision of the Supreme Court, and the acquisition of territory carries with it the power to govern the territory, and the power to govern includes the power to regulate slavery.

He believed negro slavery would be as effectually excluded by this bill as if the Wilmot proviso, or any other bill, had passed. He had a respect for the Supreme Court, but he was

---

[1] The repressive "black laws" of Ohio were wiped out by the legislature in the course of the following year.

not willing to leave the decision of the question to a court, so large a portion of which were opposed to slavery.

MR. DIX defended the State of New York against the charge of refusing to surrender fugitives from justice, claimed under requisition from the State of Virginia. He alleged that this was not the act of the State, but of the governor. He read the resolutions adopted by the legislature, of which he was a member, which condemned the course of the governor.

The bill was adopted in the Senate on July 26 by a vote of 33 to 22. It then went to the House, where, on motion of Alexander H. Stephens [Ga.] it was laid on the table by a vote of 112 to 97, 8 Southern Whigs and 31 Northern Democrats voting with all the Northern Whigs in the affirmative. The charge was made by some of the Democrats that these Southern Whigs were acting in the interest rather of their party than of their section, but this Mr. Stephens repelled, saying that the Supreme Court, to whom the bill left the decision, was certain to pronounce against the claim that slavery was allowable in the Territories solely by virtue of the Constitution; he cited many opinions of the Court,[1] showing that it had repeatedly upheld this view, namely, that "the Constitution recognizes and guarantees slavery wherever it exists by *local* law, but establishes it nowhere where it is prohibited by law."

In lieu of the bill Stephens urged that the Southern Representatives refuse to make any appropriations for carrying out the treaty with Mexico until the rights of the South in regard to taking their slaves into the Territories had been secured.

The House having tabled the Senate bill proceeded to organize a territorial government for Oregon alone. A bill to this effect incorporating the prohibition of slavery as set forth in the Ordinance of 1787 was passed on August 2, 1848, by a vote of 129 to 71.

On August 3 the House bill came before the Senate. It was debated until August 10, when it was passed with an amendment offered by Stephen A. Douglas [Ill.],

[1] Wheaton's Rep., VIII, p. 589; XII, pp. 528-535; Peters' Rep., I, pp. 517, 542, 544, VI, p. 712; VII, pp. 86, 87; VIII, pp. 444, 465; IX, pp. 133, 736, 747-749; X, pp. 305, 330, 721, 732; XII, p. 412.

by a vote of 33 to 21. On the following day the House
refused to concur in the amendment, and the Senate,
on August 12, accepted the House bill intact by a vote
of 29 to 25. The reason for this acceptance was the
nomination at Buffalo, N. Y., on August 9 of Free Soil
candidates for President and Vice-President, Martin
Van Buren [N. Y.] and Charles Francis Adams
[Mass.] pledged against the extension of slavery into
any of the Territories, California and New Mexico, as
well as into Oregon. The Liberty party was now
merged with the Free Soil party.

On the debates in the Senate the following were the
chief speakers: pro-slavery, James M. Mason [Va.],
Andrew P. Butler [S. C.], John C. Calhoun [S. C.], John
Bell [Tenn.], General Samuel Houston [Tex.] and W.
Johnson [Ga.]; anti-slavery, William L. Dayton [N. J.],
Daniel Webster [Mass.] and John M. Niles [Conn.].

THE OREGON BILL

SENATE, AUGUST 3-12, 1848

SENATOR MASON attributed to the committee the design to
evade the slavery question. He referred to the convention
about to be assembled at Buffalo, for the choice of a standard-
bearer. But one god was to be worshiped there, and that
god was power—the power to trample down the Constitution
of the country. He referred to the recent decision of Virginia
not to regard any law of the United States which should prevent
her citizens from carrying their slaves into any of the Territories.
He and his constituents were willing to be bound by the principle
of the compromise, but it was not to be expected that they
would go one single step beyond it. It would be to expect them
to submit to insult.

SENATOR DAYTON replied, to the threats held out by the Senator from Virginia, that if she was to be forced another step, she
would proclaim nullification. He repudiated for the Whig
party this question as the great issue to be tried at the coming
election. The questions of free soil and slavery were not the
great questions of the Whig party. They constituted too narrow
a ledge for that party to stand on. Nor would it be generally
understood that this was the great issue with the Democratic
party.

SENATOR WEBSTER said that his objection to slavery was irrespective of lines and points of latitude; it took in the whole country, and the whole question. He was opposed to it in every shape, and in every qualification, and was against any compromise of the question.

As to California and New Mexico, he said it was easy to foresee to what the acquisition of this territory would lead. He congratulated himself that he had taken no part in the late war, except to oppose its commencement with all his might, and at the close to oppose the treaty with all his might. He believed the war itself to be a calamity, and he greatly feared that the treaty would turn out to be the most permanent calamity.

SENATOR BUTLER disapproved of this policy of giving especial protection to the Territories north of the Missouri line of compromise, and giving to the North all that valuable portion of the Union. The resolutions of the State of Virginia, which were referred to the other day by a Senator from that State [Mr. Mason], had been responded to by all the Southern States of the Union. He would tell the Senate that his advice to his constituents would be to go to these new Territories with arms in their hands; to go as armed communities and take possession of the lands which they had helped to acquire and see who would attempt to dispossess them. Would the military force of the United States shoot down the plowman at his plow? So help him God, he would so advise his constituents, to take with them their property there, and settle at all hazards. The subtleties and sophisms of the laws of nations would be feeble barriers to the spirit which would show itself in the South. Times and circumstances had changed the character of this bill for the establishment of a Territory in Oregon from what it was two years ago. Then it was comparatively innocent; now he regarded it as a masked battery, from behind which the institutions of the South were to be assailed with a firm determination to subdue them. The South would not fear a contest. She was ready to meet her opponents in a fair and open manner, but she would rise indignant against these covert attacks. He was ready to embark in the boat with his State, and to trust it to the care of Heaven.

SENATOR CALHOUN referred to the insurrection of the slaves in the West India Islands; and the same spirit, though suppressed, exists here. He dreaded the result which would follow if the same spirit which now animated the North should continue to grow and spread. He referred to the positions taken by the South and the North on the slave question. The latter had been unable to meet the arguments of the Southern Senators, and turned out of the direct course to discuss the question of the extension of territory, which was not connected with the subject, and was not advocated by a single Representative from his State. He would now tell the people of the South that they

JOSHUA [CALHOUN] COMMANDING THE SUN [THE PRESS] TO STAND STILL [1848]

From the collection of the New York Historical Society

can never settle this question until they take it into their own hands. He admitted that the South was poor in comparison with the North. Slavery had benefited all mankind—all countries but the South. Slavery, like the waters of the Nile, had spread its fertilizing influence over all the world. It had benefited all but the Southern planter, who had been the tutor, the friend, as well as the master, of the slave, and had raised him up to civilization.

SENATOR NILES said that the movement of the North was forced upon them by the Southern attempt to mix up this slavery question with the politics of the country. It had been given out by the South that no candidate for the Presidency should be supported there who did not pledge himself against the Wilmot proviso. Now, when this course was taken it was incumbent on the North to make a counteracting movement.

SENATOR BUTLER said the South did not take this course until ten of the Northern States had pledged themselves in an opposite manner.

SENATOR NILES admitted that this was true. But here was the distinction: the Northern States merely asserted their opinions as a principle, while the South follow up their pledge by an awful threat of nullification if their wishes are not complied with.

SENATOR WEBSTER said that he had been among the earliest to oppose acquisition of foreign territory. He referred to the maxim of Lord Bacon—that the best way to avoid any domestic disputes or difficulties was to avoid the occasion for them; and said that, in accordance with this maxim, he [Mr. W.] had always opposed the acquisition of foreign territory. There were wiser heads than Lord Bacon's now. There are persons who will provoke occasions, or certainly will meet them, and adopt circumstances as they may arise. He enumerated the difficulties in which this acquisition of territory had plunged us. He was not apprehensive of any disunion. He never contemplated its possibility. He was not one of those who accustom themselves to speak of such a contingency. An earthquake may come, a volcano may burst forth; but human foresight can do nothing to prevent such calamities. So the dissolution of the Union is among those possible calamities. He believed there was a disposition everywhere to support the Union, and that five out of six of our citizens would be glad to give back the new Territories we have acquired.

SENATOR JOHNSON said that the South honestly held the opinion that Congress has no power to prohibit slavery. He believed the contrary opinion was entertained with equal honesty in the North. If the North, having the majority, insist on exercising the power, what can follow but the degradation of the South, or the dissolution of the Union? The only remedy was a just and honorable compromise.

SENATOR CALHOUN said: The North is determined to exclude the property of the slaveholder, and of course the slaveholder himself, from its territory. The effect of this determination of the North was to convert all the Southern population into slaves; and he would never consent to entail that disgrace on his posterity. He denounced any Southern man who would not take the same course. Gentlemen were greatly mistaken, if they supposed the Presidential question in the South would override this more important one. The separation of the North and the South is completed. The South has now a most solemn obligation to perform—to herself—to the Constitution—to the Union. She is bound to come to a decision not to permit this to go on any further, but to show that, dearly as she prizes the Union, there are questions which she regards as of greater importance than the Union.

Gentlemen may do with this bill as they please. If they will not give now what the South asks as a compromise, she will, at the next session, demand all, and will not be satisfied with anything less.

SENATOR BELL believed that the Senator from South Carolina, and those who concurred with him, had placed the South in a wrong position, when they assumed that, by the decision of this question, the die would be cast, and the issue must now be made which involves the dissolution of the Union. Until a vote of Congress should, on the subject of the Southern Territories, actually separate the Union, he never would believe that such a vote could be given.

SENATOR HOUSTON was ready to vote for the admission of Oregon, even with the prohibition of slavery attached to it, as it could never affect the southern Territories. He remembered the cry of disunion and nullification when the high tariff was imposed. That cry reached him in the wilderness, an exile from kindred, and friends and sections; but it rung in his ears, and wounded his heart. He had heard the menaces and cries of disunion until he had become familiar with them, and they had now ceased to produce alarm in his bosom. He had no fear of the dissolution of the Union, when he recollected how it had been established, and how it had been defended. It could not be the interest of the North to destroy the South, notwithstanding the papers signed by old men, and old women, and pretty little girls, praying for abolition—these could not ruffle the Union. The intelligent and manly spirits of the North would rise up to defend the Union. He wished no separation of the States. He had too much confidence in the North to fear any injury from that section. And he thought the South—and he was a Southern man—should make some sacrifice for the purpose of reconciliation with the North. Oregon cannot obtain protection and good government, except from Congress; and he hoped these would be extended to her.

MR. JOHNSON, in reply to the Senator from Texas, declared that the South could not with any propriety rely on the magnanimity of the North. He also took exception to the course of the Senator from Tennessee [Mr. Bell], who, as a Southern man, looked forward to the day when the South would be saved by Northern generosity. The incendiary publications which had been circulated, as blood in the human body, through every vein and artery, with numerous other acts of notoriety, might be quoted to show the character of Northern generosity.

The South had asked us only to keep off legislative action on this subject. They asked only that the question should be submitted to the Supreme Court, to be decided upon in conformity with the Constitution. But the compromise based on this principle had been laid on the table by the other House—rejected without any of that courtesy and magnanimity which the Senators from Missouri and Texas had promised to us.

SENATOR WEBSTER said: Although slavery as attached to the South exists in other countries, he knew not that slaves transferable as chattels, to be separated from the glebe, were to be found but in America, and in the colonies of America. He remembered when this was regarded as an evil fixed on us by the mother country, and it must be considered as an entailment. He referred to the original introduction of slavery in the South, and assumed that no one, as far as he could gather from the acts and debates in Congress, had contemplated any extension of it to new territory. In the Convention, and in the first Congress, it was conceded that slavery was a State institution, and that Congress had no power over it. He was of this opinion, and he would countenance no efforts to produce excitement by the introduction of these questions.

As the Senator from Georgia desires to leave the question to the decision of the civilized world, and as he acquiesced in that course, how would it then stand? The Southern Senators say we deprive them of the right to go into these newly acquired

Territories with their property. We certainly do not prevent them from going into these Territories with what is in general law called property. But these States have by their local laws created a property in persons, and they cannot carry these local laws with them. Slavery is created and exists by a local law, which is limited to a certain section; and it is asked that Congress shall establish a local law in other Territories, to enable Southern Senators to carry their particular law with them. No man can be held as a slave, except the local law shall accompany him. The slave is held to be free, until evidence shall be presented to prove that he is a slave.

He was not willing to extend the area of slavery, or to increase the slave representation in the other House. He thought enough had been yielded when twenty representatives from slave States, elected by three-fifths, were in the House of Representatives.

President Polk approved the bill, but in doing so sent a special message to Congress in which he advocated the submission to the people of California and New Mexico of the question whether these territories should be organized with or without slavery.

POPULAR SOVEREIGNTY

PRESIDENT POLK

Ought we now to disturb the Missouri and Texas compromises? Ought we, at this late day, in attempting to annul what has been so long established and acquiesced in, to excite sectional divisions and jealousies; to alienate the people of different portions of the Union from each other, and to endanger the existence of the Union itself?

Why should our institutions be endangered, because it is proposed to submit to the people of the remainder of our newly acquired territory lying south of thirty-six degrees thirty minutes, embracing less than four degrees of latitude, the question whether, in the language of the Texas compromise, they "shall be admitted (as a State) into the Union with or without slavery"? Is this a question to be pushed to such extremities by excited partisans on the one side or the other, in regard to our newly acquired distant possessions on the Pacific, as to endanger the union of thirty glorious States which constitute our Confederacy? I have an abiding confidence that the sober reflec-

tion and sound patriotism of the people of all the States will
bring them to the conclusion that the dictate of wisdom is to
follow the example of those who have gone before us, and settle
this dangerous question on the Missouri compromise, or some
other equitable compromise, which would respect the rights of
all, and prove satisfactory to the different portions of the Union.

The Democratic party had met in convention at Balti-
more May 22, 1848, and nominated Senator Lewis Cass
[Mich.] for President and William O. Butler [Ky.] for
Vice-President.

The principle of popular or "squatter" sovereignty
was almost unanimously repudiated in the convention,
and that of non-interference by the Federal Government with the "rights of property" (i. e., slavery) in
the States was defeated by a vote of 246 to 36; yet,
before Congress, then in session, dispersed, the rejected
principles, as we have seen, became, the one the leading
tenet of the party, and the other its almost equally accepted corollary.

In the ensuing election the Free Soil candidates,
while securing no electoral votes, polled 291,263 popular
votes. A majority of these were drawn from the Democratic party, this being particularly the case in New
York State, whose 36 electoral votes were thereby thrown
to the Whig candidates, and determined their election,
the electoral vote being 163 for Taylor and Fillmore,
and 127 for Cass and Butler. Although the political
views of General Taylor were little known (he had
never voted at any election, though he professed himself a Whig), owing to the fact that he was a Louisianian
it was assumed by many in the South that he would not
antagonize that section by his position on slavery, and
he accordingly received the votes of Delaware, Maryland, North Carolina, Georgia, Kentucky, Tennessee,
Louisiana, and Florida, whereat the Northern Democrats in Congress were incensed, and decided to cut
loose from their Southern colleagues on the question
of slavery in the Territories.

In his annual message at the opening of the next
session of Congress (December 5, 1848) President Polk

repeated his recommendations about organizing the new Territories with the following addition:

> If Congress, instead of observing the course of non-interference, leaving the adoption of their own domestic institutions to the people who may inhabit these Territories; or if, instead of extending the Missouri compromise line to the Pacific, shall

THE LIBERTY CHARIOT

Cass and Butler (horses) with Uncle Sam (driver) enter the White House gate, drawing the North and South, in the Union chariot, over the prostrate Van Buren, whose mount (the negro) is trampled upon by the Whig "hack" bearing Taylor and Fillmore

From the collection of the New York Historical Society

prefer to submit the legal and constitutional questions which may arise to the decision of the judicial tribunals, as was proposed in a bill which passed the Senate at your last session, an adjustment may be effected in this mode. If the whole subject be referred to the judiciary, all parts of the Union should cheerfully acquiesce in the final decision of the tribunal created by the Constitution for the settlement of all questions which may arise under the Constitution, treaties, and laws of the United States.

Congress is earnestly invoked, for the sake of the Union, its harmony, and our continued prosperity as a nation, to adjust at its present session this, the only dangerous question which lies in our path.

The House, on December 13, by a vote of 108 to 80 instructed the Committee on Territories to bring in territorial bills for California and New Mexico "excluding slavery therefrom." One week later (December 20) the committee reported such a bill for California, and on January 3, 1849, another for New Mexico. On February 27 the California bill was passed by an almost sectional vote of 126 to 87. The New Mexico bill was not reached during the session.

Owing to the discovery of gold in California January 19, 1848, within a year the population had increased so rapidly that the people applied to Congress for admission to the Union. The Senate referred the matter to a select committee of which Stephen A. Douglas [Ill.] was made chairman. On January 29, 1849, Senator Douglas reported a bill to admit California as a State "upon an equal footing with the *original States in all respects whatsoever,* so soon as it shall contain the proper number of inhabitants, and they should establish for themselves a constitution and republican form of government"—an implicit recognition of the principle of "Popular Sovereignty."

On February 5 Robert M. T. Hunter [Va.] presented in the Senate resolutions of the Virginia legislature against applying the Wilmot proviso to the admission of any State or the organization of any territory south of the line established by the Missouri compromise, and against the abolition of slavery or the slave trade in the District of Columbia, threatening in either event "a determined resistance at all hazards and to the last extremity."

On these resolutions Senator Hunter spoke as follows:

PROTEST OF VIRGINIA AGAINST THE WILMOT PROVISO

SENATOR HUNTER

Some two years since, Virginia felt it to be her duty, under the circumstances which surrounded her, to declare her opinions as to the right of Congress to prohibit slavery in territory to be acquired either by conquest or treaty. These resolutions denied the power of Congress "to control, directly or indirectly," the institution of slavery, so as to impair the rights of the slaveholder; they declared that the territory to be acquired by the United States from any foreign power would be the common property of the States, and that any Federal legislation which directly or indirectly prevented the citizens of any of the States from emigrating to it with their property, of whatever description, would violate the Constitution and the rights of the States, would derogate from that perfect equality which belongs to the States of this Confederacy, and tend to subvert the Union itself; they proclaimed that if the Wilmot proviso should be adopted, in disregard of the spirit and principles of the Missouri compromise, and of every consideration of right, justice, and fraternal feeling, the people of Virginia could have no difficulty in choosing between the only alternatives that would then remain—of abject submission to aggression and outrage on the one hand, or determined resistance on the other, at all hazards and to the last extremity. They declared it to be the duty of every man from every section of this Confederacy, if he loves the Union, to oppose the passage of such a law; and, in the event of its enactment, they warned the slaveholding States, and every citizen thereof, that it would be their duty, as they valued their dearest privileges, their sovereignty, their independence, and their rights of property, to take firm, united, and concerted action in that emergency. Again, at the present session of the legislature, these resolutions have been solemnly reaffirmed.

Sir, we have been taught to believe that our Constitution, if administered truly, and in a spirit of justice and fraternal feeling, contained more securities for human happiness and the liberty of the citizen than any other instrument ever devised by the art of man. But the Union which we love is a confederacy of equals. The Constitution which we cherish makes no invidious distinction between States or citizens, but distributes equally its blessings and its burdens. Such is the Union and such is the Constitution which the blood of our fathers was shed to procure; and shall their sons so far fail in reverence to it as to agree to the subversion of the very principle which lies at the foundation of the structure? Sir, this cannot, ought not to be. The South cannot consent to be made the Jamaica or even the Ireland of this Confederacy, without an effort to prevent it. It would not be for the glory or even for the interest of the non-slaveholding States to force us to such extremities if they could. Sir, they can have no interest in forcing us to extremities; and

I believe that they would pause in that progress which is inevitably leading to such a result, if they understood fully how we think and feel on this subject. Alas! sir, that it should be so; but we have ceased to study and consider the feelings and opinions of each other in the true spirit of fraternal affection.

On February 20, 1849, Isaac P. Walker [Wis.] moved in the Senate to amend a general appropriation bill by extending the Constitution of the United States to the Territories. Upon this a constitutional debate, one of the most important in American history, arose between Daniel Webster [Mass.] and John C. Calhoun [S. C.].

EXTENSION OF THE CONSTITUTION TO THE TERRITORIES

SENATE, FEBRUARY 4, 1849

SENATOR WEBSTER said: Mr. President, it is of importance that we should seek to have clear ideas and correct notions of the question which this amendment of the member from Wisconsin has presented to us; and especially that we should seek to get some conception of what is meant by the proposition, in a law, to "extend the Constitution of the United States to the Territories." Why, sir, the thing is utterly impossible. All the legislation in the world, in this general form, could not accomplish it. There is no cause for the operation of the legislative power in such a manner as that. The Constitution—what is it? We extend the Constitution of the United States by law to a Territory! What is the Constitution of the United States? Is not its very first principle that all within its influence and comprehension shall be represented in the legislature which it establishes, with not only a right of debate and a right to vote in both Houses of Congress, but a right to partake in the choice of the President and Vice-President? And can we by law extend these rights, or any of them, to a Territory of the United States? Everybody will see that it is altogether impracticable. Well, sir, the amendment goes on, and says that the revenue laws shall, so far as they are suitable, be applied in the Territories. Now, with respect to that qualification, made by the honorable member from Wisconsin, I shall like to know if he understands it as I suppose he does. Does the expression, "as far as suitable," apply to the Constitution or the revenue laws, or both?

SENATOR WALKER.—It was not the proposition to extend the Constitution beyond the limits to which it was applicable.

SENATOR WEBSTER.—It comes to this, then, that the Constitution is to be extended as far as practicable; but how far that is is to be decided by the President of the United States, and therefore he is to have absolute and despotic power. He is the judge of what is suitable and what is unsuitable, and what he thinks is suitable is suitable, and what he thinks unsuitable is unsuitable. He is *"omnis in hoc"*; and what is this but to say, in general terms, that the President of the United States shall govern this territory as he sees fit till Congress makes further provision? Now, if the gentleman will be kind enough to tell me what principle of the Constitution he supposes suitable, what discrimination he can draw between suitable and unsuitable, which he proposes to follow, I shall be instructed. Let me say that in this general sense there is no such thing as extending the Constitution. The Constitution is extended over the United States and over nothing else, and can extend over nothing else. It cannot be extended over anything except over the old States and the new States that shall come in hereafter, when they do come in. There is a want of accuracy of ideas in this respect that is quite remarkable among eminent gentlemen, and especially professional and judicial gentlemen. It seems to be taken for granted that the right of trial by jury, the *habeas corpus,* and every principle designed to protect personal liberty is extended by force of the Constitution itself over every new Territory. That proposition cannot be maintained at all. How do you arrive at it by any reasoning or deduction? It can be arrived at only by the loosest of all possible constructions. It is said this must be so, else the right of the *habeas corpus* would be lost. Undoubtedly these rights must be conferred by law before they can be enjoyed in a Territory.

Sir, if the hopes of some gentlemen were realized, and Cuba were to become a possession of the United States by cession, does anybody suppose that the *habeas corpus* and the trial by jury would be established in it by the mere act of cession? Why more than election laws and the political franchises, or popular franchises? Sir, the whole authority of Congress on this subject is embraced in that very short provision that Congress shall have power to make all needful rules and regulations respecting the *Territories* of the United States. The word is *Territories;* for it is quite evident that the compromises of the Constitution looked to no new acquisitions to form new Territories. But, as they had been acquired from time to time, new Territories have been regarded as coming under that general provision for making rules for *Territories*. We have never had a *Territory* governed as the United States are governed. The legislature and judiciary of Territories have always been established by a law of Congress. I do not say that, while we sit here to make laws for these Territories, we are not bound by every one of those great principles which are intended as general securities for public liberty. But they do not exist in Territories till introduced by the authority of Congress. These principles do not, *proprio vigore*, apply to any one of the Territories of the United States, because that Territory, while a Territory, does not become a part, and is no part, of the United States.

SENATOR CALHOUN.—I am very happy, sir, to hear this proposition thus asserted, for it will have the effect of narrowing very greatly the controversy between the North and the South, as it regards the slavery question in connection with the Territories. It is an implied admission that, if the Constitution does extend to the Territories, the South will be protected in the enjoyment of its property—that it will be under the shield of the Constitution. You can put no other interpretation upon the proposition which the gentlemen have made, that the Constitution does not extend to the Territories.

Then the simple question is, does the Constitution extend to the Territories, or does it not extend to them? Why, the Constitution interprets itself. It pronounces itself to be the supreme law of the land.

SENATOR WEBSTER.—What land?

SENATOR CALHOUN.—The land; the Territories of the United States are a part of the land. It is the supreme law, not within the limits of the States of this Union merely, but wherever our flag waves—wherever our authority goes, the Constitution in part goes, not all its provisions certainly, but all its suitable provisions. Why, can we have any authority beyond the Constitution? I put the question solemnly to gentlemen: if the Constitution does not go there, how are we to have any authority or jurisdiction whatever? Is not Congress the creature of the Constitution? does it not hold its existence upon the tenure of the continuance of the Constitution; and would it not be annihilated upon the destruction of that instrument, and the consequent dissolution of this confederacy? And shall we, the creature of the Constitution, pretend that we have any authority beyond the reach of the Constitution? Sir, we were told a few days since that the courts of the United States had made a decision that the Constitution did not extend to the Territories without an act of Congress. I confess that I was incredulous, and I am still incredulous that any tribunal pretending to have a knowledge of our system of government, as the courts of the United States ought to have, could have pronounced such a monstrous judgment. I am inclined to think that it is an error which has been unjustly attributed to them; but, if they have made such a decision as that, I for one say that it ought not and never can be respected. The Territories belong to us; they are ours; that is to say, they are the property of the thirty States of the Union; and we, as the representatives of those thirty States, have the right to exercise all that authority and jurisdiction which ownership carries with it.

Sir, there are some questions that do not admit of lengthened discussion. This is one of them. The mere statement is sufficient to carry conviction with it. And I am rejoiced to hear gentlemen acknowledge that, if the Constitution is there, we are under its shield. The South wants no higher ground to stand upon. The gentlemen have put us upon high ground by the admission that their only means of putting their claims above ours is to deny the existence of the Constitution in California and New Mexico. Now, is there a more fundamental principle than that the States of which this Federal Union is composed have a community of interest in all that belongs to the Union in its federative character? And that the territory of the United States belongs to the Union in that capacity is declared by the Constitution, and that there shall be, in all respects, perfect equality among all the members of the confederacy. There is no principle more distinctly set forth than that there shall be no discrimination in favor of one section over another, and that the Constitution shall have no halfway operation in regard to one portion of the Union, while it shall have full force and effect in regard to another portion.

SENATOR WEBSTER.—The honorable Senator from South Carolina alludes to some decision of the United States courts as affirming that the Constitution of the United States does not extend to the Territories. I can assure him that the same thing has been decided by the United States courts over and over again for the last thirty years.

The Constitution, as the gentleman contends, extends over the Territories. How does it get there? I am surprised to hear a gentleman so distinguished as a strict constructionist affirming that the Constitution of the United States extends to the Territories without showing us any clause in the Constitution in any way leading to that result; and to hear the gentleman maintaining that position without showing us any way in which such a result could be inferred increases my surprise.

The Constitution of the United States extending over the Territories and no other law existing there! Why, I beg to know how any government could proceed, without any other authority existing there than such as is created by the Constitution of the United States? Does the Constitution of the United States settle titles to land? Does it regulate the rights of property? Does it fix the relations of parent and child, guardian and ward? The Constitution of the United States establishes what the gentleman calls a confederation for certain great purposes, leaving all the great mass of laws which is to govern society to derive their existence from State enactments. That is the just view of the state of things under the Constitution. And a State or a Territory that has no law but such as it derives from the Constitution of the United States must be entirely without any State or territorial government. The honorable Senator from South Carolina, conversant with the subject as he must be, from his long experience in different branches of the Government, must know that the Congress of the United States have established principles in regard to the Territories that are utterly repugnant to the Constitution. The Constitution of the United States has provided for them an independent judiciary; for the judge of every court of the United States holds his office upon the tenure of good behavior. Will the gentleman say that in any court established in the Territories the judge holds his office in that way? He holds it for a term of years, and is removable at executive discretion. How did we govern Louisiana before it was a State? Did the writ of *habeas corpus* exist in Louisiana during its territorial existence? Or the right to trial by jury? Who ever heard of trial by jury there before the law creating the territorial government gave the right to trial by jury? No one. When new territory has been acquired it has always been subject to the laws of Congress, to such law as Congress thought proper to pass for its immediate government, for its government during its territorial existence, during the preparatory state in which it was to remain until it was ready to come into the Union as one of the family of States.

The honorable Senator from South Carolina argues that the Constitution declares itself to be the law of the land, and that, therefore, it must extend over the Territories. "The land," I take it, means the land over which the Constitution is established, or, in other words, it means the States united under the

Constitution. But does not the gentleman see at once that that argument would prove a great deal too much? The Constitution no more says that the Constitution itself shall be the supreme law of the land than it says that the laws of Congress shall be the supreme law of the land. It declares that the Constitution and the laws of Congress passed under it shall be the supreme law of the land.

SENATOR CALHOUN.—The laws of Congress made in pursuance of its provisions.

SENATOR WEBSTER.—Well, I suppose the revenue laws are made in pursuance of its provisions; but, according to the gentleman's reasoning, the Constitution extends over the Territories as the supreme law, and no legislation on the subject is necessary. This would be tantamount to saying that the moment territory is attached to the United States, all the laws of the United States, as well as the Constitution of the United States, become the governing will of men's conduct and of the rights of property. Sir, this is a course of reasoning that cannot be maintained. The Crown of England often makes conquests of territory. Who ever heard it contended that the constitution of England, or the supreme power of Parliament, because it is the law of the land, extended over the territory thus acquired, until made to do so by a special act of Parliament? The whole history of colonial conquests shows entirely the reverse. Until provision is made by act of Parliament for a civil government, the territory is held as a military acquisition. It is subject to the control of Parliament, and Parliament may make all laws that they deem proper and necessary to be made for its government; but until such provision is made the territory is not under the dominion of English law. And it is exactly upon the same principle that territories coming to belong to the United States by acquisition or by session, as we have no *jus coloniæ*, remain to be made subject to the operation of our supreme law by an enactment of Congress.

SENATOR CALHOUN.—I shall be extremely brief in noticing the arguments of the honorable Senator from Massachusetts, and I trust decisive. His first objection is, as I understand it, that I show no authority by which the Constitution of the United States is extended to the Territories. How does Congress get any power over the Territories?

SENATOR WEBSTER.—It is granted in the Constitution in so many words: the power to make laws for the government of the Territories.

SENATOR CALHOUN.—Well, then, the proposition that the

Constitution does not extend to the Territories is false to that extent. How else does Congress obtain the legislative power over the Territories? And yet the honorable Senator says I assign no reason for it. I assigned the strongest reason. If the Constitution does not extend there, you have no right to legislate or to do any act in reference to the Territories.

Well, as to the next point. The honorable Senator states that he was surprised to hear from a strict constructionist the proposition that the Constitution extends itself to the Territories. I certainly never contended that the Constitution was of itself sufficient for the government of Territories without the intervention of legislative enactments. It requires human agency everywhere; it cannot extend itself within the limits of any State, in the sense of which the gentleman speaks of it. It is, nevertheless, the supreme law, in obedience to which, and in conformity with which, all legislative enactments must be made. And the proposition that the Constitution of the United States extends to the Territories so far as it is applicable to them is so clear a proposition that even the Senator from Massachusetts, with his profound talent, cannot disprove it. I will put the case of some of the negative provisions of the Constitution. Congress shall make no law concerning religion, nor create titles of nobility. Can you establish titles of nobility in California? If not, if all the negative provisions extend to the Territories, why not the positive? I do not think it necessary to dwell any longer upon this point.

SENATOR WEBSTER.—The precise question is whether a Territory, while it remains in a territorial state, is a part of the United States. I maintain it is not. And there is no stronger proof of what has been the idea of the government in this respect than that to which I have alluded, and which has drawn the honorable member's attention. Now, let us see how it stands. The judicial power of the United States is declared by the Constitution to be "vested in one Supreme Court and in such inferior courts as Congress shall from time to time ordain and establish." The whole judicial power, therefore, of the United States is in these courts. And the Constitution declares that "all the judges of these courts shall hold their offices during good behavior." Then the gentleman must admit that the legislation of Congress heretofore has not been altogether in error; that these territorial courts do not constitute a part of the judicial power of the United States, because the whole judicial power of the United States is to be vested in one Supreme Court, and such inferior courts as Congress shall establish, and the judges of all these courts are to have a life tenure under the law; and we do not give such tenure, nor never did, to the judges of these territorial courts. That has gone on the presumption and true idea, I suppose, that the territories are not even part of the United States, but are subject to their legislation. Well, where do they get this power of legislation? Why, I have already stated that the Constitution says "the Congress shall have power to dispose of, and make all needful rules and regulations respecting, the territory or other property belonging to the United States"; and it is under that clause, and that clause only, that the legislation of Congress in respect to the Territories has been conducted. And it is apparent from our history that no other provision was intended for territorial government, inasmuch as it is highly probable, I think certain, that no acquisition of foreign territory was ever contemplated.

And again: there is another remarkable instance. The honorable gentleman, and his friends who act with him on these subjects, hold that the power of internal improvement within the United States does not belong to Congress. They deny that we can pass any law for internal improvements within any State of this Union, while they all admit that the moment we get out of the State into a Territory we can make just as much improvement as we choose. There is not an honorable gentleman on that side of the chamber who has not, time and again, voted money out of the public treasury for internal improvements out of the Union, in Territories, under the conception that, under that provision of the Constitution to which I have referred, they do not constitute any portion of the Union—that they are not parts of the Union.

Sir, there is no end to illustrations that might be brought upon this subject; our history is full of them. Our history is uniform in its course. It began with the acquisition of Louisiana. It went on after Florida became a part of the Union. In all cases, under all circumstances, by every proceeding of Congress on the subject, and by all judicature on the subject, it has been held that Territories belonging to the United States were to be governed by a constitution of their own, framed by a convention, and in approving that constitution the legislation of Congress was not necessarily confined to those principles that bind it when it is exercised in passing laws for the United States itself. But, sir, I take leave of the subject.

SENATOR CALHOUN.—Mr. President, a few words. First, as to the judiciary. If Congress has decided the judiciary of the Territories to be part of the judiciary of the United States, Congress has decided wrong. It may be that it is a part of the judiciary of the United States, though I do not think so.

SENATOR WEBSTER (in his seat).—Nor I.

SENATOR CALHOUN.—Again: the honorable gentleman from Massachusetts says that the Territories are not a part of the United States—are not of the United States. I had supposed that all the Territories were a part of the United States. They are called so.

SENATOR WEBSTER (in his seat).—Never.

SENATOR CALHOUN.—At all events, they belong to the United States.

SENATOR WEBSTER (still in his seat).—That is another thing. The colonies of England belong to England, but they are not a part of England.

SENATOR CALHOUN.—Whatever belongs to the United States, they have authority over, and England has authority over whatever belongs to her. We can have no authority over anything that does not belong to the United States, I care not in what light it may be placed.

But, sir, as to the other point raised by the Senator—internal improvements. The Senator says there is not a member on this side of the chamber but what has voted to appropriate money out of the public treasury for internal improvements in the Territories. I know that a very large portion of the gentlemen on this side have voted to appropriate money out of the public treasury for improvements in Territories, upon the principle of ownership; that the land in the Territories in which improvements are made has an increased value in proportion to the sums appropriated, and the appropriations have, in every case, been given in alternate sections. But many gentlemen here have even utterly denied our right to make them under that form. But that question comes under another category altogether. It comes under the category whether we have a right to appropriate funds out of the common treasury at all for internal improvements.

Sir, I repeat it, that the proposition that the Constitution of the United States extends to the Territories is so plain a one, and its opposite—I say it with all respect—is so absurd a one, that the strongest intellect cannot maintain it. And I repeat that the gentlemen acknowledge, by implication, if not more than that, that the extension of the Constitution of the United States to the Territories would be a shield to the South upon the question in controversy between us and them. I hold it to be a most important concession. It narrows the ground of contro-

STUDYING POLITICAL ECONOMY

From the collection of the New York Historical Society

versy between us. We then cannot be deprived of our equal participation in those Territories without being deprived of the advantages and rights which the Constitution gives us.

Senator John M. Berrien [Ga.] offered a modification of Senator Walker's amendment to the effect that the Constitution, *insofar as its provisions* can be applied to the condition of a Territory, should extend to the Territories; this was accepted by the mover, and the amendment so modified was adopted by a vote of 29 to 27.

Senator Webster made a determined effort to have the Walker amendment dropped, and succeeded in doing so only on the last day of the session. The Senate sat until the early morning hours of March 4, 1849, when Webster's motion was passed by a vote of 38 to 7, and the appropriations went through with no proviso about the new territories. President Polk at once signed the bill—perhaps unconstitutionally, for it is a disputed point as to whether his Administration had terminated at midnight, even though this hour had been conventionally advanced by the Senate to the close of their deliberations.

President Taylor, at the opening of the session of Congress (December 3, 1849), gave Robert Toombs [Ga.], a member of the House of Representatives, who approached him on the subject, clearly to understand that he would not veto a bill for the admission of the Territories with the Wilmot proviso.

The Southern Representatives then made a determined effort to elect one of themselves (Howell Cobb of Georgia) Speaker, in order, so far as possible, to prevent the passage of the proviso. Owing to the fact that a majority of the votes cast were required to elect, a deadlock ensued, and the feelings of the Southern Representatives were wrought up to a high pitch. On December 13 Richard K. Meade [Va.] made threats of secession from the Union by the South, which were more strongly repeated by Mr. Toombs, Alexander H. Stephens [Ga.], and William F. Colcock [S. C.].

RULE OR RUIN

HOUSE OF REPRESENTATIVES, DECEMBER 13, 1849

MR. MEADE.—Sir, let a proposition be made and supported by those who are desirous of crushing this demon of discord, for the purpose of uniting the conservatism on both sides, in opposition to any measure which shall look to the abolition of slavery in the District, or a prohibition of it in the Territories. If such a proposition should be adopted, I should be willing to take a Speaker from either side of the House, relying upon him to carry out the views thus expressed by a majority of this body.

But, sir, if the organization of this House is to be followed by the passage of these bills, if these outrages are to be committed upon my people, I trust in God, sir, that my eyes have rested upon the last speaker of the House of Representatives.

If the North generally, whose big prosperity is the result of unrestricted intercourse with the South, refuse the terms we prescribe, let us talk no more about the blessings of Union.

MR. TOOMBS.—I do not hesitate to avow before this House, and the country, and in the presence of the living God, that if by your legislation you seek to drive us from the Territories of California and New Mexico, purchased by the common blood and treasure of the whole people, and to abolish slavery in this district, thereby attempting to fix a national degradation upon half the States of this confederacy, *I am for disunion*, and, if my physical courage be equal to the maintenance of my convictions of right and duty, I will devote all I am and all I have on earth to its consummation.

MR. STEPHENS.—I concur in every word uttered by my colleague [Mr. Toombs], and, furthermore, I declare that, from the moment a concerted attack, made by the North upon the rights of the South, is an accomplished fact, the Union is thereby dissolved.

MR. COLCOCK.—As soon as the abolition of slavery in the District of Columbia is resolved upon, or the Wilmot proviso is passed, that moment I shall move for the dissolution of the Union.

These threats did not materialize, since Cobb, after all, was elected Speaker. On December 22 the question of the contest was referred to a committee which reported that a plurality should decide. This was agreed to by a vote of 113 to 106, and on the next day Cobb was elected by a vote of 102, Robert C. Winthrop [Mass.], a Whig, receiving 99 votes, and David Wilmot [Pa.], the choice of the Free Soilers, 8 votes. Thus, through a division of the North, the South won its point.

On December 31 Joseph M. Root [O.] moved to instruct the Committee on Territories to bring in a bill for the organization of New Mexico with the Wilmot proviso. Of this proposition Thomas L. Clingman [N. C.] remarked on January 22, 1850:

"Attempt to trample on us and we part company. Remember, sir, that this very territory was acquired by conquest, and that while the South, according to its population, would have been required to furnish only one-third of the troops, it in point of fact did furnish two-thirds of the men that made the conquest. And the North, deficient comparatively as it was in the struggle, now says that its conscience, or its cupidity, will not permit us to have the smallest portion of that territory. Why, sir, this is the most impudent proposition that was ever maintained by any respectable body of men!"

CHAPTER V

THE OMNIBUS BILL

[DEBATES ON THE CLAY COMPROMISE MEASURES]

Message of President Taylor on Admission of California—Henry Clay's Resolutions in the Senate in Favor of Compromise on Slavery—Debate: in Favor of the Resolution, Clay, Thomas H. Benton [Mo.], Daniel Webster [Mass.]; Opposed, Henry S. Foote [Miss.], James M. Mason [Va.], Jefferson Davis [Miss.], John C. Calhoun [S. C.]—Resolutions Are Referred to a Committee of Thirteen—Death of Senator Calhoun—Report of the Committee Proposing Bills; These Are Amended and Combined in an "Omnibus Bill," and Passed—Protest of Southern Senators.

PRESIDENT TAYLOR, in a special message to Congress January 21, 1850, urged the admission of California under the Constitution which she had prepared, announcing himself in favor of the principle of Popular Sovereignty.

THE RIGHT OF A STATE TO SELF-GOVERNMENT

PRESIDENT TAYLOR

Should Congress, when California shall present herself for incorporation into the Union, annex a condition to her admission as a State affecting her domestic institutions contrary to the wishes of her people, and even compel her temporarily to comply with it, yet the State could change her constitution at any time after admission, when to her it should seem expedient. Any attempt to deny to the people of the State the right of self-government in a matter which peculiarly affects themselves will infallibly be regarded by them as an invasion of their rights; and, upon the principles laid down in our own Declaration of Independence, they will certainly be sustained by the great mass of the American people. To assert that they are a conquered people, and must as a State submit to the will of their conquerors, in this regard, will meet with no cordial response among American freemen. Great numbers of them are native citizens of the United States, and not inferior to the rest of our countrymen in intelligence and patriotism; and no language of menace to restrain them in the exercise of an undoubted right, substantially guaranteed to them by the treaty of cession itself, shall ever be uttered by me, or encouraged and sustained by persons acting under my authority. It is to be expected that in the residue of the territory ceded to us by Mexico the people residing there will, at the time of their incorporation into the Union as a State, settle all questions of domestic policy to suit themselves.

On January 29 Henry Clay [Ky.], who had returned to the Senate for this express purpose, presented to that body his famous compromise resolutions on the subject of slavery. Upon them a prolonged debate occurred in which the chief speakers in favor of the resolutions, besides Senator Clay, were Thomas H. Benton [Mo.], Daniel Webster [Mass.]; those opposed to them were Henry S. Foote [Miss.], James M. Mason [Va.], Jefferson Davis [Miss.] and John C. Calhoun [S. C.].

SENATOR CLAY'S COMPROMISE RESOLUTIONS

SENATE, JANUARY 29-MARCH 7, 1850

SENATOR CLAY.—Mr. President, I hold in my hand a series of resolutions which I desire to submit to the consideration of this body. Taken together, in combination, they propose an amicable arrangement of all questions in controversy between the free and the slave States, growing out of the subject of slavery. The preamble and first resolution are as follows:

It being desirable for the peace, concord, and harmony of the Union of these States to settle and adjust amicably all existing questions of controversy between them arising out of the institution of slavery, upon a fair, equitable, and just basis: Therefore
1st. *Resolved*, That California ought, upon her application, to be admitted as one of the States of this Union, without the imposition by Congress of any restriction in respect to the exclusion or introduction of slavery within those boundaries.

The second resolution, sir, is as follows:

2d. *Resolved*, That as slavery does not exist by law, and is not likely to be introduced into any of the territory acquired by the United States from the Republic of Mexico, it is inexpedient for Congress to provide by law either for its introduction into or exclusion from any part of the said territory; and that appropriate territorial governments ought to be established by Congress in all of the said territory, not assigned as the boundaries of the proposed State of California, without the adoption of any restriction or condition on the subject of slavery.

This resolution, sir, proposes a declaration of two truths—one of law and the other of fact. The truth of law which it declares is that there does not exist, at this time, slavery within any portion of the territory acquired by the United States from Mexico.

The next truth which the resolution asserts is that slavery is not likely to be introduced into any portion of that territory. That is a matter of fact. California, of all other portions acquired by us from Mexico that country into which it would have been most likely that slavery should have been introduced, California herself has met in convention, and, by a unanimous vote, embracing slaveholders from Mississippi, as well as from other parts, who concurred in the resolution, has declared against the introduction of slavery within her limits. I think, then, that, taking this leading fact in connection with all the evidence we have from other sources on the subject, I am warranted in the conclusion which constitutes the second truth which I have stated in this resolution.

The third resolution fixes the boundaries of the State, and the fourth provides for the assumption by the United States Government of California's obligations to Texas.

The fifth resolution, sir, and the sixth, like the third and fourth, are somewhat connected together. They are as follows:

5th. *Resolved*, That it is inexpedient to abolish slavery in the District of Columbia, while that institution continues to exist in the State of Maryland, without the consent of that State, without the consent of the people of the District, and without just compensation to the owners of slaves within the District.

6th. *But Resolved*, That it is expedient to prohibit within the District the slave-trade, in slaves brought into it from States or places beyond the limits of the District, either to be sold therein as merchandise, or to be transported to other markets without the District of Columbia.

The first of these resolutions, Mr. President, in somewhat different language, asserts substantially no other principle than that which was asserted by the Senate of the United States twelve years ago (1838) upon resolutions which I then offered, and which passed—at least the particular resolution passed—by a majority of four-fifths of the Senate.

The next resolution proposed deserves a passing remark. It is that the slave trade within the District ought to be abolished, prohibited. I do not mean by that the alienation and transfer of slaves from the inhabitants within this District—the sale by one neighbor to another of a slave which the one owns and the other wants, that a husband may perhaps be put along with his wife, or a wife with her husband. I do not mean to touch at all the question of the right of property in slaves among persons living within the District; but the slave trade to which I refer was, I think, pronounced an abomination more than forty years ago by one of the most gifted and distinguished sons of Virginia, the late Mr. Randolph. And who is there who is not shocked at its enormity? Sir, it is a great mistake at the North if they suppose that gentleman living in the slave States look upon one who is a regular trader in slaves with any particular favor or kindness. They are often—sometimes unjustly, perhaps—excluded from social intercourse. But, then, what is this trade? It is a good deal limited since the retrocession (in 1846) of the portion of the District formerly belonging to Virginia. Let the slave dealer who chooses to collect his slaves in Virginia and Maryland go to ports in these States; let him not come here and establish his jails and put on his chains, and sometimes shock the sensibilities of our nature by a long train of slaves passing through that avenue leading from this Capitol to the house of the Chief Magistrate of one of the most glorious republics that ever existed. Why should he not do it? Sir, I am sure I speak the sentiments of every Southern man, and every man coming from the slave States, when I say let it terminate, and that it is an abomination; that there is no occasion for it; it ought no longer to be tolerated.

The seventh resolution relates to a subject embraced in a bill now under consideration by the Senate. It is as follows:

7th. *Resolved*, That more effectual provisions ought to be made by law, according to the requirement of the Constitution, for the restitution and delivery of persons bound to service or labor in any State who may escape into any other State or Territory in the Union.

Sir, that is so evident and has been so clearly shown by the debate which has already taken place on the subject, that I have not now occasion to add another word.

The last resolution of the series of eight is as follows:

And 8th. *Resolved*, That Congress has no power to prohibit or obstruct the trade in slaves between the slaveholding States; but that the admission or exclusion of slaves brought from one into another of them depends exclusively upon their own particular laws.

It is obvious that no legislation is necessary or intended to follow that resolution. It merely asserts a truth, established by the highest authority of law in this country, and in conformity with that decision I trust there will be one universal acquiescence.

Mr. President, you have before you the whole series of resolutions, the whole scheme of arrangement and accommodation of these distracting questions, which I have to offer, after having bestowed on these subjects the most anxious, intensely anxious, consideration ever since I have been in this body. How far it may prove acceptable to both or either of the parties on these great questions it is not for me to say. I think it ought to be acceptable to both. There is no sacrifice of any principle, proposed in any of them, by either party. The plan is founded upon mutual forbearance, originating in a spirit of conciliation and concession; not of principles, but of matters of feeling.

Sir, although I believe this project contains about an equal amount of concession and forbearance on both sides, I might have asked from the free States of the North a more liberal and extensive concession than should be asked from the slave States. And why? You are numerically more powerful than the slave States, and greatness and magnanimity should ever be allied together.

But there are other reasons why concession upon such a subject as this should be more liberal, more expansive, coming from the free than from the slave States. It is a sentiment, a sentiment of humanity and philanthropy on your side. Aye, sir, and when a sentiment of that kind is honestly and earnestly cherished, with a disposition to make sacrifices to enforce it, it is a noble and beautiful sentiment; but, sir, when the sacrifice is not to be made by those who cherish that sentiment and inculcate it, but by another people, in whose situation it is impossible, from their position, for you to sympathize and to share all and everything that belongs to them, I must say to you, Senators from the free States, it is a totally different question. On your side it is a sentiment without sacrifice, a sentiment without danger, a sentiment without hazard, without peril, without loss. But how is it on the other side, to which, as I have said, a greater amount of concession ought to be made in any scheme of compromise?

In the first place, sir, there is a vast and incalculable amount of property to be sacrificed, and to be sacrificed, not by your sharing in the common burdens, but exclusive of you. And this is not all. The social intercourse, habit, safety, property, life, everything is at hazard in a greater or less degree in the slave States.

Behold, Mr. President, that dwelling house now wrapped in flames. Listen, sir, to the rafters and beams which fall in succession, amid the crash; and the flames ascending higher and higher as they tumble down. Behold those women and children who are flying from the calamitous scene, and with their shrieks and lamentations imploring the aid of high Heaven. Whose house is that? Whose wives and children are they? Yours in the free States? No. You are looking on in safety and security, while the conflagration which I have described is raging in the slave States, and produced, not intentionally by you, but produced from the inevitable tendency of the measures which you have adopted, and which others have carried far beyond what you have wished.

In the one scale, then, we behold sentiment, sentiment, sentiment alone; in the other, property, the social fabric, life, and all that makes life desirable and happy.

Senator Clay closed his speech with the relation of an incident. A man, he said, had come to his lodgings that very morning and presented him with a precious relic.

And what, Mr. President, do you suppose it is? It is a fragment of the coffin of Washington—a fragment of that coffin in which now repose in silence, in sleep, and speechless, all the earthly remains of the venerated Father of his Country. Was it portentous that it should have been thus presented to me? Was it a sad presage of what might happen to that fabric which Washington's virtue, patriotism, and valor established? No, sir, no. It was a warning voice, coming from the grave to the Congress now in session to beware, to pause, to reflect before they lend themselves to any purposes which shall destroy that Union which was cemented by his exertions and example. Sir, I hope an impression may be made on your mind such as that which was made on mine by the reception of this precious relic.

SENATOR FOOTE.—Mr. President, I know well that the honorable Senator's intentions are pure and patriotic—that he designs only the safety and happiness of the whole Republic; and yet I do verily believe that if the resolutions now introduced by him shall be adopted, accompanied by the remarks which he has just uttered in our hearing, without any response, or even suggestion of objection from any Southern Senator, a presumption of *acquiescence* might arise which would be deeply detrimental to a cause which I hold dearer than life itself.

If I understand the resolutions properly, they are objectionable, as it seems to me:

1. Because they only assert that it is not *expedient* that Congress should abolish slavery in the District of Columbia; thus allowing the implication to arise that Congress has power to legislate on the subject of slavery in the District, which may hereafter be exercised if it should become expedient to do so; whereas, I hold that Congress has, under the Constitution, no such legislative power at all, and any attempt thus to legislate would be a gross fraud upon all the States of the Union.

2. The resolutions of the honorable Senator assert that slavery does not now exist by law in the territories recently acquired from Mexico; whereas I am of opinion that the treaty with the Mexican Republic carried the Constitution, *with all its guarantees,* to all the territory obtained by treaty, and secured the privilege to every Southern slaveholder to enter any part of it, attended by his slave property, and to enjoy the same therein free from all molestation or hindrance whatsoever.

3. Whether slavery is or is not likely to be introduced into these territories, or into any one of them, is a proposition too uncertain, in my judgment, to be at present positively affirmed; and I am unwilling to make a solemn legislative declaration on the point. *Let the future provide the appropriate solution of this interesting question.*

4 and 5.   *   *   *   *

6. As to the abolition of the *slave trade* in the District of Columbia, I see no particular objection to it, provided it is done in a delicate and judicious manner, and is not a concession to menaces or demands of factionists and fanatics. If other questions can be adjusted, this one will, perhaps, occasion but little difficulty.

7. The resolutions which provide for the restoration of fugitives from labor or service, and for the establishment of territorial governments free from all restriction on the subject of slavery, have my hearty approval. The last resolution—which asserts that Congress has no power to prohibit the trade in slaves from State to State—I equally approve.

8. If all other questions connected with the subject of slavery can be satisfactorily adjusted, I see no objection to admitting all California above the line of 36 degrees and 30 minutes into the Union; provided another new slave State can be laid off within the present limits of Texas, so as to keep up the

present *equiponderance* between the slave and the free States of the Union; and provided, further, all this is done by way of *compromise*, and in order to save the Union (as dear to me as to any man living).

SENATOR MASON.—Sir, I regret deeply that, in the earnest and honest desire which I have no doubt the Senator entertains to have these disturbing questions composed, he has felt it his duty, representing one of the slaveholding States, to offer such a proposition. I would go with him who went furthest, but within the limits of strict duty, in adjusting these unhappy differences; but I do not feel at liberty to move one step toward such a compromise, if constitutional right is invaded in the slightest degree.

Sir, so far as I have read these resolutions, there is but one proposition to which I can give a hearty assent, and that is the resolution which proposes to organize territorial governments at once in these Territories, without a declaration one way or the other as to their domestic institutions. But there is another which I deeply regret to see introduced into this Senate by a Senator from a slaveholding State; it is that which assumes that slavery now does not exist by law in those countries. I understand one of these propositions to declare that by law slavery is now abolished in New Mexico and California. That was the very proposition advanced by the non-slaveholding States at the last session, combated and disproved, as I thought, by gentlemen from the slaveholding States, and which the compromise bill was framed to test. So far I regarded the question of law as disposed of, and it was clearly and satisfactorily shown to be against the spirit of the resolution of the Senator from Kentucky. If the contrary is true, I presume the Senator from Kentucky would declare that, if a law is now valid in the Territories abolishing slavery, it could not be introduced there even if a law was passed creating the institution or repealing the statutes already existing; a doctrine never assented to, so far as I know, until now, by any Senator representing one of the slaveholding States. Sir, I hold the very opposite, and with such confidence that at the last session I was willing and did vote for a bill to test this question in the Supreme Court. Yet this resolution assumes the other doctrine to be true, and our assent is challenged to it as a proposition in law.

I deem it my duty to enter a decided protest on the part of Virginia against such doctrines. They concede the whole question at once, that our people shall not go into the new Territories and take their property with them; a doctrine to which I never will assent, and for which, sir, no law can be found. There are other portions of the resolutions, for which, if they could be separated, I should be very willing to vote. That respecting fugitive slaves, and that respecting the organization of governments in these Territories, I should be willing to vote for, and I am happy to declare the gratification I experience at finding the Senator from Kentucky differing so much on this subject from the executive message recently laid before the Senate. I beg not to be understood as having spoken in any spirit of unkindness toward the Senator from Kentucky, for whom I entertain the warmest and most profound respect; but I cannot but express also my regret that he has felt it to be his duty, standing as he does before this people, and representing the people he does, to introduce into this body resolutions of this kind.

SENATOR DAVIS.—As it has been made an historical question as to what the position of the Senate was twelve years ago, and as with great regret I see this, the conservative branch of the Government, tending toward that fanaticism which seems to prevail with the majority in the United States, I wish to read from the journals of that date the resolutions then adopted, and to show that they went further than the honorable Senator from Kentucky has stated. I take it for granted, from the date to which the honorable Senator has alluded, he means the resolutions introduced by the honorable Senator from South Carolina [Mr. Calhoun], not now in his seat, and to which the Senator from Kentucky proposed certain amendments.

Senator Davis read the resolutions with Senator Clay's amendments.

Here, then, was fully and broadly asserted the danger resulting from the interference in the question of slavery in the District of Columbia, as trenching upon the rights of the slaveholding States. Twelve years only have elapsed, yet this brief period has swept away even the remembrance of principles then deemed sacred and necessary to secure the safety of the Union. Now an honorable and distinguished Senator, to whom the country has been induced to look for something that would heal the existing dissensions, instead of raising new barriers against encroachment, dashes down those heretofore erected, and augments the existing danger. A representative from one of the slaveholding States raises his voice for the first time in disregard of this admitted right.

But, sir, we are called on to receive this as a measure of compromise! Is a measure in which we of the minority are to receive nothing a measure of compromise? I look upon it as but a modest mode of taking that the claim to which has been more boldly asserted by others; and that I may be understood upon this question, and that my position may go forth to the country in the same columns that convey the sentiments of the Senator from Kentucky, I here assert that never will I take less than the Missouri compromise line extended to the Pacific Ocean, with the specific recognition of the right to hold slaves in the territory below that line; and that, before such territories are admitted into the Union as States, slaves may be taken there from any of the United States at the option of their owners. I can never consent to give additional power to a majority to commit further aggressions upon the minority in this Union; and will never consent to any proposition which will have such a tendency, without a full guarantee or counteracting measure is connected with it. I forbear commenting at any further length upon the propositions embraced in the resolutions at this time.

SENATOR CLAY.—I am extremely sorry that this premature, and—allow me to say—in my opinion unnecessary, discussion has taken place. Whenever the Senator who has just resumed his seat chooses to meet me in argument at a proper time, I pledge myself to show him that there is not the slightest discrepancy in my course in 1838 and now.

SENATOR DAVIS.—Now is the time.

SENATOR CLAY.—I choose not to give way now.

SENATOR DAVIS.—The Senator asked me to name my time; and I say now.

SENATOR CLAY.—Not until I am done. I am reminded of my coming from a slave State. I tell the Senator from Mississippi, and I tell the Senator from Virginia, that I know my duty, and that I mean to express the opinions that I entertain, fearless of all mankind.

But, sir, as I do not choose that what I consider a mistaken representation of my sentiments in 1838 should go out, I will simply state what they were then, and what they are now.

Sir, there is not a word in that resolution that implies that any faith was pledged to the States, other than to Virginia and to Maryland, that Congress would not abolish slavery in this District. The resolution says that the agitation of the question of abolition by people living out of the District is, in its tendency, dangerous to the slave States; and that the abolition of slavery in the District of Columbia would be just cause of alarm, not merely to Virginia and Maryland, but to all the slave States. And why? What was it that Abolitionists then proposed? It was abolition without compensation; it was to take the slaves without paying for them. And would it not in that form have been a just cause of alarm to the other States of the Union owning property of that description? The assertion, therefore, of opinion which I made then was that, by the nature and object of the cession of the ten-miles-square by Virginia and Maryland, it could not have been anticipated by either of those States that the power conveyed to the general Government over the ten-miles-square would be so exercised as to abolish slavery within those States respectively; and, further, that slavery, continuing in Virginia and Maryland, if such an abolition were to take place in the District of Columbia, and without compensation to the slaveholder, it would be, as it undoubtedly would have been, a just cause of alarm to the owners of that description of property, wherever situated. Now, sir, that was my doctrine in 1838, and that is my doctrine still.

Sir, I do not regard the mere phraseology of the resolution. I will not substitute the word "unconstitutional" for the word "inexpedient," for I do not believe it to be unconstitutional. I cannot believe it. If a power to legislate in all cases whatever be granted to Congress, does it not comprehend the power to legislate on the subject of slavery as well as upon all other subjects? The power is there; but there is an implied faith connected with the power, resulting from the circumstances to which I have referred, imposing on Congress the obligation not to exercise the power as long as slavery in Virginia and Maryland exists. And now that Virginia has separated from the District, such abolition may not take place without the consent of the people of the District and of Maryland, and also without, what I contended for in 1838, compensation to the owners of the slaves for their property thus liberated.

I am extremely sorry to hear the Senator from Mississippi say that he requires, first, the extension of the Missouri compromise line to the Pacific, and also that he is not satisfied with that, but requires, if I understood him correctly, a positive provision for the admission of slavery south of that line. And now, sir, coming from a slave State, as I do, I owe it to myself, I owe it to truth, I owe it to the subject, to say that no earthly power could induce me to vote for a specific measure for the introduction of slavery where it had not before existed, either south or north of that line. Coming as I do from a slave State, it is

IV—13

my solemn, deliberate, and well-matured determination that no
power, no earthly power, shall compel me to vote for the positive introduction of slavery either south or north of that line.
Sir, while you reproach, and justly, too, our British ancestors
for the introduction of this institution upon the continent of
America, I am, for one, unwilling that the posterity of the
present inhabitants of California and of New Mexico shall reproach us for doing just what we reproach Great Britain for
doing to us. If the citizens of those Territories choose to establish slavery, and if they come here with constitutions establishing slavery, I am for admitting them with such provisions in
their constitutions; but then it will be their own work, and not
ours, and their posterity will have to reproach them, and not
us, for forming constitutions allowing the institution of slavery
to exist among them. These are my views, sir, and I choose to
express them; and I care not how extensively or universally
they are known. The honorable Senator from Virginia has expressed his opinion that slavery exists in these Territories, and
I have no doubt that opinion is sincerely and honestly entertained by him; and I would say, with equal sincerity and honesty, that I believe that slavery nowhere exists within any portion of the territory acquired by us from Mexico.

SENATOR DAVIS.—The Senator from Kentucky rose with an
announcement that he wanted to know my time for meeting
him in argument, and I have told him that my time is now.
Several times has he regretted this premature discussion; but
pray, sir, who introduced it? The Senator submitted his resolutions, discussed them *seriatim*, and then concluded with a set
speech. Are we to understand that all this was done without in-
tending to influence opinion? Was it a mere volley of blank
cartridges that he was firing, in order that he might come up
under cover of the smoke, and make a charge upon us before we
saw him?

The Senator has set up his own cob-house, to show how skil-
fully he could knock it down. It is no fabric of mine. We
maintain that it is the right of the people of the South to
carry this species of property to any portion of the Territories
of the United States; that it rests, under the Constitution, upon
the same basis as other property; but, when speaking of a compromise, it was the ultimatum I announced. It is strange that
the Senator from Kentucky should be so much surprised; it
certainly was not a new question with him, nor with his colleague, with whom, on a former occasion, a similar proposition
originated. It is a partial recognition of a right we claim to be

coextensive with the Territories of the United States; but which we are willing, in a spirit of compromise, and in compliance with the past acquiescence of the States, to restrict by the parallel of 36 degrees 30 minutes north.

Now, this is conceding a great deal. If the line were established upon any great principle arising from climate or productions, it would be different; then the line would not extend upon the same parallel of latitude. If it were a line of temperature, then, as the isothermal line bends upward, it would go north of that parallel of latitude. It is out of respect to the past, and from anxious desire peaceably to adjust a most vexatious and dangerous question, that we agree to adopt this arbitrary line. And this compromise, upon which most of his fame rests, originated, under like circumstances, with the Senator who now with such settled purpose declares his opposition to a fair application of its principle to the present case. Then all the territory involved, that of Missouri, was slave territory; the compromise act prohibited slavery in a part of the territory. Now, according to the position of the Senator, slavery is excluded from the whole territory of California and New Mexico. What, then, would the application of the spirit of the Missouri compromise require? Clearly that in running the line the question should be put at rest by declaring that below said line slavery should be permitted. It is common property of the States, and, if it be proposed to make a division of it, fairness and future peace require that the rights and conditions of each part should be prescribed. Less than this would but narrow the ground and preserve the controversy. And, unless that compromise was founded in fraud, we expect its application in this case, where all is disputed—express provisions on both sides of the line. We cannot agree to leave the question open, especially after what has been said to-day. It is the effect and not the form which I consider it my duty to examine. What matters it whether it be under cover of the acts of the Mexican Government, or by the operation of Congressional law, that slavery is excluded? The effect is the same, under the rule the Senator from Kentucky adopts, as would result from an act of prohibition by the Congress of the United States. I can only say that whenever the Senator chooses to make his argument I shall be ready to meet it.

SENATOR CALHOUN.—I have, Senators, believed from the first that the agitation of the subject of slavery would, if not prevented by some timely and effective measure, end in disunion. Entertaining this opinion, I have on all proper occasions endeavored to call the attention of each of the two great parties which divide the country to adopt some measure to prevent so great a disaster, but without success. The agitation has been permitted to proceed, with almost no attempt to resist it, until it has reached a period when it can no longer be disguised or denied that the Union is in danger. You have thus had forced upon you the greatest and the gravest question that can ever come under your consideration: How can the Union be preserved?

To give a satisfactory answer to this mighty question, it is indispensable to have an accurate and thorough knowledge of the nature and the character of the cause by which the Union is endangered. The first question, then, is: What is it that has endangered the Union?

To this question there can be but one answer: that the immediate cause is the almost universal discontent which pervades all the States composing the southern section of the Union. This widely extended discontent is not of recent origin. It commenced with the agitation of the slavery question, and has been increasing ever since. The next question, going one step further back, is: What has caused this widely diffused and almost universal discontent?

It is a great mistake to suppose, as is by some, that it originated with demagogues, who excited the discontent with the intention of aiding their personal advancement, or with the disappointed ambition of certain politicians, who resorted to it as the means of retrieving their fortunes. On the contrary all the great political influences of the section were arrayed against excitement, and exerted to the utmost to keep the people quiet. The great mass of the people of the South were divided, as in the other section, into Whigs and Democrats. The leaders and the presses of both parties in the South were very solicitous to prevent excitement and to preserve quiet; because it was seen that the effects of the former would necessarily tend to weaken, if not destroy the political ties which united them with their respective parties in the other section. Those who know the strength of party ties will readily appreciate the immense force which this cause exerted against agitation and in favor of preserving quiet. But as great as it was, it was not sufficiently so to prevent the widespread discontent which now pervades the section. No, some cause far deeper and more powerful than the one supposed must exist to account for discontent so wide and deep. The question then recurs: What is the cause of this discontent? It will be found in the belief of the people of the

Southern States, as prevalent as the discontent itself, that they cannot remain as things now are consistently with honor and safety in the Union. The next question to be considered is: What has caused this belief?

One of the causes is, undoubtedly, to be traced to the long-continued agitation of the slave question on the part of the North, and the many aggressions which they have made on the rights of the South during the time.

There is another, lying back of it, with which this is intimately connected, that may be regarded as the great and primary cause. That is to be found in the fact that the equilibrium between the two sections of the Government as it stood when the Constitution was ratified and the Government put in action has been destroyed.

On February 5 the debate was resumed.

Senator Benton.—Mr. President, it has been affirmed and denied on this floor that slavery was abolished in Mexico. I am one of those who affirm its abolition; and I propose now to read some passages from Mexican law for the purpose of supporting my opinion.

[Senator Benton read these passages.] I think everyone must see that slavery was abolished throughout the Mexican territory before the cession of California and New Mexico to the United States, and that slavery cannot exist there now by virtue of Mexican law. This is enough, in my opinion, to show the Wilmot proviso, in relation to these countries, to be a thing of nothing—an empty provision—a cloud without rain—unless it be a rain of blood.

Senator Calhoun, being indisposed, had put his speech in writing; it was read by Senator James M. Mason [Va.].

Senator Calhoun spoke of the growing political preponderance of the free States. Five new States would in all probability shortly be added to their number, making twenty free States to fifteen slave, for there was no prospect of an increase in the latter number.

This great increase of Senators added to the great increase of members of the House of Representatives and the electoral college on the part of the North, which must take place under the next decade, will effectually and irretrievably destroy the equilibrium which existed when the Government commenced.

Had this destruction been the operation of time, without the interference of Government, the South would have had no reason to complain; but such was not the fact. It was caused by the legislation of this Government, which was appointed as the common agent of all, and charged with the protection of the interests of and security of all. The legislation by which it has been effected may be classed under three heads. The first is that series of acts by which the South has been excluded from the common territory belonging to all of the States, as the members of the Federal Union, and which have had the effect of extending vastly the portion allotted to the Northern section, and restricting within narrow limits the portion left the South; the next consists in adopting a system of revenue and disbursements, by which an undue proportion of the burden of taxation has been imposed upon the South and an undue proportion of its proceeds appropriated to the North; and the last is a system of political measures by which the original character of the Government has been radically changed.

The Senator stated that the legislative acts to which he referred were the Ordinance of 1787, the Missouri compromise, and the Oregon act. He did not include the territory recently acquired from Mexico. If slavery were also debarred here, the North would have acquired three-fourths of the acquired domain since the formation of the nation.

Taking up the second cause of the destruction of the equilibrium between the two sections of the country, the revenue system, Senator Calhoun showed that the South paid far more revenue than the North, and received far less disbursements of it, with the result that the North was increasing in wealth and population (for this wealth attracted immigration) at the expense of the South.

The third cause of the destruction of the equilibrium he declared was the change of the Federal Republic into a consolidated democracy, "as despotic in its tendency as any absolute government that ever existed."

However, even these aggrandizements and changes might be acquiesced in by the South were not her peculiar institution [slavery] also attacked in its home.

Every portion of the North entertains views and feelings

more or less hostile to it. Those most opposed and hostile regard it as a sin, and consider themselves under the most sacred obligation to use every effort to destroy it. Indeed, to the extent that they conceive they have the power, they regard themselves as implicated in the sin, and responsible for suppressing it by the use of all and every means. Those less opposed and hostile regard it as a crime, an offence against humanity, as they call it; and, although not so fanatical, feel themselves bound to use all efforts to effect the same object; while those who are least opposed and hostile regard it as a blot and a stain on the character of what they call the nation, and feel themselves accordingly bound to give it no countenance or support. On the contrary, the Southern section regards the relation as one which cannot be destroyed without subjecting the two races to the greatest calamity, and the section to poverty, desolation, and wretchedness; and accordingly they feel bound by every consideration of interest and safety to defend it.

Is it not certain that, if something decisive is not now done to arrest the agitation for the abolition of slavery, the South will be forced to choose between it and secession? Indeed, as events are now moving, it will not require the South to secede to dissolve the Union. Agitation will of itself effect it, as I shall proceed to show.

It is a great mistake to suppose that disunion can be effected by a single blow. The cords which bind these States together in one common union are far too numerous and powerful for that. Disunion must be the work of time. It is only through a long process, and successively, that the cords can be snapped, until the whole fabric falls asunder. Already the agitation of the slavery question has snapped some of the most important, and has greatly weakened all the others.

Here the Senator referred to the division of the religious denominations into Northern and Southern branches on the subject of slavery.

Parties, too, were breaking up on the issue.

If the agitation goes on, the same force, acting with increased intensity, will finally snap every cord, until nothing will be left to hold the States together except force.

He then asked: How can the Union be saved? In introducing this subject he first discussed how the Union could not be saved.

It cannot be saved by eulogies on the Union, however splendid or numerous. The cry of "Union, Union, the glorious Union!" can no more prevent disunion than the cry of "Health, health, glorious health!" on the part of the physician can save a patient lying dangerously ill. So long as the Union, instead of being regarded as a protector, is regarded in the opposite character, by not much less than a majority of the States, it will be in vain to attempt to conciliate them by pronouncing eulogies on it.

Besides, this cry of Union comes commonly from those whom we cannot believe to be sincere; it usually comes from our assailants. But we cannot believe them to be sincere; for, if they loved the Union, they would necessarily be devoted to the Constitution. It made the Union, and to destroy the Constitution would be to destroy the Union. But the only reliable and certain evidence of devotion to the Constitution is to abstain, on the one hand, from violating it, and to repel, on the other, all attempts to violate it.

But how stands the profession of devotion to the Union by our assailants, when brought to this test? Have they abstained from violating the Constitution? Let the many acts passed by the Northern States to set aside and annul the clause of the Constitution providing for the delivery up of fugitive slaves answer.

Nor can the Union be saved by invoking the name of the illustrious Southerner whose mortal remains repose on the western bank of the Potomac. He was one of us—a slaveholder and a planter. We have studied his history, and find nothing in it to justify submission to wrong. On the contrary, his great fame rests on the solid foundation that, while he was careful to avoid doing wrong to others, he was prompt and decided in repelling wrong. I trust that, in this respect, we profited by his example.

Nor can we find anything in his history to deter us from seceding from the Union, should it fail to fulfil the objects for which it was instituted, by being permanently and hopelessly converted into the means of oppressing instead of protecting us. On the contrary, we find much in his example to encourage us, should we be forced to the extremity of deciding between submission and disunion.

There existed then, as well as now, a union—that between a parent country and her then colonies. It was a union that had much to endear it to the people of the colonies. Washington was born and grew up to manhood under that Union. He acquired his early distinction in its service, and there is every reason to believe that he was devotedly attached to it. But his devotion was a rational one. He was attached to it, not as an end, but as a means to an end. When it failed to fulfil its end, and, instead of affording protection, was converted into the means of oppressing the colonies, he did not hesitate to draw his sword, and head the great movement by which that union was forever severed, and the independence of these States established. This was the great and crowning glory of his life, which has spread his fame over the whole globe, and will transmit it to the latest posterity.

Nor can the plan proposed by the distinguished Senator from Kentucky, nor that of the Administration, save the Union. I shall pass by, without remark, the plan proposed by the Senator, and proceed directly to the consideration of that of the Administration. I, however, assure the distinguished and able Senator that, in taking this course, no disrespect whatever is intended to him or to his plan. I have adopted it, because so many Senators of distinguished abilities have already replied to him.

The plan of the Administration cannot save the Union, because it can have no effect whatever toward satisfying the States composing the Southern section of the Union that they can, consistently with safety and honor, remain in the Union. It is, in fact, but a modification of the Wilmot proviso. It proposes to effect the same object, to exclude the South from all territory acquired by the Mexican treaty. It is well known that the South is united against the Wilmot proviso, and has committed itself by solemn resolutions to resist should it be adopted. Its opposition *is not to the name*, but that which it *proposes to effect.* That the Southern States hold to be unconstitutional, unjust, inconsistent with their equality as members of the common Union, and calculated to destroy irretrievably the equilibrium between the two sections. These objections equally apply to what, for brevity, I will call the executive proviso. There is no difference between it and the Wilmot, except in the mode of effecting the object, and in that respect I must say that the latter is much the least objectionable. It goes to its object openly, boldly, and distinctly. It claims for Congress unlimited power over the Territories, and proposes to assert it over the territories acquired from Mexico by a positive prohibition of slavery. Not so the executive proviso. It takes an indirect course, and, in order to elude the Wilmot proviso, and thereby avoid encountering the united and determined resistance of the South, it denies, by implication, the authority of Congress to legislate for the Territories, and claims the right as belonging exclusively to the inhabitants of the Territories. But to effect the object of excluding the South, it takes care, in the meantime, to let in emigrants freely from the Northern States, and all other quarters, except from the South, which it takes special care to exclude by holding up to them the danger of having their slaves liberated under the Mexican laws. The necessary consequence is to exclude the South from that territory, just as effectually as would the Wilmot proviso.

In claiming the right for the inhabitant, instead of Congress, to legislate for the Territories, in the executive proviso, it assumes that the sovereignty over the Territories is vested in the former; or, to express it in the language used in a resolution offered by one of the Senators from Texas [General Houston, now absent], they have "the same inherent right of self-government as the people in the States." The assumption is utterly unfounded, unconstitutional, without example, and contrary to the entire practice of the Government, from its commencement to the present time, as I shall proceed to show.

The recent movement of individuals in California to form a constitution and a State government, and to appoint Senators and Representatives, is the first fruit of this monstrous assumption. It was the United States who conquered California, and finally acquired it by treaty. The sovereignty of that territory, of course, is vested in them, and not in the individuals who have attempted to form a constitution and a State, without their consent.

Now, if the sovereignty over the Territories is vested in the United States—that is, in the several States composing the Union—and the power of legislating over them is expressly vested in Congress, it follows that the individuals in California who have undertaken to form a constitution and a State have usurped the sovereignty of the State and the authority of Congress, and have acted in open defiance of them both. In other words, what they have done is revolutionary and rebellious in its character, anarchical in its tendency, and calculated to lead to the most dangerous consequences. Had they acted from premeditation and design, it would have been, in fact, actual rebellion; but such is not the case. The blame lies much less upon them than upon those who have induced them to take a course so unconstitutional and dangerous. They have been led into it by language held here, and the course pursued by the executive branch of the Government.

But, it may be asked, what is to be done with California should she not be admitted? I answer, remand her back to the territorial condition, as was done in the case of Tennessee in the early stage of the Government.

Having now shown what cannot save the Union, I return to the question with which I commenced, How can the Union be saved? There is but one way by which it can with any certainty; and that is by a full and final settlement, on the principle of justice, of all the questions at issue between the two sections. The South asks for justice, simple justice, and less she ought not to take. She has no compromise to offer but the Constitution, and no concession or surrender to make. She has already surrendered so much that she has little left to surrender. Such a settlement would go to the root of the evil, and remove all cause of discontent, by satisfying the South, that she could remain honorably and safely in the Union, and thereby it would restore the harmony and fraternal feelings between the sections which existed anterior to the Missouri agitation. Nothing else can, with any certainty, finally and forever settle the questions at issue, and so terminate agitation, and save the Union.

But can this be done? Yes, easily; not by the weaker party, for it can of itself do nothing—not even protect itself—but by the stronger. The North has only to will it to accomplish it—to do justice by conceding to the South an equal right in the acquired territory, and to do her duty by causing the stipulations relative to fugitive slaves to be faithfully fulfille l—to cease the agitation of the slave question, and to provide for the insertion of a provision in the Constitution, by an amendment, which will restore to the South in substance the power she possessed of protecting herself, before the equilibrium between the sections was destroyed by the action of this Government. There will be no difficulty in devising such a provision—one that will protect the South, and which at the same time will improve and strengthen the Government, instead of impairing and weakening it.

But will the North agree to do this? It is for her to answer this question. But, I will say, she cannot refuse, if she has half the love of the Union which she professes to have, or without justly exposing herself to the charge that her love of power and aggrandizement is far greater than her love of the Union. At all events, the responsibility of saving the Union rests on the North, and not the South. The South cannot save it by any act of hers, and the North may save it without any sacrifice whatever, unless to do justice, and to perform her duties under the Constitution, should be regarded by her as a sacrifice.

It is time, Senators, that there should be an open and manly avowal on all sides as to what is intended to be done. If the question is not now settled, it is uncertain whether it ever can hereafter be; and we, as the representatives of the States of this Union, regarded as governments, should come to a distinct understanding as to our respective views, in order to ascertain whether the great questions at issue can be settled or not. If you, who represent the stronger portion, cannot agree to settle them on the broad principle of justice and duty, say so; and let the States we both represent agree to separate and part in peace. If you are unwilling we should part in peace, tell us so, and we shall know what to do, when you reduce the question to submission or resistance. If you remain silent, you will compel us to infer by your acts what you intend. In that case, California will become the test question. If you admit her, under all the difficulties that oppose her admission, you compel us to infer that you intend to exclude us from the whole of the acquired territories, with the intention of destroying irretrievably the equilibrium between the two sections. We would be blind not to perceive, in that case, that your real objects are power and aggrandizement, and infatuated not to act accordingly.

Having faithfully done my duty to the best of my ability, both to the Union and my section, throughout this agitation, I shall have the consolation, let what will come, that I am free from all responsibility.

Senator Webster replied to the arguments of Senator Calhoun.

Mr. President, I wish to speak to-day, not as a Massachusetts man, nor as a Northern man, but as an American, and a member of the Senate of the United States.

It is fortunate that there is a Senate of the United States; a body not yet moved from its propriety, not lost to a just sense of its own dignity and its own high responsibilities, and a body to which the country looks with confidence for wise, moderate, patriotic, and healing counsels. It is not to be denied that we live in the midst of strong agitations, and surrounded by very considerable dangers to our institutions of government. The imprisoned winds are let loose. The east, the west, the north, and the stormy south all combine to throw the whole ocean into commotion, to toss its billows to the skies, and to disclose its

J C Calhoun

profoundest depths. I do not expect, Mr. President, to hold, or to be fit to hold, the helm in this combat of the political elements; but I have a duty to perform, and I mean to perform it with fidelity—not without a sense of the surrounding dangers, but not without hope. I have a part to act, not for my own security or safety, for I am looking out for no fragment upon which to float away from the wreck, if wreck there must be, but for the good of the whole, and the preservation of the whole; and there is that which will keep me to my duty during this struggle, whether the sun and the stars shall appear or shall not appear for many days. I speak to-day for the preservation of the Union. "Hear me for my cause." I speak to-day, out of a solicitous and anxious heart, for the restoration to the country of that quiet and that harmony which make the blessings of this Union so rich and so dear to us all. These are the topics that I propose to myself to discuss; these are the motives, and the sole motives, that influence me in the wish to communicate my opinions to the Senate and the country; and if I can do anything, however little, for the promotion of these ends I shall have accomplished all that I desire.

Senator Webster then related the circumstances which made it imperative that California have an organized government—chiefly the great rush of settlers to the gold country.

It became a very important subject for legislative consideration and legislative decision to provide a proper territorial government for California, yet differences of opinion in the counsels of the Government prevented the establishment of any such territorial government for California at the last session of Congress. Under this state of things, the inhabitants of San Francisco and California—then amounting to a great number of people—in the summer of last year thought it to be their duty to establish a local government. Under the proclamation of General Riley, the people chose delegates to a convention. That convention met at Monterey. They formed a constitution for the State of California, and it was adopted by the people of California in their primary assemblages. Desirous of immediate connection with the United States, its Senators were appointed and Representatives chosen, who have come hither, bringing with them the authentic constitution of the State of California; and they now present themselves, asking in behalf of their State that the State may be admitted into this Union as one of the

United States. This constitution, sir, contains an express prohibition against slavery or involuntary servitude in the State of California. It is said, and I suppose truly, that of the members who composed that convention some sixteen were natives, and had been residents of the slaveholding States, and about twenty-two were from the non-slaveholding States, and the remaining ten members were either native Californians, or old settlers in that country. This prohibition against slavery, it is said, was inserted with entire unanimity.

And it is this circumstance, sir, the prohibition of slavery by that convention, which has contributed to raise—I do not say it has wholly raised—the dispute as to the propriety of the admission of California into the Union under this Constitution. It is not to be denied, Mr. President, whatever reasons were assigned at the commencement of the late war with Mexico, that it was prosecuted for the purpose of the acquisition of territory. And, as the acquisition was to be south of the line of the United States, in warm climates and countries, it was naturally expected by the South that whatever acquisitions were made in that region would be added to the slaveholding portion of the United States. Events have turned out as was not expected, and that expectation has not been realized; and therefore some degree of disappointment and surprise has resulted. In other words, it is obvious that the question which has so long harassed the country, and at times very seriously alarmed the minds of wise and good men, has come upon us for a fresh discussion—the question of slavery in these United States.

Now, sir, upon the general nature, and character, and influence of slavery there exists a wide difference between the Northern portion of this country and the Southern. It is said, on the one side, that, if not the subject of any injunction or direct prohibition in the New Testament, slavery is a wrong; that it is founded merely in the right of the strongest; and that it is an oppression, like all unjust wars—like all those conflicts by which a mighty nation subjects a weaker nation to their will; and that slavery, in its nature, whatever may be said of it in the modifications which have taken place, is not in fact according to the meek spirit of the Gospel. It is not kindly affectioned. It does not "seek another's and not its own." It does not "let the oppressed go free." These are sentiments that are cherished, and recently with greatly augmented force, among the people of the Northern States. It has taken hold of the religious sentiment of that part of the country, as it has more or less taken hold of the religious feelings of a considerable portion of mankind. The South, upon the other side, having been accustomed to this relation between the two races all their lives, from their birth; having been taught in general to treat the subjects of this bondage with care and kindness—and I believe, in general, feeling for them great care and kindness—have yet not taken this view of the subject which I have mentioned. There are thousands of religious men, with consciences as tender as any of their brethren at the North, who do not see the unlawfulness of slavery, and there are more thousands, perhaps, that, whatsoever they may think of it in its origin, and as a matter depending upon natural right, yet take things as they are, and, finding slavery to be an established relation of the society where they live, can see no way in which—let their opinions on the abstract question be what they may—it is in the power of the present generation to relieve themselves from this relation. And, in this respect, candor obliges me to say that I believe they are just as conscientious, many of them—and, of the religious people, all of them—as they are in the North, in holding different opinions.

Senator Webster here referred to the division of religious denominations on slavery. He had read the proceedings of the Methodist Episcopal separation, and had seen no real ground for it. It was the nature of religious men to become warm in such matters, and to go to extremes.

These persons are disposed to mount upon some duty as a war-horse, and to drive furiously on, and upon, and over all other duties that may stand in the way.

There are men who, in times of that sort, and disputes of that sort, deal with morals as with mathematics, thinking what is right may be distinguished from what is wrong with the precision of an algebraic equation. They have, therefore, none too much charity toward others who differ with them. They are apt, too, to think that nothing is good but what is perfect, and that there are no compromises or modifications to be made in submission to difference of opinion, or in deference to other men's judgment. If their perspicacious vision enables them to detect a spot on the face of the sun, they think that a good reason why the sun should be struck down from heaven. They prefer the chance of running into utter darkness to living in heavenly light, if that heavenly light be not absolutely without any imperfection. These are impatient men—too impatient always to give heed to the admission of St. Paul, "that we are not to do evil that good may come"—too impatient to wait for the slow progress of moral causes in the improvement of mankind. They do not remember that the doctrines and the miracles of Jesus Christ have in eighteen hundred years converted only a small portion of the human race; and among the nations that are converted to Christianity they forget how many vices and crimes, public and private, still prevail, and that many of them—public crimes especially, which are offences against the Christian religion—pass without exciting particular regret or indignation. Thus wars are waged, and unjust wars. I do not deny that there may be just wars. There certainly are, but it was the remark of an eminent person, not many years ago, on the other side of the Atlantic, that it was one of the greatest reproaches to human nature that wars were sometimes necessary. The defence of nations sometimes causes a war against the injustice of other nations.

Now, sir, in this state of sentiment, upon the general nature of slavery, lies the cause of a great portion of those unhappy divisions, exasperations, and reproaches which find vent and support in different parts of the Union.

And now let us consider, sir, what was the state of sentiment, North and South, in regard to slavery at the time this Constitution was adopted. Now, it will be found, sir, if we will carry ourselves by historical research back to that day, and ascertain men's opinions by authentic records still existing among us, that there was no great diversity of opinion between the North and the South upon the subject of slavery; and it will be found that both parts of the country held it equally an evil—a moral and political evil. It will not be found that, either at the North or at the South, there was much, though there was some, invective against slavery as inhuman and cruel. The great ground of objection to it was political; that it weakened the social fabric; that, taking the place of free labor, society was less strong and labor was less productive; and, therefore, we find, from all the eminent men of the time, the clearest expression of their opinion that slavery was an evil. And they ascribed it, not without truth, and not without some acerbity of temper and force of language, to the injurious policy of the mother country, who, to favor the navigator, had entailed these evils upon the colonies. The eminent men of the South held that slavery was an evil, a blight, a blast, a mildew, a scourge, and a curse. There are no terms of reprobation of slavery so vehement in the North of that day as in the South. The North was not so much excited against it as the South, and the reason is, I suppose, because there was much less at the North; and the people did not see, or think they saw, the evils so prominently as they were seen, or thought to be seen, at the South.

The Convention reflected the judgment and sentiments of the great men of the South. The question was how to deal with it, and how to deal with it as an evil? Well, they came to this general result. They thought that slavery could not be continued in the country if the importation of slaves were made to cease, and therefore they provided that, after a certain period, the importation might be prevented by the act of the new Government. Twenty years was proposed by some gentlemen—a Northern gentleman, I think—and many of the Southern gentlemen opposed it as being too long. Mr. Madison, especially, was somewhat warm against it. He said it would bring too much of this mischief into the country to allow the importation of slaves for such a period, because we must take along with us, in the whole of this discussion, when we are considering the sentiments and opinions in which this constitutional provision originated, that the conviction of all men was that, if the importation of slaves ceased, the white race would multiply faster than the black race, and that slavery would therefore gradually wear out and expire. It may not be improper here to allude to that —I had almost said celebrated—opinion of Mr. Madison. You observe, sir, that the term slave, or slavery, is not used in the Constitution. The Constitution does not require that "fugitive slaves" shall be delivered up. It requires that "persons bound to service in one State, and escaping into another, shall be delivered up." Mr. Madison opposed the introduction of the term slave, or slavery, into the Constitution; for he said he did not wish to see it recognized by the Constitution of the United States of America that there could be property in men. Now, it was in the summer of 1787, the very time when the convention in Philadelphia was framing this Constitution, that the Congress in New York was framing the Ordinance of 1787. They passed that ordinance on the 13th of July, 1787, at New York, the very month—perhaps the very day—on which these questions about the importation of slaves, and the character of slavery, were debated in the convention at Philadelphia. And, so far as we can now learn, there was a perfect concurrence of opinion between these respective bodies; and it resulted in this ordinance of 1787, excluding slavery, as applied to all the territory over which the Congress of the United States had jurisdiction, and that was all the territory northwest of the Ohio.

IV—14

An honorable member, whose health does not allow him to be here to-day——

A SENATOR.—He is here. (Referring to Mr. Calhoun.)

MR. WEBSTER.—I am very happy to hear that he is—may he long be in health and the enjoyment of it to serve his country—said the other day that he considered this ordinance as the first in the series of measures calculated to enfeeble the South, and deprive them of their just participation in the benefits and privileges of this Government. He says, very properly, that it was done under the old Confederation, and before this Constitution went into effect; but my present purpose is only to say, Mr. President, that it was done with the entire and unanimous concurrence of the whole South.

But soon a change began at the North and the South, and a severance of opinion soon showed itself—the North growing much more warm and strong against slavery, and the South growing much more warm and strong in its support. Sir, there is no generation of mankind whose opinions are not subject to be influenced by what appears to them to be their present, and emergent, and exigent interest. I impute to the South no particularly interested view in the change which has come over her. I impute to her certainly no dishonest view. All that has happened has been natural.

Senator Webster ascribed the change in Southern sentiment to the sudden uprising and growth of the cotton industry.

The age of cotton became a golden age for our Southern brethren. It gratified their desire for improvement and accumulation at the same time that it excited it. The desire grew by what it fed upon, and there soon came to be an eagerness for other territory—a new area or new areas for the cultivation of the cotton crop; and measures were brought about, somewhat rapidly, one after another, under the lead of Southern men at the head of the Government—they having a majority in both branches of the Government—to accomplish their ends. In 1802, in pursuit of the idea of opening a new cotton region, the United States obtained a cession from Georgia of the whole of her Western territory, now embracing the rich and growing State of Alabama. In 1803 Louisiana was purchased from France, out of which the States of Louisiana, Arkansas, and Missouri have been framed, as slaveholding States. In 1819 the cession of Florida was made, bringing another cession of slaveholding property and territory. Sir, the honorable member from South Carolina thought he saw in certain operations of the Government, such as the manner of collecting the revenue, and the tendency of those measures to promote emigration into the country, what accounts for the more rapid growth of the North than the South. He thinks they were not the operation of time, but of the system of government established under this Constitution. That is a matter of opinion. To a certain extent it may be so; but it does not seem to me that, if any operation of the Government could be shown in any degree to have promoted the population, and growth, and wealth of the North, it is much more sure that there are sundry important and distinct operations of the Government, about which no man can doubt, tending to promote, and which absolutely have promoted, the increase of the slave interest and the slave territory of the South. Allow me to say that it was not time that brought in Louisiana; it was the act of men. It was not time that brought in Florida; it was the act of men. And, lastly, sir, to complete those acts of men who have contributed so much to enlarge the area and the sphere of the institution of slavery, Texas—great, and vast, and illimitable Texas—was added to the Union, as a slave State, in 1845; and that, sir, pretty much closed the whole chapter and settled the whole account.

And I now say, sir, as the proposition upon which I stand this day, and upon the truth and firmness of which I intend to act until it is overthrown, that there is not, at this moment, within the United States, or any Territory of the United States, a single foot of land, the character of which, in regard to its being free-soil territory or slave territory, is not fixed by some law, and some irrepealable law, beyond the power of the action of this Government.

Now, as to California and New Mexico, I hold slavery to be excluded from those Territories by a law even superior to that which admits and sanctions it in Texas—I mean the law of nature—of physical geography—the law of the formation of the earth. That law settles forever, with a strength beyond all terms of human enactment, that slavery cannot exist in California or New Mexico. This country is fixed for freedom to as many persons as shall ever live there by as irrepealable, and a more irrepealable, law than the law that attaches to the right of holding slaves in Texas; and I will say further that, if a resolution, or a law, were now before us to provide a territorial government for New Mexico, I would not vote to put any prohibition into it whatever. The use of such a prohibition would be idle as it respects any effect it would have upon the Territory, and I would not take pains to reaffirm an ordinance of nature, nor to reënact the will of God. And I would put in no Wilmot proviso for the purpose of a taunt or a reproach. I would put into it no evidence of the votes of superior power, to wound the pride, even whether a just pride, a rational pride, or an irrational pride—to wound the pride of the gentlemen who belong to the Southern States. I propose to inflict no such wound upon anybody, unless something essentially important to the country and efficient to the preservation of liberty and freedom is to be effected.

The Senator then discussed the mutual recrimination of North and South as tending to alienate the sections. Passing by as matters of dispute the other complaints of the South which had been enumerated by Senator Calhoun, he admitted that one complaint was just, namely, the Northern State legislatures had tried to evade the constitutional obligation to return fugitive slaves.

I have always thought that the Constitution addressed itself to the legislatures of the States themselves, or to the States themselves. When it is said that a person escaping into another State and becoming, therefore, within the jurisdiction of that State shall be delivered up, it seems to me the import of the passage is that the State itself, in obedience to the Constitution, shall cause him to be delivered up. But, when the subject, some years ago, was before the Supreme Court of the United States, the majority of the judges held that the power to cause fugitives from service to be delivered up was a power to be exercised under the authority of this Government. I do not know, on the whole, that it may not have been a fortunate decision. My habit is to respect the result of judicial deliberations and the solemnity of judicial decisions. But, as it now stands, the business of seeing that these fugitives are delivered up resides in the power of Congress and the national judicature, and my friend at the head of the Judiciary Committee has a bill on the subject now before the Senate, with some amendments to it, which I propose to support, with all its provisions, to the fullest extent. And I put it to all the sober and sound minds at the North as a question of morals and a question of conscience: What right have they, in all their legislative capacity, or any other, to endeavor to get round this Constitution, to embarrass the free exercise of the rights secured by the Constitution to the persons whose slaves escape from them? None at all—none at all. Wherever I go and whenever I speak on the subject— and when I speak here I desire to speak to the whole North— I say that the South has been injured in this respect, and has a right to complain; and the North has been too careless of what I think the Constitution peremptorily and emphatically enjoins upon it as a duty.

Complaint has been made against certain resolutions that emanate from legislatures at the North, and are sent here to us, not only on the subject of slavery in this District, but some- times recommending Congress to consider the means of abolish- ing slavery in the States. I should be sorry to be called upon to present any resolutions here which could not be referable to any committee or any power in Congress, and, therefore, I should be unwilling to receive from the legislature of Massachu- setts any instructions to present resolutions expre. ive of any opinion whatever on the subject of slavery, as it exists at the present moment in the States, for two reasons: because, first, I do not consider that the legislature of Massachusetts has any- thing to do with it; and, next, I do not consider that I, as her representative here, have anything to do with it. Sir, it has become, in my opinion, quite too common; and, if the legisla- tures of the States do not like that opinion, they have a great deal more power to put it down than I have to uphold it. I will simply say this: if there be any matter of interest pending in this body while I am a member of it in which Massachusetts has an interest of her own not adverse to the general interest of the country, I shall pursue her instructions with gladness of heart and with all the efficiency which I can bring to it. But, if the question be one which affects her interest and at the same time affects the interests of all other States, I shall no more regard her political wishes or instructions than I would regard the wishes of a man who might appoint me an arbitrator or referee to decide some question of important private right and who might *instruct* me to decide in his favor. If ever there was a government upon earth, it is this Government; if ever there was a body upon earth, it is this body, which should consider itself as composed by agreement of all, appointed by some, but organized by the general consent of all, sitting here under the solemn obligations of oath and conscience to do that which they think is best for the good of the whole.

The Senator then discussed the Abolition societies. Though he knew that thousands of their members were honest, well-meaning persons, he deplored the results of their agitation as wholly mischievous, defeating, indeed, their professed purpose. Instead of winning the South to their views, they stirred up resentment in that quarter against them until it was now forbidden to speak in any way against slavery, whereas before the abolition societies were organized the subject was freely discussed.

Let any gentleman who doubts of this recur to the debates in the Virginia House of Delegates in 1832 and he will see with what freedom a proposition, made by John Randolph, for the gradual abolition of slavery was discussed in that body. Every one spoke of slavery as he thought; very ignominious and disparaging names and epithets were applied to it. The debates in the House of Delegates on that occasion, I believe, were all published. They were read by every colored man who could read, and, if there were any who could not read, those debates were read to them by others. At that time Virginia was not unwilling nor afraid to discuss this question and to let that part of her population know as much of it as they could learn. That was in 1832. These abolition societies commenced their course of action in 1835. It is said—I do not know how true it may be—that they sent incendiary publications into the slave States; at any event, they attempted to arouse, and did arouse, a very strong feeling; in other words, they created great agitation in the North against Southern slavery. Well, what was the result? The bonds of the slaves were bound more firmly than before; their rivets were more strongly fastened. Public opinion, which, in Virginia, had begun to be exhibited against slavery and was opening out for the discussion of the question, drew back and shut itself up in its castle. I wish to know whether anybody in Virginia can now talk as Mr. Randolph, Governor McDowell, and others talked there openly and sent their remarks to the press in 1832. We all know the fact, and we all know the cause, and everything that this agitating people have done has been, not to enlarge but to restrain, not to set free but to bind faster the slave population of the South.

It is my firm opinion that, within the last twenty years, as much money has been collected and paid to the abolition societies, abolition presses, and abolition lecturers as would purchase the freedom of every slave—man, woman, and child—in the State of Maryland, and send them all to Liberia. I have no doubt of it. But I have yet to learn that the benevolence of these abolition societies has at any time taken that particular turn. [Laughter.]

Again, sir, the violence of the press is complained of. The press violent! Why, sir, the press is violent everywhere. There are outrageous reproaches in the North against the South, and there are reproaches in not much better taste in the South against the North. Sir, the extremists of both parts of this country are violent; they mistake loud and violent talk for eloquence and for reason. They think that he who talks loudest reasons the best. And this we must expect when the press is free, as it is here—and I trust always will be—for, with all its licentiousness and all its evil, the entire and absolute freedom of the press is essential to the preservation of government on the basis of a free Constitution. Wherever it exists there will be foolish paragraphs and violent paragraphs in the press, as there are, I am sorry to say, foolish speeches and violent speeches in both Houses of Congress. In truth, sir, I must say that, in my opinion, the vernacular tongue of the country has become greatly vitiated, depraved, and corrupted by the style of our congressional debates. [Laughter.] And, if it were possible for our debates in Congress to vitiate the principles of the people as much as they have depraved their taste, I should cry out "God save the Republic!"

There are also complaints of the North against the South. The first and gravest is that the North adopted the Constitution, recognizing the existence of slavery in the States, and recognizing the right, to a certain extent, of representation of the slaves in Congress, under a state of sentiment and expectation which do not now exist; and that, by events, by circumstances, by the eagerness of the South to acquire territory and extend their slave population, the North finds itself, in regard to the influence of the South and the North, of the free States and the slave States, where it never did expect to find itself when they entered the compact of the Constitution. They complain, therefore, that, instead of slavery being regarded as an evil, as it was then, an evil which all hoped would be extinguished gradually, it is now regarded by the South as an institution to be cherished and preserved and extended—an institution which the South has already extended to the utmost of her power by the acquisition of new territory. Well, then, passing from that, everybody in the North reads; and everybody reads whatsoever the newspapers contain; and the newspapers, some of them—especially those presses to which I have alluded—are careful to spread about among the people every reproachful sentiment

uttered by any Southern man bearing at all against the North
—everything that is calculated to exasperate, to alienate; and
there are many such things, as everybody will admit, from the
South, or some portion of it, which are spread abroad among
the reading people; and they do exasperate, and alienate, and
produce a most mischievous effect upon the public mind at the
North. An honorable member from Louisiana addressed us the
other day on this subject. I suppose there is not a more amiable
and worthy gentleman in this chamber, nor a gentleman who
would be more slow to give offence to anybody, and he did not
mean in his remarks to give offence. But what did he say?
Why, sir, he took pains to run a contrast between the slaves
of the South and the laboring people of the North, giving the
preference in all points of condition, and comfort, and happiness,
to the slaves of the South. The honorable member doubtless
did not suppose that he gave any offence, or did any injustice.
He was merely expressing his opinion. But does he know how
remarks of that sort will be received by the laboring people of
the North? Why, who are the laboring people of the North?
They are the North. They are the people who cultivate their
own farms with their own hands—freeholders, educated men,
independent men. And what can these people think when so
respectable and worthy a gentleman as the member from Louisiana undertakes to prove that the absolute ignorance, and the
abject slavery, of the South is more in conformity with the high
purposes and destinies of immortal, rational human beings than
the educated, the independent free laborers of the North?

There is a more tangible and irritating cause of grievance at
the North. Free blacks are constantly employed in the vessels of
the North, generally as cooks and stewards. When the vessel ar-
rives these free colored men are taken on shore by the police or
municipal authority, imprisoned and kept in prison till the vessel is again ready to sail. This is not only irritating but exceedingly inconvenient in practice, and seems altogether unjustifiable
and oppressive. The mission of Samuel Hoar, of Massachusetts,
some time ago to South Carolina was a well-intended effort to
remove this cause of complaint. The North thinks such imprisonment illegal and unconstitutional; as the cases occur constantly
and frequently, they think it is a great grievance.

Now, sir, so far as any of these grievances have their foundation in matters of law they can be redressed, and ought to
be redressed; and, so far as they have foundation in matters
of opinion, in sentiment, in mutual crimination and recrimination, all that we can do is to endeavor to allay the agitation

and cultivate a better feeling and more fraternal sentiments between the South and the North.

Mr. President, I should much prefer to have heard from every member on this floor declarations of opinion that this Union should never be dissolved than the declaration of opinion that, in any case, under the pressure of any circumstances, such a dissolution was possible. I hear with pain, and anguish, and distress the word secession, especially when it falls from the lips of those who are eminently patriotic and known to the country and known all over the world for their political services. Secession! Peaceable secession! Sir, your eyes and mine are never destined to see that miracle. The dismemberment of this vast country without convulsion! The breaking up of the fountains of the great deep without ruffling the surface! Who is so foolish—I beg everybody's pardon—as to expect to see any such thing? Sir, he who sees these States now revolving in harmony around a common center and expects to see them quit their places and fly off without convulsion, may look the next hour to see the heavenly bodies rush from their spheres and jostle against each other in the realms of space without producing the crush of the universe. There can be no such thing as a peaceable secession. Peaceable secession is an utter impossibility. Is the great Constitution under which we live here—covering this whole country—is it to be thawed and melted away by secession as the snows on the mountain melt under the influence of a vernal sun—disappear almost unobserved, and die off? No, sir! no, sir! I will not state what might produce the disruption of the States; but, sir, I see it as plainly as I see the sun in heaven—I see that disruption must produce such a war as I will not describe in its twofold characters.

Peaceable secession! peaceable secession! The concurrent agreement of all the members of this great Republic to separate! A voluntary separation with alimony on one side and on the other. Why, what would be the result? Where is the line to be drawn? What States are to secede? What is to remain American? What am I to be—an American no longer? Where is the flag of the Republic to remain? Where is the eagle still to tower? or is he to cower, and shrink, and fall to the ground? Why, sir, our ancestors—our fathers, and our grandfathers, those of them that are yet living among us with prolonged lives—would rebuke and reproach us; and our children, and our grandchildren would cry out: Shame upon us! if we, of this generation, should dishonor these ensigns of the power of the Government and the harmony of the Union, which is every day felt

among us with so much joy and gratitude. What is to become
of the army? What is to become of the navy? What is to become of the public lands? How is each of the thirty States
to defend itself? I know, although the idea has not been
stated distinctly, there is to be a Southern confederacy. I
do not mean, when I allude to this statement, that any
one seriously contemplates such a state of things. I do
not mean to say that it is true, but I have heard it suggested elsewhere that that idea has originated in a design to
separate. I am sorry, sir, that it has ever been thought of,
talked of, or dreamed of in the wildest flights of human imagina-
tion. But the idea must be of a separation, including the slave
States upon one side and the free States on the other. Sir,
there is not—I may express myself too strongly perhaps—but
some things, some moral things, are almost as impossible as
other natural or physical things; and I hold the idea of a separation of these States—those that are free to form one government and those that are slaveholding to form another—as a
moral impossibility. We could not separate the States by any
such line if we were to draw it. We could not sit down here
to-day and draw a line of separation that would satisfy any
five men in the country. There are natural causes that would
keep and tie us together, and there are social and domestic
relations which we could not break if we would, and which we
should not if we could. Sir, nobody can look over the face of
this country at the present moment—nobody can see where its
population is the most dense and growing—without being ready
to admit, and compelled to admit, that, ere long, America will
be in the valley of the Mississippi.

Well, now, sir, I beg to inquire what the wildest enthusiast
has to say on the possibility of cutting off that river and leaving free States at its source and its branches and slave States
down near its mouth? Pray, sir—pray, sir, let me say to the
people of this country that these things are worthy of their
pondering and of their consideration. Here, sir, are five millions of freemen in the free States north of the River Ohio: can
anybody suppose that this population can be severed by a line
that divides them from the territory of a foreign and an alien
government down somewhere, the Lord knows where, upon the
lower banks of the Mississippi? What will become of Missouri?
Will she join the arrondissement of the slave States? Shall the
man from the Yellowstone and the Platte be connected in the
new republic with the man who lives on the southern extremity
of the Cape of Florida? Sir, I am ashamed to pursue this line

of remark. I dislike it—I have an utter disgust for it. I would rather hear of natural blasts and mildews, war, pestilence, and famine than to hear gentlemen talk of secession. To break up! to break up this great Government! to dismember this great country! to astonish Europe with an act of folly such as Europe for two centuries has never beheld in any government! No, sir; no, sir! There will be no secession. Gentlemen are not serious when they talk of secession.

And now, Mr. President, instead of speaking of the possibility or utility of secession, instead of dwelling in these caverns of darkness, instead of groping with those ideas so full of all that is horrid and horrible, let us come out into the light of day; let us enjoy the fresh air of liberty and union; let us cherish those hopes which belong to us; let us devote ourselves to those great objects that are fit for our consideration and our action; let us raise our conceptions to the magnitude and the importance of the duties that devolve upon us; let our comprehension be as broad as the country for which we act, our aspirations as high as its certain destiny; let us not be pigmies in a case that calls for men.

Never did there devolve on any generation of men higher trusts than now devolve upon us for the preservation of this Constitution, and the harmony and peace of all who are destined to live under it. Let us make our generation one of the strongest, and the brightest, links in that golden chain which is destined, I fully believe, to grapple the people of all the States to this Constitution for ages to come. It is a great popular constitutional Government, guarded by legislation, by law, by judicature, and defended by the whole affections of the people. No monarchical throne presses these States together; no iron chain of despotic power encircles them; they live and stand upon a government popular in its form, representative in its character, founded upon principles of equality, and calculated, we hope, to last forever. In all its history it has been beneficent; it has trodden down no man's liberty; it has crushed no State. Its daily respiration, its liberty and patriotism; its yet youthful veins are full of enterprise, courage, and honorable love of glory and renown. It has received a vast addition of territory. Large before, the country has now, by recent events, become vastly larger. This Republic now extends with a vast breadth across the whole continent. The two great seas of the world wash the one and the other shore. We realize on a mighty scale the beautiful description of the ornamental edging of the buckler of Achilles—

"Now the broad shield complete the artist crowned,
With his last hand, and poured the ocean round;
In living silver seemed the waves to roll,
And beat the buckler's verge, and bound the whole."

On motion of Senator Henry S. Foote [Miss.] the
Clay resolutions were, on March 12, 1852, referred to
a Committee of Thirteen, who were instructed to "mature some scheme of compromise for the adjustment of

WEBSTER STEALING CLAY'S THUNDER WHILE FOOTE IS TALKING THE SENATE
TO SLEEP

From the collection of the New York Historical Society

all pending questions growing out of the institution of
slavery."

The question of this reference was warmly debated,
developing into a discussion of all the aspects of slavery.
While interesting, the discussion brought forward no
new arguments and is here omitted.

The debate on the Clay compromise was interrupted
by the death of Senator Calhoun on March 31, 1850. Extended tributes were paid to him in the Senate and the

House by his Northern political opponents as well as by the statesmen of the South.

On April 3 John Bell [Tenn.] submitted in the Senate certain resolutions along the line of those of Senator Clay, but more favorable to the South, and more specific, especially in the matter of the return of fugitive slaves. They were referred to the Committee of Thirteen if it should be appointed.

Finally on April 18, 1850, the question was put to form the Committee of Thirteen and decided in the affirmative by a vote of 30 to 22. Henry Clay [Ky.] was appointed chairman of the committee. The other members were representative equally of the North and the South.

On May 8 Senator Clay presented the report of the committee, of which the following is a digest. In the first recommendation alone the committee was unanimous.

REPORT OF THE COMMITTEE OF THIRTEEN

1. In the case of a new State to be carved out of Texas, the initiative to be taken by the State and the question of slavery therein settled by a vote of the inhabitants. Constitutionality of the admission of States (including Texas) in the Louisiana Purchase not to be inquired into, the country having acquiesced in former admissions.

2. Irregularity of California's actions in applying for admission (such as the formation of a constitution) to be overlooked for similar reasons and her application to be granted.

3. New Mexico and Utah to be organized as Territories.

4. The admission of California into the Union and the territorial organization of New Mexico and Utah to be combined in one bill because of the common condition of acquisition by the United States, their common boundaries being fixed by the act, and because of the fact that certain Senators would not vote for the admission of the State except upon condition of the organization of the Territories. "Every measure," says the report, "may contain objectionable features to some." The question to be decided is, whether the good the measure contains is of greater amount and neutralizes anything exceptionable in it. "As nothing human is perfect, for the sake of that harmony so desirable in such a confederacy as this, we must be reconciled to secure as much as we can of what we wish."

5. Omission in the joint bill of the Wilmot proviso on the one hand and any provision for the introduction of slavery on the other, the proviso being practically needless and its insertion an affront to the South, and the introduction of slavery being impracticable and an affront to the people of California who have declared against it. Recommendation that, in future legislation of this character the question of slavery be left to the people of the region affected, and so remove a source of discord from the Union. "As for California," says the report, "far from feeling her sensibility affected by her being associated with other kindred measures—she ought to rejoice and be highly gratified that, in entering into the Union, she may have contributed to the tranquillity and happiness of the great family of States of which, it is to be hoped, she may one day be a distinguished member."

6. Proposal that Texas relinquish territorial claims made by New Mexico for a pecuniary consideration made by the United States Government, the Government reimbursing itself by the sales of these relinquished lands. This boundary question to be incorporated in the joint bill aforesaid.

7. Amendment of the existing law (of 1793) more effectually to provide for the recovery of fugitive slaves, and, at the same time, to prevent abuses in such recovery. The report says:

"The text of the Constitution is quite clear: 'No person held to labor or service in one State, *under the laws thereof,* escaping into another, shall, in consequence of any law or regulation therein, be discharged from such service or labor, but *shall be delivered up* on the claim of the party to whom such service or labor may be due.'

"It is now well known and incontestable that citizens in slaveholding States encounter the greatest difficulty in obtaining the benefit of this provision of the Constitution. The attempt to recapture a fugitive is almost always a subject of great irritation and excitement, and often leads to most unpleasant, if not perilous, collisions. An owner of a slave, it is quite notorious, cannot pursue his property, for the purpose of its recovery, in some of the States, without imminent personal hazard. This is a deplorable state of things which ought to be remedied. The law of 1793 has been found wholly ineffectual and requires more stringent enactments. There is, especially, a deficiency in the number of public functionaries authorized to afford aid in the seizure and arrest of fugitives. Various States have declined to afford aid and coöperation in the surrender of fugitives from labor, as the committee believe, from a misconception of their duty arising under the Constitution of the United States. It is true that a decision of the Supreme Court of the United States has given countenance to them in withholding their assistance. But the committee cannot but believe that the intention of the Supreme Court has been misunderstood. They cannot but think that that court merely meant that laws of the several States which created obstacles in the way of the recovery of fugitives were not authorized by the Constitution, and not that State laws affording facilities in the recovery of fugitives were forbidden by that instrument.

"The non-slaveholding States, whatever sympathies any of their citizens may feel for persons who escape from other States, cannot discharge themselves from an obligation to enforce the Constitution of the United States. All parts of the instrument being dependent upon, and connected with, each other ought to be fairly and justly enforced. If some of the States may seek to exonerate themselves from one portion of the Constitution, other States may then endeavor to evade the performance of other portions of it; and thus the instrument, in some of its most important provisions, might become inoperative and invalid.

"In all cases of the arrest, within a State, of persons charged with offences; in all cases of the pursuit of fugitives from justice from one State to another State; in all cases of extradition provided for by treaties between foreign powers—the proceeding uniformly is summary. It has never been thought necessary to apply in cases of that kind the forms and ceremonies of a final trial. And, when that trial does take place, it is in the State or country from which the party has fled, and not in that in which he has found refuge. By the express language of the Constitution, whether the fugitive is held to service or labor or not, is to be determined *by the laws of the State from which he fled;* and, consequently, it is most proper that the tribunals of that State should expound and administer its own laws. If there have been any instances of abuse in the erroneous arrest of fugitives from service or labor the committee have not obtained knowledge of them. They believe that none such have occurred, and that such are not likely to occur. But, in order to guard against the possibility of their occurrence, the committee have prepared, and herewith report, a section to be added to the fugitive bill now pending before the Senate. According to this section, the owner of a fugitive from service or labor is, when practicable, to carry with him to the State in which the person is found, a record, from a competent tribunal, adjudicating the facts of elopement and slavery, with a general description of the fugitive.''

The committee submitted a bill for the form of trial of fugitives in the States whence they had fled. In concluding comment on the Fugitive Law, it said:

''If, in its practical operation, it shall be found insufficient, and, if no adequate remedy can be devised for the restoration to their owners of fugitive slaves, those owners will have a just title to indemnity out of the treasury of the United States.''

8. Slavery should not be abolished in the District of Columbia because, without entering in the question of the power of Congress to do so, this is inexpedient, as it would excite alarm in the slave States. Besides, the number of slaves in the District is rapidly diminishing. The slave trade, however, should be abolished in the District.

Bills were presented by the committee to execute its several recommendations.

The anti-slavery sentiment in the country was outraged by the abandonment, on the part of some of the Northern members of the committee, of the Wilmot proviso. The indignation was especially directed against Daniel Webster, who had voted with the Southern Senators on this point. The anti-slavery press charged him with treason to the cause of freedom, and John Greenleaf Whittier, rather in sorrow than in anger, wrote a poem upon his defection entitled ''Ichabod,'' i. e., ''The glory has departed.''

The debate on the ''Omnibus Bill,'' as the compromise measure of the Committee of Thirteen was now generally termed, was resumed in the Senate on July 22. Henry Clay made a long and eloquent plea in favor of its passage. In the course of his remarks he inferentially alluded to Representative R. Barnwell Rhett [S. C.] as a ''disunionist.'' This was replied to by Senator R. W. Barnwell [S. C.], who drew from Senator Clay the affirmation that if Mr. Rhett put into execution the threats to which he (Senator Clay) had alluded he would be a traitor.

The forebodings of Senator Clay that the ''Omnibus Bill'' would not be passed were thoroughly realized. One by one it was shorn of its members until all that remained of it was the provision for the territorial organization of Utah. It was received in this form on July 31 by roars of laughter from the Senate. On August 7 the bill fixing the boundaries of Texas was passed in the Senate, and on August 12 the bill to admit California into the Union (by a vote of 34 to 18). A number of Southern Senators entered a protest against

"NO HIGHER LAW"
From the collection of the New York Historical Society

the conditions of the California bill on the ground that "an odious discrimination was made against the property of the fifteen slaveholding States, who are thus deprived of the equality which the Constitution manifestly designs" and that the precedent was thereby established for the future admission of States into the Union with a virtual exclusion of the rights of Southern citizens to carry their slaves thither. This protest was laid on the table on August 15 by a vote of 22 to 19.

On the same day the bill organizing New Mexico was passed in the Senate by a vote of 27 to 10. The bill organizing Utah was also passed. The House concurred in these bills with an amendment that no citizen in the Territories "should be deprived of his life, liberty, or property except by judgment of his peers or the laws of the land." On September 9 this amendment was accepted by the Senate, and the bills received the signature of Millard Fillmore, who had succeeded to the presidency on the death of Zachary Taylor, July 9, 1850.

CHAPTER VI

The Fugitive Slave Law

Passage of the Fugitive Act of 1850—Personal Liberty Laws Passed by Northern States to Nullify the Act—Passage of Bill to Suppress the Slave Trade in the District of Columbia—"A New Alignment of Parties on Slavery": Speech in the House of Joshua R. Giddings [O.], on the Fugitive Slave Law—The Nashville Convention "Fire-Eaters" vs. Unionists in the South—The Union Party in the North—Manifesto of Representative Alexander H. Stephens [Ga.], Senator Henry Clay [Ky.], et al., Against Agitating the Slavery Question—Rescue of the Fugitive Slave Shadrach: Proclamation and Message Concerning It by President Fillmore—Debate in the Senate on the Message: in Favor, Clay, Jeremiah Clemens [Ala.], Stephen A. Douglas [Ill.], John M. Berrien [Ga.], Solomon U. Downs [La.]; Opposed, John P. Hale [N. H.], John Davis [Mass.], Salmon P. Chase [O.], R. Barnwell Rhett [S. C.], Jefferson Davis [Miss.]—Secession Declaration of the Southern Rights Association—Triumph of the Union Party in the South—Joint Debate Between Henry S. Foote (Unionist) and Jefferson Davis (Conditional Secessionist) in Gubernatorial Campaign in Mississippi—Speaking Tour of Daniel Webster in New York and Virginia, Upholding Fugitive Slave Law—Election of Charles Sumner [Mass.] and Benjamin Wade [O.], Anti-Slavery Men, to the Senate—President Fillmore in Annual Message (1851) Again Urges Enforcement of the Fugitive Slave Law.

EARLY in the session of 1849-50 the Judiciary Committee of the Senate reported a bill on the subject of the return of fugitive slaves. After various substitutions and amendments the bill was passed late in the session by a vote of 27 to 12, more than 20 Senators dodging the issue by refraining from voting.

As approved by President Fillmore September 18, 1850, the bill consisted of ten sections, an abstract of which is as follows: (1) the powers of judges under the act of 1793 were now given to United States commissioners; (2) the territorial courts were also to have

227

the power of appointing such commissioners; (3) all United States courts were so to enlarge the number of commissioners as to give facilities for the arrest of fugitive slaves; (4) commissioners were to have concurrent jurisdiction with United States judges in giving certificates to claimants and ordering the removal of fugitive slaves; (5) United States marshals and deputies were required to execute writs under the act, the penalty for refusal being a fine of $1,000, the marshal being further liable on his bond for the full value of any slave escaping from his custody "with or without the assent" of the marshal or his deputies; the commissioners or officers appointed by them were empowered to call the bystanders to help execute writs, and all good citizens were required to aid and assist when required; (6) on affidavit before any officer authorized to administer an oath, United States courts or commissioners were to give the claimant a certificate and authority to remove his fugitive slave whence he had escaped; in no case was the testimony of the fugitive to be admitted in evidence, and the certificate, with the seal of the court, was to be conclusive evidence of the claimant's title, thus cutting off any real benefit of the writ of *habeas corpus* from the fugitive; (7) imprisonment for six months, a fine of $1,000 and civil damages of $1,000 to the claimant were to be the punishment for obstructing an arrest, attempting a rescue, or harboring a fugitive after notice; (8) commissioners were to be paid fees of $10 when a certificate was granted, and of $5 when their decision was in favor of the alleged fugitive; fees of other officers were to follow the rules of the court; (9) on affidavit by the claimant that he apprehended a rescue, the marshal was not to surrender the fugitive to the claimant at once, but was first to take him to the State whence he had fled, employing any assistance necessary to overcome the rescuing force; (10) any claimant, by affidavit before any court of record in his own State or territory, might obtain a record with a general description of the fugitive, and an authenticated copy of such record was to be conclusive evidence, on proof of the identity of the fugitive, for issuing a certificate in any State or Territory to which the slave had fled.

The passage of the act, says Alexander Johnston in his "American Political History," gave a sudden and great impetus to the search for fugitive slaves in the North which was accompanied by various revolting circumstances, brutality in the captors, bloodshed by the captors or captured, or both, and attempted suicide to avoid arrest. From many localities in the North, persons who had long been residents were suddenly seized and taken South as fugitive slaves; and these latter arrests were more efficacious than the former in rousing Northern opposition to the law, for they seemed to show that not merely the execution but the principle of the law was unjust and illegal. Margaret Garner's attempted murder of her children in Ohio to save them from slavery,[1] and Anthony Burns's arrest in Boston,[2] were the cases which made most noise at the time.

The political consequence of the passage of the Fugitive Slave law of 1850 was the demand, first by the Free Soil party, and then by many members of the Republican party, for the repeal of the Fugitive Slave law, which the South considered irrepealable, as part of a compromise. The success of the Republican party in 1860 by a vote of the North was therefore construed by secessionists at the South as a final refusal by the North to enforce the Compromise of 1850, and was the principal excuse for secession.

The Fugitive Slave law was not finally repealed until June 28, 1864.

PERSONAL LIBERTY LAWS

In order to nullify the act within a few years after its passage many Northern States passed "Personal Liberty" laws.

These laws generally prohibited the use of the State's jails for detaining fugitives; provided State officers under various names throughout the State to act as counsel for persons alleged to be fugitives; se-

[1] January 27, 1856.
[2] May 27, 1854.

cured to all such persons the benefits of *habeas corpus* and trial by jury; required the identity of the fugitive to be proved by two witnesses; forbade State judges and officers to issue writs or give any assistance to the claimant, and imposed a heavy fine and imprisonment for the crime of forcibly seizing or representing as a slave any free person with intent to reduce him to slavery.

The Fugitive Slave law and the Personal Liberty laws, says Professor Johnston, together show plainly that the Compromise of 1850 was far worse than labor lost. It gave the South a law to which it had no title; even R. Barnwell Rhett, in the South Carolina secession convention, declared that he had never considered the Fugitive Slave law constitutional. It thus provoked the passage of the equally unconstitutional Personal Liberty laws in the North. Each section, ignoring the other's complaints, exhausted its own patience in calling for a redress which neither was willing to accord first.

SUPPRESSION OF SLAVE TRADE IN DISTRICT OF COLUMBIA

With the Fugitive Slave bill was passed that for the suppression of the slave trade in the District of Columbia.

In his annual message at the opening of Congress in December, 1850, President Fillmore declared himself in favor of the enforcement of the Fugitive Slave law.

Upon this declaration and the high officer who made it Joshua R. Giddings [O.] spoke as follows in the House of Representatives on December 9:

A NEW ALIGNMENT OF PARTIES ON SLAVERY

JOSHUA R. GIDDINGS, M. C.

No man had ever come into the presidential chair who so unceremoniously cast aside and repudiated the important pledges of his friends and his party. No public man of high standing, from the free States, has so suddenly and so boldly abjured the cause of freedom and, before the world, pledged fealty to the slave power, saving and excepting his Secretary of State [Daniel Webster], whose counsels he appears to have adopted.

Mr. Giddings charged the President with partiality toward the South in the execution of the laws. He had not removed nor even reproved Federal officers in that section who had violated the mails, seeking to suppress anti-slavery literature.

He sees the free colored citizens of the free States seized, imprisoned, and sold into bondage by Southern men. He witnesses this transcendent outrage upon the laws, upon the Constitution, and upon humanity in perfect silence; he does not even hint at their existence. He has seen the agents of Massachusetts driven by mob violence from South Carolina and Louisiana when sent there to sustain the legal rights of the citizens of that State now held in slavery. He knew that no Northern State nor individual could rescue those citizens from the chains of servitude. Upon outrages more aggravated than any that have ever occurred under this Government he makes no comment.

Sir, the House and the country must see that the only sympathy exhibited in the message is for *slavery;* he has none for freedom.

Mr. Chairman, our opposition to the fugitive law is based upon the soundest principles of ethics and of law, as well as the dictates of the common sense of mankind. While the Southern men are thus seizing Northern freemen, enslaving and brutalizing them, they turn round and call on us to leave our employments, give chase, arrest, and return their fugitive slaves. While violating our national compact in its most vital features, they ask us not merely to observe and keep our stipulations, but to go far beyond our covenants to uphold their slavery.

Now, sir, these Southern men have no claim whatever on us to observe the compact, while they disregard and trample upon it. Such are the dictates of law, and of justice, and the teachings of common sense. A compliance with such demand would constitute us the mere subsidiaries, the appendages of Southern slavery. This feeling has thus far been suppressed by our intelligent people, hoping that Congress would relieve them from the position in which they have long been placed. If this fugitive law be kept in force, and Congress shall exert its power and influence to degrade our people, I, sir, will not predict the consequences. They may be read in our past history. One thing may be regarded as admitted truth—while Northern freemen are held in Southern chains the people of the free States will not arrest nor return fugitive slaves.

The President, continued Mr. Giddings, assures us that the power of the army and navy will be used to shoot down Northern freemen if necessary to enforce this law. This attempt at menace is unworthy of a President. It will be fruitless. He may send his troops—his Swiss guards of slavery; he may drench our free land with blood; he may entitle himself to the appellation of a second *"Haynau"*;[1] but he will *never compel them to obey that law.* They will obey every constitutional enactment; but they will discard and repudiate this fugitive bill.

The President should have learned ere this that public sentiment, with an enlightened and patriotic people, is stronger than armies or navies; that he himself is but the creature of the people's will—their servant—elected to execute their purposes. In the enactment of this law, their feelings were not consulted, their honor was disregarded, and their wishes were treated with scorn. Sir, a large portion of the Northern people were not represented in this body at the passage of that law. Their servants fled from this hall, and left the interests, the rights, and the honor of their constituents to be disposed of by slaveholders and their obsequious allies. This law "was conceived in sin," and literally "brought forth in iniquity." It is due to our Southern friends that we should inform them distinctly that the law *cannot* and *will not* be enforced. Our people, sir, know what constitutes law. This enactment I call a law merely for convenience, because our language furnishes no proper term in which to characterize it. It has the *form*, but is entirely destitute of the spirit—the essence of law. It *commands* the perpetration of crimes, which no human enactment can justify. In passing it, Congress overstepped the limits of civil government, and attempted to usurp powers which belong only to God. In this attempt to involve our people in crimes forbidden by inspiration, by every impulse of humanity, and to command one portion of the people to wage a war upon another, Congress was guilty of tyranny unexampled.

Mr. Giddings declared that the law would be a "dead letter," like many other acts of Congress. It was already ineffectual. Of 15,000 fugitives not 10 had been returned.

Julius Jakob, Baron von Haynau (1786-1853), an Austrian general, had made his name a synonym of cruelty by his rigorous acts in suppressing revolution.

When Mr. Jefferson came into power, he found men imprisoned under the sedition law, which he deemed unconstitutional. He did not hesitate to pardon them. But Mr. Fillmore pledges himself to exert his power to punish every man who assists his fellow man to regain his liberty. Such, sir, is the difference between Mr. Jefferson and Mr. Fillmore.

If there be any one feature of the Constitution, which the whole history of its adoption has made plain, it is that slavery is a *State institution, over which Congress has no control*—with which this Federal Government *has no legitimate powers to interfere.* We, sir, of the North, will not be constrained, even by your fugitive law, to interfere with it. The slavery of Virginia belongs to her. If she possess the power and the disposition to uphold it, we cannot put it down or abolish it. If she sees fit to abolish it, we have no power to interfere to sustain it.

Neither the law of 1793, nor the Constitution, contemplated the organization of Northern freemen into a constabulary force for catching negroes. Nor did it give the master a guard and assistance to carry back his slave at the *expense of the nation.* Such provisions could never have been approved by Washington, who signed the law of 1793, nor by his associates who had aided in framing the Constitution, and who also voted for that law. They understood their constitutional duties.

The extent of our powers consists in prohibiting the people from interfering between the master and slave. And this fugitive law is unconstitutional to the full extent to which it attempts to exert its powers in aid of slavery. The appointment of officers, making it their duty to issue process, to pursue the slave, to arrest, to carry him back, and the paying expenses from the treasury, all are unconstitutional acts. They, sir, interfere with slavery, and are repugnant to the whole spirit of the Constitution. The President unintentionally condemns these acts. I condemn them, the country condemns them, humanity condemns them.

All who read this message must see that the only interference with slavery which the President professes to deprecate is that which tends to *loosen* the chains of bondage; he appears to have no objection to that interference which rivets them closer. Could he have believed that the intelligent freemen of the North would fail to detect the palpable contradiction between that portion of the message which deprecates interference with slavery, and that which urges the continuance of this law, which was enacted for the very purpose of interfering in support of that institution?

But this law goes further; it not only attempts to strike down God's law, which commands us "to feed the hungry," but it attempts to convert every freeman of the North into a savage. If a fugitive from oppression reaches my door amid the ragings of the storm, half clad, and benumbed with cold, fainting and weary, sick and in distress, and asks to warm himself by my fire, this law interferes, and forbids me, under heavy pains and penalties, to comply with his request. If I obey the law, I must drive him from my door, to perish with hunger and cold. If I receive him to my habitation, warm him by my fire—if I feed him, and give him drink, and restore him, so that he pursues his journey and escapes, I am subjected, under this law, to a fine of one thousand dollars and to six months' imprisonment. This law the President *approves,* and advises us to *continue it in force.* I reply, in his own language: "Every citizen who truly loves the Constitution will resolutely and firmly resist" the interference which this law enjoins.

Sir, our people will continue to feed the hungry, to clothe the naked, to visit the sick, and to relieve the oppressed; and no interference of this fugitive law will prevent this compliance with the dictates of our religion, with that law which came from God himself, and which no enactment of slaveholders and doughfaces can repeal or nullify. I speak for no one but myself and constituents; others will choose whether to obey God or the oppressors of mankind; but, as for us, we will obey that higher law of kindness, benevolence, and humanity, which was implanted in the breast of every human being, and written upon the hearts and consciences of mankind by the finger of our Creator.

The common law holds him who aids in a murder as guilty as he who strikes the knife to the heart of the victim. And will anyone suppose that he who assists in arresting and sending a fugitive slave to torture and death will be less guilty than he under whose lash the victim expires?

Sir, we will not commit this crime. No! The freemen of Ohio will never turn out to chase the panting fugitive; they will never be metamorphosed into bloodhounds, to track him to his hiding-place, and seize and drag him out, and deliver him to his tormentors. They may be shot down; the cannon and bayonet and sword may do their work upon them; they may drown the fugitives in the blood of freemen; but never will freemen stoop to the degradation of catching slaves.

Let no man tell me there is no higher law than this fugitive bill. We feel there is a law of right, a law of justice, of freedom, implanted in the breast of every intelligent human being, that bids him look with scorn upon this miscalled law.

The speaker then referred to persons, including ministers of the gospel, who claimed that there was no moral guilt in obeying the law, since the responsibility rested with Congress.

I hesitate not to say that, for its barbarity, that law is unequaled in the history of civilized legislation. Will preachers of righteousness tell them to submit, to let the slave dealer rivet the chains upon the father, tear the mother from her children, and doom her to a life of wretchedness? Will such preachers advise the daughter *peacefully* to surrender herself into the hands of slave hunters and submit to a life of pollution and shame? And will such men be called promoters of *holiness and purity*? I trust there are few such teachers in this American land. Sir, all good men must detest this law. God has no attribute which will permit him to look upon it except with abhorrence.

Yet the President assures us that it ought not to be repealed; that it should be kept in force; that these outrages should and ought to continue; that he regards this law as a *final* settlement of the slave question; and that it is wrong farther to agitate the subject. Vain advice. Agitation will never cease until the law ceases. While such crimes are authorized by statute the American people will not keep silence.

The public meetings of the people of all parties throughout the free States, the spirited resolutions which they have sent forth, are but feeble manifestations of the popular mind. Throughout the North, where free schools have been encouraged, where newspapers circulate and intelligence is disseminated, there public sentiment is loud in condemnation of this law. This feeling is increasing and extending, and rolling forward, and gaining strength and impetus, and will continue to do so until that law shall be repealed and numbered among the things that were.

There is no lingering doubt, no difficulty, no obscurity resting on the party which supports this Administration. All the Whigs throughout the country (and I speak it with some degree of feeling, for I once had the pleasure of acting with them when they had principles; then we avowed and acted upon the doctrines I have stated to-day)—all the Whigs throughout the country must now feel that their unity is gone. They see that the party has departed from its doctrines and principles, and has descended, step by step, from its former position until the remnant has literally become a slave-catching party.

I, sir, rejoice at the prospect of seeing every public man, and every elector of the nation, take his position either for freedom or for slavery. The President has come out boldly and manfully on the side of oppression, in favor of compelling the people of the North to become the catchers of Southern slaves. He calls on his friends to take position with him. They will do so. We shall soon have but two political parties. One will contend for the emancipation of the free States and this Government from the control of the slave power; to restore vitality to the Constitution; to give that instrument effect; to maintain the rights of all the States under it; to secure all men under our exclusive jurisdiction in the enjoyment of life, liberty, and happiness. With Gouverneur Morris, and those who assisted in framing the Constitution, that party *"never will concur in upholding domestic slavery."* With Mr. Gerry, "while they have nothing to do with it in the States, *they will lend no sanction to it."* With Mr. Sherman, they *"can see no more propriety in seizing and surrendering a fugitive slave than a horse."*

With these framers of the Constitution the party of freedom will stand. These principles they will maintain and carry out; they will separate and purify themselves from the sin and the shame of slavery; they will redeem this government from its support; they will leave it within the States where it exists. The judgment and conscience of the people are with us! they know our doctrines to be correct. The popular heart beats for freedom. Party prejudices are giving way. Truth is doing its legitimate work. A great political revolution is going forward. No partisan influence can stay its progress. The history of the last few months and years must bear to every reflecting mind a consciousness that the principles of justice, of righteousness, of humanity must triumph. The moral sentiment of the nation demands the repeal of those acts of Congress which authorize and enjoin the commission of crimes. *They will be repealed,* and the Government will be redeemed from its present position; and its laws and influence will be exerted for the benefit, for the elevation, of man.

The Nashville Convention

On November 14, 1850, a Southern convention which had met at Nashville, Tenn., during the discussion on the Clay compromise, to agree upon a united policy for the South, reassembled with delegates from Virginia, South Carolina, Georgia, Florida, Alabama, Mississippi, and Tennessee. It declared that all the evils anticipated by the South had been realized by the Clay compromise, and therefore it recommended that the South abstain from social, commercial, and political intercourse with the North until Southern rights were rendered safe. It proclaimed that if such a time should not come, and the North, by its violations of the Constitution, endangered the peace and existence of the South, it would have "the right, as States, there being no common arbiter, to secede from the Federal Union."

Governor J. A. Quitman [Miss.] convoked the State legislature for November 18 with the intention of laying before it a proposition for secession. On this date, however, Senator Henry S. Foote [Miss.] addressed a mass meeting at Jackson, the State capital, upholding the compromise so persuasively that the meeting decided in favor of the measure. This was the beginning of a Union party in the State which held in check the "Fire-Eaters," as the secessionists were called. Similar Union parties arose in the other Southern States, and came together in a constitutional Union party, which over-weighed the secessionist sentiment.

In the North efforts were also making to form a Union party on the basis of the compromise. Such an organization in New York came within 258 votes of electing Horatio Seymour governor, Washington Hunt, the Whig candidate, being elected.

On January 22, 1851, Alexander H. Stephens, a Representative from Georgia, drew up a manifesto on the slavery question which was signed by 44 Senators and Representatives, Senator Henry Clay [Ky.] at the head. It inveighed against the renewal at any time of the sectional quarrel, declaring that the subscribers would not support any candidate for a Federal office who did not condemn further agitation of the slavery question.

On February 15, 1851, at Boston a fugitive slave by name Shadrach, while the question of his extradition under the Fugitive Slave law was under discussion before a commissioner, was forcibly taken from custody by a crowd of negroes, set at liberty, and smuggled safely into Canada. Two days later Henry Clay [Ky.] introduced a resolution in the Senate asking the President for information as to what measures he had taken to enforce the act, and whether, in his opinion, additional legislation on the subject was necessary. On February

PRACTICAL ILLUSTRATION OF THE FUGITIVE SLAVE LAW

From the collection of the New York Historical Society

18 President Fillmore, by the advice of Daniel Webster, Secretary of State, issued a proclamation commanding all military and civil officers, and entreating all citizens, to aid in executing the law. This was followed (February 21) by a special message to Congress in which he pledged himself to use all his constitutional powers to this end. An extended discussion of the message followed in the Senate, participated in by the following supporters of the President: Henry Clay [Ky.], Stephen A. Douglas (Ill.), and John M. Berrien [Ga.]; leading speakers in opposition were John P. Hale [N. H.], Salmon P. Chase [O.], R. Barnwell Rhett

[S. C.], and Jefferson Davis [Miss.]. As a striking illustration of the fact that politics like misery sometimes makes strange bedfellows it will be noted that the two extremes of American statesmen on the slavery question, Southern "Fire-Eaters" such as Rhett and Davis, and Northern anti-slavery men, such as Hale and Chase, here joined in denouncing the Fugitive Slave law as unconstitutional.

STRANGE BEDFELLOWS—"FIRE-EATERS" AND ABOLITIONISTS

DEBATE ON THE FUGITIVE SLAVE LAW, SENATE, FEBRUARY 21-24, 1851

SENATOR HALE.—I am glad that the document which has been read has been sent to us for one reason, and but one. It satisfies me most conclusively that the President thinks and feels pretty sure that he is rendering his Administration ridiculous, and that his proclamation has done it; and he sent us a long labored essay, as I understand it, to vindicate the propriety of what cannot be vindicated. The idea of the President of the United States issuing a formal proclamation, calling upon all the naval and military force of the Government to hold themselves in readiness, and all officers and good citizens everywhere, to defend this great Republic against a handful of negroes in Boston! I do not know how it strikes others, but to my mind it is ridiculous in the extreme; and I am determined, as far as I am concerned, I will have no part nor lot in it.

SENATOR CLAY.—What is the aim of the Senator? To consider this mob as an isolated affair, as an affair of the two or three hundred negroes only. Is there any other man in the Senate who believes that it originated among these negroes? Do we not all know the ramified means which are employed by the Abolitionists openly, by word and by print everywhere, to stimulate these negroes to acts of violence, recommending them to arm themselves and to slay, murder, and kill anybody in pursuit of them in order to recover and call them back to the duty and service from which they had escaped?

The proclamation is not aimed solely at the miserable negroes, who are without the knowledge and without a perfect consciousness of what became them or what was their duty. They are urged on and stimulated by speeches, some of which are made on this floor and in the House of Representatives, and by prints which are scattered broadcast throughout the whole country.

The proclamation, then, has higher and greater aims. It aims at the maintenance of the law; it aims at putting down all those who would put down the law and the Constitution, be they black or white.

SENATOR CHASE.—Sir, it seems to me somewhat remarkable that the very Senator [Mr. Clay] who has most vehemently denounced agitation and agitators should himself have furnished the occasion of almost every debate on slavery topics during this session. And yet peace and quiet and harmony were promised us. I have never believed, I do not believe, and, unless the future developments shall convince me of error, I never shall believe that the measures to which the sanction of this body was given at the last session will be productive of quiet and harmony. We have been told here to-day that those measures in the series which the South approved were passed by Southern votes, and those which received the approbation of the North by Northern votes. Well, sir, are quiet and harmony to be expected when the parties who are to form the compromise are neither of them satisfied with its terms? If each party rejects that portion of the compromise which offends its particular section, how can it be considered as a settlement? Sir, it is no settlement. It has none of the attributes of a settlement. This very fugitive slave law, to which the attention of the Senate has now been called, will, of itself, produce more agitation than any other which has ever been adopted by Congress.

Mr. President, here in my place I opposed the passage of this fugitive act. I opposed it for the reason, among others, because I believed that the obligations which the Constitution imposed in respect to fugitives from labor devolved upon the States. I agree with the Senator from Virginia [Mr. Mason] that the clause relating to fugitives from service creates "a *federal* obligation." And I concur with the Senator from South Carolina [Mr. Butler] in the opinion that it constitutes "a compact between the States." It is a compact to be executed by the States, just as the other compacts in the same article are to be executed in good faith, but each State is to judge of the extent of its own obligations, and of the particular legislation required to fulfill them. Now, sir, let us refer to the state of things some twelve years ago. From the ocean almost to the base of the Rocky Mountains stretched an unbroken chain of State legislation providing for the reclamation of escaping servants. This being the state of affairs, the Supreme Court, in the case of Prigg against Pennsylvania, decided that the States have no constitutional power to legislate upon the subject. That decision swept the whole of this legislation from the statute books. Then, of course, it became impossible to reclaim fugitives. The decision of the Supreme Court made it impossible, and I believed then, and I believe now, that that decision practically expunged the fugitive servant clause from the Constitution.

And now, sir, what is the particular transaction to which our attention is invoked by the Senator from Kentucky? What is this *nodus Deo vindice dignus?*[1] Why, sir, in Massachusetts, in the city of Boston, it so happened the other day that an individual claimed as a fugitive slave was arrested and taken before a commissioner. In the progress of the investigation fifteen or twenty colored people lingered about the door. These persons, it seems, formed and executed, upon the spot and at the moment, the purpose of rescuing the prisoner. They burst open the door, took the man out, and set him at liberty. There was no organized mob—no general concert of action—the whole affair was confined to the few immediate participants.

Well, sir, what is there strange or unusual in a rescue by force from legal custody? Such infractions of law occur not unfrequently, and in every State. Does it not seem ridiculous to fulminate proclamations and legislation against a few negroes upon an occasion like this? Surely something more than this must be designed. The proclamation and the contemplated legislation must be intended to operate upon the public sentiment of the country, to subjugate the people to the execution of the law. There can be no practical legislation except in two directions. We may provide for the erection of jails; to which no person could object, since Massachusetts has denied, as she had an undoubted right to deny, the use of her prisons for the confinement of persons arrested under national laws. Were there not existing provisions in the statute books authorizing marshals, in such circumstances, to hire temporary places of confinement? We may go further and authorize the President to call out the militia. But I ask Senators to consider where that will end. Call out the militia! March troops to Boston! You cannot prevent the occurrence of such cases as that at Boston by all the military force in the world. You cannot suppress the spirit of the people, unless you are prepared to establish, and the people are ready to receive, a military despotism. Governor Gage tried the experiment of a proclamation upon the people of Boston some seventy-five years ago. It resulted, not in the suppression of public sentiment, but in a revolution. The proclamation of President Fillmore will not, indeed, lead to any out-

[1] "Knot worthy of a Divine adjudication."

IV—16

break; but I feel quite sure that it can do no good. Sir, the ordinary authorities and processes are entirely adequate to every such case as that which has occurred; and it will be useless, and much worse than useless, in my judgment, to clothe the President with any such extraordinary powers as seem to be contemplated by the advocates of this reference. I shall not, however, object to the reference proposed. Let the committee act; and, if Senators think fit to waste any more time of the session upon this matter, let us have their report and another debate. I desire to see, and the country will desire to see, how far it is proposed to go, not in the execution of law by its ordinary processes and officers, but in this strange attempt to suppress discussion, to prevent agitation, to restore peace, tranquillity, and harmony to the country, by the employment of military force!

SENATOR DOUGLAS.—The Senator from Ohio refers to the decision of the Supreme Court of the United States in the case of Prigg *vs.* the State of Pennsylvania, and says that that decision practically expunged from the Constitution of the United States the clause in relation to the surrender of fugitives from labor. I presume the Senator does not mean that the Supreme Court of the United States intended to expunge it. I presume he does not mean that anything they have said in their decision does expunge it. I presume he does not mean that that decision is in conflict with that provision of the Constitution of the United States. But I understand him to mean that, if it could be held that the Congress of the United States had no right to legislate upon the subject, and that therefore the power was reserved exclusively to the States, the free States of this Union would not execute the law. I understand him to mean that while the Constitution of the United States requires every member of a legislature in every State in the Union to take an oath to support that Constitution; while no man can be a judge, a justice of the peace, a constable, a sheriff, or any other officer under a State government without first taking an oath to support the Constitution of the United States, yet when his constituents—the legislature of his State—have elected him to this body, they may be so recreant to their duties under the Constitution, so false to their God, as to vary from their oath in order to violate the Constitution of the country. That is what I understand him to mean.

SENATOR CHASE.—The decision in the case of Prigg *vs.* the State of Pennsylvania denies to the legislatures of the States the power to legislate upon this subject. What does the Senator mean when he talks about a State legislature being recreant to its public duty and to God, when it simply declines to exercise a power which the decision of the Supreme Court denies to it? I say that, when that decision denied to the legislatures of the States the power to execute this article of the Constitution, it swept from the statute book all State legislation upon the subject; and, inasmuch as it then devolved upon Congress to carry into effect this power, and as those laws must be carried into effect, if at all, by the power and officers of the general Government, it would be, in my judgment, impracticable to execute them so as to give them full effect. I did not intimate, and never intimated, that there would be any organized opposition, publicly sanctioned, to the law; but, in the midst of a reluctant community, every man knows you cannot practically execute a Federal law, such a law as this is, unaided by the officers of the general Government. And, therefore, because that decision devolved upon Congress the duty of legislation which it denied to the States, it did, in my judgment, practically expunge the clause from the Constitution. I respect the judges of the Supreme Court as highly as any man. I believe that they decided the case as they believed the Constitution required. I think, however, and I know that very many intelligent citizens of the slave States concur in the opinion, that the decision was, in its practical effect upon the right of reclamation, an extremely unfortunate one for parties interested in that right.

SENATOR DOUGLAS.—The Senator says that decision practically nullifies the fugitive provision in the Constitution of the United States. How does it practically nullify it? That decision declares that it is the duty of the Congress of the United States to pass laws for carrying into effect that provision of the Constitution. If the Senator had obeyed that decision, and had obeyed the Constitution of the United States according to it, he would have been here the advocate of the fugitive law instead of its enemy, for that would have been his duty under the decision to which he refers. But that decision goes further. It says that the Constitution is imperative, conferring the right to reclaim the slave; that the master has a right to go and reclaim him, and that no citizen has a right to obstruct him. Then how could that decision make that clause of the Constitution a dead letter? How could it expunge that clause from the Constitution, unless the Senator means to intimate that there are men in this country who are prepared to disregard the Constitution—who are prepared to disregard the laws of the land. That decision says that Congress must pass a law to carry the clause of the Constitution into effect. It says that every citizen is bound to aid in its enforcement. If the Senator, and those who act with him, would obey that decision, the fugitives from labor would certainly be sent back according to the Constitution. When the Senator says they will not, he casts an imputation upon the people of the free States of this Union that they disregard the Constitution, disregard their oath to support it, disregard the decisions of the Supreme Court of the United States, and that they will take the law into their own hands and raise the standard of rebellion against the Federal Government. That is what I understand to be the direct and legitimate consequences of the argument which he has made, and it was against that I intended to make my protest. I believe it to be a calumny upon the free States of this Union to say that their sons are not prepared to perform every obligation under the Constitution. I do not believe that the free States of this Union ever sent, or ever will send, four Senators to this Chamber who claim that there is a "law higher" than the Constitution which authorizes them to commit perfidy to their God and treason to their country by disobeying the Constitution which they have sworn to support.

I must follow the Senator a few steps further. He can see no necessity for the proclamation of the President. I will not argue that point. He looks upon the matter of the rescue of a fugitive at Boston as an ordinary and a trivial transaction. I do not; and the reason I do not regard it in that light is this: It is well known that there has been a systematic organization throughout many of the free States of this Union to evade the obligations of the Constitution of the United States and to prevent the enforcement of the laws of the United States in relation to fugitive slaves. This organization has been general throughout most of the States, although it does not embrace one in a hundred of the citizens of those States. But it has men of talent, men of genius, men of energy and of daring and of desperate purpose at its head; and the opposition to this fugitive law has been a combined and concerted action. It is in the nature of a conspiracy against the Government. It is a conspiracy to violate the supreme law of the land, to the intent that it shall not be obeyed. I say, therefore, that these conspirators are responsible for all that any of their number may do in resistance to this law. The doctrine of confederates applies to them. Sir, I hold white men now within the range of my sight responsible for the violation of the law at Boston. It was done under their advice, under their teaching, under their sanction, under the influence of their speeches. I do not mean that they advised it in this particular instance; but I say that any negro who came into possession of speeches made in our presence during the last session would have felt himself authorized and justified, by the express direction of men high in authority, to go and set the Constitution and the laws at defiance. These negroes have only done what their white confederates have prompted them to do. The negro has been put forward as the active instrument, while the instigators had not the moral courage to show themselves in the front rank. When these trials shall come on, when the majesty of the law shall be asserted, when the judgment of the court shall be pronounced, I trust it will fall upon the conspirators themselves; upon the leading, distinguished white men who put them up to it, instead of upon the ignorant, simple-minded, and abused tools and instruments that they use to carry out their designs.

. SENATOR BERRIEN.—Sir, if the resistance to this law shall still continue, and the people of the free States shall turn a deaf ear to remonstrances uttered in no spirit of menace and with no feelings of hostility, but with a sincere desire to cultivate and cherish those kindly relations which ought to exist between States thus intimately associated—if these agitations shall continue, and shall result (in the language of the people of Georgia) "in the disruption of every tie which binds her to the Union," in the destruction of our constitutional charter, and the Union of which it is the guaranty—then, sir, I have to say that the people of Georgia will stand acquitted of all participation in this outrage upon the principles of regulated liberty—this utter prostration of the cherished hopes of the votaries of freedom throughout the world. Giving expression to the feelings of my constituents, I say, to the people of the free States, the fate of the Union is in your hands; uttering their deliberate opinion and adopting their language, I say, "upon the faithful execution of the Fugitive Slave law by the proper authorities depends the preservation of our much-loved Union."

SENATOR RHETT.—Sir, the law is not always a law. There is no lawyer who does not know that. A law, to have its practical effect, must move in harmony with the opinions and feelings of the community where it is to operate. In this case no one can doubt that the feeling of the whole and entire North—whatever may be their submission to what they may consider to be the supreme law of the land—is opposed to the institution of slavery and opposed to this law. Now, you may multiply officers as much as you please; you may make every ship a prison; you may make every custom house a guard-room; you

may, in all your great central points, make every effort you
can for the purpose honestly of enforcing the law; nay, you
may have a large majority in all the free States in favor of its
enforcement; and yet, if there be a formidable minority that
determine upon the defeat of the operation of the law, they
can defeat it, and they will defeat it. The recovery of a fugitive slave is not merely the case of a person coming into court.
It is not merely a case in which the law should be enforced
by courts. The fugitive slave may be concealed or sworn out
of court; a thousand artifices and expedients may be resorted
to by which the slaveholder will be unable to recapture his
slave or the slave, when regained, will be rescued. Although
the Government may be perfectly honest in its determination to
enforce the law, although you may legislate with the utmost
rigor, yet, after all, the statutes may be nothing more than so
much waste paper, of no use but to deceive those who are
willing to be deceived. As my honorable colleague very correctly said the other day, out of fifteen thousand slaves at the
North—and I have seen a statement myself putting the number
at thirty thousand—how many have been recaptured? Some
fifteen have been taken in eight or nine months; and in every
case in which there was any dispute it cost the master more than
the worth of the slave.

It is on an examination of these facts that I have come to
the conclusion that this law cannot and will not be so enforced
as practically to secure the rights of the South. With this conviction I have looked most carefully into this matter since it
arose here in debate; and I have come to the conclusion that,
from the beginning of the legislation of Congress on this whole
subject to this day, we of the South have been wronged and
have been made to abandon a better and more efficient remedy
which the Constitution provides.

Every man in the free States must be bound, as a party to
the constitutional compact, to deliver up to him his slave on
his mere *"claim."* This is the great, efficient remedy provided
in the Constitution for the recovery of fugitive slaves; and, the
claim being made, it rested with the State or the State authorities to do one of two things—"deliver up" the slave or pay
for him.

As a substitute—and an exclusive substitute—for this peaceable and more efficient redress under the Constitution, Congress
has usurped the power of legislating upon this subject. It has
undertaken to thrust the powers of the general Government into
the matter and secure to us our fugitive slaves.

Sir, I protest against this doctrine. I protest against this usurpation on the part of Congress. It is fatal to the rights of the South. I maintain that, by the Constitution, we have the faith of the States as sovereigns to a compact with us; and that by that compact the government of every free State, every man in every free State, is bound, morally and constitutionally, to aid in the recovery and restoration of our fugitive slaves.

But Congress has determined otherwise, and the Supreme Court has determined otherwise. I have great respect, personally, for the judges of that court. I believe them to be able and upright; but they are men—very fallible men; and I cannot but remember that, in all times, the judiciary of a country has always been on the side of the Government.

I hold in my hand a compendium of their decisions on this subject and their reasons sustaining them. I will not name the judges delivering the decisions, but quote simply the decisions themselves.

"It cannot be doubted," says the court, "that the Constitution requires the delivery of the fugitive 'on claim' of the master; and the natural inference certainly is that the National Government is clothed with appropriate authority and functions to enforce it." This is very cool. It claims power by nature for the general Government—a new source of authority, certainly. I should say that, as the Constitution does not even mention Congress, much less the National Government, the National Government has nothing to do with it. The decision goes on: "The fundamental principle applicable to all cases of this sort would seem to be that, where the end is required, the means are given." Certainly no one will dispute this position. But the question is, has any power over the end (the recovery of fugitive slaves in a State) been given to Congress by the Constitution? "The clause relating to fugitive slaves is found in the National Constitution, and not in that of any State." Here is a reason as original as it is profound. Where should any of the terms of agreement between the States be found but in their constitutional compact? Did the constitution of any nation ever contain its compacts with other nations? How absurd, then, to attempt to argue that because the States did not, because they could not, insert into their separate constitutions their compact concerning fugitive slaves, that therefore Congress has exclusive jurisdiction over it!

"It might well be deemed an unconstitutional exercise of the power of interpretation to insist that the States are bound to provide means to carry into effect the duties of the National Government, nowhere delegated or intrusted to them by the Constitution. On the contrary, *the natural,* if not the necessary, conclusion is that the National Government, *in the absence of all possible provisions to the contrary,* is bound, through its own proper departments, legislative, executive, or judicial, as the case may require, to carry into effect all the rights and duties imposed upon it by the Constitution.''

Here again the whole question is begged. It is taken for granted that it is the duty of the general Government to enforce the recovery of fugitive slaves. The learned judge declares the powers of the *"National* Government," not from any specified grants in the Constitution, but "in the absence of all provisions to the contrary." He proceeds:

"If this be so, it would seem, upon just principles of construction, that the legislation of Congress, if constitutional, must *supersede all State legislation upon the subject,* and, by *necessary implication, prohibit it.* For if Congress have a constitutional power to regulate a particular subject, and they actually regulate it in a given manner, and in a certain form, it cannot be that the State legislatures have the right to interfere. Where Congress have an *exclusive power* over a subject it is not competent for State legislation *to interfere.''*

Here is the doctrine by which Congress not only possesses the power of legislating on the subject of fugitive slaves, but all legislation on the part of the States is *prohibited.* The same doctrine is reiterated in another case:

"The right to seize and retake fugitive slaves, and the duty to deliver them up, in whatever State of the Union they may be found, is, under the Constitution, recognized as an absolute, positive right and duty, pervading the whole Union with an equal and supreme force, *uncontrolled and uncontrollable by State sovereignty or State legislation.''*

State sovereignty, which alone, under the Constitution, according to its plain purport, had anything to do with the rendition of fugitive slaves, is thus arbitrarily put aside; and State legislation, the only efficient means of enforcing their recovery, is prohibited.

Sir, I know very well that it will be said that these few remarks tend to support the abolitionists; and I should not at all be surprised if I should consequently be denounced by some of the papers of the country, not very far from Washington, as having a very close understanding with the abolitionists. Such imputations are to be expected. He who would be useful as a statesman must be prepared, as the only efficient means of vindication, to act down and live down all imputations on his motives or policy. I think the abolitionists have their way, according to the Constitution as it is construed and administered. I do not think they would be very unwilling that the existing laws should continue without being materially modified or changed. They would infinitely prefer that you should send an army to Boston to enforce them, and thus make our rights under the Constitution incompatible with the independence and sovereignty of the States. Why, you may pass your laws; but a handful of people—it does not require a majority—can baffle your authority in every town in the United States, and thus nullify your law, deride your proclamation, and put your army and navy at defiance. Senators on the other side of the Chamber, not I, are on the side of the abolitionists. Sir, what is the foundation of abolitionism in this Union? It is consolidation. I remember many years since that he who filled the seat I now occupy [Senator Calhoun], and whose shoe-latchets as a statesman I am unworthy to loose, said to the Senator from Massachusetts, now no longer in this body [Mr. Webster], in the great debate that occurred in 1833:

"If the principles you contend for are correct, you will wake up a spirit of abolition in the North; you will make your people believe they are responsible for this institution; and the day that that principle gets into their minds, and that feeling into their hearts, this Union will be at an end. And you yourself will be the very first to feel the effects of the doctrine you are now maintaining by being ostracized and scorned."

Although that great statesman did not live to see the fulfillment of his prophecy, we now see it. Where is the great statesman of Massachusetts in Massachusetts?

The greatest friends of abolition in this country are the consolidationists. They are the fathers of it; they have made it. From their corrupt constructions of the Constitution this hideous monster has arisen, now shaking this Union to its center and, in my opinion, destined to overthrow it.

Sir, what did this Congress do at the last session? Consolidation carried its triumphant career unchecked over the rights and honor of the South, and the rights also of the North. By the compromise, as it was called, you stripped the South, having an equal right in the whole of our vast territories, conquered by us in common with you, of any participation in them. You ignominiously ejected us, but admitted freely not only all the people of the North, but the people of every other land and tongue, even to the convicts of Botany Bay. They are fit to be your compeers in holding that magnificent country; but we—we, your equals in this Confederacy—are spurned and thrust aside. That was one branch of your mighty measures of consolidation. And what else did you do? You passed the Fugitive Slave bill, another measure of consolidation, as I humbly conceive, although not injurious to the North. And after you had done this you then cried out: "All hail! here is peace; there is to be no more contention; the lamb and the wolf are to lie down together; satisfaction, and peace, and quietude prevail all over the Union! the South is satisfied, the North is satisfied; we are all satisfied."

Sir, the South has succumbed far beyond what she expected, or anybody else expected, after the solemn committals she had made. She had resolved that she would resist, at every hazard and to the last extremity, if you perpetrated over her this enormous spoliation of her ejection from California. She has, nevertheless, apparently succumbed—all at least but two States. But the North for whom you plundered us—the North who had triumphed by your consolidation, instead of being satisfied with what she had gained, was dissatisfied with the poor boon the South acquired for the recapture of fugitive slaves. If the Constitution was violated by this law, they should not have complained, for they had more than its equivalent in the unconstitutional appropriation of California and the subjection of the South. Swollen with the arrogance of predominating power, however, they have risen up and said you shall not enforce this law. We see now this singular state of things: While the South—the wronged, the insulted party—is sinking lower and lower the spirit of the North is rising every day and saying, with its accustomed potency, you shall not enforce this law, until at length we are now deliberately debating whether we shall stretch the Union to the utmost tension of its powers to put down their dissatisfaction and resistance.

There is not a mathematical problem in Euclid more clear than this. Just in proportion as you limit the sphere of the operations of the general Government according to the simple purport of the Constitution, in that proportion you strengthen the Union; and just in proportion as you enlarge the sphere of the operations of the general Government by construction, in that proportion you endanger the stability of the Union. Those who adopt the policy of enlarging the powers of the general Government by construction have only to go on, and they will consummate that prediction made by a distinguished statesman on this floor, if it is not done already, that we would soon become, not one people, but a divided people, a people frowning at and hating each other. You have by this course of consolidation destroyed the bond of peace and brotherly love that has so long united us together. I do not know what other gentlemen may say, but I, for one, can speak for my constituency as to the effect of your legislation upon them. They look upon this Union, in the manner in which the representatives of the North carry out its operations, as a curse rather than a blessing. They deem the course of policy which you have pursued, in your measures of compromise and spoliation, to be inconsistent with their honor and inconsistent with their rights and safety.

One word before I close to my Democratic friends. Sir, I have been a humble follower of that party for more than twenty years. For thirteen years I have been standing up here in Congress endeavoring to bring it back to the original principles upon which it was placed. It was placed there by mighty men. The genius of Jefferson and Madison founded it. It was based not only on principles of policy, but on the fixed and immutable principles of truth and justice. But at the last session of Congress they surrendered to their enemies; they went over in the free States to the consolidationists, in order that together they might spoil the South. They took the honorable Senator from Kentucky as their leader—he who for twenty years has been the leader of the great Federal or Whig party— and an abler leader they have never had or ever will possess. Every step they took under such a leader toward consummating these measures of compromise they strengthened the Federal or consolidation party and weakened themselves. Now where are they? Where are the principles of the Democratic party? They are gone—they are destroyed. The Whig or Federal party is the only party that possesses power in this Union, and those of our Democratic friends who thought proper to coöperate with them in their measures of consolidation of the last Congress must sink into their embraces or sink beneath their feet. There may yet be recuperative power in the country if it could be brought forth; but I have waited here, a watcher of the night, and have looked long and long for the streaks of day. Shall that bright day ever again come, when the Democratic party, chastised by its errors and disciplined by defeat, shall again be clothed in its ancient armor and fighting for their principles, and the noble faith of the Constitution once more mount to victory? I fear not. I fear they are gone, gone forever; and that this Union will soon come to an end, under the mighty sweep of the free States, with the consolidation principles which they have ever advocated and enforced. The wheel is destined to roll on, crushing beneath its weight interest after interest, all faith, brotherhood, and peace, until the whole fabric falls, a vast pile of ruin and desolation.

SENATOR CLAY.—The speech of the Senator reminds me of a remark of the late Chief Justice of the United States, when a learned counsel from one of the distant States began to argue, and went as far back as the Flood, laying down certain fundamental rules of the law which he thought essential to be known by the Supreme Court. With that blandness and mildness that characterized that illustrious man, he said: "Why, Mr. Counsel, I really think there are some things which this court may be presumed to understand." The whole difficulty with the Senator and his school is that they undertake to say what are the granted powers, and what is and what is not necessary to carry into effect the granted powers. And if all others do not concur with them they are consolidationists, Federalists, Whigs, precipitating the country into ruin. They dispose of all precedent. What is a precedent? A precedent is the deliberate judgment of a court or a deliberative body upon questions which arise before that court or before that body. It is the opinion of the court or of the body upon the subject matter which is before them. It is, therefore, always entitled to respect, and he who sets aside precedents, he who rejects them all, says, in substance, I am wiser than all men who have pronounced these opinions and established these precedents, and therefore I pay no respect to them. During the last week I heard a Senator, who is not now in his place, I believe, reject in one general mass all precedents upon a particular subject, and immediately afterward shelter himself behind the opinion of the illustrious and lamented Senator from South Carolina [Mr. Calhoun], which he thought was superior to all other opinions and all other precedents. So it is with the whole school. They will tell you that the Supreme Court of the United States know nothing about the Constitution; that Congress has been violating it from 1793 down to this day. But if they can find an opinion of the lamented individual to whom I have referred, sanctioning their views, why it is worth all the precedents and the opinions of the Washingtons, Jeffersons, Madisons, Monroes, and all the other Presidents of the United States. The learned Senator has contended that there was no power in the Government of the United States to pass the fugitive slave law. It is not among the most remarkable features of the times that there are certain coincidences between extremes in this body and in the country. The honorable Senator from South Carolina, who, I believe, holds

extreme doctrines upon the subject of slavery and considers
that institution as a blessing, and the honorable Senator from
Ohio [Mr. Chase], who holds directly opposite opinions, both
unite in expressing the opinion that there is no power in the
Congress of the United States to pass the Fugitive Slave law,
and that Washington and all of us, from the commencement of
the Government down to this time, have been wrong; that the
Supreme Court has been wrong, and that the Congress of 1793
were wrong. Yet the colleague of the Senator from South Carolina, I believe, originally introduced the bill, and it was per-
fected by the Senator from Virginia [Mr. Mason].

The Senator from South Carolina says the more you limit
the Constitution the more you add strength to it. Then, I
suppose, if all the powers of the Government are to be taken
away in this process of limitation, it would make the Union
stronger. He says the more you stretch the Constitution the
more you increase the danger to the perpetuity of the Union.
But who is to decide the question of stretching the powers of
the Constitution, and of limiting them? What man, mortal,
fallible, weak, erring man, can get up here and say the Constitution means this or that, and all others who give it a different interpretation are traitors, consolidationists, Whigs, or
Federalists? I have never heard a man get up here and talk
about his being a State rights man emphatically and exclusively,
per se, a Simon Pure, that I did not feel those emotions which
Junius describes whenever he saw a Scotchman smile. [Laugh-
ter.] The honorable Senator from Ohio and others who concur
with him in opinion anticipated a vast and boundless fund of
agitation if the compromise measures were passed. Instead of
that, peace has been produced to an extent surpassing even my
most sanguine anticipations. There was one exception. It was
predicted by myself and others, at least, that the ultra abolitionists would not be tranquillized; that they would go on and
agitate; and they would denounce the existence of the Union.
Did the Senator suppose we had undertaken the herculean task
of pacifying his friends, or at least those who think with him
on the general subject of abolition?

SENATOR CHASE.—Does the Senator mean to enumerate me
among those who ever expressed a wish for the dissolution of
the Union?

SENATOR CLAY.—No, sir; I only mean to say that the Senator is in bad company. [Laughter.] If the Senator will disavow and repudiate the abolitionists of all shades and colors, I
should be truly happy to hear him.

SENATOR CHASE.—I do disavow most emphatically all association or connection with any class of persons who desire the dissolution of this Union. I say now, as I said at the last session, that "we of the West are in the habit of looking upon this Union as we look upon the arch of heaven; without a thought that it can ever decay or fall." I am aware that there are some abolitionists or anti-slavery men—names are of little consequence—who regard the Constitution as at war with moral obligation and the supreme law. I am not of them. But if the Senator, when denouncing abolitionists, means to include in his reproaches all those citizens who, within the limits of constitutional obligation, seek to rescue this Government from all connection with slavery, I can claim no exemption. I am one of those who mean to exercise all legitimate constitutional power to restrict slavery within the limits of the slave States, and in all places under the exclusive jurisdiction of the National Government to maintain every person, of whatever race or origin, in the enjoyment of personal freedom. That is my position.

SENATOR DAVIS.—If the action of the negro mob in the city of Boston be sustained and adopted by the State of Massachusetts; if she has resolved to cast off the obligation of the Constitution and to absolve herself from the duties which devolve upon her as a member of the Union, then she is, of her own free will and sovereign act, virtually out of it. I, for one, will never give a dollar to coerce her back. In saying this I make no special attack upon that State. I attack no State. Though those with whom I am most identified have suffered most grievous wrongs from the State of Massachusetts; though she has been in the lead in that agitation, the object of which has been to deprive us of our property, still I remember the earlier and more glorious portions of her history. Still, if I could have the faintest ray of hope, I would say, despite my wrongs, I love thee still. If we can only have such a ray of hope furnished by the action of the Governor of that State; if he, with the militia of Massachusetts, will put down the mob and enforce the laws made under the Constitution, how much better, more peaceful, efficient, and permanent it would be than any remedy applied by the army and navy. And I reject the idea of the coercion of the State by the power of the Federal Government. If the State will not act thus, it can only be said she has dissolved the bonds that connected her to the other States by repudiating the Constitution. If so, I say let her go—go in peace, go in good will, go with all the kind and proud remembrances which cluster about her early history; go, if she will not maintain her obligations to the Constitution, as becomes a sovereign State and an equal member of the Union.

I know, Mr. President, that this doctrine which I entertain of the freedom of the State from coercion by the Federal Government will be by some identified with the doctrine of nullification, to which it bears no resemblance. I deny the power of Massachusetts to nullify the law and remain in the Union. But I concede to her the right, I am willing she should exercise it, if she deliberately desires it, to retire from the Union—to take the "extreme medicine," secession.

When I become convinced that this Union solely depends for its preservation on the measures which politicians may suggest, I shall look upon its days as numbered. The charm which invests and binds it with far greater force than bands of brass and steel must have been dissolved, and the efforts of any puny arm to forge fetters to replace the magic power which had passed away would only provoke contempt if it did not heighten the catastrophe. This Union is held together by historical associations and national pride. It is held together by mutual attachments and common interests. It is held together by social links, from the fact that fathers and sons, mothers and daughters, brothers and sisters, and boyhood friends, live in extreme ends of the Union. These States are held together by so many unseen, close, and daily increasing points of contact that it can be rent in twain only by something which loosens these rivets, and permits the use of a lever as powerful as that which has been recently introduced. When it depends upon politicians to manufacture bonds to hold the Union together, it is gone—worthless as a rope of sand.

The Southern Rights Association of South Carolina held a convention in Charleston early in May, 1851, and passed resolutions declaring that the State would not submit to injustice from the Federal Government, and would "relieve herself therefrom whether with or without the coöperation of the other Southern States," and calling for a "Secession Congress" of those States, which call was ratified by the State legislature. The other Southern States did not respond, and the Virginia legislature expressly declined to take any steps which should endanger the Union, and strongly warned South Carolina to desist from her course. A reaction took place in South Carolina, and at the October election of delegates in that State to the Secession Congress the secessionists were completely defeated. During the same month the Union party in Mississippi elected Henry S. Foote governor over the secession candidate, Jefferson Davis, by 999 votes, after a campaign in which the two candidates debated with each other in meetings held throughout the State. Even Davis was only a moderate secessionist, holding that, so long as a State was in the Union, it had no right to nullify a Federal law.

During May and June, 1851, Daniel Webster, Secretary of State, made a speaking tour through New York and Virginia, defending in brilliant oratory the Fugitive Slave law, yet unintentionally giving evidence of its ineffectiveness by his denunciation of its defiance by Massachusetts, Ohio, and other Northern States.

The reply to Webster by Massachusetts and Ohio was the election to the Senate by the former State of Charles Sumner, an even more radical anti-slavery man than his colleague, John Davis, and by the latter State of Benjamin Wade, equally as fervent in the cause as his colleague, Salmon P. Chase.

On August 26 Senator Sumner established his reputation as the leading orator of the anti-slavery cause by a long and brilliant speech in which he declared "Freedom National and Slavery Sectional." It was replied to by George E. Badger [N. C.]. As the argument of the debate is abstract, being only incidentally connected with the Fugitive Act, it has been omitted.

In his annual message at the opening of Congress on December 2, 1851, President Fillmore referred as follows to the Fugitive Slave law:

ENFORCEMENT OF THE FUGITIVE SLAVE LAW

PRESIDENT FILLMORE

The act of Congress for the return of fugitives from labor is one required and demanded by the express words of the Constitution. This injunction of the Constitution is as peremptory and as binding as any other. Some objections have been urged against the details of the act for the return of fugitives from labor; but it is worthy of remark that the main opposition is aimed against the Constitution itself, and proceeds from persons and classes of persons, many of whom declare their wish to see that Constitution overturned. They avow their hostility to any law which shall give full and practical effect to this requirement of the Constitution. Fortunately, the number of these persons is comparatively small, and is believed to be daily diminishing, but the issue which they present is one which involves the supremacy and even the existence of the Constitution.

Cases have heretofore arisen in which individuals have denied the binding authority of acts of Congress, and even States have proposed to nullify such acts, upon the ground that the Constitution was the supreme law of the land, and that those acts of Congress were repugnant to that instrument; but nullification is now aimed, not so much against particular laws as being inconsistent with the Constitution as against the Constitution itself; and it is not to be disguised that a spirit exists and has been actively at work to rend asunder this Union, which is our cherished inheritance from our revolutionary fathers.

IV—17

CHAPTER VII

REPEAL OF THE MISSOURI COMPROMISE

President Pierce's Inaugural—His Allusion to the Finality of the Compromise of 1850—The Platte Country—Proposal to Organize It as the Territory of Nebraska—Stephen A. Douglas [Ill.] Introduces Bill in the Senate to This Effect—His Report on the Bill Questions Validity of the Missouri Compromise—Debate on the Bill: in Favor, Douglas, Archibald Dixon [Ky.], George E. Badger [N. C.], Andrew P. Butler [S. C.]; Opposed, Salmon P. Chase [O.], Charles Sumner [Mass.], William H. Seward [N. Y.], Benjamin Wade [O.]—Bill Is Passed— Douglas Justifies His Action in Speech at Springfield, Ill.—Abraham Lincoln Replies to Him.

BY the overwhelming election of Franklin Pierce to the presidency the Whig party received a mortal blow and its disintegration was only a matter of a few years. During the campaign it had lost its greatest leaders by death, Henry Clay passing away on

GREAT FOOT-RACE FOR THE PRESIDENTIAL PURSE ($100,000 AND PICKINGS)
OVER THE UNION COURSE, 1852
From the collection of the New York Historical Society

258

June 29, 1852, and Daniel Webster on October 23, 1852. There now began the political division on the issue of slavery, which these great compromises had sought to avoid. More than any other it was a woman, Harriet Beecher Stowe, who made the issue inevitable, her great anti-slavery novel, "Uncle Tom's Cabin," published in 1851-52, furnishing the chief wedge that was to cleave the country in two during the coming Administrations.

So great was the curiosity to hear what position the new and comparatively unknown President would take on the slavery question, which, though it had been taken out of the campaign, so far as possible, by the Whig and Democratic conventions, still remained the burning issue of the period, that a greater crowd than had ever before assembled in Washington flocked to the capital on March 4, 1853, to hear the inaugural address.

Slavery a Constitutional Right

President Pierce

To every theory of society or government, whether the off-spring of feverish ambition or of morbid enthusiasm, calculated to dissolve the bonds of law and affection which unite us, I shall interpose a ready and stern resistance. I believe that involuntary servitude, as it exists in different States of this confederacy, is recognized by the Constitution. I believe that it stands like any other admitted right, and that the States where it exists are entitled to efficient remedies to enforce the constitutional provisions. I hold that the laws of 1850, commonly called the "compromise measures," are strictly constitutional, and to be unhesitatingly carried into effect. I believe that the constituted authorities of this Republic are bound to regard the rights of the South in this respect as they would view any other legal and constitutional right, and that the laws to enforce them should be respected and obeyed, not with a reluctance encouraged by abstract opinions as to their propriety in a different state of society, but cheerfully, and according to the decisions of the tribunal to which their exposition belongs. Such have been and are my convictions, and upon them I shall act. I fervently hope that the question is at rest, and that no sectional, or ambitious, or fanatical excitement may again threaten the durability of our institutions or obscure the light of our prosperity.

THE NEBRASKA BILL

The hope of the President was quickly to be destroyed, and that by his own consent and even connivance.

West of Missouri and Iowa and extending to the Rocky Mountains was a great plain called, from the chief river which traversed it, the "Platte country." The eastern portion alone was considered desirable for habitation, and this consisted largely of Indian reservations upon which, as late as 1850, whites had been forbidden to settle. Although the Platte country was traversed by two great highways to the Far West, the Santa Fé and Oregon trails, no emigrants stopped to settle the semi-arid central and western portions which now, as a result of cultivation and irrigation, are flourishing agricultural regions.

By the terms of the Missouri compromise this entire country had been dedicated to freedom. Nevertheless the pact had been broken in part in 1836, when a strip of land along the Missouri frontier was added to that State (so quietly that little notice of the annexation was taken at the time), and six counties were formed of it wherein slavery was introduced.

In the Congress of 1851-52 petitions were presented from the sparse population of the western portion for a territorial organization of the country. No action, however, was taken, until the next session, when, on December 13, 1852, Willard P. Hall [Mo.] submitted in the House of Representatives a bill organizing the Territory of Platte, comprising the whole region. This was referred to the Committee on Territories, and, on February 2, 1853, William A. Richardson [Ill.], of the committee, reported a bill organizing the region under the name of the Territory of Nebraska. While the bill did not mention slavery, nevertheless the restriction against it in the Missouri Compromise was implied, and therefore the Southern Representatives, with the exception of those from Missouri, opposed the measure stoutly. It was, however, passed by the House on February 10 by a vote of 98 to 43. It then went to the Senate, where it was reported by Stephen A. Douglas [Ill.], chairman of the Committee on Territories, on February 11. On March 2 it was laid on the table by a vote of 23 to 17, every Southern Senator but those from Missouri voting in the affirmative. David R. Atchison, from that State, a strong pro-slavery man, clearly intimated that he was voicing the will of his constituents rather than of himself by his vote, and that it was the policy of the South to delay the organization of the Territory until some counterpoise could be found, such as the partition of Texas into several slave States and Territories.

The bill was brought before the Senate of the next Congress on December 14, 1853, by Augustus C. Dodge [Ia.], and was referred to the Committee on Territories, from which Senator Douglas reported it on January 4, 1854, with certain amendments, none of which, however, touched the question of slavery. Nevertheless, Senator Douglas's report on the bill questioned the validity of the 8th section in the Missouri Compromise, which prohibited slavery north of 36 degrees 30 minutes north latitude. The report said:

"Under this section, as in the case of the Mexican law in New Mexico and Utah, it is a disputed point whether slavery is prohibited in the Nebraska country by *valid* enactment. The decision of this question involves the constitutional power of Congress to pass laws prescribing and regulating the domestic institutions of the various Territories of the Union. In the opinion of those eminent statesmen who hold that Congress is invested with no rightful authority to legislate upon the subject of slavery in the Territories, the 8th section of the act preparatory to the admission of Missouri is null and void; while the prevailing sentiment in large portions of the Union sustains the doctrine that the Constitution of the United States secures to every citizen an inalienable right to move into any of the Territories with his property, of whatever kind and description, and to hold and enjoy the same under the sanction of law. Your committee do not feel themselves called upon to enter upon the discussion of these controverted questions. They in-

volve the same grave issues which produced the agitation, the
sectional strife, and the fearful struggle of 1850. As Congress
deemed it wise and prudent to refrain from deciding the matters in controversy then, either by affirming or repealing the
Mexican laws, or by an act declaratory of the true intent of
the Constitution, and the extent of the protection afforded by
it to slave property in the Territories, so your committee are
not prepared to recommend a departure from the course pursued on that memorable occasion, either by affirming or repealing the 8th section of the Missouri act, or by any act declaratory
of the meaning of the Constitution in respect to the legal points
in dispute.''

Nevertheless, near the close the report said:

''From these provisions it is apparent that the compromise
measures of 1850 affirm and rest upon the following proposition:
''That all questions pertaining to slavery in the Territories
and the new States to be formed therefrom are to be left to the
decision of the people residing therein, by their appropriate
representatives, to be chosen by them for that purpose.''

The bill thus reported was soon after, on Mr. Douglas's motion, recommitted, and on the 23d reported again
by him from his Committee on Territories, with material
alterations. For, meantime (on January 16, 1854),
Archibald Dixon [Ky.] had given due notice that, whenever this bill should come up, he would offer the following amendment:

''That the 8th section of the Missouri compromise *shall not
be so construed as to apply to the Territory contemplated by
this act, or to any other Territory of the United States;* but
that the citizens of the several States or Territories shall be
at liberty to take and hold their slaves within any of the Territories or States to be formed therefrom, as if the said act,
entitled as aforesaid, and approved as aforesaid, had never been
passed.''

This blunt proposition, says Horace Greeley in his
''American Conflict,'' that the Missouri Compromise,
in so far as its stipulations favored the consecration of
the Territories to free labor, be utterly repudiated, now

that so much of it as strengthened slavery had taken full and vigorous effect, was received with more surprise than satisfaction by the engineers of the original measure. The *Union,* then the Democratic organ at Washington, promptly denounced it as a Whig device to divide and disorganize the Democratic party. It received no hearty welcome from any quarter—certainly none from Senator Douglas, or any supporter of his Presidential aspirations. It had evidently been expected by them that his proposal to organize these territories, so expressly contemplated and covered by the inhibition of bondage contained in the Missouri act, in blank silence on the subject of slavery, would be deemed a concession to Southern prejudices, if not to Southern interests. Yet, in the presence of this bolder, stronger, larger, and more practical concession, that of Senator Douglas dwindled by contrast into insignificance.

Senator Douglas, thus outbid, resolved to start afresh. On the 23d aforesaid he reported from his committee a bill so different from its predecessor as hardly to resemble it, save that it contemplated the same region. Instead of one Territory, to be called Nebraska, and stretching from the parallel of 36 degrees 30 minutes north latitude on the south to that of 43 degrees 30 minutes on the north, and from the western boundary of Missouri and Iowa on the east to the crests of the Rocky Mountains on the west, he now proposed to create *two* Territories, one to be composed of so much of said region as was directly west of the State of Missouri, to be known as Kansas, the other to comprise the residue and be known as Nebraska. And, with reference to slavery, the new bill contained these provisions:

"Sec. 21. That, in order to avoid all misconstruction, it is hereby declared to be the true intent and meaning of this act, so far as the question of slavery is concerned, to carry into practical operation the following propositions and principles, *established by the compromise measures of 1850,* to wit:

"First. That all questions pertaining to slavery in the Territories and in the new States to be formed therefrom are to be left to the decision of the people residing therein, through their appropriate representatives.

"Second. That 'all cases involving title to slaves' and 'questions of personal freedom' are referred to the adjudication of the local tribunals, with the right of appeal to the Supreme Court of the United States.

"Third. That the provisions of the Constitution and laws of the United States, in respect to fugitives from service, are to be carried into faithful execution in all the 'organized Territories,' the same as in the States."

Proceeding to that section which provides for the election of a delegate to Congress from Kansas, instead of the original stipulation—

"That the Constitution and all laws of the United States which are not locally inapplicable shall have the same force and effect within the said Territory as elsewhere in the United States"—

the following important reservation was now added:

"Except the section of the act preparatory to the admission of Missouri into the Union, approved March 6, 1820, which was superseded by the principles of the legislation of 1850, commonly called the compromise measures, and is declared inoperative."

The section which authorized Nebraska to send a delegate was amended in precisely the same manner.

The amended bill thus reported by Senator Douglas was debated at length by Senators Douglas, Dixon, James C. Jones [Tenn.], George E. Badger [N. C.], Andrew P. Butler [S. C.], and several others in favor, and Senators Salmon P. Chase [O.], Charles Sumner [Mass.], William H. Seward [N. Y.], Benjamin Wade [O.], and others, in opposition.

REPEAL OF THE MISSOURI COMPROMISE

SENATE, JANUARY 30, 1854

SENATOR DOUGLAS.—Upon the question of slavery in the Territories, the committee took the principles established by the compromise act of 1850 as our guide, and intended to make each and every provision of the bill accord with those principles. Those measures established and rest upon the great principle of self-government—that the people should be allowed to decide the questions of their domestic institutions for themselves, subject only to such limitations and restrictions as are imposed by the Constitution of the United States, instead of having them determined by an arbitrary or geographical line.

The original bill reported by the committee, as a substitute for the bill introduced by the Senator from Iowa [Mr. Dodge], was believed to have accomplished this object. The amendment which was subsequently reported by us was only designed to render that clear and specific which seemed, in the minds of some, to admit of doubt and misconstruction. In some parts of the country the original substitute was deemed and construed to be an annulment or a repeal of what has been known as the Missouri compromise, while in other parts it was otherwise construed. As the object of the committee was to conform to the principles established by the compromise measures of 1850, and to carry those principles into effect in the Territories, we thought it was better to recite in the bill precisely what we understood to have been accomplished by those measures, viz: That the Missouri compromise, having been superseded by the legislation of 1850, has become inoperative, and hence we propose to leave the question to the people of the States and the Territories, subject only to the limitations and provisions of the Constitution.

Senator Douglas, having explained the bill, referred to aspersions that had been cast on the committee for its action, particularly in an article in the Abolition paper, the *National Era,* which was signed by Senator Salmon P. Chase, Senator Charles Sumner, Representative Joshua R. Giddings, and other anti-slavery statesmen. He read part of the article:

''We arraign this bill as a gross violation of a sacred pledge; as a criminal betrayal of precious rights; as part and parcel of an atrocious plot to exclude from a vast unoccupied region emigrants from the Old World, and free laborers from our own States, and convert it into a dreary region of despotism, inhabited by masters and slaves.''

Then speaking of the Committee on Territories, these confederates use this language:

"The *pretences*, therefore, that the Territory, covered by the positive prohibition of 1820, sustains a similar relation to slavery with that acquired from Mexico, covered by no prohibition except that of disputed constitutional or Mexican law, and that the compromises of 1850 require the incorporation of the pro-slavery clauses of the Utah and New Mexico bill in the Nebraska act, are mere *inventions, designed to cover up from public reprehension meditated bad faith.*"

Again:

"Servile demagogues may tell you that the Union can be maintained only by submitting to the demands of slavery."

Then there is a postscript added, equally offensive to myself, in which I am mentioned by name. The address goes on to make an appeal to the legislatures of the different States, to public meetings, and to ministers of the Gospel in their pulpits, to interpose and arrest the vile conduct which is about to be consummated by the Senators who are thus denounced. That address, sir, bears date Sunday, January 22, 1854. Thus it appears that on the holy Sabbath, while other Senators were engaged in attending divine worship, these abolition confederates were assembled in secret conclave, plotting by what means they should deceive the people of the United States and prostrate the character of brother Senators. This was done on the Sabbath day, and by a set of politicians, to advance their own political and ambitious purposes, in the name of our holy religion.

But this is not all. It was understood from the newspapers that resolutions were pending before the legislature of Ohio, proposing to express their opinions upon this subject. It was necessary to hasten the action of the Ohio legislature, under a misapprehension, to state that it was signed, not only by the abolition confederates, but by the whole Whig representation, and a portion of the Democratic representation in the other House from the State of Ohio.

SENATOR CHASE.—Mr. President, the Senator misstates the facts——

SENATOR DOUGLAS.—Sir, if the Senator does interpose, in violation of the rules of the Senate, to a denial of the fact, it may be that I shall be able to nail that denial, as I shall the statements here which are over his own signature, as a base falsehood, and prove it by the solemn legislation of this country.

SENATOR CHASE.—I call the Senator to order.

The VICE-PRESIDENT.—The Senator from Illinois is certainly out of order.

SENATOR DOUGLAS.—Then I will only say that I shall confine myself to this document, and prove its statements to be false by the legislation of the country. Certainly that is in order.

SENATOR CHASE.—You cannot do it.

SENATOR DOUGLAS.—The argument of this manifesto is predicated upon the assumption that the policy of the Fathers of the Republic was to prohibit slavery in all the territory ceded by the old States to the Union and made United States territory, for the purpose of being organized into new States. I take issue upon that statement.

The Senator here stated that in the organization of the Territories of Mississippi, Louisiana, and Missouri slavery was not restricted.

This continued to be the condition of the country in the Missouri Territory up to 1820, when the celebrated act which is now called the Missouri compromise act was passed. Slavery did not exist in, nor was it excluded from, the country now known as Nebraska. There was no code of laws upon the subject of slavery either way: First, for the reason that slavery had never been introduced into Louisiana and established by positive enactment. It had grown up there by a sort of common law, and been supported and protected. When a common law grows up, when an institution becomes established under a usage, it carries it so far as that usage actually goes and no further. If it had been established by direct enactment, it might have carried it so far as the political jurisdiction extended; but, be that as it may, by the act of 1812, creating the Territory of Missouri, that Territory was allowed to legislate upon the subject of slavery as it saw proper, subject only to the limitations which I have stated; and the country not inhabited or thrown open to settlement was set apart as Indian country, and rendered subject to Indian laws. Hence the local legislation of the State of Missouri did not reach into that Indian country, but was excluded from it by the Indian code and Indian laws. The municipal regulations of Missouri could not go there until the Indian title had been extinguished and the country thrown open to settlement. Such being the case, the only legislation in existence in Nebraska Territory at the time that the Missouri act was passed, namely, the 6th of March, 1820, was a provision in effect that the people should be allowed to do as they pleased upon the subject of slavery.

The Territory of Missouri having been left in that legal condition, positive opposition was made to the bill to organize a State government, with a view to its admission into the Union; and a Senator from my State, Mr. Jesse B. Thomas, introduced an amendment, known as the eighth section of the bill, in which it was provided that slavery should be prohibited north of 36° 30' north latitude, in all that country which we had acquired from France. What was the object of the enactment of that eighth section? Was it not to go back to the original policy of prescribing boundaries to the limitation of free institutions, and of slave institutions, by a geographical line, in order to avoid all controversy in Congress upon the subject? Hence they extended that geographical line through all the territory purchased from France, which was as far as our possessions then reached. It was not simply to settle the question on that piece of country, but it was to carry out a great principle, by extending that dividing line as far west as our territory went, and running it onward on each new acquisition of territory. True, the express enactment of the eighth section of the Missouri act, now called the Missouri compromise act, only covered the territory acquired from France; but the principles of the act, the objects of its adoption, the reasons in its support, required that it should be extended indefinitely westward, so far as our territory might go, whenever new purchases should be made.

Thus stood the question up to 1845, when the joint resolution for the annexation of Texas passed. There was inserted in that a provision, suggested in the first instance and brought before the House of Representatives by myself, extending the Missouri compromise line indefinitely westward through the Territory of Texas. Why did I bring forward that proposition? Why did the Congress of the United States adopt it? Not because it was of the least practical importance, so far as the question of slavery within the limits of Texas was concerned, for no man ever dreamed that it had any practical effect there. Then why was it brought forward? It was for the purpose of preserving the principle, in order that it might be extended still further westward, even to the Pacific Ocean, whenever we should acquire the country that far.

It will be seen that the joint resolution for the annexation of Texas contains a very remarkable provision, which is that, when States lying north of 36° 30' apply for admission, slavery shall be prohibited in their constitutions. I presume no one pretends that Congress could have power thus to fetter a State applying for admission into this Union; but it was necessary to preserve the principle of the Missouri compromise line in order that it might afterward be extended; and it was supposed that, while Congress had no power to impose any such limitation, yet, as that was a compact with the State of Texas, that State could consent for herself that, when any portion of her own territory, subject to her own jurisdiction and control, applied for a constitution, it should be in a particular form; but that provision would not be binding on the new State one day after it was admitted into the Union. The other provision was that such States as should lie south of 36° 30′ should come into the Union with or without slavery, as each should decide in its constitution. Then, by that act, the Missouri compromise was extended indefinitely westward, so far as the State of Texas went, that is, to the Rio del Norte; for our Government at the time recognized the Rio del Norte as its boundary. We recognized it in many ways, and among them by even paying Texas for it, in order that it might be included in and form a portion of the Territory of New Mexico.

Then, sir, in 1848 we acquired from Mexico the country between the Rio del Norte and the Pacific Ocean. Immediately after that acquisition the Senate, on my own motion, voted into a bill a provision to extend the Missouri compromise indefinitely westward to the Pacific Ocean, in the same sense and with the same understanding with which it was originally adopted. That provision passed this body by a decided majority and went to the House of Representatives, and was there defeated by Northern votes.

Now, sir, let us pause and consider for a moment. The first time that the principles of the Missouri compromise were ever abandoned, the first time they were ever rejected by Congress, was by the defeat of that provision in the House of Representatives in 1848. By whom was that defeat effected? By Northern votes, with Free-Soil proclivities. It was the defeat of that Missouri compromise that reopened the slavery agitation with all its fury. It was the defeat of that Missouri compromise that created the tremendous struggle of 1850. It was the defeat of that Missouri compromise that created the necessity for making a new compromise in 1850. Had we been faithful to the principles of the Missouri compromise in 1848, this question would not have arisen. Who was it that was faithless? I undertake to say it was the very men who now insist that the Missouri compromise was a solemn compact, and should never be violated or departed from. Every man who is now assailing the principle of the bill under consideration, so far as I am advised, was opposed to the Missouri compromise in 1848. The very men who now arraign me for a departure from the Missouri compromise are the men who successfully violated it, repudiated it, and caused it to be superseded by the compromise measures of 1850. Sir, it is with rather bad grace that the men who proved false themselves should charge upon me and others, who were ever faithful, the responsibilities and consequences of their own treachery.

Then, sir, as I before remarked, the defeat of the Missouri compromise in 1848 having created the necessity for the establishment of a new one in 1850, let us see what that compromise was.

The leading feature of the compromise of 1850 was congressional non-intervention as to slavery in the Territories; that the people of the Territories and of all the States were to be allowed to do as they pleased upon the subject of slavery, subject only to the provisions of the Constitution of the United States.

That, sir, was the leading feature of the compromise measures of 1850. Those measures, therefore, abandoned the idea of a geographical line as the boundary between free States and slave States; abandoned it because compelled to do it from an inability to maintain it; and, in lieu of that, substituted a great principle of self-government which would allow the people to do as they thought proper. Now, the question is, when that new compromise, resting upon that great fundamental principle of freedom, was established, was it not an abandonment of the old one—the geographical line? Was it not a supercedure of the old one within the very language of the substitute for the bill which is now under consideration? I say it did supersede it, because it applied its provisions as well to the north as to the south of 36° 30'. It established a principle which was equally applicable to the country north as well as south of the parallel of 36° 30'—a principle of universal application.

In order to refute the presumption that the Missouri compromise was abandoned and superseded by the principles of the compromise of 1850, these confederates cite the following amendment, offered to the bill to establish the boundary of Texas and create the Territory of New Mexico in 1850:

"*Provided*, That nothing herein contained shall be construed to impair or qualify anything contained in the third article of the second section of the joint resolution for annexing Texas to the United States, approved March 1, 1845, either as regards the number of States that may hereafter be formed out of the State of Texas or otherwise."

After quoting this proviso, they make the following statement, and attempt to gain credit for its truth by suppressing material facts which appear upon the face of the same statute, and, if produced, would conclusively disprove the statement:

"It is solemnly declared in the very compromise acts 'that *nothing herein contained shall be construed to impair or qualify'* the prohibition of slavery north of 36° 30'; and yet, in the face of this declaration, that sacred prohibition is said to be overthrown. Can presumption further go!"

I will now proceed to show that presumption could not go further than is exhibited in this declaration.

They suppress the following material facts, which, if produced, would have disproved their statement: They first suppress the fact that the same section of the act cuts off from Texas and cedes to the United States all that part of Texas which lies north of 36° 30'. They then suppress the further fact that the same section of the law cuts off from Texas a large tract of country on the west, more than three degrees of longitude, and adds it to the territory of the United States. They then suppress the further fact that this territory thus cut off from Texas, and to which the Missouri compromise line did apply, was incorporated into the Territory of New Mexico. And then what was done? It was incorporated into that Territory with this clause:

"That, when admitted as a State, the said Territory, or any portion of the same, shall be received into the Union with or without slavery, as their constitution may prescribe at the time of its adoption."

Yes, sir, the very bill and section from which they quote cuts off all that part of Texas which was to be free by the Missouri compromise, together with some on the south side of the line, incorporates it into the Territory of New Mexico, and then says that that Territory, and every portion of the same, shall come into the Union with or without slavery, as it sees proper.

Now, I ask those Senators, do not those provisions repeal the Missouri compromise so far as it applied to that country cut off from Texas? Do they not annul it? Do they not supersede it? If they do, then the address which has been put forth to the world by these confederates is an atrocious falsehood. If they do not, then what do they mean when they charge me with having, in the substitute first reported from the committee, repealed it, with having annulled it, with having violated it, when I only copied those precise words? I copied the precise words into my bill as reported from the committee which were contained in the New Mexico bill. They say my bill annuls the Missouri compromise. If it does, it had already been done before by the act of 1850, for these words were copied from the act of 1850.

SENATOR WADE.—Why did you do it over again?

SENATOR DOUGLAS.—I will come to that point presently and explain why we did it over again. I am now dealing with the truth and veracity of a combination of men who have assembled in secret caucus upon the Sabbath day, to arraign my conduct and belie my character.

In order to give greater plausibility to this falsification of the terms of the compromise measures of 1850, the confederates also declare in their manifesto that they (the territorial bills for the organization of Utah and New Mexico) "applied to the territory acquired from Mexico, and to that only. They were intended as a settlement of the controversy growing out of that acquisition, and of that controversy only. They must stand or fall by their own merits."

Sir, so far as the Utah and New Mexico bills included the territory which had been subject to the Missouri compromise provision, to that extent they absolutely annulled the Missouri compromise. As to the unorganized territory not covered by those bills, it was superseded by the principles of the compromise of 1850. We all know that the object of the compromise measures of 1850 was to establish certain great principles, which would avoid the slavery agitation in all time to come. Was it our object simply to provide for a temporary evil? Was it our object just to heal over an old sore, and leave it to break out again? Was it our object to adopt a mere miserable expedient to apply to that territory, and that alone, and leave ourselves entirely at sea without compass when new territory was acquired, or new territorial organizations were to be made? Was that the object for which the eminent and venerable Senator from Kentucky [Mr. Clay] came here and sacrificed even his last energies upon the altar of his country? Was that the object for which Webster, Clay, Cass, and all the patriots of that day struggled so long and so strenuously? Was it merely the application of a temporary expedient in agreeing to stand by past and dead legislation that the Baltimore platform pledged us to sustain the compromise of 1850? Was it the understanding of the Whig party, when they adopted the compromise measures of 1850 as an article of political faith, that they were only agreeing to that which was past, and had no reference to the future? If that was their meaning—if that was their object—they palmed off an atrocious fraud upon the American people. Was it the meaning of the Democratic party, when we pledged ourselves to stand by the compromise of 1850, that we spoke only of the past and had no reference to the future? If so, it was then a fraud. When we pledged our President to stand by the compromise measures, did we not understand that we pledged him as to his future action? Was it as to his past conduct? If it had been in relation to past conduct only, the pledge would have been untrue as to a very large portion of the Democratic party. Men went into that convention who had been opposed to the compromise measures—men who abhorred those measures when they were pending—men who never would have voted affirmatively on them. But inasmuch as those measures had been passed, and the country had acquiesced in them, and it was important to preserve the principle in order to avoid agitation in the future, these men said to the President, we waive our past objections, and we will stand by you and with you in carrying out these principles in the future.

Such I understood to be the meaning of the two great parties at Baltimore. Such I understand to have been the effect of their pledges. If they did not mean this, they meant merely to adopt resolutions which were never to be carried out, and which were designed to mislead and deceive the people for the mere purpose of carrying an election.

I hold, then, that as to the territory covered by the Utah and New Mexico bills, there was an express annulment of the Missouri compromise; and as to all the other unorganized territories, it was superseded by the principles of that legislation, and we are bound to apply those principles in the organization of all new Territories, to all which we now own, or which we may hereafter acquire. If this construction be given, it makes that compromise a final adjustment. No other construction can possibly impart finality to it. By any other construction the question is to be reopened the moment you ratify a new treaty acquiring an inch of country from Mexico. By any other construction you reopen the issue every time you make a new territorial government. But, sir, if you treat the compromise measures of 1850 in the light of great principles, sufficient to remedy temporary evils, at the same time that they prescribe rules of action applicable everywhere in all time to come, then you avoid the agitation forever, if you observe good faith to the provisions of these enactments, and the principles established by them.

Mr. President, I repeat that, so far as the question of slavery is concerned, there is nothing in the bill under consideration which does not carry out the principle of the compromise measures of 1850, by leaving the people to do as they please, subject only to the provisions of the Constitution of the United States. If that principle is wrong, the bill is wrong. If that principle is right, the bill is right. It is unnecessary to quibble about phraseology or words; it is not the mere words, the mere phraseology, that our constituents wish to judge by. They wish to know the legal effect of our legislation.

The legal effect of this bill, if it be passed as reported by the Committee on Territories, is neither to legislate slavery into these Territories nor out of them, but to leave the people to do as they please, under the provisions and subject to the limitations of the Constitution of the United States. Why should not this principle prevail? Why should any man, North or South, object to it? I will especially address the argument to my own section of the country, and ask why should any Northern man object to this principle? If you will review the history of the slavery question in the United States, you will see that all the great results in behalf of free institutions which have been worked out have been accomplished by the operation of this principle, and by it alone.

Let me ask you where have you succeeded in excluding slavery by an act of Congress from one inch of the American soil? You may tell me that you did it in the Northwest Territory by the ordinance of 1787. I will show you by the history of the country that you did not accomplish any such thing. You prohibited slavery there by law, but you did not exclude it in fact. Illinois was a part of the Northwest Territory. With the exception of a few French and white settlements, it was a vast wilderness, filled with hostile savages, when the ordinance of 1787 was adopted. Yet, sir, when Illinois was organized into a territorial government it established and protected slavery, and maintained it in spite of your ordinance, and in defiance of its express prohibition. It is a curious fact that, so long as Congress said the Territory of Illinois should not have slavery, she actually had it; and on the very day when you withdrew your congressional prohibition, the people of Illinois, of their own free will and accord, provided for a system of emancipation.

But, sir, these abolition confederates, in their manifesto,

have also referred to the wonderful results of their policy in the State of Iowa. Here again they happen to be in fault as to the laws of the land. The act to organize the Territory of Iowa did not prohibit slavery, but the people of Iowa were allowed to do as they pleased under the territorial government. Iowa, when she came to form a constitution and State government, preparatory to admission into the Union, considered the subject of free and slave institutions calmly, dispassionately, without any restraint or dictation, and determined that it would be to the interest of her people in their climate, and with their productions, to prohibit slavery, and hence Iowa became a free State by virtue of this great principle of allowing the people to do as they please, and not in obedience to any Federal command.

The abolitionists are also in the habit of referring to Oregon as another instance of the triumph of their abolition policy. There again they have overlooked or misrepresented the history of the country. Sir, for about twelve years you failed to give Oregon any government or any protection; and during that period the inhabitants of that country established a government of their own, and by virtue of their own laws, passed by their own representatives before you extended your jurisdiction over them, prohibited slavery by a unanimous vote.

How was it in regard to California? Every one of these abolition confederates who have thus arraigned me and the Committee on Territories before the country, who have misrepresented our position, and misquoted the law and the fact, predicted that, unless Congress interposed by law and prohibited slavery in California, it would inevitably become a slave-holding State. Congress did not interfere; Congress did not prohibit slavery. There was no enactment upon the subject; but the people formed a State constitution and then prohibited slavery.

So it was in regard to Utah and New Mexico. We established the territorial governments of Utah and New Mexico without any prohibition. We gave to these abolitionists a full opportunity of proving whether their predictions were true or false. Years have rolled round and the result is before us. The people there have not passed any law recognizing, or establishing, or introducing, or protecting slavery in the Territories.

I know of but one Territory of the United States where slavery does exist, and that one is where you have prohibited it by law, and it is this very Nebraska Territory. In defiance of the eighth section of the act of 1820, in defiance of congressional dictation, there have been, not many but a few, slaves introduced. I heard a minister of the Gospel the other day conversing with a member of the Committee on Territories upon this subject. This preacher was from that country; and a member put this question to him: "Have you any negroes out there?" He said there were a few held by the Indians. I asked him if there were not some held by white men? He said there were a few, under peculiar circumstances, and he gave an instance: An abolition missionary, a very good man, had gone there from Boston, and he took his wife with him. He got out into the country, but could not get any help; hence he, being a kind-hearted man, went down to Missouri and gave $1,000 for a negro, and took him up there as "help." [Laughter.] So, under peculiar circumstances, when these Free-Soil and abolition preachers and missionaries go into the country, they can buy a negro for their own use, but they do not like to allow anyone else to do the same thing. [Renewed laughter.] I suppose the fact of the matter is simply this: There the people can get no servants, and, from the necessity of the case, they must do the best they can, and for this reason a few slaves have been taken there. I have no doubt that, whether you organize the Territory of Nebraska or not, this will continue for some time to come. It certainly does exist, and it will increase as long as the Missouri Compromise applies to the Territory; and I suppose it will continue for a little while during their territorial condition, whether a prohibition is imposed or not. But when settlers rush in—when labor becomes plenty, and therefore cheap, in that climate, with its productions, it is worse than folly to think of its being a slave-holding country. I do not believe there is a man in Congress who thinks it could be permanently a slave-holding country. All I have to say on that subject is that, when you create them into a Territory, you thereby acknowledge that they ought to be considered a distinct political organization. And, when you give them in addition a legislature, you thereby confess that they are competent to exercise the powers of legislation. If they wish slavery they have a right to it. If they do not want it, they will not have it, and you should not force it upon them.

I do not like, I never did like, the system of legislation on our part by which a geographical line, in violation of the laws of nature, and climate, and soil, and of the laws of God, should be run to establish institutions for a people; yet, out of a regard for the peace and quiet of the country, out of respect for past pledges, and out of a desire to adhere faithfully to all compromises, I sustained the Missouri compromise so long as it was in force, and advocated its extension to the Pacific. Now, when that has been abandoned, when it has been superseded, when a great principle of self-government has been substituted for it, I choose to cling to that principle, and abide in good faith, not only by the letter but by the spirit of the last compromise.

SENATOR CHASE.—Mr. President, the Senator from Illinois charges that the address, upon which he has been pleased to· comment in terms which befit any other place than the Senate Chamber—however low that place may be—was concocted in what he chooses to call an abolition caucus held upon Sunday. Ay, sir, with a generosity peculiarly his own, he has availed himself of a mere error of date, and piously holds up to public reprobation the gentlemen who have signed that address as violating the sacredness of the Sabbath day, that day for which he cherishes, doubtless, a peculiar reverence.

Well, sir, the Senator further charges that a false statement has been put forth in connection with this address. That false statement, as he alleges, was this: That the appeal was signed by a majority of the members from the State of Ohio. He thinks that the design was to catch some "soft-footed Democrats." "Soft-footed Democrats!" Ay, that is the phrase by which he chooses to mark all Democrats who will vote against this bill. I trust he will find that such Democrats are a little more numerous than he seems now to imagine.

The simple facts are these: The address bears no signatures other than those of the Independent Democrats, whom the Senator chooses to style "the abolition confederates." By no one of them was it ever represented to be otherwise signed. Some gentlemen connected with the press, however, hearing of the purpose that it should be signed by more or less of the delegation from Ohio, have sent it abroad with a statement that it was thus signed in fact.

Well, sir, the Senator proceeded to take exception to the character and scope of the whole document. He says that we, forsooth, have held him up to the country in this address as guilty of certain great and enormous crimes. Why, sir, any man who reads the address will see that in no part of it, from first to last, except in a brief note appended, is the Senator mentioned at all. So far as I am responsible for the document, either by signature or authorship, I tell the Senator he was not in all my thoughts. He exaggerates his importance when he supposes that we had him, rather than any other member of the committee, specially in view. Sir, I know the gigantic stature of the Senator; [1] I know the weight and importance which he possesses in the country; I know that he has a great and powerful party surrounding him; and I know also the great disadvantages under which I enter into any controversy which he provokes. I am in a minority. I know that full well. It is no very pleasant position. But I dare do that which I should like to see the Senator also do. I dare adhere to principle, even though that adherence must carry me into a minority.

Sir, our offence is that we deny the nationality of slavery. No man can show that we have ever sought to interfere with the legislation of any State of the Union upon that subject. All that we have ever insisted upon is that the Territories of this Union shall be preserved from slavery; and that where the general Government exercises exclusive jurisdiction its legislation shall be on the side of liberty. It is because we defend these positions that the Senator from Illinois attacks us. He thinks that he can take advantage of his position in the country—that he can take advantage of his connection with a great and powerful political organization, and assail us with little hazard. It is safe to attack opponents who stand, as we stand, without the supports he counts upon. Ay, sir, that shows courage, that shows chivalry, that shows high honor, that shows lofty manhood—to assail the few and the unsupported. I tell the Senator from Illinois that we did not assail him. We did not say a word about him from the beginning to the end of our appeal. He was named only in the postscript, and then merely as the author of the bill. We spoke of the bill. We spoke of its character. We said nothing about the character of the individuals who were its authors; anybody may see that who chooses to read the address.

In the whole discussion of the matter in controversy, we confined ourselves in that appeal strictly and closely to the merits of the case. And now, sir, here, in this Chamber, before this audience, I reaffirm every word and every syllable of that appeal. I make no personal imputations; I make no personal charges; I do not follow the example which has been set here to-day, but which, in my judgment, is not fit to be followed anywhere; but I reaffirm and reiterate, distinctly and emphatically, every word and every syllable of that address. I thank the Senator from Illinois for having brought it so prominently before the country. It will now reach thousands and tens of

[1] Senator Douglas was short in stature, and therefore was called by his followers the "Little Giant," in implicit compliment to his intellectual eminence among his fellow statesmen.

thousands who would not have read it but for the discussion which has taken place here to-day. It will be seen, read, and judged by the people, and they will determine for themselves whether or not its doctrine is sound and its facts are truly stated.

In this appeal "we arraign this bill as a gross violation of a sacred pledge." The Senator from Illinois thinks that the pledge of the Missouri compromise was nothing worth. We think it was of vast consequence, and absolutely binding; and, as the bill proposes to abrogate it, we do not choose soft words, but characterize it at once as it deserves. We arraign it also as "a criminal betrayal of precious rights." Well, what rights are precious if those secured to free labor and free laborers in that vast Territory are not? What can be criminal, if it be not criminal to subvert these rights for the purpose of giving room to slavery? When the bill proposes to reach this bad end by the baseless declaration that the Missouri prohibition is superseded by the principles of the legislation of 1850—a singular mode of repeal that—we call it "a criminal betrayal of precious rights."

The appeal goes on to denounce the bill as "part and parcel of an atrocious plot to exclude from a vast unoccupied region emigrants from the Old World and free laborers from our own States, and convert it into a dreary region of despotism, inhabited by masters and slaves." Well, suppose this Territory opened to slavery. Who does not know that upon the western borders of Missouri there are many slaveholders restrained now by the prohibition, but eager to enter the new Territory with their slaves? Who does not know that the effect of the introduction of slaves will be the exclusion of free laborers, and, to a great extent, of the emigrants from Europe? Why, sir, in my judgment, a concerted movement by slavery confederates to open this great Territory, larger by twelve times than the whole State of Ohio—larger than all the existing free States, with the exception of California—to the ingress of slavery is mildly characterized by the language of the appeal. But I will not further review this document. It will appear with these remarks and will speak for itself.

On February 3, 1854, Senator Chase moved to strike out so much of the bill as declared the restriction regarding slavery in the Missouri compromise "superseded" by the compromise of 1850. He spoke as follows upon the amendment:

Let Us Maintain Our Plighted Faith

Senator Chase

Mr. President, I had occasion a few days ago to expose the utter groundlessness of the personal charges made by the Senator from Illinois [Mr. Douglas] against myself and the other signers of the Independent Democratic appeal. I now move to strike from this bill a statement which I will to-day demonstrate to be without any foundation in fact or history. I intend afterward to move to strike out the whole clause annulling the Missouri prohibition.

I enter into this debate, Mr. President, in no spirit of personal unkindness. The issue is too grave and too momentous for the indulgence of such feelings. I see the great question before me, and that question only.

Sir, these crowded galleries, these thronged lobbies, this full attendance of the Senate prove the deep, transcendent interest of the theme.

A few days only have elapsed since the Congress of the United States assembled in this Capitol. Then no agitation seemed to disturb the political elements. Two of the great political parties of the country, in their national conventions, had announced that slavery agitation was at an end, and that henceforth that subject was not to be discussed in Congress or out of Congress. The President, in his annual message, had referred to this state of opinion, and had declared his fixed purpose to maintain, as far as any responsibility attached to him, the quiet of the country.

And so, sir, the country was at peace. As the eye swept the entire circumference of the horizon and upward to midheaven not a cloud appeared.

But suddenly all is changed. Rattling thunder breaks from the cloudless firmament. The storm bursts forth in fury. Warring winds rush into conflict.

> "Eurus, Notusque ruunt, creberque procellis,
> Africus."

"Yes, sir, "*creber procellis Africus*"—the south wind thick with storm. And now we find ourselves in the midst of an agitation, the end and issue of which no man can foresee.

Now, sir, who is responsible for this renewal of strife and controversy? Not we, for we have introduced no question of

territorial slavery into Congress—not we who are denounced as
agitators and factionists. No, sir; the quietists and the finalists
have become agitators; they who told us that all agitation was
quieted, and that the resolutions of the political conventions
put a final period to the discussion of slavery.

This will not escape the observation of the country. It is
slavery that renews the strife. It is slavery that again wants
room. It is slavery, with its insatiate demands for more slave
territory and more slave States.

And what does slavery ask for now? Why, sir, it demands
that a time-honored and sacred compact shall be rescinded—a
compact which has endured through a whole generation—a compact which has been universally regarded as inviolable, North
and South—a compact the constitutionality of which few have
doubted, and by which all have consented to abide.

It will not answer to violate such a compact without a
pretext. Some plausible ground must be discovered or invented
for such an act; and such a ground is supposed to be found in
the doctrine which was advanced the other day by the Senator
from Illinois, that the compromise acts of 1850 "superseded"
the prohibition of slavery north of 36° 30', in the act preparatory for the administration of Missouri.

It is against this statement, untrue in fact and without
foundation in history, that the amendment which I have proposed is directed.

The Senator from Illinois attempts to show that the original
policy of the country was one of indifferentism between slavery
and freedom; and that, in pursuance of it, a geographical line
was established reaching from the eastern to the western limit
of the original States—that is to say, to the Mississippi River.
Sir, if anything is susceptible of absolute historical demonstration, I think it is the proposition that the founders of this Republic never contemplated any extension of slavery.

Senator Chase here adduced the anti-slavery opinions of Thomas Jefferson and his part in the organization of the Territorial domain. Jefferson had been a
member of the first committee to report an ordinance
on the subject. In this early ordinance the proviso was
made that slavery should be abolished after 1800 in all
the territory belonging to the Government.

Well, what was the action of Congress upon this proviso? The States stood six to three in its favor, four States

being either divided or not voting. Of the twenty-three delegates present, sixteen were for the proviso and seven against
it. But under the provisions of the Articles of Confederation,
which then controlled the legislation of Congress, the votes of a
majority of all the States were necessary to retain the proviso
in the ordinance. It failed, consequently. Sir, if that doctrine
of the rights of majorities, of which we hear so much and see
in actual practice so little, had then been recognized—if the
wishes of a majority of the States, and of the majority of the
delegates, had prevailed—if the almost universal sentiment of
the people had been respected, the question of slavery in this
country would have been settled that day forever. All the
territory acquired by the Union would have been covered with
the impenetrable ægis of freedom. But then, as now, there was
a slave interest in the country—then, as now, there was a slave
power. The interest was comparatively small and the power
comparatively weak; but they were sufficient, under the then
existing Government, to defeat the proviso, and transfer the
great question of slavery to future discussion. The facts which
I have detailed, however, are sufficient to show what was the
general sentiment, and what was the original policy of the
country in respect to slavery. It was one of limitation, dis-
couragement, repression.

What next occurred? The subject of organizing this Territory remained before Congress. Mr. Jefferson, in 1785, went
to France. His great influence was no longer felt in the coun-
cils of the country, but his proviso remained, and in 1787 was
incorporated into the ordinance for the government of the territory northwest of the River Ohio. I beg the Senate to observe that this territory was, at that moment, the whole territory
belonging to the United States. I will not trouble the Senate
by reading the proviso of the ordinance. It is enough to say
that the Jefferson proviso of 1784, coupled with a provision
saving to the *original* States of the Union a right to reclaim
fugitives from service, was incorporated into the ordinance, and
became a fundamental law over every foot of national territory.
What was the policy indicated by this action by the Fathers of
the Republic? Was it that of indifferentism between slavery
and freedom?—that of establishing a geographical line, on one
side of which there should be liberty and on the other side
slavery, both equally under the protection and countenance of
the Government? No, sir; the furthest thing possible from
that. It was the policy of excluding slavery from all national
territory. It was adopted, too, under remarkable circumstances.

Slavery was already in the territory under the French colonial law, and also, if the claim of Virginia was well founded, under the laws of that State. These facts prove that the first application of the original policy of the Government converted slave territory into free territory.

And now, sir, let me ask the attention of the Senate to the Constitution itself. That charter of our Government was not formed upon pro-slavery principles, but upon anti-slavery principles. It nowhere recognizes any right of property in man. It nowhere confers upon the Government which it creates any power to establish or to continue slavery.

Not only was the idea of property in men excluded from the Constitution; not only was there no power granted to Congress to authorize or enable any man to hold another as property, but an amendment was afterward ingrafted upon the Constitution which especially denied all such power.

The history of that amendment is worth attention. The State which the Senators from Virginia so ably represent on this floor was one of those which immediately after the adoption of the Constitution proposed amendments of it. One of the amendments which she proposed was this:

"No *freeman* ought to be taken, imprisoned, or deprived of his freehold, liberties, or franchises, or outlawed, or exiled, or in any manner deprived of his life, liberty, or property, but by the law of the land."

Did Congress adopt that amendment? No, sir; it adopted and proposed to the States a very different amendment. It was this:

"No person * * * shall be deprived of life, liberty, or property, without due process of law."

Now, sir, in my judgment, this prohibition was intended as a comprehensive guaranty of personal freedom, and denies absolutely to Congress the power of legislating for the establishment or maintenance of slavery. This amendment of itself, rightly interpreted and applied, would be sufficient to prevent the introduction of slaves into any territory acquired by the United States. At all events, taken in connection with the ordinance, and with the original provision of the Constitution, it shows conclusively the absence of all intention upon the part of the founders of the Government to afford any countenance or protection to slavery outside of State limits. Departure from the true interpretation of the Constitution has created the necessity for positive prohibition.

My general view upon this subject is simply this: Slavery is the subjection of one man to the absolute disposal of another man by force. Master and slave, according to the principles of the Declaration of Independence, and by the law of nature, are alike men, endowed by their Creator with equal rights. Sir, Mr. Pinckney was right when, in the Maryland House of Delegates, he exclaimed, "By the eternal principles of justice, no man in the State has a right to hold his slave for a single hour." Slavery then exists nowhere by the law of nature. Wherever it exists at all, it must be through the sanction and support of municipal or State legislation.

Upon this state of things the Constitution acts. It recognizes all men as persons. It confers no power, but, on the contrary, expressly denies to the Government of its creation all power to establish or continue slavery. Congress has no more power under the Constitution to make a slave than to make a king; no more power to establish slavery than to establish the Inquisition.

At the same time the Constitution confers no power on Congress; but, on the contrary, denies all power to interfere with the internal policy of any State, sanctioned and established by its own constitution and its own legislation, in respect to the personal relations of its inhabitants. The States under the Constitution are absolutely free from all interference by Congress in that respect, except, perhaps, in the case of war or insurrection; and may legislate as they please within the limitations of their own constitutions. They may allow slavery if they please, just as they may license other wrongs. But State laws, by which slavery is allowed and regulated, can operate only within the limits of the State, and can have no extra-territorial effect.

Sir, I could quote the opinions of Southern judges *ad infinitum,* in support of the doctrine that slavery is against natural right, absolutely dependent for existence or continuance upon State legislation. I might quote the scornful rejection by Randolph of all aid from the general Government to the institution of slavery within the States. I might quote the decision of the celebrated Chancellor George Wythe, of Virginia—overruled afterward, I know, in the court of appeals—that slavery was so against justice that the presumption of freedom must be allowed in favor of every alleged slave suing for liberty, and that the onus of proving the contrary rested upon the master.

I think I have now shown that the Ordinance of 1787, and

the Constitution of the United States, were absolutely in harmony one with the other; and that if the ordinance had never been adopted, the Constitution itself, properly interpreted, and administered, would have excluded slavery from all newly acquired territory. But, sir, whatever opinion may be entertained in respect to the interpretation of the Constitution which I defend, one thing is absolutely indisputable, and that is that it was the original policy of the country to exclude slavery from all national territory.

The Senator continued his historical review of slavery in the United States, showing that there was no thought of establishing a geographical line (such as Senator Douglas had claimed was drawn at that early period) until the Missouri compromise. Having related the history of this adjustment of the question, he said:

Here then is a compact, complete, perfect, irrepealable, so far as any compact, embodied in a legislative act, can be said to be irrepealable. It had the two sections of the country for its parties, a great Territory for its subject, and a permanent adjustment of a dangerous controversy for its object. It was forced upon the free States. It has been literally fulfilled by the free States. It is binding, indeed, only upon honor and conscience; but, in such a matter, the obligations of honor and conscience must be regarded as even more sacred than those of constitutional provisions.

Mr. President, if there was any principle which prevailed in this arrangement, it was that of permitting the continuance of slavery in the localities where it actually existed at the time of the acquisition of the territory, and prohibiting it in the parts of territory in which no slaves were actually held. This was a wide departure from the original policy which contemplated the exclusion of slavery from territories in which it actually existed at the time of acquisition. But the idea that slavery could ever be introduced into free territory, under the sanction of Congress, had not, as yet, entered into any man's head.

Senator Chase continued with his review, taking up the history of the Wilmot proviso. The North's position, he stated, was that territory already free, south of the Compromise line, should remain free. Therefore the free States defeated Senator Douglas's proposal to extend the line to the Pacific, with the effect that slavery would be introduced in all territory to the south, whatever its previous condition, whether slave or free.

The Senator then came to the Clay Compromise.

What, then, was the principle, if any, upon which this controversy was adjusted? Clearly this: That, when free territory is acquired, that part of it which is ready to come in as a free State shall be admitted into the Union, and that part which is not ready shall be organized into territorial governments, and its condition in respect to slavery or freedom shall be left in doubt during the whole period of its territorial existence.

It is quite obvious, Mr. President, how very prejudicial such a doubt must be to the settlement and improvement of the territory. But I must not pause upon this.

The truth is that the compromise acts of 1850 were not intended to introduce any principle of territorial organization applicable to any other Territory except that covered by them. The professed object of the friends of the compromise acts was to compose the whole slavery agitation. There were various matters of complaint. The non-surrender of fugitives from service was one. The existence of slavery and the slave trade here in this District and elsewhere, under the exclusive jurisdiction of Congress, was another. The apprehended introduction or prohibition of slavery in the Territories furnished other grounds of controversy. The slave States complained of the free States, and the free States complained of the slave States. It was supposed by some that this whole agitation might be stayed, and finally put at rest by skillfully adjusted legislation. So, sir, we had the Omnibus bill, and its appendages the Fugitive Slave bill, and the District Slave Trade Suppression bill. To please the North—to please the free States—California was to be admitted, and the slave depots here in the District were to be broken up. To please the slave States, a stringent fugitive slave act was to be passed, and slavery was to have a chance to get into the new Territories. The support of the Senators and Representatives from Texas was to be gained by a liberal adjustment of boundary, and by the assumption of a large portion of their State debt. The general result contemplated was a complete and final adjustment of all questions relating to slavery. The acts passed. A number of the friends of the acts signed a compact, pledging themselves to support no man for any office who would in any way renew the agitation. The country was required to acquiesce in the settlement as an absolute finality. No man concerned in carrying those measures through Congress, and least of all the distinguished man whose efforts mainly contributed to their success, ever imagined that in the territorial acts, which formed a part of the series, they were planting the germs of a new agitation. Indeed, I have proved that one of these acts contains an express stipulation which precludes the revival of the agitation in the form in which it is now thrust upon the country, without manifest disregard of the provisions of those acts themselves.

I have thus proved beyond controversy that the averment of the bill, which my amendment proposes to strike out, is untrue. Senators, will you unite in a statement which you know to be contradicted by the history of the country? Will you incorporate into a public statute an affirmation which is contradicted by every event which attended or followed the adoption of the compromise acts? Will you here, acting under your high responsibility as Senators of the States, assert as fact, by a solemn vote, that which the personal recollection of every Senator who was here during the discussion of those compromise acts disproves? I will not believe it until I see it. If you wish to break up the time-honored compact embodied in the Missouri compromise, transferred into the joint resolution for the annexation of Texas, preserved and affirmed by these compromise acts themselves, do it openly—do it boldly. Repeal the Missouri prohibition. Repeal it by a direct vote. Do not repeal it by indirection. Do not "declare" it "inoperative," "because superseded by the principles of the legislation of 1850."

Senator Chase closed his speech with a philosophical analysis of the history of slavery in the country, dividing the period covered into eras. The *Era of Enfranchisement* was the first. It continued until the Louisiana Purchase, when, owing to the acquisition of territory where slavery already existed, it waned into the *Era of Conservatism,* in which the subject of slavery was "let alone," *e. g.,* the possession of slaves in Illinois was winked at, while the ordinance of 1787 was continued nominally in force.

The Era of Conservatism passed, also by imperceptible gradations, into the *Era of Slavery Propagandism.* Under the influences of this new spirit we opened the whole territory acquired from Mexico, except California, to the ingress of slavery. Every foot of it was covered by a Mexican prohibition; and yet, by the legislation of 1850, we consented to expose it to the introduction of slaves. Under the evil influences of the same spirit, we are now called upon to reverse the original policy of the Republic; to subvert even a solemn compact of the conservative period, and open Nebraska to slavery.

Sir, I believe that we are upon the verge of another era. That era will be the *Era of Reaction*. The introduction of this question here, and its discussion, will greatly hasten its advent. We, who insist upon the denationalization of slavery, and upon the absolute divorce of the general Government from all connection with it, will stand with the men who favored the compromise acts, and who yet wish to adhere to them, in their letter and in their spirit, against the repeal of the Missouri prohibition. But you may pass it here. You may send it to the other House. It may become law. But its effect will be to satisfy all thinking men that no compromises with slavery will endure, except so long as they serve the interests of slavery; and that there is no safe and honorable ground for non-slaveholders to stand upon, except that of restricting slavery within State limits, and excluding it absolutely from the whole sphere of Federal jurisdiction. The old questions between political parties are at rest. No great question so thoroughly possesses the public mind as this of slavery. This discussion will hasten the inevitable reorganization of parties upon the new issues which our circumstances suggest. It will light up a fire in the country which may, perhaps, consume those who kindle it.

I cannot believe that the people of this country have so far lost sight of the maxims and principles of the Revolution, or are so insensible to the obligations which those maxims and principles impose, as to acquiesce in the violation of this compact. Sir, the Senator from Illinois tells us that he proposes a final settlement of all territorial questions in respect to slavery, by the application of the principle of popular sovereignty. What kind of popular sovereignty is that which allows one portion of the people to enslave another portion? Is that the doctrine of equal rights? Is that exact justice? Is that the teaching of enlightened, liberal, progressive democracy? No, sir; no! There can be no real democracy which does not fully maintain the rights of man, as man. Living, practical, earnest democracy imperatively requires us, while carefully abstaining from unconstitutional interference with the internal regulations of any State upon the subject of slavery, or any other subject, to insist upon the practical application of its great principles in all the legislation of Congress.

I repeat, sir, that we who maintain these principles will stand shoulder to shoulder with the men who, differing from us upon other questions, will yet unite with us in opposition to the violation of plighted faith contemplated by this bill. There are men, and not a few, who are willing to adhere to the compromises of 1850. If the Missouri prohibition, which those compromises incorporate and preserve among their own provisions, shall be repealed, abrogated, broken up, thousands will say, Away with all compromises; they are not worth the paper on which they are printed; we will return to the old principles of the Constitution. We will assert the ancient doctrine, that no person shall be deprived of life, liberty, or property, by the legislation of Congress, without due process of law. Carrying out that principle into its practical applications, we will not cease our efforts until slavery shall cease to exist wherever it can be reached by the constitutional action of the Government.

Sir, I trust that the result of this discussion will show that the American Senate will sanction no breach of compact. Let us strike from the bill that statement which historical facts and our personal recollections disprove, and then reject the whole proposition which looks toward a violation of the plighted faith and solemn compact which our fathers made, and which we, their sons, are bound by every tie of obligation sacredly to maintain.

On the next day (February 4) Senator Dixon replied to Senator Chase. His chief argument was the familiar one that the Territories belonged in common to the people of the entire Union, and no discrimination, therefore, should be made against the South by Federal restriction of slavery therein.

The debate was renewed on February 6, Senator Wade having the floor. The Senator claimed that the "conspiracy" to overturn the Missouri compromise had been "hatched" within the previous six weeks. When the compromise of 1850 had been proposed the delicate question of whether or not it superseded the compromise of 1820 had been carefully avoided.

But, sir, notwithstanding their extraordinary silence, Senators have discovered that the legislation of 1850 had, in some

IV—19

mysterious manner, superseded the most stern and stubborn law of Congress, which was formed upon a compromise as sacred as could be made between conflicting sections of this Union, and concurred in on all hands for at least one-third of a century. They declare that it is superseded by a new "principle." Now, as a lawyer, I hardly know what a man means when he tells me that an act of legislation is superseded by a principle. I thought it took an act of Congress to repeal, or annul, or suspend, a former act.

SENATOR DOUGLAS.—I contend that by the acts of 1850 a great principle of self-government was substituted for a geographical line; and hence, by the use of the words "superseded by," I mean which was "inconsistent with" the compromise of 1850. If the gentleman prefers the words "inconsistent with," I will put them in with a great deal of pleasure, and that will avoid all the trouble in regard to the use of the word "supersede."

SENATOR WADE.—The Senator made a very simple declaration in his speech upon this point. It was that the Missouri compromise was annulled to the extent to which Congress, in running the boundary lines of New Mexico and Utah, might take for the sake of convenience any little piece of territory which was covered by the Missouri compromise. That certainly was a truism; but the idea that the acts to organize Utah and New Mexico repealed or superseded the Missouri compromise as to the remainder of the territory acquired by the Louisiana cession is an idea from which I am glad to see that the gentleman now recedes.

SENATOR DOUGLAS.—Not at all.

SENATOR WADE.—What does the Senator mean, then, by saying that the Missouri compromise was superseded by the principles of the compromise measures of 1850? Suppose you run a line with your neighbor, and the line has become uncertain, and in order to straighten it you run another, and in running this other line may possibly take in a little land that belonged to him, or you may leave out a little belonging to yourself; if you find you have entered wrongfully on his land, does the principle of running that line supersede his title to the balance, and therefore can you lay title to the whole of his land? Indeed, the gentleman informed us, in the report, that this was a matter too grave even for Congress to decide, and much too grave for a committee, and therefore they would not do it; and yet in nineteen days afterward they come in with what is equivalent to a total repeal of the compromise.

I will not answer for the consequences of the legislation of this day, sir; but I anxiously desire to inquire if nothing can be established in this Government? Is there nothing too sacred to be overhauled for some miserable party or other purpose?

Why, sir, Henry Clay is scarcely in his grave before another generation comes up that knows not what he had done, and some even pretend that in what he himself did, in 1850, he seemed to concede that the compromise of 1820 was not to be lived up to. I tell the gentlemen there is not a word, nor a syllable, that goes to indicate that anyone supposed that anything was done then to overthrow the time-honored compromise of 1820. Not one word, sir; but, on the contrary, if they could recur to this compromise, they indorsed it and reaffirmed it in 1850 beyond all gainsaying.

But, sir, I need not refer further to the speech of the Senator from Illinois. My colleague [Mr. Chase] so entirely pulverized that speech that there is not enough of it left upon which a man can possibly hang an idea. [Laughter.] In fact, there was nothing to begin with. It was a bare afterthought; after the report of the committee had been made, and the bill had been altered, it was necessary to get up some other reason or pretext than was set forth in the report, in order to show why it was proposed to repeal the Missouri compromise.

Here is a Territory large as an empire. It is pure as nature; it is beautiful as the garden of God. There is nothing now to prevent us doing with it what will minister to the best interests of the people now and hereafter. Our forefathers expressed their opinion as to what was best to be done with it. They believed it should be fenced up from the intrusion of this accursed scourge of mankind, human slavery. They have done this effectually in this Territory. Shall we undo their work? The Southern States have had the benefit of the Missouri compromise for thirty years? Has any Northern man stepped forward, Senators of the South, to impair your rights in that compromise? No, sir, it is not pretended; and now the period is drawing near when that part of this great bargain which is beneficial to us at the North is approaching, and I call upon you as honorable men to fulfill it. The Senator from Kentucky [Mr. Dixon] told us that this came from the North, and therefore the South were absolved from their obligation. I must say I think you understand well that the North know nothing about this base conspiracy to betray them. When did it come up? Did you let it go before the people, that they might pass upon the question? Why, sir, in the presidential election, triumphant as the Democracy were, I ask any gentleman of the North, suppose you had staked the election of Mr. Pierce upon this question, how many votes could he have received in the North? Not one. You gave us no notice of any such thing. The people of the North, even now, do not know what nefarious projects are afoot here in the Capitol. You of the South are not absolved, because one or two men, very honorable men, stand forth here and say, "I am ready to go in and make this monstrous proposition." Sir, in the days of the Revolution, Major André was hung by the neck until he was dead, for accepting a proposition not more base than this, which is a gross betrayal of the rights of the whole North.

Gentlemen seek to extend the market for human beings; and hence the object of this bill. I say it does not consist with the welfare of this Union to do so.

You may call me an abolitionist if you will; I care but little for that; for if an undying hatred to slavery or oppression constitutes an abolitionist, I am that abolitionist. Not, sir, that I ever went with that particular party; but I did not differ from them on these points; but because they did not make their opposition effectual, in my judgment; for I would have gone with those who would have reached your institutions, wherever the Constitution gave us a right to reach them, without encroaching one hair's breadth where we had no right. There I do not undertake, and never shall undertake, to trench, upon them. I admit that in the States you have full control over it. You may do with it as seems to you good. You never found me, you never found the party to which I belong in the North, pretending to do anything adverse to your right to make such laws and regulations with regard to this institution as you please. We hoped that you would see that the system did not work to your best advantage; we were in hopes you would see that a gradual system of emancipation, just such as made the vast difference between the progress of the State of New York and old Virginia, would wake up every sensible man to follow in the track, and to do likewise. We hoped that, but we claimed no right to interfere. You must do with this as seems to you good.

Mr. President, this is an exceedingly dangerous issue. I know the Senator from Kentucky said he did not think there would be very much of a storm after all. He was of opinion that the Northern mind would immediately lie down under it, that the North would do as they have frequently done, submit to it, and finally become indifferent in regard to it. But I tell the gentleman that I see indications entirely adverse to that. I see a cloud, a little bigger now than a man's hand, gathering in the North, and in the West, and all around, and soon the whole northern heavens will be lighted up with a fire that you cannot quench. The indications of it are rife now in the heavens, and any man who is not blind can see it. There are meetings of the people in all quarters; they express their alarm, their dismay, their horror at the proposition which has been made here. You cannot make them believe that the thing is seriously contemplated here. How is it? You of the South, all of you, propose to go for repudiating this obligation. Do you not see that you are about to bring slavery and freedom face to face, to grapple for the victory, and that one or the other must die? I do not know that I ought to regret it, but I say to gentlemen you are antedating the time when that must come. It has always been my opinion that principles so entirely in opposition to each other, so utterly hostile and irreconcilable, could never exist long in the same Government.

I tell you, sir, if you precipitate such a conflict as that, it will not be liberty that will die in the nineteenth century. This is a progressive age; and if you make this fight you must be ready for the consequences. I regret it. I am an advocate for the continuance of this Union; but, as I have already said, I do not believe this Union can survive ten years the act of perfidy that will repudiate the great compromise of 1820.

On February 14, George E. Badger [N. C.] spoke as follows:

My position has never been an extreme one upon this subject. I was always content with the Missouri compromise line—always anxious for it—always voted for it; but my own individual opinion upon the subject always was that the principles adopted in 1850 are the true principles.

We have among us a population of three millions of slaves. They are here. They are slaves. They cannot remain here except as slaves. Everybody knows that. They cannot, by any operation of man's wit, be put into any situation in our country which will not be vastly more injurious to them, physically and morally, than the identical state and condition which they now occupy. They cannot be sent away. Where are your means to come from to make an exodus across the ocean of three millions of slaves—to buy them, and to remove them? And if you could buy them, and remove them, permit me to say that a more cruel act of tyranny and oppression could not

be perpetrated upon any body of men. A very large proportion of them would reject with horror the idea of being transported to those barbarous and foreign climes of Africa, for
which, though their fathers came from them, they cherish no
feeling of attachment; for this is their country as well as ours.

What, then, are you going to do? Is it not obvious that
the true policy, as well as the true Christian philanthropy, involved in this matter is to allow this population to diffuse itself
in such portions of the Territories as from climate and soil are
adapted to slave cultivation? You can have no injurious competition with your free labor. Slave labor will not be profitable,
and largely employed anywhere, except upon the great staples
of the South—tobacco, cotton, sugar, and rice. Will white
men make these products for exportation? They will not. Will
your Northern people compete with Southern slaves for the
privilege of making rice, and sugar, and cotton, and tobacco?
No, sir. Where that cultivation ceases, rely upon it, a slave population is not going to spread itself. We shall have no conflict,
no embarrassment from the meeting of two tides of laborers
from the North and South; for the kind of soil and climate
which suits us and our slave cultivation does not suit yours.

Here, then, is the great fact we have to deal with. Why not
let it adjust itself? Cease to quarrel and wrangle with each
other. Live in your free States. Rejoice in the possession of
the many advantages you have. But if there is a strip of land
belonging to the United States, upon which a Southern planter
can make cotton or sugar, why grudge it to him? He reduces
no man from freedom to slavery in order to make it. He transfers his slaves from the banks of the Mississippi, or the Cooper,
or the Cape Fear, or any of our Southern rivers, to another
place; and he certainly will not do it unless the lands are better, the crops larger, and he and his slaves can live more com-
fortably, and have a more abundant supply of the necessaries
of life; and I will ask, in the name of Heaven, whom does it
hurt? You love freedom. We do not ask you to make freemen
slaves. You profess to have a regard for the black man; can
you resist the only measure which can enable us to make a progressive improvement of his condition as the amount of black
population increases?

I think, Mr. President, it is in the highest degree probable
that, with regard to these Territories of Nebraska and Kansas,
there will never be any slaves in them. It is possible some gentlemen may go there and take a few domestic servants with
them; and I would say that if those domestic servants were

faithful and good ones, and the masters did not take them with them, the masters would deserve the reprobation of all good men. What would you have them do? Would you have me to take the servants who wait upon me, and live with me, and to whom I have as strong attachments as to any human beings on this earth out of my own immediate relations and connections, and, because I want to move to Kansas, put them in. the slave market and sell them? Sir, I would suffer my right arm to be cut off before I would do it. Why, therefore, if some Southern gentleman wishes to take the nurse that takes charge of his little baby, or the old woman that nursed him in childhood, and whom he called "mammy" until he returned from college, and perhaps afterward, too, and whom he wishes to take with him in her old age when he is moving into one of these new Territories for the betterment of the fortunes of his whole family, why, in the name of God, should anybody prevent it? Do you wish to force us to become hard-hearted slave dealers? Do you wish to aggravate the evils, if there are evils existing in this relation? Do you wish that we shall no longer have a mutual feudal feeling between our dependants and ourselves? Do you want to make us mercenary and hard-hearted? Or will you allow us, having, as I trust we have, some touch of humanity, and some of the beneficial and love-breathing spirit of Christianity, to let these beings go forth as they are accustomed to do, and us to rejoice when we look out and see our slaves happy and cheerful around us, when we hear the song arising from their dwellings at night, or see them dressed in their neat clothes and going to attend their churches on Sunday, and realizing, as they look at us, that we are the best friends they have upon earth?

To the "old mammy" argument Senator Wade replied pertinently: "We have not the least objection to the Senator's migrating to Kansas and taking his old mammy along with him. We only insist that he shall not be empowered to *sell* her after taking her there."

On February 17 William H. Seward [N. Y.] made a long and carefully prepared speech, in the beginning of which he thus paid his respects to Senator Badger:

The honorable and very acute Senator from North Carolina has wooed us most persuasively to waive our objections to the new principle, as it is called, of non-intervention, by assuring us that the slaveholder can use slave labor only where the soils and climates favor the culture of tobacco, cotton, rice, and sugar. To which I reply: None of them find these congenial soils or climates at the sources of the Mississippi, or in the valleys of the Rocky Mountains. Why, then, does he want to remove the inhibition there?

But again: That Senator reproduces a pleasing fiction of the character of slavery from the Jewish history, and asks, Why not allow the *modern patriarchs* to go into new regions with their slaves, as their ancient prototypes did, to make them more comfortable and happy? And he tells us, at the same time, that this indulgence will not increase the number of slaves. I reply by asking, first, whether slavery has gained or lost strength by the diffusion of it over a larger surface than it formerly covered? Will the Senator answer that? Secondly, I quite admire the simplicity of the patriarchal times. But they nevertheless exhibited some peculiar institutions quite incongruous with modern republicanism, not to say Christianity; namely, that of a latitude of construction of the marriage contract, which has been carried by one class of so-called patriarchs into Utah. Certainly no one would desire to extend that peculiar institution into Nebraska. Thirdly, slaveholders have also a peculiar institution, which makes them *political* patriarchs. They reckon five of their slaves as equal to three freemen in forming the basis of Federal representation. If these patriarchs insist upon carrying their institution into new regions, north of thirty-six degrees thirty minutes, I respectfully submit that they ought to reassume the modesty of their Jewish predecessors, and relinquish this political feature of the system they thus seek to extend. Will they do that?

On February 24, 1854, Senator Sumner delivered a long and eloquent address against the bill.

THE LANDMARK OF FREEDOM

SENATOR SUMNER

The primal truth of the equality of men, as proclaimed in our Declaration of Independence, has been assailed, and this great charter of our country discredited. Sir, you and I will soon pass away, but that will continue to stand, above impeachment or question. The Declaration of Independence was a Declaration of Rights, and the language employed, though general in its character, must obviously be restrained within the design and sphere of a Declaration of Rights, involving no such

absurdity as was attributed to it yesterday by the Senator from
Indiana [John Pettit [1]]. Sir, it is a palpable fact that men are
not born equal in physical strength or in mental capacities, in
beauty of form or health of body. These mortal cloaks of flesh
differ, as do these worldly garments. Diversity or inequality, in
these respects, is the law of creation. But, as God is no re-
specter of persons, and as all are equal in his sight, whether
Dives or Lazarus, master or slave, so are all equal in natural
inborn rights; and pardon me if I say it is a vain sophism
to adduce in argument against this vital axiom of Liberty the
physical or mental inequalities by which men are characterized, or the unhappy degradation to which, in violation of a
common brotherhood, they are doomed. To deny the Declaration of Independence is to rush on the bosses of the shield of
the Almighty, which, in all respects, the supporters of this
measure seem to do.

To the delusive suggestion of the Senator from North Carolina [Mr. Badger], that, by the overthrow of this prohibition,
the number of slaves will not be increased; that there will be
simply a beneficent diffusion of slavery, and not its extension, I
reply at once that this argument, if of any value, would equally
justify and require the overthrow of the prohibition of slavery
in the free States, and, indeed, everywhere throughout the world.
It is clear, beyond dispute, that, by the overthrow of this prohibition, slaves will be multiplied, while new "room and verge"
will be secured for the gloomy operations of slave law, under
which free labor will droop, and a vast territory be smitten
with sterility. Sir, a blade of grass would not grow where the
horse of Attila had trod; nor can any true prosperity spring up
in the footprints of the slave.

But it is argued that slaves will not be carried into Nebraska
in large numbers, and that, therefore, the question is of small
practical moment. Sir, the census shows that it is of vital consequence. There is Missouri at this moment, with Illinois on
the east and Nebraska on the west, all covering nearly the same
spaces of latitude, and resembling each other in soil, climate,
and productions. Mark now the contrast! By the potent efficacy of the ordinance of the Northwestern Territory, Illinois is
now a free State, while Missouri has 87,422 slaves; and the simple question which challenges an answer is whether Nebraska
shall be preserved in the condition of Illinois or surrendered to
that of Missouri? Surely this cannot be treated lightly. But
for myself, I am unwilling to measure the exigency of the pro-

[1] Senator Pettit called the Declaration "a self-evident lie."

hibition by the number of persons, whether many or few, whom it may protect. Human rights, whether in a vast multitude or a solitary individual, are entitled to an equal and unhesitating support.

And now, sir, in the name of that public faith which is the very ligament of civil society, and which the great Roman orator tells us it is detestable to break even with an enemy, I arraign this scheme, and hold it up to the judgment of all who hear me.

Sir, the proposition before you involves not merely the repeal of an existing law, but the infraction of solemn obligations originally proposed and assumed by the South, after a protracted and embittered contest, as a covenant of peace— with regard to the Louisiana Purchase. This arrangement in its stipulations for slavery was justly repugnant to the conscience of the North, and ought never to have been made; but it has on that side been performed. And now the unperformed outstanding obligations to freedom, originally proposed and assumed by the South, are resisted.

Years have passed since these obligations were embodied in the legislation of Congress and accepted by the country. This extraordinary lapse of time, with the complete fruition by one party of all the benefits belonging to it, under the compact, gives to the transaction an added and most sacred strength. Prescription steps in with new bonds to confirm the original work; to the end that, while men are mortal, controversies shall not be immortal. Death, with inexorable scythe, has mowed down the authors of this compact; but, with conservative hourglass, it has counted out a succession of years, which now defile before us, like so many sentinels, to guard the sacred landmark of freedom.

A subtle German has declared that he could find heresies in the Lord's Prayer—and I believe it is only in this spirit that any flaw can be found in the existing obligations of this compact. As late as 1848, in the discussions of this body, the Senator from Virginia [Mr. Mason], while condemning it in many aspects, says:

"Yet as it was agreed to as a compromise by the South for the sake of the Union, *I would be the last to disturb it.*"

This act, under all the circumstances attending its passage, also by long acquiescence and the complete performance of its conditions by one party, has become a part of our fundamental law, irrepealable by any common legislation. As well might Congress at this moment undertake to overhaul the original purchase of Louisiana, as unconstitutional,[1] and now, on this account, thrust away that magnificent heritage, with all its cities, States, and Territories, teeming with civilization. The Missouri compact, in its unperformed obligations to freedom, stands at this day as impregnable as the Louisiana Purchase.

I appeal to Senators about me not to disturb it. I appeal to the Senators from Virginia to keep inviolate the compact made in their behalf by James Barbour and Charles Fenton Mercer. I appeal to the Senators from South Carolina to guard the work of John Gaillard and William Lowndes. I appeal to the Senators from Maryland to uphold the compromise which elicited the constant support of Samuel Smith, and was first triumphantly pressed by the unsurpassed eloquence of Pinkney. I appeal to the Senators from Delaware to maintain the landmark of freedom in the Territory of Louisiana, early espoused by Louis McLane. I appeal to the Senators from Kentucky not to repudiate the pledges of Henry Clay. I appeal to the Senators from Alabama not to break the agreement sanctioned by the earliest votes in the Senate of their late most cherished fellow-citizen, William Rufus King. Sir, I have heard of an honor that felt a stain like a wound. If there be any such in this chamber—as surely there is—it will hesitate to take upon itself the stain of this transaction.

Sir, Congress may now set aside this obligation, repudiate this plighted faith, annul this compact; and some of you, forgetful of the *majesty of honest dealing*, in order to support slavery, may consider it advantageous to use this power. To all such let me commend a familiar story: An eminent leader in antiquity, Themistocles, once announced to the Athenian Assembly that he had a scheme to propose highly beneficial to the state, but which could not be expounded to the many. Aristides, surnamed the Just, was appointed to receive the secret, and to report upon it. His brief and memorable judgment was that, while nothing could be more advantageous to Athens, nothing could be more unjust; and the Athenian multitude, responding at once, rejected the proposition. It appears that it was proposed to burn the combined Greek fleet, which then rested in the security of peace in a neighboring sea, and thus confirm the naval supremacy of Athens. A similar proposition is now brought before the American Senate. You are asked to destroy a safeguard of freedom, consecrated by solemn compact, under which the country is now reposing in the security of peace, and

---

[1] Opponents of the Purchase declared at the time that it was unconstitutional. See Volume II, chapter iv.

thus confirm the supremacy of slavery. To this institution and its partisans the proposition may seem to be advantageous; but nothing can be more unjust. Let the judgment of the Athenian multitude be yours.

Mr. President, it is not only as an infraction of solemn compact, embodied in ancient law, that I arraign this bill. I arraign it also as a flagrant and extravagant departure from the original policy of our fathers, consecrated by their lives, opinions, and acts.

Sir, the original policy of the country, begun under the Confederation, and recognized at the initiation of the new Government, is clear and unmistakable. Compendiously expressed, it was *non-intervention by Congress with slavery in the States, and its prohibition in all the national domain.* In this way, the discordant feelings on this subject were reconciled. Slave masters were left at home in their respective States to hug slavery, under the protection of local laws, without any interference from Congress, while all opposed to it were exempted from any responsibility therefor in the national domain. This, sir, is the common ground on which our political fabric was reared; and I do not hesitate to say that it is the only ground on which it can stand in permanent peace.

But the original policy of the Government did not long prevail. The generous sentiments which filled the early patriots, giving to them historic grandeur, gradually lost their power. The blessings of freedom being already secured to themselves, the freemen of the land grew indifferent to the freedom of others. They ceased to think of the slaves. The slave masters availed themselves of this indifference, and, though few in numbers, compared with the non-slaveholders, even in the slave States (according to the late census they are fewer than three hundred thousand), they have, under the influence of an imagined self-interest, by the skillful tactics of party, and especially by an unhesitating, persevering union among themselves —swaying, by turns, both the great political parties—succeeded, through a long succession of years, in obtaining the control of the National Government, bending it to their purposes, compelling it to do their will, and imposing upon it a policy friendly to slavery; offensive to freedom only, and directly opposed to the sentiments of its founders. Our Republic has swollen in population and power; but it has shrunk in character. It is now what it was at the beginning, a republic merely permitting, while it regretted, slavery; tolerating it only where t could not be removed, and interdicting it where it did not exist—but a mighty propagandist openly favoring and vindicating it; visiting, also, with displeasure all who oppose it.

The Senator then opposed the arguments in favor of the bill.

I am unwilling to admit, sir, that the prohibition of slavery in the Territories is, in any just sense, an infringement of the local sovereignty. Slavery is an infraction of the immutable law of nature, and, as such, cannot be considered a natural incident to any sovereignty, especially in a country which has solemnly declared, in its Declaration of Independence, the inalienable right of all men to life, *liberty,* and the pursuit of happiness. In an age of civilization, and in a land of rights, slavery may still be tolerated in fact; but its prohibition, within a municipal jurisdiction, by the Government thereof, as by one of the States of the Union, cannot be considered an infraction of natural rights; nor can its prohibition by Congress in the Territories be regarded as an infringement of the local sovereignty, founded, as it must be, on natural rights.

But another argument is pressed, most fallacious in its character. It is asserted that, inasmuch as the Territories were acquired by the common treasure, they are the common property of the whole Union; and, therefore, no citizen can be prevented from moving into them with his slaves, without an infringement of the equal rights and privileges which belong to him as a citizen of the United States. But it is admitted that the people of this very Territory, when organized as a State, may exclude slaves, and in this way abridge an asserted right founded on the common property in the Territory. Now, if this can be done by the few thousand settlers who constitute the State government, the whole argument founded on the acquisition of the Territories by a common treasure seems futile and evanescent.

But this argument proceeds on an assumption which cannot stand. It assumes that slavery is a national institution, and that property in slaves is recognized by the Constitution of the United States. Nothing can be more false. By the judgment of the Supreme Court of the United States, and also by the principles of the common law, slavery is a local municipal institution, which derives its support exclusively from local municipal laws, and beyond the sphere of these laws it ceases to exist, except so far as it may be preserved by the clause for the rendition of fugitives from labor. Madison thought it wrong to admit into the Constitution the idea that there can be no property in man; and I rejoice to believe that no such idea can be found there. The Constitution regards slaves always as "persons," with the rights of "persons," never as property. When it is said, therefore, that every citizen may enter the national domain with his property, it does not follow by any rule of logic or of law that he may carry his slaves. On the contrary, he can only carry that property which is admitted to be such by the universal law of nature, written by God's own finger on the heart of man.

Again. The relation of master and slave is sometimes classed with the domestic relations. Now, while it is unquestionably among the powers of any State, within its own jurisdiction, to change the existing relation of husband and wife, and to establish polygamy, I presume no person would contend that a polygamous husband, resident in one of the States, would be entitled to enter the national territory with his harem—his property, if you please—and there claim immunity. Clearly, when he passes the bounds of that local jurisdiction, which sanctions polygamy, the peculiar domestic relation would cease; and it is precisely the same with slavery.

Sir, I dismiss these considerations. The prohibition of slavery in the Territory of Nebraska stands on foundations of adamant, upheld by the early policy of the Fathers, by constant precedent and time-honored compact. It is now in your power to overturn it; you may remove the sacred landmark, and open the whole vast domain to slavery. To you is committed this high prerogative. Our fathers, on the eve of the Revolution, set forth in burning words among their grievances, that George III, "in order to keep open a market where men should be bought and sold, had prostituted his negative for suppressing every legislative attempt to prohibit or restrain this execrable commerce." Sir, like the English monarch, you may now prostitute your power to this same purpose. But you cannot escape the judgment of the world, nor the doom of history.

It will be in vain that, while doing this thing, you plead, in apology, the principle of *self-government*, which you profess to recognize in the Territories. Sir, this very principle, when truly administered, secures equal rights to all, without distinction of color or race, and makes slavery impossible. By no rule of justice, and by no subtlety of political metaphysics, can the right to hold a fellow-man in bondage be regarded as essential to self-government. The inconsistency is too flagrant. It is apparent on the bare statement. It is like saying *two* and *two* make *three*. In the name of liberty you open the door to slavery. With professions of equal rights on the lips, you trample on the rights of human nature. With a kiss upon the brow of that fair Territory you betray it to wretchedness and shame. Well did the patriot soul exclaim, in bitter words, wrung out by bitter experience: "Oh, liberty! what crimes are done in thy name!"

In vain, sir, you will plead that this measure proceeds from the North, as has been suggested by the Senator from Kentucky [Mr. Dixon].

It is true that the race of men, "white slaves of the North," described and despised by a Southern statesman, is not yet extinct there. It is one of the melancholy tokens of the power of slavery, under our political system, and especially through the operations of the National Government, that it loosens and destroys the character of Northern men, even at a distance—like the black magnetic mountain in the Arabian story, under whose irresistible attraction the iron bolts, which held together the strong timbers of a stately ship, were drawn out, till the whole fell apart, and became a disjointed wreck. Alas! too often those principles, which give consistency, individuality, and form to the Northern character, which render it staunch, strong, and seaworthy, which bind it together as with iron, are drawn out, one by one, like the bolts of the ill-fated vessel, and from the miserable, loosened fragments is formed that human anomaly— *a Northern man with Southern principles.* Sir—no such man can speak for the North.

[Here there was an interruption of prolonged applause in the galleries.]

Mr. President, pass this bill, and it will be in vain that you say the slavery question is settled. Sir, *nothing can be settled which is not right.* Nothing can be settled which is adverse to freedom. God, nature, and all the holy sentiments of the heart repudiate any such false seeming settlement.

On the contrary, defeat the bill and you will most truly promote the harmony which you so much desire. You will establish tranquillity throughout the country. Then, at last, sir, the slavery question will be settled. Banished from its usurped foothold under the National Government, slavery will no longer enter, with distracting force, into the national politics—making and unmaking laws, making and unmaking Presidents. Confined to the States, where it was left by the Constitution, it will take its place as a local institution—if, alas! continue it must!—for which we are in no sense responsible, and against which we cannot exert any political power. We shall be relieved from our present painful and irritating connection with it. The existing antagonism between the North and South will be softened; crimination and recrimination will cease; the wishes of the Fathers will be fulfilled, and this great evil be left to the kindly influences of morals and religion, and the prevailing laws of social economy.

The North and the South, sir, as I fondly trust, amid all differences of opinion, will ever have a hand and a heart for each other; and, believing in the sure prevalence of almighty truth, I confidently look forward to the good time when both will unite, according to the sentiments of the Fathers and the true spirit of the Constitution, in declaring freedom and not slavery *national*, while slavery and freedom shall be *sectional*. Then will be achieved that Union, contemplated at the beginning, against which the storms of faction and the assaults of foreign power shall beat in vain, as upon the Rock of Ages; and Liberty, seeking a firm foothold, *will have at last whereon to stand and move the world.*

Senator Butler replied to Senator Sumner upon the same day.

SENTIMENTALITY VS. STATESMANSHIP

SENATOR BUTLER

After premising that he would (1) show that the Missouri compromise was, instead of a soothing salve, a thorn in the body of the South; (2) that, whatever benefit there was in it to the South had been nullified, and (3) was unconstitutional, he addressed himself to answering Senator Sumner.

I might begin by adopting the remark quoted by the honorable Senator from Massachusetts.

"Oh, Liberty! what crimes have been committed in thy name!"

The blood that lay in pools around the posts of the guillotine would make a historical response, but there may have been, with the French people, some excuse, at least, for their excesses. If, however, the efforts of fanatical organization shall result as that honorable Senator has indicated they must result in breaking down the distinction between the black and the white man, and elevating one, or degrading the other, to an equality, the horrors of the French Revolution, in all their frantic ferocity and cruelty, will be nothing compared to the consequences which must flow from such a state of things. The effort to confound castes between whom God has made an indelible distinction would but result in the destruction of one, or the base degradation of the higher class. It is presumptuous, arrogant, and criminal to deal with such elements in the spirit which has manifested itself in the speeches of the gentleman to whom I have referred.

Liberty! Sir, liberty is like fire, which may be used either to warm and preserve the temple in which it is kindled, or to be the means of its destruction. It may be an object of worship, or it may be a means of destruction. They who hold their hands in solemn worship at the fires of Vesta occupy a very different place from those who would light firebrands upon her altar to illuminate the temple in which they have none of the rights of priesthood, nor the spirit of worshipers. They are profane intruders, who cannot perceive the difference between dangerous heat and pure light—such as are willing to fire the edifice, in the belief that it might afford the light of delusive salvation.

There was a remark made by the Senator from Ohio [Mr. Chase] which struck me with more astonishment than any. It was that this bill ought to be defeated, because the slaveholder with his laborers, in the form of slaves, would pollute the soil upon which they settled, and might, by such settlement, exclude foreigners as well as citizens from the non-slaveholding States.

Why, sir, the slaveholder, with his slaves well governed, forms a relation that is innocent enough, and useful enough. I believe that it is a population which Iowa to-morrow would prefer to an inundation of those men coming as emigrants from a foreign country, wholly unacquainted with the institutions of this country.

I am told, however, Mr. President, by another Senator from Ohio [Mr. Wade], who, it seems to me, has taken very contradictory positions, as have the other gentlemen who have sustained him, that the black man, under the sentimental idea contained in the Declaration of Independence, has a right to claim an equality with the white man; and I think that honorable Senator said that, but for his degradation by the master, he would elevate himself to that equality. According to the argument of these gentlemen, at one moment he is the equal of the master and entitled to claim the franchises of a civilized freeman, but the next moment he is so degraded that he pollutes the very soil on which he stands, making it offensive to the white man to be even in his territorial neighborhood. The gentleman said, however, notwithstanding all this, he *guessed* there would be no difference in the races in the sight of God.

Sir, I will not invade the province of God. I will not undertake to say in what point of view the white and the black man may be regarded at the bar of His tribunal. I should regard it as profanity in me to do so. Inequality pervades the creation of this universe.

Yes, sir, with a chain of subordinate links and gradation, all existence upon this earth is connected together, from the lowest worm that crawls upon the earth to the purest angel that burns before the altar of God. Inequality seems to characterize the administration of the providence of God. I will not undertake to invade that sanctuary, but I will say that the abolitionists cannot make those equal whom God has made unequal, in human estimation. That He has made the blacks unequal to the whites, human history, as far as it can take cognizance of the matter, has pronounced its uniform judgment. The judgment of the earth and the history of mankind lead to but one judgment—revealing to us, perhaps, a melancholy truth.

Now, sir, what is the truth in relation to this matter? I am perfectly willing that the blindest fanatic should hear me in regard to it. I should be perfectly willing that even William Lloyd Garrison should hear me. He sends me his paper, and I sometimes read it as a mere matter of curiosity. I am perfectly willing that the blindest fanatic upon earth should hear me upon this subject. Is the black man equal with the white man under human judgment? All history refutes it. Who ever heard of the African astronomer, statesman, general, poet? Who ever heard of the African soaring in those regions in which the Caucasian race have made their greatest developments? Is it not perfectly true, so far as regards the statutory provisions of the Federal and State legislation, that the black man has never been, and never can be, equal with the white man? In your naturalization laws it is provided that none but a white man shall be a citizen of the United States. Under your militia laws, none but a white man can take a musket in the service of the country, or be enrolled among the militia. It is notorious that those very gentlemen who bestow so much tongue-expressed philanthropy upon the black man do not themselves regard him as an equal, and they cannot so regard him.

I appeal to those who hear me, if gentlemen who have gone

to the South, who have lived amid slaveholders, who have partaken of their hospitality, and have seen the administration of justice and all the graver forms of civilization there, are not better reconciled to the institution of slavery than that class and school of persons who read and take in their notions from "Uncle Tom's Cabin"?

Sir, there are various *isms* at the North, and there is but one of them for which I have any respect, and that is Puritanism. The Puritan, who came to this country with the sword in one hand and the Bible in the other, was an honest man, though he may have made a mistake in some of his peculiarities; but when we come to Abolitionism, to Maine-liquor-law-ism, to Strong-minded-woman-ism, Bloomerism, and all the *isms* which now pervade some portions of the North, I am far from supposing that they do infuse into the social system anything like a healthful action. No, sir; they are the cankers of theoretical conceit, of impudent intrusion, and cheerless infidelity.

The most extraordinary development of that class of persons and that temper of society that gives rise to such *isms* is to be found in conventions of women, who step from the sphere prescribed to them by God, to enter into the political arena, and claim the rights of men. I have a profound respect for woman in all the true relations for which she is fitted. Man always has a respect for woman. So long as she confines herself within the jurisdiction prescribed to her by the Almighty, she fulfills the ends of her existence; but when she passes those lines, and undertakes to intrude herself into a jurisdiction not assigned to her, I regard her as committing an impious transgression. Her sphere is higher than that of man—more sublime in spirit, and more useful in moulding society to the obligations of virtue, the influence of religion, and the happiness of affection and friendship. Hers is the sphere of love, and affection, and benevolence. What bounds are there to the sphere of a mother's love, a daughter's and sister's tenderness, or a wife's devotion? I know of none. Washington Irving has beautifully remarked, that the "heart is the woman's world." It is there her ambition should seek for empire, and her avarice seek for hidden treasures. But when she unsexes herself, and puts on the habiliments and claims to exercise the masculine functions of man in society, she has lost the position which she should occupy. When woman violates the law which God has given her, she has no law, and is the creature of hateful anarchy. She may be the worst or the best of human beings. She may approach the angel, or she may assimilate herself to the demon.

Senator Butler then paid his respects to Senator Seward, who had elevated himself to the position of protagonist of the anti-slavery cause, chiefly by his enunciation of the "higher law" of obedience to the dictates of conscience rather than to human statutes when the two are in conflict. Senator Seward first used this phrase in March, 1850, in a speech on the Omnibus bill.

I must, Mr. President, deny the claim of the Senator from New York to be the author of the law which he undertakes to administer or propagate. Sir, the teacher of that law was an ancient author. It was no less than the serpent who crept into the Garden of Eden and whispered to Eve that there was a *higher law*. She was banished from the Garden, and Paradise was lost.

At the close of his speech, having elaborated the propositions of his premise, Senator Butler praised Senator Douglas, the author of the bill, for his tactful presentation of it to the Senate and his energy in pressing it to a decision.

A wise man knows how to take advantage of circumstances —in common phrase, to strike when the iron is hot. You had better do a right thing than to content yourself by saying it ought to be done. Words produce wrangle; acts require affirmation or opposition.

If the honorable Senator from Illinois has shown that address, and that judgment, and that wisdom, let him have the honor of it. I know the aspersions which have been thrown upon him. He does not need support from me. He is sustained by his own State. But, sir, the difference between rashness and timidity was never better illustrated than in the conversation between Telemachus and Mentor. Telemachus noticed that Mentor trembled in the consideration of a measure, but became steady after his resolution to pursue it. "Why is this?" said the young man. The reply was, "I may well have trembled, because I saw the danger; but when resolved to meet it I armed myself with the resolution that would enable me to go through with success, or at once to perish." Sir, the Senator from Illinois has embarked upon this question, knowing its perils; and if he shall be sustained by the country he deserves the honor of success.

The motion of Senator Chase to strike out the clause stating that the restriction of slavery in the Missouri Compromise had been "superseded" was defeated on February 6 by a vote of 30 to 13. Senator Douglas then moved to substitute for the clause the following one:

—which being inconsistent with the principles of non-intervention by Congress with slavery in the States and Territories, as recognized by the legislation of 1850, commonly called the compromise measures, is hereby declared inoperative and void, it being the true intent and meaning of this act not to legislate slavery into any Territory or State, nor to exclude it therefrom; but to leave the people thereof perfectly free to form and regulate their domestic institutions in their own way, subject only to the Constitution of the United States."

This was adopted on February 15 by a vote of 35 to 10.

On March 2 Senator Chase moved to add to this clause the words:

"Under which the people of the Territory, through their appropriate representatives, may, if they see fit, prohibit the existence of slavery therein."

This was voted down by 36 nays to 10 yeas. The bill was passed on March 3 by a vote of 37 to 14.

In the House, says Horace Greeley in his "American Conflict," this bill was not taken up for more than two months after it had passed the Senate. There were scruples to vanquish, objections to remove or to soften, and machinery to adjust, in order to give the measure a chance of success. Meantime, the hum of public dissatisfaction rose louder and louder, and members who were soon to face Northern constituents were reasonably reluctant to vote for it, unless the Democratic majorities in their districts were well-nigh impregnable.

A House bill (nearly a copy of that of Senator Douglas) having been reported on January 31 by Mr. Richardson [Ill.], from the Committee on Territories, William H. English [Ind.]—a most unflinching Democrat—from the minority of said committee, proposed to strike out the clause which we have seen reported by Mr. Douglas to the Senate, and adopted by that body, repealing the 8th section of the Missouri act, and insert instead the following:

"*Provided,* That nothing in this act shall be so construed as to prevent the people of said Territory, through the properly constituted legislative authority, from passing such laws, in relation to the institution of slavery, as they may deem best adapted to their locality, and most conducive to their happiness and welfare; and so much of any existing act of Congress as may conflict with the above right of the people to regulate their domestic institutions in their own way, be, and the same is hereby, repealed."

It is highly probable that this proposition could not have been defeated on a call of the yeas and nays in the House—which was doubtless the reason why it was never acted on. The House bill was never taken up, save at a late day (May 8), so as to enable the Senate bill to be moved as an amendment.

There was a violent struggle in the House for and against closing the debate on this measure, and it was finally agreed that said debate should terminate on Saturday, May 20.

When the hour for closing the debate had arrived, Alexander H. Stephens [Ga.] moved *that the enacting clause of the bill be stricken out,* which was carried by a preconcerted and uncounteracted rally of the unflinching friends of the measure. Of course, all pending amendments were thus disposed of, the bill being reported as dead. Having thus got the bill out of committee and before the House, Messrs. Stephens & Co. voted, by 117 nays to 97 yeas, *not to agree to the report of the Committee of the Whole,* thus bringing the House to an immediate vote on the engrossment of the bill. Mr. Richardson now moved an amendment in the nature of a substitute (being, in effect, the Senate's bill), and thereupon called the previous question, which was seconded: Yeas, 116; nays, 90; when his amendment was adopted—yeas, 116; nays, 95; the bill ordered to be engrossed—yeas, 112; nays, 99; the previous question again ordered and sustained, and the bill finally passed: Yeas, 113; nays, 100. Thus the opponents of the measure in the House were precluded from proposing any amendments or modifications whatever, when it is morally certain that, had they been permitted to do so, some such amendment as Senator Chase's or Mr. English's would have been carried.

The free States contributed 44 votes—all cast by Democrats—to the support of this measure. From the slave States, 12 Whigs and 57 Democrats sustained it. Against it were 91 members from free States, of whom 44 were chosen as Whigs, three as "Free Soil" proper, and 44 as Democrats. So that precisely as many Democrats from free States voted for as against the final passage of the Nebraska bill. Only nine members from slave States opposed it, of whom but two had been regarded as Democrats; and of these Thomas H. Benton [Mo.] was not so regarded thereafter. Of the Whigs who so voted, but two were returned to the next House.

The bill had thus passed the House in form as an original measure of that body, although it was in essence the amended Senate bill. Being sent to the Senate as such, an attempt to amend was voted down, and the bill ordered to be engrossed, by 35 yeas to 13 nays. It was immediately passed (on May 24, 1854) and, being approved by President Pierce, became a law of the land.

At the time he proposed to Senator Dixon the repeal of the Missouri compromise Senator Douglas had prophesied that he would be reviled and, perhaps, even mobbed by his constituents for introducing the measure, but he had declared that he would carry out the project for the sake of the Union whatever might be the consequences to himself.

The results justified his prediction. The entire press and public sentiment of Chicago, his home city, were arrayed solidly against him. Nevertheless he boldly faced his fellow citizens. The term of his colleague, General James Shields, was about to expire and, in order to obtain a majority of the Illinois legislature favorable to his reëlection, Senator Douglas went to Chicago in

September and attempted to make a speech justifying the course of Shields and himself. He was unable to make himself heard, owing to the hoots and jeers of his audience. He thereupon announced that he would speak in the State capitol on October 5. He did so, presenting in varied and more popular form the arguments he had delivered in the Senate. At the close of his address it was announced that a reply would be made to it on the following day by Abraham Lincoln. Lincoln's opposition in Congress to the Mexican war had been so unpopular with his "jingo" Western constituency that he not only refused to stand for reëlection but resolved to devote himself exclusively to the law, wherein he speedily obtained local preëminence. Probably fearing that he might be impelled to break his resolution and to reënter politics he did not join his townsmen as they crowded into the State capitol to hear the bold and brilliant man who had kindled into its fiercest flame the now lambent, now latent, but ever-living issue of early American politics. However, he was irresistibly drawn to the meeting, and entered the Hall of Representatives in which it was held shortly before the close of Douglas's remarks. He probably had not realized before how deeply he felt on the violation of the national pledge in regard to the restriction of slavery in the Territories, but the sophistry of the advocate of this violation, the very sight of one toward whom he had been on principle an inveterate antagonist and whom he believed with all his heart to be the prince of demagogues,[1] caused him to throw to the winds all selfish personal considerations and, in default of an available statesman of Douglas's rank, to enter the lists himself against the redoubtable "Little Giant" as the champion of national faith and human freedom.

On the day appointed Lincoln spoke for three hours,

[1] Lincoln's mantle of "charity for all" was not wide enough to cover the "Little Giant" in the ante-bellum days. Later Lincoln learned that he had misjudged his fellow statesman. This was at the testing of souls in the spring of 1861, when Douglas came to the sorely troubled President and offered his whole-hearted services to the Union cause—an earnest of which he gave soon after in a speech at Chicago, which was the most eloquent of his career as well as his last, since he died a few weeks after delivering it.

YOUNG AMERICA

President Pierce, supported by jingo Democratic statesmen

From the collection of the New York Historical Society

313

delivering a terrible philippic against the Nebraska bill. Douglas himself declared that he had heard nothing like it in the Senate. Unfortunately for the archives of American oratory the speech was not reported. However, its argument has been preserved, and undoubtedly in more finished form, in a speech of the same tenor which Lincoln delivered at Peoria two weeks later (October 16) and in the joint debate with Douglas in 1858 [see Vol. V, chapter III].

CHAPTER VIII

"BLEEDING KANSAS"

[DEBATES ON THE ADMISSION OF KANSAS INTO THE UNION]

Foundation of the Republican Party: Its Success in the Elections of 1854—
President Pierce Sends Special Message to Congress on Kansas in Favor
of the Pro-Slavery Party—Answer in the House to the Message by
Galusha A. Grow [Pa.]—President Pierce Issues Proclamation Against
Interference in Kansas by Men of the Bordering States—House of
Representatives Sends Investigating Committee to Kansas—Its Report—
Debate on the Report: Anti-Slavery Speakers, Israel Washburn [Me.],
Samuel Galloway [O.]; Pro-Slavery Speakers, William H. English [Ind.],
Thomas F. Bowie [Md.]—Bill Introduced in the Senate to Admit Kan-
sas into the Union—Debates on the Bill: in Favor of "Popular Sov-
ereignty," Stephen A. Douglas [Ill.]; in Favor of Prohibition of Sla-
very, William H. Seward [N. Y.]—Bill to Admit Kansas Is Passed in
the House, but Rejected in the Senate.

O N May 23, 1854, the day after the passage of the
Nebraska bill, some thirty members of the House
of Representatives met together to plan their
future action on the issue. The leader of the meeting,
Israel Washburn, Jr. [Me.], assumed the existence of
a new party to which they belonged, and used the name
"Republican" to designate it—not as an innovation,
however, since it was a term already "in the air," having been suggested at a meeting of "anti-Nebraska"
men of all former parties, held in Ripon, Wis., March 20.
During the course of the year it was adopted at "anti-
Nebraska" conventions held in various Northern States.

The name, as we have seen, had been the designation of the anti-Federalists, and remained the official
name of that party long after it became popularly known
as the Democratic party. Indeed, it was still used by
a number of Southern members of that party in Congress in preference to the term Democrat.

315

After the demise of the Federalist party "Republican" was the common element in the name of the two new political factions which arose, the broad constitutional constructionists and the protective tariff men, such as Henry Clay, Daniel Webster, calling themselves "National Republicans." When the faction assumed the dimensions of a party, it officially adopted the popular designation of Whig.

Accordingly, since the "anti-Nebraska" faction was composed of the larger portion of the Northern Whigs and all of the Free Soil Democrats, there was a unanimous and spontaneous desire of these elements to assume a term which was endeared to them by former political association.

The regular Democrats, on the other hand, vigorously protested against this assumption, which they considered an unwarranted and almost sacrilegious misuse of the revered name. Accordingly, they attempted at first to fix the name "Black Republican" upon the new party. This, though it seemed most odious to themselves, rather strengthened the anti-Nebraskans with the Northern people, who were becoming more and more opposed not only to slavery in the Territories but also in the States, and so the new party was enspirited to accept the designation and to justify it by taking a more advanced position than its founders had originally intended, declaring war against slavery *per se*. While such a declaration frightened away the more timorous Whigs and Democrats, it secured the adherence of nearly all the Abolitionists, who, though fewer in numbers than the disaffected element, were ardent and successful propagandists, and soon swelled the ranks of the "Black" Republicans with converts that more than made up the balance against them.

In 1854 the new party elected eleven Senators and a plurality of Representatives. It was especially strong in the West, the Eastern men who had become dissatisfied with the old parties preferring to join the Know Nothing party, which, however, was tinged with anti-slavery sentiment and, being a movement of protest rather than fundamental principle, was ready to break away and join whatever new party would prove the most successful antagonist of the dominant one.

EVENTS IN KANSAS

Even before the passage of the Kansas-Nebraska bill preparations had been made by the South to introduce slavery into the Territory of Kansas. The only white men in the region were missionaries and Indian agents, who were all Southerners. These men had the first information of the purchase of the Indian reservations in Kansas, which was quietly made by the Government shortly before the passage of the Kansas-Nebraska bill, and they proceeded to organize for the capture of the territorial government. In aid of their project Missourians along the Kansas border formed into various societies, "Blue Lodges," "Sons of the South," etc., with intent to enter the Indian reservations at the earliest possible moment and vote for the introduction of slavery into the new Territory. They did so on the passage of the act, bringing some slaves with them, and holding meetings at which they resolved that "no protection would be afforded Abolitionist settlers in the region," and that "slavery was recognized as already existing in the Territory," and that "slaveholders should introduce their property as early as possible."

The Northern Abolitionists thereupon organized "Emigrant Aid Societies" to promote the migration of anti-slavery men to Kansas. Hearing of this the pro-slavery associations in Kansas and western Missouri held meetings at which they resolved forcibly to remove these Abolitionist immigrants from the Territory.

The first company of Northern immigrants was sent by the New England Emigrant Aid Society. It reached Kansas late in July, 1854, and located at a place which they named after the treasurer of the society [Amos A.] Lawrence. While erecting their houses they were visited by an armed party of Missourians but, on their preparing to defend themselves, their visitors retired without molesting them.

The Government of the Territory was organized in the autumn, Andrew H. Reeder [Pa.] being appointed governor by President Pierce. Although an Administration Democrat he was thought by many to be a Free Soiler. In the election held in the Territory in November John W. Whitfield, an Indian agent and a pro-slavery man, was chosen Delegate to Congress. On the advice of Senator David R. Atchison many Missourians crossed the line and voted for Whitfield. About this time a number of pro-slavery men founded a town which they named for the Senator and established a newspaper organ there, called the *Squatter Sovereign*. In an early issue this paper said:

"We can tell the impertinent scoundrels of *The Tribune* that they may exhaust an ocean of ink, their Emigrant Aid Societies spend their millions and billions, their representatives in Congress spout their heretical theories till doomsday, and His Excellency appoint abolitionist after free-soiler as our governor, yet we will continue to lynch and hang, tar and feather and drown, every white-livered abolitionist who dares to pollute our soil."

Early in 1855 Governor Reeder of Kansas ordered an election for a Territorial legislature to be held on March 30. Only two Free-Soilers were elected. Eight times as many votes were counted as there were legal voters in the Territories.

Protests were made against the election of four councilmen and thirteen representatives on the ground of fraud, and, on the presentation of evidence of this, Governor Reeder refused to issue to them certificates and ordered new elections to be held in their districts, whereupon the pro-slavery press of Missouri advocated "hemping" the "infernal scoundrel." At the second election all these districts but Leavenworth elected Free State councilmen and Representatives. These the legislature refused to admit and seated the men who had been supplanted. The legislature met at the call of the governor at Pawnee City, in the interior of the State, and immediately adjourned, over the governor's veto, to Shawnee Mission, on the Missouri border. Here

it adopted as the laws of Kansas Territory the laws of
the State of Missouri, including those maintaining
slavery and prohibiting the agitation of abolition and
punishing the agitators. These acts were vetoed by
Governor Reeder, but were passed over his veto. The
legislature petitioned the President for his removal,
which was in due time effected, Wilson Shannon, a Democrat from Ohio, who had been governor of that State,
being appointed in his stead. Shannon took an early
opportunity to declare that the acts of the legislature
were legal and to announce himself in favor of slavery
in Kansas.

In the meantime outrages were committed by pro-
slavery mobs, one paper being destroyed which had
advocated the rights of the Free Soilers under the law,
and its editor forced to flee for his life; and a lawyer
of Leavenworth, who had signed the protest against the
election in that city, being tarred and feathered, ridden
on a rail and finally sold to a negro, who was compelled
to purchase him.

The Free Soil settlers held a convention at which
they repudiated the legislature and its acts, refused to
take part in the election of a delegate to Congress,
which had been set by the legislature, and called another
delegate convention and a constitutional convention.
At the former they elected Governor Reeder as the delegate and at the latter, which was held at Topeka, they
formed a Free-State constitution, under which they
asked Congress to admit Kansas into the Union.

The events which took place in Kansas during the
session of Congress, 1855-56, and to which allusion was
made in the debates of the session, were as follows:

An armed conflict between pro-slavery and Free-
Soil men arose out of the assassination, on November
21, 1855, of a Free-State settler, William Dow. On an
appeal from the pro-slavery sheriff, Governor Shannon issued a proclamation calling out 3,000 militia to
"execute the laws." In response to this a pro-slavery
army came from the border and encamped on the banks
of the Wakarusa River at Franklin, a pro-slavery town
near Lawrence. During the encampment, Thomas W.

Barber (or Barbour), a Free State man of the neighborhood, was shot dead by some of the "militia."[1] Finally an armistice was arranged between Governor Shannon and the Free State leaders, and the Missourians dispersed. Thus ended the so-called "Wakarusa War."

Leavenworth was also the scene of many outrages. A band of Missourians entered the town on December 20, 1855, and destroyed the office of the *Territorial Register*, a Free State paper.

On January 15, 1856, the territorial election under the Topeka (Free State) constitution was held. Charles Robinson (Free State) was elected governor (subject to the approval of Congress) and a Free State legislature was chosen. The organization of the territorial government was set for March 1, 1856, to give Congress time to act, it being hoped that Kansas would be admitted into the Union with the Topeka constitution, and the elections made under it would be ratified.

Congress assembled on December 3, 1855. The Democratic majority in the Senate was considerably lessened and no party had a majority in the House. After balloting for several weeks Nathaniel P. Banks [Mass.], a Know-Nothing and anti-Nebraskan, was elected Speaker of the House.

The President in his annual message (on December 31) declared that nothing had taken place in Kansas which warranted interference by the Federal Executive, and expressed the hope that the people of the Territory, by exercising "their right to determine their own domestic institutions" under Federal protection from outside interference, would be able to suppress "organized resistance to territorial law."

On January 26, 1856, George G. Dunn [Ind.] moved in the House of Representatives to restore the Missouri compromise as a means of settling the agitation. The resolution was carried by one vote, 101 yeas to 100 nays, but failed of passage in the Senate.

Outrages by the Missourians, who were called "Border Ruffians" by the Free State men, continued. On January 21 and 22 Robinson and Gen. James H. Lane,

[1] See John G. Whittier's poem, "Burial of Barbour."

LIBERTY. THE FAIR MAID OF KANSAS—IN THE HANDS OF THE "BORDER RUFFIANS"

From the collection of the New York Historical Society

leaders of the Free State men, telegraphed to President Pierce, stating that a great invasion was preparing in Missouri and asking him to issue a proclamation against it, and employ Federal troops stationed in Leavenworth to oppose it.

On January 24 the President sent a special message to Congress on the subject. In this he blamed the Emigrant Aid Society for causing the trouble by intervening in the affairs of the Territory in order to defeat the principle of popular sovereignty, and he upheld the organization of the Territory that had been made by the pro-slavery party. He said:

"If the passionate rage of fanaticism and partisan spirit did not force the fact upon our attention, it would be difficult to believe that any considerable portion of the people of this enlightened country could have surrendered themselves to a fanatical devotion to the supposed interests of the relatively few Africans in the United States, as totally to abandon and disregard the interests of the twenty-five millions of Americans."

To this Galusha A. Grow [Pa.], on March 5, alluded at the close of a speech on Kansas:

Injury of One the Injury of All

Galusha A. Grow, M. C.

The art of the lawyer and the politician is ever to associate names made odious in the public mind with what they wish to destroy, and upon them attempt to excite the prejudice of men.

Sir, the men of the North have not *surrendered themselves to a fanatical devotion to the supposed interests of the relatively few Africans in the United States,* but they desire to gladden the heart of the patriot forever with the "contemplation of a portion of territory consecrated to freedom, whose soil shall never be moistened by the tear of the slave, or degraded by the step of the oppressor or oppressed."

The rights of the citizens of Kansas are the rights of the *twenty-five millions of Americans,* and the wrongs of the one should be adopted as the wrongs of the other. If the rights of one man in this country can be trampled upon by legislative enactment the rights of all may. When men are disfranchised by law, and deprived of their nearest and dearest rights, and that law rests upon the Government of the country for its validity and its sanction, it comes home to the bosom of every person, no matter in what part of the Republic he lives; and he who would sit quietly down and permit wrong and injustice to be done to a citizen of the country when he could prevent it is guilty of a gross dereliction of duty.

The freemen of Kansas are entitled to your protection. They are entitled to your protection against invasion of the ballot-box, to your protection against unjust laws which violate all their rights, your protection in the freedom of speech and the press. The supervision of all their legislation being under the control of Congress, let it, then, do its duty, and remove from the people these odious enactments which the President has declared must be enforced, and secure to them the free and undisturbed exercise of their civil rights and privileges.

The men of the North are but resisting the attempt to subvert the spirit and genius of the institutions of the Republic; and the effort now making to overturn its well-established policy in legislating for the Territories, the effort to reverse the decision of the courts making slavery a local, sectional institution, resting upon local law for its support, and to nationalize it by throwing over it the shield and the protection of the Constitution and the Union, wherever it goes beyond the jurisdiction of the local laws which gave it support—it is against this doctrine that the men of the North war, and not in behalf of "the relatively few Africans" in the country. Their condition, however deplorable in the States where they exist, is beyond our reach. We must therefore leave them to those who have the control of the laws under which they live. But we insist that the flag of the Union shall float, as heretofore, the emblem of freedom, and under its folds, everywhere, the freedom of speech and of the press and the inalienable rights of men shall be protected.

On February 11 the President issued a proclamation in which he warned all citizens of the States neighboring to Kansas who were contemplating armed intervention in the affairs of that Territory to lay aside their purposes on pain of suppression by the Federal troops; and on the 15th of the month Jefferson Davis, Secretary of War, sent orders to the army officers at Leavenworth to place troops at the disposal of Governor Shannon.

In the spring of 1856 Colonel Buford [Ala.] came

with a regiment of young Southerners to Kansas with the purpose of making it a slave State. Their temper may be judged from the fact that they found a Free State emigrant from South Carolina and convicted him of treason, from the mortal penalty of which he escaped with the loss of his money and his horse.

Buford's regiment and the "Platte County Rifles" led by ex-Senator David R. Atchison, General Stringfellow, and others, and armed with weapons from the Federal armory at Leavenworth, entered Lawrence and destroyed the printing offices and burned the Free State Hotel and the residence of Free State Governor Robinson.

A small body of Free State men then arose under the leadership of John Brown of Osawatomie and began to make reprisals for the pro-slavery outrages in the "Battle of Black Jack," capturing, with their plunder, a party that had just sacked Palmyra, a Free State settlement. In reprisal a pro-slavery party under John W. Whitfield, in the absence from the town of Brown and his party, burned Osawatomie on June 5.

On March 10, 1856, the House of Representatives, by a vote of 101 to 93, resolved to send a special committee to Kansas to inquire into the state of anarchy prevailing there. This committee was composed of William A. Howard [Mich.], John Sherman [O.], and Mordecai Oliver [Mo.]. These men immediately proceeded to Kansas and spent several weeks there in an investigation, an exhaustive report of which they presented to Congress on their return. Their conclusions were:

First. That every election in the Territory had been fraudulently carried by organized invasions from Missouri;

Second. That the legislature was therefore an illegal body and its acts were null and void;

Third. That its powers had been used for unlawful purposes;

Fourth. That the choice of Whitfield as delegate to Congress was illegal;

Fifth: That the election of the contesting delegate, ex-Governor Reeder, was illegal;

Sixth. That Reeder had, however, received a majority of the resident vote;

Seventh. That a fair election could not be held without a new census, a well-guarded election law, the selection of impartial judges, and the presence of Federal troops;

Eighth. That the Constitution framed by the convention held for that purpose embodied the will of a majority of the residents of the Territory.

A debate ensued in the House of Representatives on this report.

Kansas Contested Election

House of Representatives, March 14, 1856

On March 14 Israel Washburn [Me.] made a long speech in favor of the report of the committee, in the course of which he said:

Gentlemen upon the other side of the question have spoken eloquently in behalf of law and order. The simplicity and apparent sincerity with which they have insisted that law and order were to be respected in this case, by upholding a pretended legislature in Kansas—admitted to be elected in good part by non-residents; elected, as is charged—and this is the question in issue—in contempt of all law, order, and decency, by fraud, force, and unheard-of outrages; and by submitting, uncomplainingly, to the acts of such a body, sitting in fraud of the rights of the people, was indeed admirable; or the irony of their remarks, if they were so intended, was more admirable still. The law must be kept by protecting law-breakers, and sustaining their doings in open violation of all law! Order must be observed by yielding an unquestioning obedience to acknowledged mobs! Sir, we stand for law; this House, I trust, will stand for law and by law, and ascertain what the law is in so far as it is itself concerned, and bound to know and act upon it. It should inquire and investigate to this end, and be careful that the law, rather than the resolutions of marauders, shall control its decisions.

In no State or Territory, upon any question where slavery is not concerned, would such principles and doctrines as we have heard in this debate be avowed. Suppose that an invasion like the one alleged to have been made upon Kansas had been made

upon Minnesota from Canada, and that under similar circumstances of fraud and force a legislature had been imposed upon
that Territory; and then that under its pretended laws a delegate elected by Canadians had been sent here—where is the man
who would consent that Canada should be permitted in this way
to be represented in this House? Oh! sir, nothing but the system of slavery—its necessities for strange and unfounded assumptions and demands—could suggest or permit such opinions
and claims as have been set up here. They must not be tolerated
for a moment. Does any man imagine that those to whom they
are addressed do not perceive how utterly unsound and ground-
less they are? Should they submit to them they would acknowledge their unfaithfulness or incapacity, and justly become the
scorn or pity of mankind.

Mr. Speaker, for the sake of slavery solemn compacts of long
standing, deliberately entered into and with mutual considerations, have been destroyed; pledges of faith and honor have been
cast like worthless weeds away; the great writ of right, sacred
for centuries to the protection of mankind—the *habeas corpus*—
has been struck down; the trial by jury, the palladium of civil
right and personal security, born of the conflicts of liberty with
despotism, and baptized in the blood of men struggling to be
free, consecrated in our hearts as the ancient and indefeasible
heritage of the people, guarded by the Constitution, stands
against all assaults except those of slavery; and, as if these
things were not enough, we are now told that the instruments of
this sectional interest, its gangs and invading armies, may enter
and seize upon our infant Territories, our own Territories, under
the immediate and especial protection of the general Government
—subjugate the people rightfully residing there, make laws and
elect delegates for them; and this House, in its absolute and unrestricted power to judge of the elections of its members, has no
authority to inquire into their proceedings, or to resist the admission of such delegates upon this floor.

Slavery, in its claims and demands of to-day, is so much
greater and better than anything else, nay, than all things else,
that to protect and strengthen it is held to justify the destruction of whatever stands in its way. The rules of the House are
broken down by unscrupulous majorities, and less than a quorum
of members permitted to report bills from the Committee of the
Whole to the House at its call. Laws are set aside, and compromises violated for its sake, and nothing is held sacred against
its assaults. The great idea of the Declaration of Independence,
and which has given its author a name that

"Through the ages,
Living in historic pages,
Brighter grows and gleams immortal,"

is pronounced in the Senate of the United States "a self-evident lie." All memories and hopes, all possessions and rights—the Constitution, the Union, the living Gospel of "peace on earth and good will to men," are but flax and stubble when exposed to the consuming flame of this insatiate and inexorable system.

On March 17 Samuel Galloway [O.] spoke in favor of the report:

Mr. Speaker, this Kansas Legislature has, by its legislation, utterly violated the *great fundamental principle* (popular sovereignty) of the organic act of the Territory; and hence all its enactments contravening the constitutional law of the Territory are void.

Now, sir, I respectfully ask that gentleman, and all in this House who concur with him in sentiment, whether that *"fundamental principle"* is not totally subverted by these enactments against free speech in regard to slavery?

Mr. Speaker, if you, or I, to-day, in any company in Kansas, were to express the very common, and as we think very reasonable, sentiments that free labor was more profitable and vastly more pleasant that slave labor, and that the people would be richer, happier, and holier with the benefits of freedom than with the blessings of slavery, we would be liable to arrest; and, although *perfectly free*, we might in a short time have the glorious experience of the *perfection* of our freedom within the walls of a prison—a place not usually regarded as affording the largest liberty.

Suppose some meek minister of Christianity, not fully having the fear of the law in his heart, should, while declaring the whole counsel of God, in a moment of unusual spiritual excitement utter such scriptural sentiment as—"Is not this the fast that I have chosen, to loose the bands of wickedness, to undo the heavy burdens, and to let the oppressed go free, and that ye break every yoke?" "Whatsoever ye would that men should do to you, do ye even so to them"—might not some "popular sovereignty" Democrat, innocently suspecting that such words contained "innuendoes," at least calculated to excite *"disorderly and dangerous disaffections,"* arrest him, and start him in the straight and narrow way to a place where he would not be so *perfectly free* to preach the *free* gospel of "peace on earth and good-will to men," if not *in his own way*, at least in the way prescribed by the pious legislators in Kansas?

Suppose, on the 4th of July, some patriotic and fervent patriot should read from the Declaration of Independence: "We hold these truths to be self-evident: that all men are created free and equal; that they are endowed with certain inalienable rights, among which are life, liberty, and the pursuit of happiness"; might not some descendant of those sires of the Revolution who first uttered those sentiments, which then and since have been known and felt to produce *disorderly and dangerous disaffections*, arrest the imprudent orator, and put him in a place where he would be free to meditate on the blessings of liberty?

"Perfectly free?" So were those victims whom the fabled robber Procrustes placed upon his iron bed. They enjoyed a *free* use of their legs; but, if they were not adapted to the principles of his legislation, he stretched them if they were too short, and lopped them off if they were too long, to suit the length of his law in regard to *free* legs. Tantalus, also, in his fabled hell, was *perfectly free* to eat and drink. To be sure, when he undertook to exercise his liberty of drinking, the water retreated from his lips, but yet he was *free* to use what he could not get. He was *perfectly free* to eat of the rich clusters of grapes that hung above him, but when he attempted to seize them the wind blew them from his grasp. So with the *water* of political salvation, and rich clusters of the grapes of freedom around and over the people of Kansas. As soon as the thirsty and hungry for freedom attempt to eat or drink, although *perfectly free* to do so, they are seized and imprisoned for exercising their appetites *in their own way*.

Mr. Speaker, it is not many years since the thunders of the people were directed against a President and Congress of the United States for their usurpation and arbitrary stretch of power in causing to be enacted the memorable "sedition law." Thomas Jefferson, the great apostle of Democracy, and his disciples, have ever denounced it as a despotic violation of the liberty of speech and of the press. Yet, sir, that law, in all its alleged enormities, was not comparable with this sedition law of the Kansas Assembly. Under that odious law of 1798 one might offer the truth in evidence in defence: under this infamous law of 1854, enacted and advocated by the same disciples of the same Democracy, this poor privilege is denied; and the "head and front of the offending" consists in uttering the great truths of liberty.

Why, sir, if that matchless orator and matchless man, Henry Clay, were to-day alive, and were to stand up (as *he only* could stand) on the Territory of Kansas, and utter this sentiment, which a few years since he uttered in the Senate Hall—

"I repeat that I never can, and never will, vote—and no earthly power will make me vote—to spread slavery over territory where it does not exist"—

—for such a sentiment that prince among the people would be made a prisoner among debased felons. Were the eccentric and eloquent Randolph of Roanoke alive, and were he to utter in the free Territory of Kansas these thoughts, once proclaimed on this floor—

"Sir, I know there are gentlemen, not only from the Northern but from the Southern States, who think that this unhappy question—for such it is —of negro slavery, which the Constitution has vainly attempted to blink by not using the term, should never be brought into public notice, more especially into that of Congress, and most especially here. Sir, with every due respect for the gentlemen who think so, I differ from them *toto cœlo*. Sir, it is a thing which cannot be hid. It is not a dry rot, that you can cover with the carpet until the house tumbles about your ears. You might as well try to hide a volcano in full operation—it cannot be hid—it is a cancer in your face, and must be treated *secundum artem*"—

—how certain and severe would be his condemnation. Why, we *Black Republicans* could not begin to imitate and utter such thrilling thoughts and burning words, and so eminently calculated to *excite disorderly and dangerous disaffections*—certainly, such fanaticism would send him to the felon's cell.

I will not consume the time of the House with further quotations. Everybody knows that the language I have read was such as was used by the noble men of our Republic in every section of our Confederacy twenty years ago; yet, in Kansas, this day, all those men, for the utterance of such sentiments, would be branded with infamy! And can it be that the national legislature will tolerate men who thus tarnish the fair fame of their fathers, and violate the spirit and letter of our charter of rights? Will the North submit to it? Never. With the poet, we can fervently say:

"Is this the land our fathers loved?
The freedom which they fought to win?
Is this the soil they trod upon?
Are these the graves they slumber in?
Are we the sons by whom are borne
The mantles which the dead have worn?

And shall we crouch above their graves
  With craven soul and fettered lip,
Yoked in with marked and branded slaves,
  And tremble at the master's whip?
No! by their enlarging souls, which burst
  The bands and fetters round them set;
By the free pilgrim-spirit, nursed
  Within our inmost bosoms—yet
By all above, around, below,
  Be *ours* the indignant answer—No!''

On March 18 William H. English [Ind.] closed a
long speech against the report with the charge that
fraud and intimidation had been used in other places
than Kansas without a subsequent investigation by
Congress.

Sir, Kansas is not the only place where men have been deprived of their political rights, and the purity of the ballot-box
sullied by fraud and violence. Let gentlemen look nearer home.
Will they—dare they attribute to the Nebraska bill those terrible scenes which sent a thrill of horror throughout the length
and breadth of the land, enacted at the elections in some of the
States—ay, sir, in the very heart of boasted civilization and refinement—and which, for unprovoked atrocity, and for cold-
blooded and deliberate outrage, are without a parallel, and so
far exceed anything that has transpired in Kansas, even supposing the most distorted and exaggerated abolition accounts to
be true, that, in comparison, the conduct of the "border ruffians" sinks into utter insignificance?

Sir, what have we seen? We have seen eminent patriots and
statesmen denied the freedom of speech; we have seen armed
mobs placed as judges of the elective franchise; we have seen
quiet, inoffensive, and respected citizens brutally assaulted and
driven from the polls for daring to exercise, in a peaceable manner, rights secured to them by the Constitution and the laws;
we have seen the ballot-box itself—that sheet-anchor of American
freedom—seized by armed bullies, and committed to the flames,
or the ballots scattered to the winds, and trampled beneath their
ruffian feet; we have seen race arrayed against race, neighborhood against neighborhood, and religion against religion; we
have seen men driven by prejudice, intolerance, and passion to
deeds of violence and bloodshed which sicken the heart—sparing
neither age nor sex, and extending even to the sanctuary of
God! All this, sir, and more, have we seen, *outside of the Ter-*

ritory of Kansas; and if you would find its true origin look to
your secret, oath-bound, political organizations—to the doctrines
of political proscription and religious intolerance—and not to
the great principles of equality and popular sovereignty contained in the Nebraska bill.

On March 19 Thomas F. Bowie [Md.] spoke against the report, concluding as follows:

Mr. Speaker, I have heard with deep regret the denunciations of our Northern brethren against the slave States of this
Union. They speak of them as an "oligarchy of slavery," and,
in the language of Mr. Seward, "the aristocracy of slavery."
Sir, why such terms are used I cannot comprehend, unless it be
that those who employ them are themselves *aristocrats,* and *envy*
the Southern States the aristocracy of their own institutions.
Sir, I believe Mr. Seward "has let the cat out of the bag," and
that this is the true secret of all their opposition to Southern
slave-holders, *"et hinc ille lachrymæ."* [1] The aristocracy of
slavery! Sir, the aristocracy of the North is the aristocracy of
white slavery—the cold, heartless, selfish, cruel, and despotic
power of wealth—which brings to its feet, as an humble suppli-
cant, the labor of the white man. The poorer classes there are
ground down to the earth; and the only question among them
is who can make the other *work for him,* a species of *white
slavery* that I utterly abhor. Sir, I was born and have lived all
my life among Southern slaveholders, and I can tell Mr. Seward,
"et id omne genus," [2] what the aristocracy of Southern slavery
is. It is, in fact, the aristocracy of nature, and not the aristocracy of conventional deceits. It is the aristocracy of enlightened
intelligence, of love, of kindness, of magnanimity, of honor, of
generosity, of valor, of independence, of hospitality, and, above
all, of indomitable energy. And if, in the patriotism of the
North, they can hate aristocracy like this, I do not envy them
the emotion of their hearts.

Sir, if this question has been sprung upon the South for no
other purpose than to insult and abuse them, I fear the times,
indeed, forbode great evils. I warn gentlemen "to look well
before they leap," for he who soweth the storm must expect to
reap the whirlwind. If the seeds of discord and disunion are
to be scattered among the States of this our beloved and glorious
country, accursed be the evil genius that lends a helping hand!
May the arm that is now uplifted to strike down the stars and

[1] "And hence these tears."
[2] "And all that class."

stripes of this great confederacy be palsied by the benignant power of an overruling Providence! May we once more, sir, become a happy and a united people, and, living in the bonds of fraternal love, present as a living spectacle to the world an enduring monument of national greatness!

Delegate Whitfield retained his seat notwithstanding all the efforts of the Republican Representatives to expel him.

A bill inspired by Stephen A. Douglas was reported in the Senate on March 20 from the Committee on Territories, authorizing the people of Kansas to form a constitution and State government preparatory to their admission as a State when they had the requisite population (93,420). Senator William H. Seward [N. Y.] moved a substitute bill organizing the State under the Free State (Topeka) constitution. Upon the former bill Stephen A. Douglas [Ill.] spoke on April 4, denouncing the Republican Senators, Seward in particular, as inconsistent for desiring to admit Kansas under the Topeka constitution, which provided that no negro, free or slave, should be permitted within the State.

SQUATTER SOVEREIGNTY

SENATE, APRIL 4-MAY 13, 1856

SENATOR DOUGLAS.—While the Senator from New York [Mr. Seward] is portraying the beauties of negro freedom and equality, and demonstrating the propriety of sacrificing the political and constitutional rights of twenty millions of white people for the benefit of three millions of negroes, I would be glad if he would point out the advantages which the negro will derive from the admission of Kansas with the Topeka constitution. That constitution provides that as long as Kansas shall be a State, as long as water runs and grass grows, no negro, free or *slave*, shall ever live or breathe under that constitution.

SENATOR SEWARD.—Does the Senator wish me to answer now?

SENATOR DOUGLAS.—Yes, sir.

SENATOR SEWARD.—Then, my answer is that, such being the Constitution, he is wrong in his premises that I am desirous to admit the State of Kansas for the benefit of the negro. It must be for the benefit of the white man.

SENATOR DOUGLAS.—Am I to understand the Senator that he has abandoned the cause of the negro upon the ground that his freedom and equality are inconsistent with the rights of the white man? What has become of his professions of sympathy for the poor negro? What are we to think of the sincerity of his professions upon this subject?

SENATOR SEWARD.—That is another thing.

SENATOR DOUGLAS.—That is the very thing. If all other considerations are to be made to yield to the paramount object of prohibiting slavery in Kansas upon the ground that the inequality which it imposes is unjust to the negro, will that injustice be removed by adopting a constitution which in effect declares that the negro, whether free or slave, shall never tread the soil, nor drink the water, nor breathe the air of Kansas? The Senator from New York admits that the Constitution with which he proposes by his bill to admit Kansas contains such a provision. Under the code of laws enacted by the territorial legislature of Kansas, which the Senator, in common with his party, professes to consider monstrous and barbarous, a negro may go to Kansas and be protected in all his rights so long as he obeys the laws of the land. In order to get rid of those laws the Senator from New York proposes to give effect to a constitutional provision which is designed to prevent the negro forever from entering the State!

I should like to hear from the Senator from New York on this point.

SENATOR SEWARD.—I need scarcely inform the honorable Senator that I do not approve of any such provision in any constitution in the world. I never did, and I never shall, vote to approve or sanction in any constitution, or in any law, a provision which tends to keep any man, any member of the human family to which I belong, in a condition of degradation below the position which I occupy myself, except for his own fault or crime.

SENATOR DOUGLAS.—The Senator does not approve of this provision, and never can, for the reason that it does not put the negro on an equality with himself! Then, will he vote for admitting Kansas in this irregular manner, and without the requisite population, merely because her constitution has a provision which keeps slaves from going into the Territory, while in another clause "which tends to keep a man, any being, a member of the human family to which he belongs, in a condition of

degradation below the position which he occupies himself''?
Yet, if he votes for his own bill to admit Kansas with the Topeka
constitution, according to his own doctrine he does vote to sanction a provision to keep the negro out altogether; he will not
allow a negro to come in a condition either below him or above
him!

SENATOR SEWARD.—You can take it either way—above or
below.

SENATOR DOUGLAS.—Yes; he will exclude the negro absolutely if he is below or above him! He will insist upon having
the negro upon a footing of entire and perfect equality with himself. Yet, if his bill passes, and Kansas is admitted with the
constitution which has been formed and presented here, all
negroes, both free and slave, are forever prohibited from entering the State of Kansas by the terms of the instrument. He cannot escape the responsibility of this result on the plea that he
does not vote directly to indorse and sanction the constitution in
all its parts; for his doctrine, and the doctrine of his party, is
that they not only have the right, but that it is their duty, to
examine the constitution in all its parts, and vote for it or
against it, according as they approve or disapprove of its provisions, and especially those provisions which degrade the negro
below the level of the white man. He must abandon all the
principles to which his life has been devoted; he must abandon
the creed of the party of which he is the acknowledged leader,
before he can vote for his own bill. The Black Republican party
was organized and founded on the fundamental principle of
perfect and entire equality of rights and privileges between the
negro and the white man—an equality secured and guaranteed
by a law higher than the Constitution of the United States. In
your creed, as proclaimed to the world, you stand pledged
against "the admission of any more slave States";

To repeal the fugitive slave law;

To abolish the slave trade between the States;

To prohibit slavery in the District of Columbia;

To restore the prohibition on Kansas and Nebraska; and

To acquire no more territory unless slavery shall be first
prohibited.

This is your creed, authoritatively proclaimed. I trust there
is to be no evading or dodging the issues—no lowering of the
flag. Let each party stand by its principles and the issues as
you have presented them and we have accepted them. Let us
have a fair, bold fight before the people, and then let the verdict
be pronounced.

SENATOR SEWARD.—You will have it.

SENATOR DOUGLAS.—I rejoice in this assurance. I trust the Senator will be able to bring his troops up to the line, and to hold them there. I trust there is to be no lowering of the flag— no abandonment or change of the issues. There are rumors afloat that you are about to strike your colors; that you propose to surrender each one of these issues, not because you do not profess to be right, but because you cannot succeed in the right; that you propose to throw overboard all the bold men who distinguished themselves in your service in fighting the anti-Nebraska fight, and to take a new man, who, in consequence of not being committed to either side, will be enabled to cheat somebody by getting votes from both sides!

We are prepared to give you a fair fight on the issues you have tendered and we accepted. Let the presidential contest be one of principle alone; let the principles involved be distinctly stated and boldly met, without any attempts at concealment or equivocation; let the result be a verdict of approval or disapproval so emphatic that it cannot be misunderstood. One year ago you promised us a fair fight in open field, upon the principles of the Kansas-Nebraska act. You then unfurled your banner, and bore it aloft in the hands of your own favorite and tried leaders, with your principles emblazoned upon it. Are you now preparing to lower your flag, to throw overboard all your tried men who have rendered service in your cause, and issue a search warrant in hopes of finding a new man who has not antagonized with anybody, and whose principles are unknown, for the purpose of cheating somebody by getting votes from all sorts of men? Let us have an open and a fair fight. [Applause in the galleries.]

A bill to admit Kansas was prepared by the Territorial Committee of the House of Representatives. On June 30 it was rejected by one vote—106 yeas to 107 nays; later it was reconsidered and passed by a vote of 99 to 97. It was rejected by the Senate.

CHAPTER IX

THE ASSAULT ON SENATOR SUMNER

Philippic in the Senate by Charles Sumner Against the Pro-Slavery Conspirators Against Freedom in Kansas—Replies by Stephen A. Douglas [Ill.] and James M. Mason [Va.]—Representative Preston J. Brooks [S. C.] Assails Sumner in Senate Chamber—Sen. Henry Wilson Describes the Assault—A Committee of Investigation Is Appointed by the Senate—The Committee Reports That a Breach of Senatorial Privilege Was Committed, and Recommends that the Matter Be Laid Before the House of Representatives for Action; the Recommendation Is Adopted—Massachusetts Legislature Passes Resolutions Denouncing Brooks—Senator Andrew P. Butler [S. C.] Defends Brooks—House of Representatives Appoints Investigating Committee—Report of a Majority of the Committee States that a "Breach of Privilege" Had Been Committed, and Recommends Expulsion of Brooks from the House and Reprimand of Henry A. Edmunson [Va.] and Lawrence M. Keitt [S. C.], for Their Connection with the Assault—Minority Report Finds No Breach of Privilege Had Been Committed, and Recommends That No Action Be Taken—Anson Burlingame [Mass.] Denounces Brooks—House Refuses to Expel Brooks, Reprimands Keitt, and Refuses to Reprimand Edmunson—Resignation of Brooks: His Defiant Speech—His Subsequent Career.

O N May 19, 1856, Charles Sumner [Mass.], in a carefully prepared speech on the bill for admitting Kansas into the Union, delivered the most notable philippic in the annals of American forensic oratory. Dealing exhaustively with its subject, "The Crime Against Kansas," it necessarily included much of the arguments already presented. This part has therefore been omitted in favor of the special indictment in the speech of the conspirators against the liberty of Kansas—of whom the Senator particularly pilloried Senator Andrew P. Butler of South Carolina and Senator Stephen A. Douglas of Illinois.

"Conspirators" vs. "Slanderer"

Senator Sumner

Before entering upon my argument I must say something in response to what has fallen from Senators who have raised themselves to eminence on this floor in championship of human wrongs; I mean the Senator from South Carolina [Mr. Butler], and the Senator from Illinois [Mr. Douglas], who, though unlike as Don Quixote and Sancho Panza, yet, like this couple, sally forth together in the same adventure. I regret much to miss the elder Senator from his seat; but the cause against which he has run a tilt with such activity of animosity demands that the opportunity of exposing him should not be lost; and it is for the cause that I speak. The Senator from South Carolina has read many books of chivalry, and believes himself a chivalrous knight, with sentiments of honor and courage. Of course he has chosen a mistress to whom he has made his vows, and who, though ugly to others, is always lovely to him; though polluted in the sight of the world, is chaste in his sight—I mean the harlot, Slavery. For her his tongue is always profuse in words. Let her be impeached in character, or any proposition made to shut her out from the extension of her wantonness, and no extravagance of manner or hardihood of assertion is then too great for this Senator. The frenzy of Don Quixote, in behalf of his wench, Dulcinea del Toboso, is all surpassed. The asserted rights of slavery, which shock equality of all kinds, are cloaked by a fantastic claim of equality. If the slave States cannot enjoy what, in mockery of the great Fathers of the Republic, he misnames equality under the Constitution—in other words, the full power in the National Territories to compel fellow-men to unpaid toil, to separate husband and wife, and to sell little children at the auction block—then, sir, the chivalric Senator will conduct the State of South Carolina out of the Union! Heroic knight! Exalted Senator! A second Moses come for a second exodus!

But not content with this poor menace, which we have been twice told was "measured," the Senator, in the unrestrained chivalry of his nature, has undertaken to apply opprobrious words to those who differ from him on this floor. He calls them "sectional and fanatical"; and opposition to the usurpation in Kansas he denounces as "an uncalculating fanaticism." To be sure, these charges lack all grace of originality and all sentiment of truth; but the adventurous Senator does not hesitate.

He is the uncompromising, unblushing representative on this floor of a flagrant *sectionalism*, which now domineers over the Republic, and yet with a ludicrous ignorance of his own position—unable to see himself as others see him—or with an effrontery which even his white head ought not to protect from rebuke, he applies to those here who resent his *sectionalism* the very epithet which designates himself. The men who strive to bring back the Government to its original policy, when Freedom and not Slavery was national, while Slavery and not Freedom was sectional, he arraigns as *sectional*. This will not do. It involves too great a perversion of terms. I tell that Senator that it is to himself, and to the "organization" of which he is the "committed advocate," that this epithet belongs. I now fasten it upon them. For myself, I care little for names; but, since the question has been raised here, I affirm that the Republican party of the Union is in no just sense *sectional*, but, more than any other party, *national;* and that it now goes forth to dislodge from the high places of the Government the tyrannical sectionalism of which the Senator from South Carolina is one of the maddest zealots.

To the charge of fanaticism I also reply. Sir, fanaticism is found in an enthusiasm or exaggeration of opinions, particularly on religious subjects; but there may be a fanaticism for evil as well as for good. Now, I will not deny that there are persons among us loving liberty too well for their personal good in a selfish generation. Such there may be, and, for the sake of their example, would that there were more! In calling them "fanatics" you cast contumely upon the noble army of martyrs, from the earliest day down to this hour; upon the great tribunes of human rights, by whom life, liberty, and happiness on earth have been secured; upon the long line of devoted patriots, who, throughout history, have truly loved their country; and upon all who, in noble aspirations for the general good and in forgetfulness of self, have stood out before their age and gathered into their generous bosoms the shafts of tyranny and wrong, in order to make a pathway for Truth. You discredit Luther, when alone he nailed his articles to the door of the church at Wittenberg, and then, to the imperial demand that he should retract, firmly replied, "Here I stand; I cannot do otherwise, so help me God!" You discredit Hampden, when alone he refused to pay the few shillings of ship-money, and shook the throne of Charles I; you discredit Milton, when, amid the corruptions of a heartless court, he lived on, the lofty friend of Liberty, above question or suspicion; you discredit Russell and Sidney, when, for the sake of their country, they calmly turned from family and friends to tread the narrow steps of the scaffold; you discredit those early founders of American institutions, who preferred the hardships of a wilderness, surrounded by a savage foe, to injustice on beds of ease; you discredit our later fathers, who, few in numbers and weak in resources, yet strong in their cause, did not hesitate to brave the mighty power of England, already encircling the globe with her morning drum-beats. Yes, sir, of such are the fanatics of history, according to the Senator. But I tell that Senator that there are characters badly eminent, of whose fanaticism there can be no question. Such were the ancient Egyptians, who worshiped divinities in brutish forms; the Druids, who darkened the forests of oak, in which they lived, by sacrifices of blood; the Mexicans, who surrendered countless victims to the propitiation of their obscene idols; the Spaniards, who, under Alva, sought to force the Inquisition upon Holland, by a tyranny kindred to that now employed to force slavery upon Kansas; and such were the Algerines, when in solemn conclave, after listening to a speech not unlike that of the Senator from South Carolina, they resolved to continue the slavery of white Christians, and to extend it to the countrymen of Washington! Ay, sir, extend it! And in this same dreary catalogue faithful history must record all who now, in an enlightened age and in a land of boasted freedom, stand up, in perversion of the Constitution and in denial of immortal truth, to fasten a new shackle upon their fellow-men. If the Senator wishes to see fanatics let him look round among his own associates; let him look at himself.

As the Senator from South Carolina is the Don Quixote, the Senator from Illinois [Mr. Douglas] is the squire of slavery, its very Sancho Panza, ready to do all its humiliating offices. Standing on this floor, the Senator issued his rescript, requiring submission to the usurped power of Kansas; and this was accompanied by a manner—all his own—such as befits the tyrannical threat. Very well. Let the Senator try. I tell him now that he cannot enforce any such submission. The Senator, with the slave power at his back, is strong; but he is not strong enough for this purpose. He is bold. He shrinks from nothing. Like Danton, he may cry, *"l'audace! l'audace! toujours l'audace!"* [1] but even his audacity cannot compass this work. The Senator copies the British officer, who, with boastful swagger, said that with the hilt of his sword he would cram the "stamps" down the throats of the American people, and he will meet a similar

---

[1] "Boldness, boldness, always boldness."

failure. He may convulse this country with civil feud. Like
the ancient madman, he may set fire to this temple of constitutional liberty, grander than Ephesian dome; but he cannot
enforce obedience to that tyrannical usurpation.

The Senator dreams that he can subdue the North. How
little that Senator knows himself or the strength of the cause
which he persecutes! He is but a mortal man; against him is
an immortal principle. With finite power he wrestles with the
infinite, and he must fall. Against him are stronger battalions
than any marshaled by mortal arm—the inborn, ineradicable,
invincible sentiments of the human heart; against him is nature
in all her subtle forces; against him is God. Let him try to
subdue these.

At the close of his speech Senator Sumner returned
to this personal attack upon Senators Butler and Douglas, adding to the objects of his philippic Senator James
M. Mason of Virginia In connection with Butler and
Mason he attacked the character of the States which
they represented.

With regret, I come again upon the Senator from South
Carolina [Mr. Butler], who, omnipresent in this debate, over-
flowed with rage at the simple suggestion that Kansas had applied for admission as a State; and, with incoherent phrases,
discharged the loose expectoration of his speech, now upon her
representative, and then upon her people. There was no extravagance of the ancient parliamentary debate which he did not
repeat; nor was there any possible deviation from truth which
he did not make, with so much of passion, I am glad to add, as
to save him from the suspicion of intentional aberration. But
the Senator touches nothing which he does not disfigure—with
error, sometimes of principle, sometimes of fact. He shows an
incapacity of accuracy, whether in stating the Constitution or
in stating the law, whether in the details of statistics or the di-
versions of scholarship. He cannot ope his mouth but out there
flies a blunder. Surely he ought to be familiar with the life of
Franklin; and yet he referred to this household character, while
acting as agent of our fathers in England, as above suspicion;
and this was done that he might give point to a false contrast
with the agent of Kansas—not knowing that, however they may
differ in genius and fame, in this experience they are alike:
that Franklin, when intrusted with the petition of Massachusetts
Bay, was assaulted by a foul-mouthed speaker, where he could

not be heard in defence, and denounced as a "thief," even as the agent of Kansas has been assaulted on this floor, and denounced as a "forger." And let not the vanity of the Senator be inspired by the parallel with the British statesmen of that day; for it is only in hostility to freedom that any parallel can be recognized.

But it is against the people of Kansas that the sensibilities of the Senator are particularly aroused. Coming, as he announces, "from a State"—ay, sir, from South Carolina—he turns with lordly disgust from this newly formed community, which he will not recognize even as "a body-politic." Pray, sir, by what title does he indulge in this egotism? Has he read the history of "the State" which he represents? He cannot surely have forgotten its shameful imbecility from slavery, confessed throughout the Revolution, followed by its more shameful assumptions for slavery since. He cannot have forgotten its wretched persistence in the slave trade as the very apple of its eye, and the condition of its participation in the Union. He cannot have forgotten its constitution, which is republican only in name, confirming power in the hands of the few, and founding the qualifications of its legislators on "a settled freehold estate and ten negroes." And yet the Senator, to whom that "State" has in part committed the guardianship of its good name, instead of moving, with backward treading steps, to cover its nakedness, rushes forward, in the very ecstasy of madness, to expose it by provoking a comparison with Kansas. South Carolina is old; Kansas is young. South Carolina counts by centuries; where Kansas counts by years. But a beneficent example may be born in a day; and I venture to say that against the two centuries of the older "State" may be already set the two years of trial, evolving corresponding virtue, in the younger community. In the one is the long wail of slavery; in the other the hymns of freedom. And if we glance at special achievements it will be difficult to find anything in the history of South Carolina which presents so much of heroic spirit in an heroic cause as appears in that repulse of the Missouri invaders by the beleaguered town of Lawrence, where even the women gave their effective efforts to freedom. The matrons of Rome, who poured their jewels into the treasury for the public defence—the wives of Prussia, who, with delicate fingers, clothed their defenders against French invasion—the mothers of our own Revolution, who sent forth their sons, covered over with prayers and blessings, to combat for human rights, did nothing of self-sacrifice truer than did these women on this occasion. Were the whole history of South Carolina blotted out of existence, from its very beginning down to the day of the last election of the Senator to his present seat on this floor, civilization might lose—I do not say how little; but surely less than it has already gained by the example of Kansas, in its valiant struggle against oppression, and in the development of a new science of emigration. Already in Lawrence alone there are newspapers and schools, including a high school, and throughout this infant Territory there is more mature scholarship far, in proportion to its inhabitants, than in all South Carolina. Ah, sir, I tell the Senator that Kansas, welcomed as a free State, will be a "ministering angel" to the Republic when South Carolina, in the cloak of darkness which she hugs, "lies howling."

The Senator from Illinois [Mr. Douglas] naturally joins the Senator from South Carolina in this warfare, and gives to it the superior intensity of his nature. He thinks that the National Government has not completely proved its power, as it has never hanged a traitor; but, if the occasion requires, he hopes there will be no hesitation; and this threat is directed at Kansas, and even at the friends of Kansas throughout the country. Again occurs the parallel with the struggles of our Fathers, and I borrow the language of Patrick Henry, when, to the cry from the Senator, of "treason," "treason," I reply, "if this be treason, make the most of it." Sir, it is easy to call names; but I beg to tell the Senator that if the word "traitor" is in any way applicable to those who refuse submission to a tyrannical usurpation, whether in Kansas or elsewhere, then must some new word, of deeper color, be invented, to designate those mad spirits who would endanger and degrade the Republic, while they betray all the cherished sentiments of the Fathers and the spirit of the Constitution, in order to give new spread to slavery. Let the Senator proceed. It will not be the first time in history that a scaffold erected for punishment has become a pedestal of honor. Out of death comes life, and the "traitor" whom he blindly executes will live immortal in the cause.

> "For Humanity sweeps onward; where to-day the martyr stands,
> On the morrow crouches Judas, with the silver in his hands;
> While the hooting mob of yesterday in silent awe return,
> To glean up the scattered ashes into history's golden urn."[1]

Among these hostile Senators there is yet another, with all the prejudices of the Senator from South Carolina, but without his generous impulses, who, on account of his character before

[1] "The Present Crisis," by James Russell Lowell.

the country, and the rancor of his opposition, deserves to be named. I mean the Senator from Virginia [Mr. Mason], who, as the author of the Fugitive Slave bill, has associated himself with a special act of inhumanity and tyranny. Of him I shall say little, for he has said little in this debate, though within that little was compressed the bitterness of a life absorbed in the support of slavery. He holds the commission of Virginia; but he does not represent that early Virginia, so dear to our hearts, which gave to us the pen of Jefferson, by which the equality of men was declared, and the sword of Washington, by which Independence was secured; but he represents that other Virginia, from which Washington and Jefferson now avert their faces, where human beings are bred as cattle for the shambles, and where a dungeon rewards the pious matron who teaches little children to relieve their bondage by reading the Book of Life. It is proper that such a Senator, representing such a State, should rail against free Kansas.

Senators such as these are the natural enemies of Kansas, and I introduce them with reluctance simply that the country may understand the character of the hostility which must be overcome. Arrayed with them, of course, are all who unite, under any pretext or apology, in the propagandism of human slavery. To such, indeed, the time-honored safeguards of popular rights can be a name only, and nothing more. What are trial by jury, habeas corpus, the ballot-box, the right of petition, the liberty of Kansas, your liberty, sir, or mine, to one who lends himself, not merely to the support at home, but to the propagandism abroad, of that preposterous wrong, which denies even the right of a man to himself! Such a cause can be maintained only by a practical subversion of all rights. It is, therefore, merely according to reason that its partisans should uphold the usurpation in Kansas.

Senator Douglas replied to Senator Sumner's attack upon him as follows:

I shall not detain the Senate by a detailed reply to the speech of the Senator from Massachusetts. Inded, I should not deem it necessary to say one word, but for the personalities in which he has indulged, evincing a depth of malignity that issued from every sentence, making it a matter of self-respect with me to repel the assaults which have been made.

As to the argument, we have heard it all before. The Senator seems to get up a speech as in Yankee land they get up a bed quilt. They take all the old calico dresses of various colors, that have been in the house from the days of their grandmothers, and invite the young ladies of the neighborhood in the afternoon, and the young men to meet them at a dance in the evening. They cut up these pieces of old dresses and make pretty figures, and boast of what beautiful ornamental work they have made, although there was not a new piece of material in the whole quilt. [Laughter.] Thus it is with the speech which we have had rehashed here to-day in regard to matters of fact, matters of law, and matters of argument—everything but the personal assaults and the malignity.

I beg pardon; there is another point. We have had another dish of the classics served up—classic allusions, each one only distinguished for its lasciviousness and obscenity—each one drawn from those portions of the classics which all decent professors in respectable colleges cause to be suppressed, as unfit for decent young men to read. Sir, I cannot repeat the words. I should be condemned as unworthy of entering decent society if I repeated those obscene, vulgar terms which have been used at least a hundred times in that speech. It seems that his studies of the classics have all been in those haunts where ladies cannot go, and where gentlemen never read Latin. [Laughter.] I have no disposition to follow him in that part of his speech.

The Senator's endeavor seems to be an attempt to whistle to keep up his courage by defiant assaults upon us all. I am in doubt as to what can be his object. He has not hesitated to charge three-fourths of the Senate with fraud, with swindling, with crime, with infamy, at least one hundred times over in his speech. Is it his object to provoke some of us to kick him as we would a dog in the street, that he may get sympathy upon the just chastisement?

Who are the Senators thus arraigned? He does me the honor to make me the chief. It was my good luck to have such a position in this body as to enable me to be the author of a great, wise measure, which the Senate has approved, and the country will indorse. That measure was sustained by about three-fourths of all the members of the Senate. It was sustained by a majority of the Democrats and a majority of the Whigs in this body. It was sustained by a majority of Senators from the slaveholding States and a majority of Senators from the free States. The Senator by his charge of crime, then, stultifies three-fourths of the whole body, a majority of the North, nearly the whole South, a majority of Whigs, and a majority of Democrats here. He says they are infamous. If he so believed, who could suppose that he would ever show his face among such a body of men? How dare he approach one of those gentlemen to give him his hand after that act? If he felt the courtesies between men he would not do it. He would deserve to have himself spit in the face for doing so.

This charge is made against the body of which we are members. It is not a charge made in the heat of debate. It is not made as a retort growing out of an excited controversy. If it were of that nature I could make much allowance for it. I can pay great deference to the frailties and the impulses of an honorable man, when indignant at what he considers to be a wrong. If the Senator, betraying that he was susceptible of just indignation, had been goaded, provoked, and aggravated, on the spur of the moment, into the utterance of harsh things, and then apologized for them in his cooler hours, I could respect him much more than if he had never made such a departure from the rules of the Senate, because it would show that he had a heart to appreciate what is due among brother Senators and gentlemen. But, sir, it happens to be well known, it has been the subject of conversation for weeks, that the Senator from Massachusetts had his speech written, printed, committed to memory, practiced every night before the glass with a negro boy to hold the candle and watch the gestures, and annoying the boarders in the adjoining rooms until they were forced to quit the house! [Laughter.] It was rumored that he read part of it to friends, and they repeated in all the saloons and places of amusement in the city what he was going to say. The libels, the gross insults which we have heard to-day have been conned over, written with cool, deliberate malignity, repeated from night to night in order to catch the appropriate grace, and then he came here to spit forth that malignity upon men who differ from him— for that is their offence.

Mr. President, I ask what right has that Senator to come here and arraign three-fourths of the body for a dereliction of duty? Is there anything in the means by which he got here to give him a superiority over other gentlemen who came by the ordinary means? Is there anything to justify it in the fact that he came here with a deliberate avowal that he would never obey one clause of the Constitution of the United States, and yet put his hand upon the Holy Bible, in the presence of this body, and appealed to Almighty God to witness that he would be faithful to the Constitution with a pledge to perjure his soul by violating both that oath and the Constitution? He came here with a pledge to perjure himself as the condition of eligibility to the place. Has he a right to arraign us because we have felt it to be our duty to be faithful to that Constitution which he disavows —to that oath which he assumes and then repudiates?

The Senate have not forgotten the debate on the Fugitive Slave law, when that Senator said, in reply to a question whether he was in favor of carrying into effect that clause of the Constitution for the rendition of fugitive slaves—"Is thy servant a dog that he should do this thing?" A dog—to do what you swore you would do! A dog—to be true to the Constitution of your country! A dog—to be true to your oath! A dog—unless you are a traitor! That was his position; and still he comes here and arraigns us for crime, and talks about "audacity!" Did mortal man ever witness such audacity in an avowed criminal? He comes here with a pledge to defy the Constitution of his country, and the wrath of God, by not obeying his oath, and then talks about audacity. In what does my audacity, of which he speaks, consist? It consists in the fact that, coming from a free State, born in a free State, with associations all around me tinctured strongly with anti-slavery, when I was elected to the Senate, and took an oath to be true to the Constitution, I would not violate that oath, even in obedience to a popular prejudice at home. My crime consists in saying to my people, "So long as that Constitution requires the fugitive slave to go back, so long will I, as a citizen or a representative, be faithful to that clause of the Constitution, as well as to every other." I tell the people with whom I live that I do not desire a man to represent me who, for the sake of getting an office, will take an oath to be true to the Constitution, with a secret pledge to violate it. I do not wish to have a man on the bench to administer justice who, in order to get the place, will take an oath to be faithful to the Constitution and then repudiate both the Constitution and the oath. I tell my people, "If you want perjurers to represent you get the men who believe in a higher law than the Constitution! Because I am faithful to the Constitution of my country I am arraigned as a conspirator, as a traitor, as a man guilty of crime. Is there any other reason? If I would follow the popular prejudice of the section where I was born, where I live, and where I hope to die; if I would fan the flame of sectional excitement and strife to the very point of consuming this glorious temple of freedom, I should be as pure a man, and as pure a patriot, as these men who live under constitutions which they do not respect, and will not obey! I have been burned and hung in effigy under the advice and arrangement of these conspirators here because of my fidelity to the Constitution of the country, and to the principles to which I stood pledged, and which my judgment approved.

I have stood by my principles, by my pledges, by the Constitution, and by my oath. If I had abandoned them I could have had the applause of all these Black Republican leaders.

Now, sir, this dealing in general terms of insult; this talk about crime, treachery, and swindling; this indulgence in coarse, vulgar denunciation against three-fourths of the body to which you belong, does not meet the points between us. You challenged me to this great issue, which you say you have made up between the negro worshipers and the "slave power," as you call it. What you call the slave power is simply observance of the Constitution of the country, as our fathers made it. Let us have that fair issue between the parties, and let us discuss that, instead of dealing in denunciation against one another here. I wish the Senate to bear in mind that, in the many controversies in which I have been engaged since I have been a member of this body, I never had one in which I was not first assailed. I have always stood on the defensive. You arrange it on the opposite side of the House to set your hounds after me, and then complain when I cuff them over the head and send them back yelping. I never made an assault on any Senator; I have only repelled attacks.

The attack of the Senator from Massachusetts now is not on me alone. Even the courteous and the accomplished Senator from South Carolina [Mr. Butler] could not be passed by in his absence.

SENATOR MASON.—Advantage was taken of it.

SENATOR DOUGLAS.—It is suggested that advantage is taken of his absence. I think that is a mistake. I think the speech was written and practiced, and the gestures fixed; and, if that part had been stricken out, the Senator would not have known how to repeat the speech. [Laughter.] All that tirade of abuse must be brought down on the head of the venerable, the courteous, and the distinguished Senator from South Carolina. I shall not defend that gentleman here. Every Senator who knows him loves him. He, however, will be here in due time to speak for himself, and to act for himself, too. I know what will happen. The Senator from Massachusetts will go to him, whisper a secret apology in his ear, and ask him to accept that as satisfaction for a public outrage on his character! I know how the Senator from Massachusetts is in the habit of doing those things. I have had some experience of his skill in that respect.

Why these attacks on individuals by name and two-thirds

of the Senate collectively? Is it the object to drive men here to dissolve social relations with political opponents? Is it to turn the Senate into a bear garden, where Senators cannot associate on terms which ought to prevail between gentlemen? These attacks are heaped upon me by man after man. When I repel them it is intimated that I show some feeling on the subject. Sir, God grant that when I denounce an act of infamy I shall do it with feeling, and do it under the sudden impulses of feeling, instead of sitting up at night writing out my denunciation of a man whom I hate, copying it, having it printed, punctuating the proof-sheets, and repeating it before the glass, in order to give refinement to insult, which is only pardonable when it is the outburst of a just indignation.

Senator James M. Mason [Va.] replied to Senator Sumner's attack upon him as follows:

Mr. President, the necessities of our political position bring us into relations and associations upon this floor which, in obedience to a common Government, we are forced to admit. They bring us into relations and associations which, beyond the walls of this Chamber, we are enabled to avoid—associations here, whose presence elsewhere is dishonor, and the touch of whose hand would be a disgrace. They are the necessities of our political position; and yet, Mr. President, it is not easy to bear them. Representing our States here, under a Constitution which we came here to obey, we are constrained to listen, from day to day, from sources utterly irresponsible, to language to which no gentleman would subject himself elsewhere. I say it is difficult to bear. We bear it from respect to the obligations of the Constitution, and in obedience to the constitutional trust which we have undertaken to perform.

Sir, the Senator who here represents Massachusetts undertook to-day to assail the absent—to assail one honorable man who honored this Chamber when he was a member of this body, but who is no longer a member, and to assail him when he was at the distance of some two thousand miles from his presence; and to assail him how? Assuming to be the Cicero of the occasion, to denounce him as a Catiline!

I am not here to vindicate absent gentlemen. The Senator from South Carolina will return in good time to his place. I will say this, however, in the presence of the Senate, that when the Senator from Massachusetts dared, in this Chamber, and among those who know the Senator from South Carolina, to connect his name with untruth—for he did so—he presented himself here as one utterly incapable of knowing what truth is —utterly incapable of conceiving the perceptions of an honorable mind, when directed to the investigation of truth. He presented himself as the cunning artificer or forger, who knows no other use of truth than to give currency to falsehood; who uses the beaten gold to enable him to pass off the false coin; who distinguishes between that which is pure metal and that which is not so, only to enable him to deceive those who have trusted him here.

But, Mr. President, I did not intend to be betrayed into this debate. I have said that the necessity of political position alone brings me into relations with men upon this floor who elsewhere I cannot acknowledge as possessing manhood in any form. I am constrained to hear here depravity, vice in its most odious form uncoiled in this presence, exhibiting its loathsome deformities in accusation and vilification against the quarter of the country from which I come; and I must listen to it because it is a necessity of my position, under a common Government, to recognize as an equal, politically, one whom to see elsewhere is to shun and despise. I did not intend to be betrayed into this debate; but I submit to the necessity of my position. I am here now united with an honored band of patriots, from the North equally with the South, to try if we can preserve and perpetuate those institutions which others are prepared to betray, and are seeking to destroy; and I will submit to the necessity of that position at least until the work is accomplished.

Mr. President, the first criminal known to the world, in the complaint which instigated him to crime, declared only that the offering of his brother was more acceptable than his. It was the complaint of Cain against Abel, and he avenged it by putting that brother to death, and then went forth with the primeval curse upon his brow. In the fortunes of those who are enlisted with the Senator from Massachusetts against this confederation now, let them go, as Cain did, with the curse upon their brow of fraternal homicide, but with the still deeper guilt that they instigate others to shed blood when they shed none themselves.

SENATOR SUMNER replied: To the Senator from Illinois I should willingly leave the privilege of the common scold—the last word; but I will not leave to him, in any discussion with me, the last argument, or the last semblance of it. He has crowned the audacity of this debate by venturing to rise here and calumniate me. He has said that I came here, took an oath to support the Constitution, and yet determined not to support a particular clause in that Constitution. To that statement I give, to his face, the flattest denial. When it was made on a former occasion on this floor by the absent Senator from South Carolina [Mr. Butler] I then repelled it. I will read from the debate of the 28th of June, 1854, as published in the *Globe*, to show what I said in response to that calumny when pressed at that hour.

I proceeded to read from the memorable veto by President Jackson, in 1832, of the Bank of the United States. It will be remembered that to his course, at that critical time, were opposed the authority of the Supreme Court and his oath to support the Constitution, precisely as the Senator from Illinois now, with ignorance, or with a want of logic greater than his ignorance, undertakes to revile me. Here is the triumphant reply of President Jackson:

"If the opinion of the Supreme Court covers the whole ground of this act, it ought not to control the coördinate authorities of this Government. The Congress, the Executive, and the Court must each for itself be guided by its own opinion of the Constitution. *Each public officer who takes an oath to support the Constitution swears that he will support it as he understands it, and not as it is understood by others.*"

I concluded on this point in these words:

"I desire to say that, as I understand the Constitution, this clause does not impose upon me, as a Senator or citizen, any obligation to take part, directly or indirectly, in the surrender of a fugitive slave."

Sir, this is the Senate of the United States, an important body, under the Constitution, with great powers. Its members are justly supposed, from age, to be above the intemperance of youth, and from character to be above the gusts of vulgarity. They are supposed to have something of wisdom and something of that candor which is the handmaid of wisdom. Let the Senator bear these things in mind, and let him remember hereafter that the bowie-knife and bludgeon are not the proper emblems of senatorial debate. Let him remember that the swagger of Bob Acres and the ferocity of the Malay cannot add dignity to this body. The Senator has gone on to infuse into his speech the venom which has been sweltering for months—ay, for years; and he has alleged facts that are entirely without foundation, in order to heap upon me some personal obloquy. I will not go into the details which have flowed out so naturally from his tongue. I only brand them to his face as false. I say, also, to that Senator, and I wish him to bear it in mind, that no person with the upright form of man can be allowed——[Hesitation.]

SENATOR DOUGLAS.—Say it.

SENATOR SUMNER.—I will say it—no person with the upright form of man can be allowed, without violation of all decency, to switch out from his tongue the perpetual stench of offensive personality. Sir, that is not a proper weapon of debate, at least, on this floor. The noisome, squat, and nameless animal, to which I now refer, is not a proper model for an American Senator. Will the Senator from Illinois take notice?

SENATOR DOUGLAS.—I will; and therefore will not imitate you, sir.

SENATOR SUMNER.—I did not hear the Senator.

SENATOR DOUGLAS.—I said if that be the case I would certainly never imitate you in that capacity, recognizing the force of the illustration.

SENATOR SUMNER.—Mr. President, again the Senator has switched his tongue, and again he fills the Senate with its offensive odor.

I pass from the Senator from Illinois. There was still another, the Senator from Virginia, who is now also in my eye. That Senator said nothing of argument, and, therefore, there is nothing of that for response. I simply say to him that hard words are not argument; frowns not reasons; nor do scowls belong to the proper arsenal of parliamentary debate. The Senator has not forgotten that on a former occasion I did something to exhibit on this floor the plantation manners which he displayed. I will not do any more now.

SENATOR MASON.—Manners of which that Senator is unconscious.

SENATOR DOUGLAS.—I am not going to pursue this subject further. I will only say that a man who has been branded by me in the Senate, and convicted by the Senate of falsehood, cannot use language requiring reply, and therefore I have nothing more to say.

THE ASSAULT ON SUMNER

The great severity with which Senator Sumner had spoken against South Carolina and one of her Senators [Andrew P. Butler] caused Preston S. Brooks, a Representative from that State and a relative of Senator Butler, to commit a physical assault upon the offending Senator from Massachusetts two days after the speech [on May 22, 1856].

The nature of the assault was thus described by Senator Sumner's colleague, Henry Wilson, on the day following the outrage:

Mr. President, the seat of my colleague is vacant to-day. That seat is vacant to-day for the first time during five years of public service. Yesterday, after a touching tribute of respect to the memory of a deceased member of the House of Representatives, the Senate adjourned. My colleague remained in his seat,

SOUTHERN CHIVALRY—CLUBS VERSUS ARGUMENT

From the collection of the New York Historical Society

busily engaged in his public duties. While thus engaged, with pen in hand, and in a position which rendered him utterly incapable of protecting or defending himself, Mr. Preston S. Brooks, a member of the House of Representatives, approached his desk unobserved, and abruptly addressed him. Before he had time to utter a single word in reply he received a stunning blow upon the head from a cane in the hands of Mr. Brooks, which made him blind and almost unconscious. Endeavoring, however, to protect himself, in rising from his chair his desk was overthrown; and while in that condition he was beaten upon the head by repeated blows, until he sunk upon the floor of the Senate exhausted, unconscious, and covered with his own blood. He was taken from this Chamber to the ante-room, his wounds were dressed, and then by friends he was carried to his home and placed upon his bed. He is unable to be with us to-day to perform the duties that belong to him as a member of this body.

Sir, to assail a member of the Senate out of this Chamber, "for words spoken in debate," is a grave offence, not only against the rights of the Senator, but the constitutional privileges of this House; but, sir, to come into this Chamber and assault a member in his seat until he falls exhausted and senseless on this floor is an offence requiring the prompt and decisive action of the Senate.

Senators, I have called your attention to this transaction. I submit no motion. I leave it to older Senators, whose character —whose position in this body, and before the country, eminently fit them for the task of devising measures to redress the wrongs of a member of this body, and to vindicate the honor and dignity of the Senate.

On motion of William H. Seward [N. Y.] a committee of investigation was elected. On May 28 the committee made its report. After presenting the facts of the case and various parliamentary precedents and rules relating to a breach of privilege of one House of legislation by a member of another, chiefly the rule laid down by Thomas Jefferson in his "Manual of Parliamentary Practice," to the effect that complaint of the breach should be laid before the other House, and punishment be left to it, the committee gave it as its opinion that this should be the disposition of the case. This was agreed to by the Senate with only one dissenting vote, that of Robert Toombs [Ga.].

Later, upon the return of Andrew P. Butler [S. C.] to the Senate and the development in the House of Representatives of a strong opposition to the expulsion from that body of Mr. Brooks, there was manifested in the upper House a disposition to reconsider the resolution that had been passed on the recommendation of the investigating committee.

THE ASSAULT ON SUMNER

SENATE, JUNE 12, 1856

On June 12 Senator Andrew P. Butler [S. C.], aspersions upon whom had caused Mr. Brooks, who was his relative, to make the assault, spoke in behalf of the assailant, the occasion being the presentation to the Senate of resolutions, by the State of Massachusetts, condemnatory of the assault upon its Senator.

Senator Butler claimed that Senator Sumner had provoked the assault by his aspersions on South Carolina, and it was these that had aroused Brooks, as a loyal son of the State, to the only expression of resentment open to him.

What was my friend to do? Sue the libeler? Indict him? If that was the mode in which he intended to take redress he had better never go to South Carolina again. Was he to challenge him? That would have been an exhibition of chivalry having no meaning. Although he has been upon the field, both in open war and in a private affair, I should be very sorry to see any crisis requiring it again. A challenge would have been an advertisement to the world of his courage, when there was not a probability of its being tried. He would have made himself contemptible, and perhaps might have been committed to the penitentiary for sending a challenge.

Then, what course was left to him to pursue? Mr. Sumner had opportunities enough to make an apology. God knows I could not have resisted the admonitory criticism of the distinguished Senator from Michigan [Lewis Cass], perhaps the most imposing authority in the Senate. He paid no regard to him, and for a very good reason: his speech was written, and had gone out, and he could not contradict what he had sent forth to the public with malice aforethought.

Well, sir, what did Mr. Brooks do? It is said he sought Mr. Sumner in the Senate Chamber. It is the last place in which he wished to seek him. He would have met him in an open combat, on a fair field, and under a free sky, at any time. And when the legislature of Massachusetts chooses to say that his conduct is cowardly let her try him in any way she chooses. [Applause.]

THE PRESIDENT *pro tempore.*—Persons in the galleries will distinctly understand that if there be any further demonstration the galleries will be cleared of all except ladies.

WILLIAM P. FESSENDEN [Me.].—In justice to the galleries, I will suggest that the impression on this side of the House is that the disturbance came from the floor of the Senate Chamber, and not from the galleries. I hope the galleries will not be punished for the act of persons on the floor.

Sir, a man who occupies a place in the Senate, representing

a great commonwealth like Massachusetts, occupies a very high position, from which he can send forth to the public what may affect the character of any man except some one upon whose character the verdict of history has been rendered. For this reason I would never look, and I never have looked, beyond the public position of a member here, to go into his private and personal character. I would not do it because by so doing I should do a wrong which I could not redress. We are in a position which requires high considerations for the regulation of our conduct. I agree thoroughly with General Jackson, that the slanderer who involves third persons in difficulty and danger is an incendiary, against whom we should guard more than any one else, in a parliamentary point of view. I will quote General Jackson's language. He said: "Over the doors of each House of Congress, in letters of gold, should be inscribed the words, 'The Slanderer Is Worse than the Murderer.'" A single murder is horrible. It may take a single individual from society. But when I look at the mischievous influence of slander I find that it pervades a whole community; makes war in society; sets family against family; individual against individual; section against section. It is the most cowardly mode in which a war can be conducted.

With the state of opinion to which I have alluded prevailing, what did Mr. Brooks do? He thought Mr. Sumner deserved a castigation, and he undertook to give it to him according to the old-fashioned notion, by caning him. Mr. Brooks, not finding him anywhere else, came to him while he was sitting in his seat here, after the Senate had adjourned. He came to him in front —different from the statement made to the Massachusetts legislature. He was half a minute in his proem or explanation. He said: "Mr. Sumner, I have read your speech. I have read it carefully, with as much consideration, and forbearance, and fairness as I could; but, sir, I have come to punish you now for the contents of that speech, which is a libel on my State and on a gray-haired relative."

Instinct would have prompted most men to rise immediately. Mr. Sumner did rise. In the act of rising Mr. Brooks struck him across the face—not, as has been represented, over his head, for that is not the truth, nor is it borne out by the testimony. On the second stroke the cane broke. It is the misfortune of Mr. Brooks to have incurred all the epithets which have been used in regard to an assassin-like and bludgeon attack, by the mere accident of having a foolish stick, which broke. It broke again; and it was not, as I understand, until it came very near the handle, that he inflicted blows which he would not have inflicted if he had an ordinary weapon of a kind which would have been a security against breaking.

It has gone through the country that Mr. Brooks struck him after he was prostrate on the floor. None who know this young man could entertain such an idea. Notwithstanding all that has been said of his brutality, he is one of the best tempered fellows I ever knew—impetuous, no doubt, and quick in resentment—but he did not intend what has been assigned to him.

After all that has been said and done, on a *post bellum* examination, what is it? A fight in the Senate Chamber, resulting in two flesh wounds, which ought not to have detained Mr. Sumner from the Senate. Being rather a handsome man, perhaps he would not like to expose himself by making his appearance for some time; but if he had been in the army there was no reason why he should not go to the field the next day; and he would deserve to be cashiered if he did not go.

For this transaction, as I have detailed it, and without the intelligence which I have detailed being before them, the legislature of Massachusetts have sent their resolutions here. These resolutions are without a precedent in the history of this country. I hope other Senators will speak to them, for they are not only an insult to South Carolina and her representatives in Congress, but I think they assail the Constitution of the country.

Taking all these things into consideration, indicted as Mr. Brooks has been by an *ex parte* accusation, without evidence, without even the finding of a grand jury, what is his position? If a civil action were brought by Mr. Sumner against Mr. Brooks for assault and battery I pledge myself that, with all the resources he could bring to his command, he would be able to reduce the verdict to a penny damages. What would be the state of the pleadings? Mr. Brooks struck Mr. Sumner would be the allegation. It would be admitted that he struck him, and inflicted two flesh wounds. Mr. Sumner would reply, "I am a Senator of the United States; and although the Senate was not in session I was in that sacred temple, and my character is so sacred under the privileges of the Senate that I am not to be assailed." What would Mr. Brooks' counsel rejoin? The rejoinder would be, "Sir, you had profaned and disgraced the seat you occupied before you were struck."

Then the question would be, what is this privilege so much spoken of—freedom of debate? The court would examine the question, whether what was said was privileged within the rules of the Senate, or whether it was a libel. If it should be pronounced to be a libel, and I were the judge before whom an action were brought—if a man brought before me could show that another insulted his mother, or his father, or his sister, or himself, or his country, I would say to the man who inflicted the blow, "My duty is to fine you; you are not justified by the law; but it is my privilege to say that, while I will enforce the law and maintain its dignity, I shall fine you as small a sum as I possibly can within my discretion."

BREACH OF PRIVILEGE

[ASSAULT ON SENATOR SUMNER]

HOUSE OF REPRESENTATIVES, JUNE 2, 1856

The House appointed a committee consisting of three Northern and two Southern Representatives to investigate the assault and report upon it. On June 2 two reports, a majority one by the Northern Representatives, Lewis D. Campbell [O.], Francis E. Spinner [N. Y.], and Alexander M. Pennington [N. J.], and a minority one by the Southern Representatives, Howell Cobb [Ga.] and Alfred B. Greenwood [Ark.], were presented to the House. The former report declared that the assault had been committed without warning and with "a weapon of deadly character" and that "the blows were indiscriminately dealt at the hazard of the life of the assailed," and that it had been "premeditated during a period of at least two days, without any other provocation than words lawfully spoken in debate in the Senate Chamber, not ruled out of order by the President of the Senate, nor objected to by any Senator as violative of the rules . . . of that body." The majority of the committee also found that two Representatives, Henry A. Edmunson [Va.], and Lawrence M. Keitt [S. C.], had been previously informed of the intent of Mr. Brooks to commit the assault and of the time and place of its probable occurrence; that they were in a room adjoining the Senate Chamber at the time of the assault, and that Mr. Keitt "rushed up with a cane in a threatening manner when the bystanders attempted to protect Mr. Sumner from the blows of Mr. Brooks and that Mr. Edmunson entered the Chamber soon after Mr. Sumner fell.'' The majority refused ''to discuss the powers of the House to punish its disorderly members'' nor to ''argue the general question as to what constitutes a breach of privilege.'' It closed by recommending that Brooks be expelled from the House and that the House declare its disapprobation of the acts of Edmunson and Keitt.

The minority report quoted that portion of Senator Sumner's speech which related to South Carolina and Senator Butler, who was absent at the time, as the provocation for Mr. Brooks' assault, and briefly described the assault as ''repeated and severe blows'' with ''a walking stick.'' · It found that Edmunson and Keitt previously knew of the assailant's intention and did not communicate the fact to Senator Sumner, but stated that there was no evidence that they knew of the time and place at which the assault was to occur.

The minority report entered into a long discussion of ''breach of privilege,'' citing examples from the history of the British Parliament to show the construction by that body of what constitutes a breach, and the extreme penalties imposed at its sole discretion. This practice, the report contended, should not be used as a precedent by Congress.

Holding, as we do, that neither House has any privileges except those which are written and declared either in the Constitution or some law or rule passed in pursuance thereof, and that the facts developed by the evidence show no violation of any such written and recognized privileges, we recommend the adoption of the following resolution:

Resolved, That this House has no jurisdiction over the assault alleged to have been committed by the Hon. Preston S. Brooks, a member of this House from the State of South Carolina, upon the Hon. Charles Sumner, a Senator from the State of Massachusetts; and therefore deem it improper to express any opinion on the subject.

On June 21 Anson Burlingame [Mass.] spoke upon the assault on Senator Sumner.

BULLY BROOKS AND HIS GANG

ANSON BURLINGAME, M. C.

On the 19th of May it was announced that Mr. Sumner would address the Senate upon the Kansas question. The floor of the Senate, the galleries, and avenues leading thereto were thronged with an expectant audience; and many of us left our places in this House to hear the Massachusetts orator. To say that we were delighted with the speech we heard would but faintly express the deep emotions of our hearts awakened by it. I need not speak of the classic purity of its language, nor of the nobility of its sentiments. It was heard by many; it has been read by millions. There has been no such speech made in the Senate since the days when those Titans of American eloquence—the Websters and the Haynes—contended with each other for mastery.

It was severe because it was launched against tyranny. It was severe as Chatham was severe when he defended the feeble colonies against the giant oppression of the mother country. It was made in the face of a hostile Senate. It continued through the greater portion of two days; and yet, during that time, the speaker was not once called to order. This fact is conclusive as to the personal and parliamentary decorum of the speech. He had provocation enough. His State had been called hypocritical. He himself had been called "a puppy," "a fool," "a fanatic," and "a dishonest man." Yet he was parliamentary from the beginning to the end of his speech. No man knew better than he did the proprieties of the place, for he had always observed them. No man knew better than he did parliamentary law, because he had made it the study of his life. No man saw more clearly than he did the flaming sword of the Constitution, turning every way, guarding all the avenues of the Senate. But he was not thinking of these things; he was not thinking then of the privileges of the Senate nor of the guarantees of the Constitution; he was there to denounce tyranny and crime, and he did it. He was there to speak for the rights of an empire, and he did it, bravely and grandly.

So much for the occasion of the speech. A word, and I shall be pardoned, about the speaker himself. He is my friend; for many and many a year I have looked to him for guidance and light, and I never looked in vain. He never had a personal enemy in his life; his character is as pure as the snow that falls on his native hills; his heart overflows with kindness for every being having the upright form of man; he is a ripe scholar, a chivalric gentleman, and a warm-hearted, true friend. He sat at the feet of Channing, and drank in the sentiments of that noble soul. He bathed in the learning and undying love of the great jurist Story; and the hand of Jackson, with its honors and its offices, sought him early in life, but he shrank from them with instinctive modesty. Sir, he is the pride of Massachusetts. His mother commonwealth found him adorning the highest walks of literature and law, and she bade him go and grace somewhat the rough character of political life. The people of Massachusetts—the old and the young and the middle-aged—now pay their full homage to the beauty of his public and private character. Such is Charles Sumner.

On the 22d day of May, when the Senate and the House had clothed themselves in mourning for a brother fallen in the battle of life in the distant State of Missouri, the Senator from Massachusetts sat in the silence of the Senate Chamber, engaged in the employments appertaining to his office, when a member from this House, who had taken an oath to sustain the Constitution, stole into the Senate, that place which had hitherto been held sacred against violence, and smote him as Cain smote his brother.

MR. KEITT (in his seat).—That is false.

MR. BURLINGAME.—I will not bandy epithets with the gentleman. I am responsible for my own language. Doubtless he is responsible for his.

MR. KEITT.—I am.

MR. BURLINGAME.—I shall stand by mine.

One blow was enough; but it did not satiate the wrath of that spirit which had pursued him through two days. Again and again, quicker and faster fell the leaden blows, until he was torn away from his victim, when the Senator from Massachusetts fell in the arms of his friends, and his blood ran down on the Senate floor. Sir, the act was brief, and my comments on it shall be brief also. I denounce it in the name of the Constitution it violated. I denounce it in the name of the sovereignty of Massachusetts, which was stricken down by the blow. I denounce it in the name of humanity. I denounce it in the name of civilization which it outraged. I denounce it in the name of that fair play which bullies and prize-fighters respect. What! strike a man when he is pinioned—when he cannot respond to a blow! Call you that chivalry? In what code of honor did you get your authority for that? I do not believe that member has a friend so dear who must not, in his heart of hearts, condemn the act. Even the member himself, if he has left a spark of that chivalry and gallantry attributed to him, must loathe and scorn the act. God knows I do not wish to speak unkindly, or in a spirit of revenge; but I owe it to my manhood and the noble State I, in part, represent, to express my deep abhorrence of the act. But much as I reprobate the act, much more do I reprobate the conduct of those who were by, and saw the outrage perpetrated. Sir, especially do I notice the conduct of that Senator recently from the free platform of Massachusetts,[1] with the odor of her hospitality on him, who stood there, not only silent and quiet while it was going on, but, when it was over, approved the act. And worse, when he had time to cool, when he had slept on it, he went into the Senate Chamber of the United States and shocked the sensibilities of the world by approving it. Another Senator[2] did not take part because he feared his motives might be questioned, exhibiting as extraordinary a delicacy as that individual who refused to rescue a drowning mortal because he had not been introduced to him. [Laughter.] Another[3] was not on good terms; and yet, if rumor be true, that Senator has declared that himself and family are more indebted to Mr. Sumner than to any other man; yet, when he saw him borne bleeding by, he turned and went on the other side. Oh, magnanimous Slidell! Oh, prudent Douglas! Oh, audacious Toombs!

Sir, there are questions arising out of this which far transcend those of a mere personal nature. Of those personal considerations I shall speak, when the question comes properly before us, if I am permitted to do so. The higher question involves the very existence of the Government itself. If, sir, freedom of speech is not to remain to us, what is all this Government worth. If we from Massachusetts, or any other State—Senators, or members of the House—are to be called to account by some "gallant nephew" of some "gallant uncle," when we utter something which does not suit their sensitive natures, we desire to know it. If the conflict is to be transferred from this peaceful, intellectual field to one where, it is said, "honors are easy and responsibilities equal," then we desire to know it. Massachusetts, if her sons and representatives are to have the rod held over them, if these things are to continue, the time may come—though she utters no threats—when she may be called upon to withdraw them to her own bosom, where she can furnish to them that protection which is not vouchsafed to them under the flag of their common country. But, while she permits us to remain, we shall do our duty—our whole duty. We shall speak whatever we

[1] Robert Toombs [Ga.].   [2] John Slidell [La.].
[3] Stephen A. Douglas [Ill.].

choose to speak, when we will, where we will, and how we will regardless of all consequences.

Sir, the sons of Massachusetts are educated at the knees of their mothers, in the doctrines of peace and goodwill, and, God knows, they desire to cultivate those feelings—feelings of social kindness, and public kindness. The House will bear witness that we have not violated or trespassed upon any of them; but, sir, if we are pushed too long and too far there are men from the old commonwealth of Massachusetts who will not shrink from a defence of freedom of speech, and the honored State they represent, on any field where they may be assailed.

On July 14 the resolution to expel Mr. Brooks came to a vote. The yeas were 121 and the nays 95, and, since a two-thirds vote is required for expulsion, the resolution was lost. On the following day, by a vote of 106 to 96, the House "declared its disapprobation" of Mr. Keitt for his actions in connection with the assault on Senator Sumner, and, by a vote of 60 yeas to 136 nays, refused to disapprove of Mr. Edmunson's actions in the same matter.

Mr. Brooks, because the vote of a majority of his fellow Representatives in favor of his expulsion was an actual, if not a parliamentary, condemnation resigned his seat the same day, after a speech in which he justified his assault upon Senator Sumner, asserted that his virtual condemnation was a precedent which would return to plague those who had inflicted it, and defied those Representatives who had most unsparingly denounced him. Relying upon the support of his constituency, and, indeed, of the entire South, the press of which had almost unanimously applauded his action, and from which region he had received the presents of countless canes in approbation of his assault, he virtually expressed the defiance of Catiline: "I go, but I return."

"LOOK TO YOUR HEARTHS, MY LORDS!"

[RESIGNATION OF PRESTON M. BROOKS, M. C.]

Some time since a Senator from Massachusetts allowed himself, in an elaborately prepared speech, to offer a gross insult to my State and to a venerable friend, who is my State's representative, and who was absent at the time.

Not content with that, he published to the world, and circulated extensively, this uncalled-for libel on my State and my blood. Whatever insults my State insults me. Her history and character have commanded my pious veneration; and in her defence I hope I shall always be prepared, humbly and modestly, to perform the duty of a son. I should have forfeited my own self-respect, and perhaps the good opinion of my countrymen, if I had failed to resent such an injury by calling the offender in question to a personal account. It was a personal affair, and in taking redress into my own hands I meant no disrespect to the Senate of the United States or to this House. Nor, sir, did I design insult or disrespect to the State of Massachusetts. I was aware of the personal responsibilities I incurred, and was willing to meet them. I knew, too, that I was amenable to the laws of the country, which afford the same protection to all, whether they be members of Congress or private citizens. I did not, and do not now, believe that I could be properly punished, not only in a court of law, but here also, at the pleasure and discretion of the House. I did not then, and do not now, believe that the spirit of American freemen would tolerate slander in high places, and permit a member of Congress to publish and circulate a libel on another, and then call upon either House to protect him against the personal responsibilities which he had thus incurred.

But, if I had committed a breach of privilege, it was the privilege of the Senate, and not of this House, which was violated. I was answerable *there*, and not *here*. They had no right, as it seems to me, to prosecute me in these halls, nor have you the right in law or under the Constitution, as I respectfully submit, to take jurisdiction over offences committed against them. The Constitution does not justify them in making such a request, nor this House in granting it. If, unhappily, the day should ever come when sectional or party feeling should run so high as to control all other considerations of public duty or justice, how easy will it be to use such precedents for the excuse of arbitrary power, in either House, to expel members of the minority who may have rendered themselves obnoxious to the prevailing spirit in the House to which they belong.

This House, however, it would seem, from the unmistakable tendency of its proceedings, takes a different view from that which I deliberately entertain in common with many others.

So far as public interests or constitutional rights are involved, I have now exhausted my means of defence. I may, then, be allowed to take a more personal view of the question at issue. The further prosecution of this subject, in the shape it has now assumed, may not only involve my friends, but the House itself in agitations which might be unhappy in their consequences to the country. If these consequences could be confined to myself individually, I think I am prepared and ready to meet them, here or elsewhere; and, when I use this language, I mean what I say. But others must not suffer for me. I have felt more on account of my two friends who have been implicated than for myself. I will not constrain gentlemen to assume a responsibility on my account which, possibly, they would not on their own.

Sir, I cannot, on *my own account*, assume the responsibility, in the face of the American people, of commencing a line of conduct which, in my heart of hearts, I believe would result in subverting the foundations of this Government and in drenching this hall in blood. No act of mine, and on my personal account, shall inaugurate revolution; but when you, Mr. Speaker, return to your own home and hear the people of the great North—and they are a great people—speak of me as a bad man, you will do me the justice to say that a blow struck by me at this time would be followed by revolution—and this I know. [Applause and hisses in the gallery.]

The Speaker announced that, if any such demonstrations were repeated the galleries should be cleared.

MR. BROOKS (turning to the gentlemen's gallery).—If I have any friends in the gallery I appeal to them to be quiet.

At the same time, Mr. Speaker, I am not willing to see the Constitution wounded through me; nor will I submit voluntarily to a wrong if I can avoid it. I will not voluntarily give my name to countenance parliamentary misrule or constitutional aggression. If I am to be tried again for the matter now before us I will choose my own tribunal. I will appeal from this House to my own constituents. From that verdict I will not appeal. The temper of the times is not favorable for a calm and dispassionate judgment of the case; and if, by any act of mine, I can save the majority of this House from the consequences of a rash decision, the time may come when the good men who are pursuing me—and I believe there are such in the opposition—will admit that I deserve their thanks for the deed. The axe that is uplifted to strike me may fall upon others, and fall upon them after they have parted with the shield of the Constitution to protect them.

For myself I have only to say that, if I cannot preserve my self-respect and constitutional rights, together with a seat in this body, I must renounce the last rather than the former.

I have no desire, sir, to continue an argument which my friends have exhausted. The determination of the majority is fixed, and it is in vain to resist it. I will make no appeal to a *packed jury*, but I protest against its inconsistencies and its usurpations. During this session the charge was openly made by a member from the State of Pennsylvania on this floor that another [John J. Pearce], who is his colleague, had been guilty of an attempt to bribe, and no proceedings were instituted in the case. Do the majority of this House propose to instruct the American people, from their high position, that bribery is excusable, and simple assault and battery a crime? That is the lesson, and you are the teachers.

And in whose behalf is this extraordinary stretch of constitutional power invoked? Sir, I do not intend to violate any rule of this House, or of parliamentary courtesy, but it cannot be denied that he is, *par excellence*, the representative of a sovereignty which is at this instant in open, statutory rebellion— not to a simple rule of a single House, but to the Constitution and laws of the United States of America. Massachusetts sits in judgment upon me without a hearing, and presents me for a breach of privilege! Sir, is it not strange that it did not occur to that sage legislature that its *demand* upon the Congress of the United States, relative to a member, was a greater breach of privilege in them than that complained of the member himself? What right, sir, has the legislature of Massachusetts to make any demand upon this House? She has not the right of even instructing the most insignificant member from the State, and has, by her resolutions, but given additional proof that she neither comprehends the theory of our Government nor is loyal to its authority.

I have said, sir, that, if I have committed a breach of privilege, it was the privilege of the Senate. If I have, in any particular, violated the privileges or proprieties of this House, I am unconscious of it, and I challenge every member to specify a single disorderly or improper act.

And yet, sir, the vote which has just been taken transmits me to posterity as a man unworthy, in the judgment of a majority of my peers, of a seat in this Hall. And for what? The member from New Jersey [Mr. Pennington]—the prosecuting member—the thumb-paper member [laughter]—the Falstaffian member, who, like his prototype, was born about four o'clock in the morning and, if he has not the bald head, is graced with the corporeal rotundity [great laughter] of his predecessor upon his advent into this sublunary world—he says it was for making a "murderous" assault with a "bludgeon"; and he, forsooth, would have this House and the country believe, with an intent to kill.

If I desired to kill the Senator, why did not I do it? You all admit that I had him in my power. Let me tell the member from New Jersey that it was expressly to avoid taking life that I used an ordinary cane, presented to me by a friend in Baltimore nearly three months before its application to the "bare head" of the Massachusetts Senator. I went to work very deliberately, as I am charged—and this is admitted—and speculated somewhat as to whether I should employ a horsewhip or a cowhide; but, knowing that the Senator was my superior in strength, it occurred to me that he might wrest it from my hand, and then—for I never attempt anything I do not perform—I might have been compelled to do that which I would have regretted the balance of my natural life.

The question has been asked in certain newspapers why did I not invite the Senator to personal combat in the mode usually adopted. Well, sir, as I desire the whole truth to be known about the matter, I will, for once, notice a newspaper article on the floor of the House and answer here.

My answer is that I knew that the Senator would not accept a message; and, having formed the unalterable determination to punish him, I believed that the offence of "sending a hostile message," superadded to the indictment for assault and battery, would subject me to legal penalties more severe than would be imposed for a simple assault and battery.

For this act, which the Senate, with a solitary exception of a distinguished gentleman from Georgia [Mr. Toombs] have pronounced me guilty of a breach of its privileges—for this act I am complained of by that body to this House. Your committee have declared, and this House has now concurred in the opinion, that my offence is to the Senate, and that no rule or order of this body have I violated.

Now, sir, let me ask why the Senate did not protect its own rights? The argument has been made here that *ex necessitate* this House must have the power to protect itself. If that principle be true in its application *here*, why has not the Senate the same powers of protection? But what right has this House to punish me for offences committed out of its presence? They tell me that my responsibility to this House is because of the general responsibility which attaches to every member. Where do you stop in this question of authority of the House over its members? If your authority goes into the Senate Chamber, and even when the Senate is not in session, why should it not go into the ante-rooms and down the steps of the Capitol? Why not pursue me into the avenue—into the steamboat—to my plantation? Why, sir, if I go to my home and find that one of my slaves has behaved badly in my absence and I direct him to be flogged, I may be charged with—to use the language which is familiar here—"crime the blackest and most heinous"; and when I come back—and come back I will—may be punished myself for inflicting a chastisement which, by the common law and the constitutional laws of my country, I have the right to inflict upon my slave, who is my property.

Now, sir, let me inform the honorable members who have been pursuing me so fiercely that my present attitude was long since foreseen, and that I am altogether prepared for any of its emergencies. I knew with whom I had to deal, and my resignation has been for more than ten days in the hands of the Governor of South Carolina, to take effect the very instant that I announce my resignation upon this floor. But, before I make the announcement, I desire to say a word or two in reference to what has been said of me in debate and elsewhere.

Your amiable colleague [Chauncey L. Knapp], who was presented by his constituents with a revolver, intended for my particular benefit, yesterday declared that Massachusetts would "take her own time and place" to resent what he and she both pronounced to be an insult and an injury. I do not intend, Mr. Speaker, to utter an offensive, unkind, or even a rough word to that gentleman—for he is a gentleman, socially, I know—but I wish to say this to him, that I will never plead the statute of limitations in bar of the wrath of Massachusetts.

I now desire the attention of my *quondam* friend from Massachusetts [Linus B. Comins]. From his place in this House—in his representative character, and at the time armed to the teeth, he quoted the language and indorsed the sentiment of Chevalier Webb, of poor Jonathan Cilley notoriety, as follows:

"Looking at it solely as an insult to the country, a trampling upon the Constitution, and an outrage upon the sanctity of the Senate Chamber, it was an outrage which merited death on the spot from any patriot present who was in a position to inflict the punishment."

Now, sir, I say to that gentleman that no man has the right to wear arms who does not dare to use them. In my country the cock that crows and won't fight is despised by the hens and even by the pullets, who know a thing or two instinctively. [Great laughter.] His chivalric spurs dwindle before the charges of the valorous gout, and his place is—out of sight. I feel, sir, that "the blood more stirs to hunt the lion than to chase the hare"; but, if my *quondam* friend has any ambition, under the directions of the Chevalier Webb, to play the *"patriot,"* let him or *le preux chevalier,* separately or together, or backed by the whole Black Republican crew, come take the life which they say is forfeited.

Now, Mr. Speaker, I have nearly finished what I intended to say. If my opponents, who have pursued me with unparalleled bitterness, are satisfied with the present conditions of this affair, I am. I return my thanks to my friends, and especially to those who are from non-slaveholding States, who have magnanimously sustained me, and felt that it was a higher honor to themselves to be just in their judgment of a gentleman than to be a member of Congress for life. In taking my leave, I feel that it is proper that I should say that I believe some of the votes which have been cast against me have been extorted by an outside pressure at home, and that their votes do not express the feelings or opinions of the members who gave them.

To such of these as have given their votes and made their speeches on the constitutional principles involved, and, without indulging in personal vilification, I owe my respect. But, sir, they have written me down upon the history of the country as worthy of expulsion and in no unkindness I must tell them that for all future time my self-respect requires that I shall pass them as strangers.

And now, Mr. Speaker, I announce to you and to this House that I am no longer a member of the Thirty-Fourth Congress.

Mr. Brooks then walked out of the House of Representatives.

Shortly after his resignation Brooks selected from his detractors Anson Burlingame, the Representative from Massachusetts who had particularly charged him with cowardice, and challenged him to a duel, which Burlingame accepted. The affair was arranged to take place on the Canadian side of Niagara Falls in order to be out of the jurisdiction of this country, most of the States of which had passed laws against dueling. Brooks finally declined to fight at the place designated, for the reason that to reach it he would have to pass through a State (New York) which was inimical to him. Brooks was sent back to Congress by his constituents and took an active part in its deliberations before his career was cut short by death, which occurred in the following year (1857).

Senator Sumner never entirely recovered from the assault—indeed, it hastened his death. It was not until December, 1859, that he resumed his seat; he took little part in the debates until the middle of the session, when he delivered a notable speech on the "Barbarism of Slavery," which aroused, if possible, even greater animosity against him on the part of the South than he had brought upon himself by his speech on "The Crime Against Kansas."

CHAPTER X

THE DRED SCOTT DECISION

Presidential Campaign of 1856 Fought on the Popular Sovereignty Issue—
President Pierce Writes a Message on "The Defeat of Sectionalism"—
Reply by John P. Hale [N. H.]—President Buchanan, in His Inaugural
Address, Prepares the Public to Accept the Forthcoming Dred Scott De-
cision by the Supreme Court—Horace Greeley's Account of the Case:
Opinions of Chief Justice Roger B. Taney, and of Other Justices, Who
Concurred in the Decision; Opinions of Justices John McLean and Ben-
jamin R. Curtis, Who Dissented from the Decision—Senator Stephen A.
Douglas Accepts the Decision in a Speech at Springfield, Ill.—Abraham
Lincoln Replies to Him: "The Sacredness of Judicial Decisions."

I N the Presidential campaign of 1856 the question of
popular sovereignty was the chief issue. The
American (Know Nothing) convention, which met
in Philadelphia on February 22, declared for this principle, causing about fifty "anti-Nebraska" delegates to
secede. Ex-President Millard Fillmore [N. Y.], noted
for his deprecation of "sectionalism," was nominated
for President, and Andrew Jackson Donelson [Tenn.]
for Vice-President.

The Democratic national convention met at Cincin-
nati, O., on June 2. James Buchanan [Pa.] was nominated for President and John C. Breckinridge [Ky.]
for Vice-President. The platform declared in favor
of popular sovereignty in the Territories, "as embody-
ing the only sound and safe solution of the slavery
question, upon which the great national idea of the
people of this whole country can repose in its determined
conservation of the Union," and in favor of "non-interference of Congress with slavery in the Territories or
in the District of Columbia."

The Republican national convention was held at
Philadelphia on June 17. John C. Frémont [Cal.] was
nominated for President on the first ballot. William

370

L. Dayton [N. J.] was nominated for Vice-President on the first ballot by 259 votes to 110 cast for Abraham Lincoln [Ill.] and 180 scattering. The platform contained, among other resolutions, the following:

"*Resolved,* That, with our republican fathers, we hold it to be a self-evident truth that all men are endowed with the in-

THE RIGHT MAN FOR THE RIGHT PLACE
Frémont on left, Fillmore in center, Buchanan on right
From the collection of the New York Historical Society

alienable rights to life, liberty, and the pursuit of happiness; and that the primary object and ulterior design of our Federal Government were to secure these rights to all persons within its exclusive jurisdiction; that, as our republican fathers, when they had abolished slavery in all our national territory, ordained that no person should be deprived of life, liberty, or property, without due process of law, it becomes our duty to maintain this provision of the Constitution against all attempts to violate it for the purpose of establishing slavery in any territory of the United States by positive legislation, prohibiting its existence and extension therein. That we deny the authority of Congress, of a territorial legislature, of any individual or association of

individuals to give legal existence to slavery in any Territory of
the United States while the present Constitution shall be maintained.

"*Resolved,* That the Constitution confers upon Congress sovereign power over the Territories of the United States for their
government; and that, in the exercise of this power, it is both
the right and the duty of Congress to prohibit in the Territories those twin relics of barbarism—polygamy and slavery."

In the ensuing election 174 Democratic and 114 Republican electors were chosen, and the American party
carried Maryland with 8 electoral votes.

In his annual message at the opening of Congress,
December 2, 1856, President Pierce began, not with
the discussion of foreign affairs, as had been the custom, but with the burning question of the hour, the Kansas situation. This he treated from an extreme partisan point of view, justifying the course of the Administration in the matter, denouncing the policy of the
opposition, and exulting over its defeat in the presidential election.

The Defeat of Sectionalism

President Pierce

It is impossible to misapprehend the great principles which,
by their recent political action, the people of the United States
have sanctioned and announced.

They have asserted the constitutional equality of each and
all of the States of the Union as States; they have affirmed the
constitutional equality of each and all of the citizens of the
United States as citizens, whatever their religion, wherever their
birth, or their residence; they have maintained the inviolability
of the constitutional rights of the different sections of the Union;
and they have proclaimed their devoted and unalterable attachment to the Union and the Constitution, as objects of interest
superior to all subjects of local or sectional controversy, as the
safeguard of the rights of all, as the spirit and the essence of
the liberty, peace, and greatness of the Republic.

In doing this, they have, at the same time, emphatically
condemned the idea of organizing in these United States mere

geographical parties; of marshaling in hostile array toward each other the different parts of the country—North or South, East or West.

Schemes of this nature, fraught with incalculable mischief, and which the considerate sense of the people has rejected, could have had countenance in no part of the country, had they not been disguised by suggestions plausible in appearance, acting upon an excited state of the public mind, induced by causes temporary in their character and, it is to be hoped, transient in their influence.

Perfect liberty of association for political objects and the widest scope of discussion are the received and ordinary conditions of government in our country. Our institutions, framed in the spirit of confidence in the intelligence and integrity of the people, do not forbid citizens, either individually or associated together, to attack by writing, speech, or any other methods short of physical force the Constitution and the very existence of the Union. Under the shelter of this great liberty, and protected by the laws and usages of the Government they assail, associations have been formed in some of the States of individuals who, pretending to seek only to prevent the spread of the institution of slavery into the present or future inchoate States of the Union, are really inflamed with desire to change the domestic institutions of existing States. To accomplish their objects, they dedicate themselves to the odious task of depreciating the Government organization which stands in their way, and of calumniating, with indiscriminate invective, not only the citizens of particular States with whose laws they find fault, but all others of their fellow citizens throughout the country who do not participate with them in their assaults upon the Constitution, framed and adopted by our fathers, and claiming for the privileges it has secured, and the blessings it has conferred, the steady support and grateful reverence of their children. They seek an object which they well know to be a revolutionary one. They are perfectly aware that the change in the relative condition of the white and black races in the slaveholding States, which they would promote, is beyond their lawful authority; that to them it is a foreign object; that it cannot be effected by any peaceful instrumentality of theirs; that for them, and the States of which they are citizens, the only part to its accomplishment is through burning cities, and ravaged fields, and slaughtered populations, and all there is most terrible in foreign, complicated with civil and servile, war; and that the first step in the attempt is the forcible disruption of a country embracing in its broad bosom a degree of liberty, and an amount of individual and public prosperity, to which there is no parallel in history, and substituting in its place hostile governments, driven at once and inevitably into mutual devastation and fractricidal carnage, transforming the now peaceful and felicitous brotherhood into a vast permanent camp of armed men, like the rival monarchies of Europe and Asia. Well knowing that such, and such only, are the means and the consequences of their plans and purposes, they endeavor to prepare the people of the United States for civil war by doing everything in their power to deprive the Constitution and the laws of moral authority, and to undermine the fabric of the Union by appeals to passion and sectional prejudice, by indoctrinating its people with reciprocal hatred, and by educating them to stand face to face as enemies, rather than shoulder to shoulder as friends.

It is by the agency of such unwarrantable interference, foreign and domestic, that the minds of many, otherwise good citizens, have been so inflamed into the passionate condemnation of the domestic institutions of the Southern States, as at length to pass insensibly to almost equally passionate hostility toward their fellow citizens of those States, and thus, finally, to fall into temporary fellowship with the avowed and active enemies of the Constitution. Ardently attached to liberty in the abstract, they do not stop to consider practically how the objects they would attain can be accomplished, nor to reflect that, even if the evil were as great as they deem it, they have no remedy to apply, and that it can be only aggravated by their violence and unconstitutional action. A question which is one of the most difficult of all the problems of social institution, political economy, and statesmanship they treat with unreasoning intemperance of thought and language. Extremes beget extremes. Violent attack from the North finds its inevitable consequence in the growth of a spirit of angry defiance at the South. Thus, in the progress of events, we had reached that consummation which the voice of the people has now so pointedly rebuked, of the attempt of a portion of the States, by a sectional organization and movement, to usurp the control of the Government of the United States.

On December 2, 1856, Senator John P. Hale [N. H.] replied to the President's message.

Under the grant of the Constitution by which he may, from time to time, give to Congress information of the state of the

Union, and recommend to their consideration such measures as he may judge expedient, the President undertakes to set himself up as an arbiter and to pronounce *ex cathedrâ* upon what were the issues involved in the last presidential election, and to tell what the people have decided. I will tell him, to begin with, that there was one thing which they decided before they went into the contest, and that was, let who would be chosen, they would not have a second edition of him.

In his inaugural address (March 4, 1857) President Buchanan presented his policy upon the Kansas question.

SUPPRESS THE AGITATION

INAUGURAL ADDRESS OF PRESIDENT BUCHANAN

We have recently passed through a presidential contest in which the passions of our fellow-citizens were excited to the highest degree by questions of deep and vital importance; but, when the people proclaimed their will the tempest at once subsided and all was calm. The voice of the majority, speaking in the manner prescribed by the Constitution, was heard, and instant submission followed. Our own country could alone have exhibited so grand and striking a spectacle of the capacity of man for self-government.

What a happy conception, then, was it for Congress to apply this simple rule—that the will of the majority shall govern—to the settlement of the question of domestic slavery in the Territories! Congress is neither "to legislate slavery into any Territory or State, nor to exclude it therefrom; but to leave the people thereof perfectly free to form and regulate their domestic institutions in their own way, subject only to the Constitution of the United States." As a natural consequence Congress has also prescribed that, when the Territory of Kansas shall be admitted as a State, it "shall be received into the Union with or without slavery, as their constitution may prescribe at the time of their admission."

A difference of opinion has arisen in regard to the point of time when the people of a Territory shall decide this question for themselves. This is, happily, a matter of but little practical importance. *Besides, it is a judicial question which legitimately belongs to the Supreme Court of the United States, before whom it is now pending, and will, it is understood, be speedily and finally settled.* To their decision, in common with all good citizens, I shall cheerfully submit, whatever this may be, though it has ever been my individual opinion that, under the Nebraska-Kansas act, the appropriate period will be when the number of actual residents in the Territory shall justify the formation of a constitution with a view to its admission as a State into the Union. But, be this as it may, it is the imperative and indispensable duty of the Government of the United States to secure to every resident inhabitant the free and independent expression of his opinion by his vote. This sacred right of each individual must be preserved. That being accomplished, nothing can be fairer than to leave the people of a Territory free from all foreign interference to decide their own destiny for themselves, subject only to the Constitution of the United States.

The whole territorial question being thus settled upon the principle of popular sovereignty—a principle as ancient as free government itself—everything of a practical nature has been decided. No other question remains for adjustment; because all agree that under the Constitution slavery in the States is beyond the reach of any human power except that of the respective States themselves wherein it exists. May we not, then, hope that the long agitation on this subject is approaching its end, and that the geographical parties to which it has given birth, so much dreaded by the Father of his Country, will speedily become extinct? Most happy will it be for the country when the public mind shall be diverted from this question to others of more pressing and practical importance. Throughout the whole progress of this agitation, which has scarcely known any intermission for more than twenty years, while it has been productive of no positive good to any human being, it has been the prolific source of great evils to the master, to the slave, and to the whole country. It has alienated and estranged the people of the sister States from each other, and has even seriously endangered the very existence of the Union.

Nor has the danger yet entirely ceased. Under our system there is a remedy for all mere political evils in the sound sense and sober judgment of the people. Time is a great corrective. Political subjects which but a few years ago excited and exasperated the public mind, have passed away, and are now nearly forgotten. But this question of domestic slavery is of far graver importance than any mere political question, because, should the agitation continue, it may eventually endanger the personal safety of a large portion of our countrymen where the institution exists. In that event, no form of government, however admirable in itself, and however productive of material benefits, can compensate for the loss of peace and domestic security around the family altar. Let every Union-loving man, therefore, exert his best influence to suppress this agitation, which, since the recent legislation of Congress, is without any legitimate object.

The question to which the President referred as pending before the Supreme Court, and as shortly to be decided, was the Dred Scott case. Undoubtedly he had private information as to what the decision would be and was preparing the public for it.

The Dred Scott Case

Dred Scott, a negro, was, previously to 1834, held as a slave in Missouri by Dr. Emerson, a surgeon in the U. S. Army. In that year the doctor was transferred to the military post at Rock Island, in the State of Illinois, and took his slave with him. Here Major Taliaferro (also of the army) had, in 1835, in his service a negress known as Harriet, whom he likewise held as his slave. The major was transferred that year to Fort Snelling, on the other side of the Mississippi, in what is now known as Minnesota, but was then an unorganized territory of the United States, expressly covered by the slavery prohibition embodied in the Missouri compromise of 1820. Dr. Emerson was likewise transferred to Fort Snelling in 1836, and here bought Harriet of Major Taliaferro and held her and Dred as his slaves; they being married to each other with his consent soon after his arrival at the fort. Two children were born to them north of the Missouri line. The doctor, with Dred, Harriet, and Eliza, returned thence to St. Louis, and he there continued to hold them as his slaves, until he sold them, several years later, to John F. A. Sanford, of the city of New York. Finally Dred brought suit for his freedom, on the above state of facts, in the State Circuit Court of St. Louis County, Missouri, and obtained a verdict and judgment in his favor. But this was reversed by a judgment on a writ of error to the Supreme

Court of that State, from which an appeal was taken to the courts of the United States, and the case came to trial in May, 1854. Having been fully heard by the Supreme Court at Washington, that court was about to decide at its term of 1855-6, but the controlling majority of its judges concluded, in view of the pending presidential election and the strong excitement which the Nebraska bill and the Kansas outrages had aroused throughout the free States, to defer rendering judgment until its next session.

"It is quite probable that its action in the premises, if made public at the time originally intended, would have reversed the issue of that presidential election," observes Horace Greeley in his "American Conflict," from which these facts have been taken.

On March 11, 1857, the decision and opinions of this court in the Dred Scott case were made public. Chief-Justice Roger B. Taney, in pronouncing the decision of the court, which nullified the Missouri restriction, or *any* restriction by Congress on the boundless diffusion of slavery throughout the Territories of the Union, commenced by denying to Dred Scott, or to any person "whose ancestors were imported to this country and sold as slaves," any right to sue in a court of the United States. He said:

"The question before us is: whether the class of persons described in the plea in abatement compose a portion of this people and are constituent members of this sovereignty? We think they are not, and that they are not included, and were not intended to be included, under the word 'citizen' in the Constitution, and can therefore claim none of the rights and privileges which that instrument provides for and secures to citizens of the United States. On the contrary, they were at that time considered as a subordinate and inferior class of beings, who had been subjugated by the dominant race, and, whether emancipated or not, yet remained subject to their authority, and had no rights or privileges but such as those who held the power and the Government might choose to grant them."

The Chief-Justice proceeded to affirm not only that no persons who had been or whose ancestors had been slaves were regarded as citizens previously to, or at the time of, adopting the Federal Constitution, but that —no State has, or can have, any right to confer citizenship on such persons.

"In the opinion of the court the legislation and history of the times, and the language used in the Declaration of Independence, show that neither the class of persons who had been imported as slaves, nor their descendants, whether they had become free or not, were then acknowledged as a part of the people, nor intended to be included in the general words used in that memorable instrument.

"It is difficult at this day to realize the state of public opinion in relation to that unfortunate race which prevailed in the civilized and enlightened portions of the world at the time of the Declaration of Independence and when the Constitution of the United States was framed and adopted. But the public history of every European nation displays it in a manner too plain to be mistaken.

"They had, for more than a century before, been regarded as beings of an inferior order and altogether unfit to associate with the white race, either in social or political relations; and so far inferior that *they had no rights which the white man was bound to respect;* and that the negro might justly and lawfully be reduced to slavery for his benefit. He was bought and sold and treated as an ordinary article of merchandise and traffic whenever a profit could be made by it. This opinion was, at that time, fixed and universal in the civilized portion of the white race. It was regarded as an axiom in morals, as well as in politics, which no one thought of disputing or supposed to be open to dispute; and men of every grade and position in society daily and habitually acted upon it in their private pursuits, as well as in matters of public concern, without doubting for a moment the correctness of this opinion.

"And in no nation was this opinion more firmly fixed or more uniformly acted upon than by the English Government and English people. They not only seized them on the coast of Africa and sold them or held them in slavery for their own use, but they took them as ordinary articles of merchandise to every country where they could make a profit on them, and were far more engaged in this commerce than any other nation in the world.

"The opinion thus entertained and acted upon in England was naturally impressed upon the colonies they founded on this side of the Atlantic. And, accordingly, a negro of the African race was regarded by them as an article of property and held and bought and sold as such in every one of the thirteen colonies which united in the Declaration of Independence and afterward formed the Constitution of the United States. The slaves were more or less numerous in the different colonies, as slave labor was found more or less profitable. But no one seems to have doubted the correctness of the prevailing opinion of the time.''

Chief-Justice Taney then quoted the preamble of the Declaration of Independence.

''The general words above quoted would seem to embrace the whole human family; and, if they were used in a similar instrument at this day, would be so understood. But it is too clear to dispute that the enslaved African race were not intended to be included and formed no part of the people who framed and adopted this Declaration; for, if the language, as understood in that day, would embrace them, the conduct of the distinguished men who framed the Declaration of Independence would have been utterly and flagrantly inconsistent with the principles they asserted; and, instead of the sympathy of mankind, to which they so confidently appealed, they would have deserved and received universal rebuke and reprobation.

''Yet the men who framed this declaration were great men— high in literary acquirements—high in their sense of honor— and incapable of asserting principles inconsistent with those on which they were acting. They perfectly understood the meaning of the language they used and how it would be understood by others; and they knew that it would not, in any part of the civilized world, be supposed to embrace the negro race; which, by common consent, had been excluded from civilized governments and the family of nations and doomed to slavery. They spoke and acted according to the then established doctrines and principles, and in the ordinary language of the day and no one misunderstood them. The unhappy black race were separated from the white by indelible marks and laws long before established, and were *never thought of or spoken of except as property,* and when the claims of the owner or the profit of the trader were supposed to need protection.

''This state of public opinion had undergone no change when the Constitution was adopted, as is equally evident from its provisions and language.''

Chief-Justice Taney then proceeded to argue that slavery was abolished by our fathers, not at all because it was felt to be wrong, but because it was found to be unprofitable in this particular locality. On this point he said:

"It is very true that, in that portion of the Union where the labor of the negro race was found to be unsuited to the climate and unprofitable to the master, but few slaves were held at the time of the Declaration of Independence; and, when the Constitution was adopted, it had entirely worn out in one of them and measures had been taken for its gradual abolition in several others. But this change had not been produced by any change of opinion in relation to this race, but because it was discovered from experience that slave labor was unsuited to the climate and productions of these States; for some of these States where it had ceased, or nearly ceased, to exist were actively engaged in the slave trade, procuring cargoes on the coast of Africa and transporting them for sale to those parts of the Union where their labor was found to be profitable and suited to the climate and productions. And this traffic was openly carried on and fortunes accumulated by it without reproach from the people of the States where they resided. And it can hardly be supposed that, in the States where it was then countenanced in its worst form—that is, in the seizure and transportation—the people could have regarded those who were emancipated as entitled to equal rights with themselves."

The Chief-Justice then declared that no State can make its black people citizens, because that would be very inconvenient and unsafe for the slaveholders of other States. "For," he says:

"If they were so received, and entitled to the privileges and immunities of citizens, it would exempt them from the operation of the special laws and from the police regulations which they considered to be necessary for their own safety. It would give to persons of the negro race who were recognized as citizens in any one State of the Union the right to enter every other State whenever they pleased, singly or in companies, without pass or passport; and, without obstruction, to sojourn there as long as they pleased; to go where they pleased at every hour of the day or night without molestation, unless they committed some violation of law for which a white man would be punished; and it would give them the full liberty of speech in public and private upon all subjects upon which its own citizens might speak; to hold public meetings upon political affairs, and to keep and carry arms wherever they went. And all of this would be done in the face of the subject race of the same color, both free and slaves, and inevitably producing discontent and insubordination among them, and endangering the peace and safety of the State.''

Having thus determined that Dred Scott, being a negro and descended from slaves, had no right to bring this suit and no standing in the Federal courts, and that the court has no authority in the premises, the Chief-Justice proceeded to uphold the right of Congress to exclude slavery from any Territory. To this end he affirmed that that clause of the Constitution (Art. IV, Sec. 3) which says ''Congress shall have power to dispose of and make all needful rules and regulations respecting the territory or other property belonging to the United States,'' applies only to such territory as belonged to the United States at the time the Constitution was framed. The territory covered by the Missouri restriction, having all been acquired *since* that time, is not, in his view, subject to this provision.

He proceeded to affirm that, by the mere fact of our acquiring territory, ''the Government and the citizen both enter it under the authority of the Constitution''; in other words, that the Constitution takes effect upon any territory that our Government may acquire, at the instant of such acquisition, in such manner as to create and uphold the right of every slaveholder to take his slaves thither and hold them there as property. But this particular and only clause of the Constitution relating to territory has no application or substituting validity; because, if it had, it might enable Congress to prohibit slavery therein. The Chief-Justice therefore nullified the Missouri restriction and all kindred restrictions in the following terms.

''Upon these considerations it is the opinion of the court that the act of Congress which prohibited a citizen from holding property of this kind in the territory of the United States north of the line therein mentioned is not warranted by the Constitution, and it is therefore void; and that neither Dred Scott himself, nor any of his family, were made free by being carried into this territory, even if they had been carried there by the owner with the intention of becoming a permanent resident."

But Dred's freedom was claimed on still another ground, *viz.*: that he had been taken by his master to the Free State of Illinois and there retained some two or three years. But this the Chief-Justice disposed of by declaring that his claim was not properly before the court; that the question raised by it was to be adjudged by the tribunals of Missouri alone; and he concluded as follows:

"Upon the whole, therefore, it is the judgment of this court that it appears by the record before us that the plaintiff in error is not a citizen of Missouri, in the sense in which that word is used in the Constitution; and that the Circuit Court of the United States, for that reason, had no jurisdiction in the case and could give no judgment in it. Its judgment for the defendant must, consequently, be reversed and a mandate issued directing the suit to be dismissed for want of jurisdiction."

Associate-Justice James Moore Wayne, of Georgia, concurred "entirely in the opinion of the court as written and read by the Chief-Justice, without any qualification of its reasoning or its conclusions."

Associate-Justice Samuel Nelson, of New York, concurred also in the conclusion of the court. He said:

"If Congress possesses power, under the Constitution, to abolish slavery in a Territory it must necessarily possess the like power to *establish* it. It cannot be a one-sided power, as may suit the convenience or particular views of the advocates. It is a power, if it exist at all, over the whole subject."

Associate-Justice Robert Cooper Grier, of Pennsylvania concurred in the opinion delivered by Justice Nelson.

"I also concur with the opinion of the court, as delivered by the Chief-Justice, that the act of Congress of 6th of March, 1820, is unconstitutional and void; and that, assuming the facts as stated in the opinion, the plaintiff cannot sue as a citizen of

Missouri in the courts of the United States. But, that the record shows a *prima facie* case of jurisdiction, requiring the court to decide all the questions properly arising in it; and, as the decision of the pleas in bar shows that the plaintiff is a slave, and therefore not entitled to sue in a court of the United States, the form of the judgment is of little importance; for, whether the judgment be affirmed or dismissed for want of jurisdiction, it is justified by the decision of the court and is the same in effect between the parties to the suit."

Associate-Justice Peter Vivian Daniel, of Virginia, asserted that slaves were property.

"Now, the following are truths which a knowledge of the history of the world and particularly of that of our own country, compels us to know—that the African negro race have never been acknowledged as belonging to the family of nations; that, as among them there never has been known or recognized by the inhabitants of other countries anything partaking of the character of nationality, or civil or political polity; that this race has been by all the nations of Europe regarded as subjects of capture or purchase, as subjects of commerce or traffic; and that the introduction of that race into every section of this country was not as members of civil or political society, but as slaves—as *property*, in the strictest sense of the term."

He proceeded to deny the right or power of any State to elevate persons (or, as he would say, *property*) of African descent to citizenship of the United States, "by any direct or indirect proceeding," so as to entitle them to sue, or be sued, in the Federal tribunals. Justice Daniel, pushing his doctrines to their legitimate result, pronounced the Ordinance of 1787 only equal in constitutionality and validity with the Missouri restriction—that is to say, essentially null and void.

Associate-Justice John A. Campbell, of Alabama, followed with a general assent to the views of Chief-Justice Taney.

Associate-Justice John Catron, of Tennessee, concurred with Justice Nelson that Dred Scott had no right to freedom at the hands of the Supreme Court on the ground of his two years' residence in Illinois; but he dissented from the Chief Justice's notion that the power over the Territories, expressly given to Congress by the Constitution, has no force or application *beyond* the territory possessed by us when that Constitution was framed. In fact, as he had been hanging men for the last twenty years under this very power, he could not well do otherwise. He says:

"It is due to myself to say that it is asking much of a judge, who has for nearly twenty years been exercising jurisdiction from the western Missouri line to the Rocky Mountains, and, on this understanding of the Constitution, inflicting the extreme penalty of death for crimes committed where the direct legislation of Congress was the only rule, to agree that he had all the while been acting in mistake, and as an usurper.

"More than sixty years have passed away since Congress has exercised power to govern the Territories by its legislation directly, or by territorial charters subject to repeal at all times; and it is now too late to call that power in question if this court could disregard its own decisions, which it cannot do, as I think."

He concluded that that clause of the Constitution which provides that "the citizens of each State shall be entitled to all privileges and immunities of citizens in the several States" gives slaveholders an indefeasible right to carry their slaves into, and hold them in, the Territories.

Associate-Justice John McLean, of Ohio, in his opinion dissenting from that of the court, said:

"Will it be said that the slave is taken as property, the same as other property which the master may own? To this I answer, that colored persons are made property by the law of the State, and no such power has been given to Congress. Does the master carry with him the law of the State from which he removes into the Territory? and does that enable him to coerce his slave in the Territory? Let us test this theory: If this may be done by a master from one slave State, it may be done by a master from every other slave State. This right is supposed to be connected with the person of the master by virtue of the local law. Is it transferable? May it be negotiated as a promissory note or bill of exchange? If it be assigned to a man from a free State may he coerce the slave by virtue of it? What shall this thing be denominated? Is it personal or real property? Or is it an indefinable fragment of sovereignty which every person carries with him from his late domicile? One thing is certain, that its origin has been very recent and it is unknown to the laws of any civilized country. It is said that the Territories are the common property of the States, and that every man has a right to go there with his property. This is not controverted. But the court say a slave is not property beyond the operation of the local law which makes him such. Never was a truth more authoritatively and justly uttered by man. Suppose a master of a slave in a British island owned a million of property in England; would that authorize him to take his slaves with him to England? The Constitution, in express terms, recognizes the *status* of slavery as founded on the municipal law: 'No person held to service or labor in one State, *under the laws thereof,* escaping to another shall,' etc. Now, unless the fugitive escape from a place where, by the municipal law, he is held to labor, this provision affords no remedy to the master. What can be more conclusive than this? Suppose a slave escape from a Territory where slavery is not authorized by law, can he be reclaimed? In this case a majority of the court have said that a slave may be taken by his master into a Territory of the United States, the same as a horse, or any other kind of property. It is true this was said by the court, as also many other things which are of no authority. Nothing that has been said by them which has not a direct bearing on the jurisdiction of the court against which they decided can be considered as authority. I shall certainly not regard it as such. The question of jurisdiction, being before the court, was decided by them authoritatively, but nothing beyond that question. A slave is not a mere chattel. He bears the impress of his Maker and is amenable to the laws of God and man, and he is destined to an endless existence.''

To the same effect Associate-Justice Benjamin R., Curtis, of Massachusetts, in his dissenting opinion, thus traversed the judgment of the court:

''Is it conceivable that the Constitution has conferred the right on every citizen to become a resident on the territory of the United States with his slaves and there to hold them as such, but has neither made nor provided for any municipal regulations which were essential to the existence of slavery? Is it not more rational to conclude that they who framed and adopted the Constitution were aware that persons held to service under the laws of a State are property only to the extent and under the conditions fixed by those laws, and that they must cease to be available as property when their owners voluntarily place them permanently within another jurisdiction where no municipal laws on the subject of slavery exist?

"Moreover, if the right exists, what are its limits, and what are its conditions? If citizens of the United States have a right to take their slaves to a Territory and hold them there as slaves, without regard to the laws of the Territory, I suppose this right is not to be restricted to the citizens of slaveholding States. A citizen of a State which does not tolerate slavery can hardly be denied the power of doing the same thing. And what law of slavery does either take with him to the Territory? If it be said to be those laws respecting slavery which existed in the particular State from which each slave last came, what an anomaly is this! Where else can we find under the laws of any civilized country the power to introduce and permanently continue diverse systems of foreign municipal law for holding persons in slavery?"

In reply to Chief-Justice Taney's disquisition as to the opinions and views of our Revolutionary statesmen, Justice Curtis said:

"To determine whether any free persons descended from Africans held in slavery were citizens of the United States under the Confederation and, consequently, at the time of the adoption of the Constitution of the United States, it is only necessary to know whether such persons were citizens of either of the States under the Confederation, at the time of the adoption of the Constitution.

"Of this there can be no doubt. At the time of the ratification of the Articles of Confederation all free, native-born inhabitants of the States of New Hampshire, Massachusetts, New York, New Jersey, and North Carolina, though descended from African slaves, were not only citizens of those States, but such of them as had the other necessary qualifications possessed the franchise of electors, on equal terms with other citizens."

He proceeded to cite, in support of this averment, the judgment of the Supreme Court of North Carolina in the case of the *State against Manual,* wherein William Gaston—by far the most eminent jurist of whom that State could ever boast—pronounced the opinion of the court in the following terms:

"According to the laws of this State all human beings within it who are not slaves fall within one of two classes. Whatever distinctions may have existed in the Roman laws between citizens and free inhabitants, they are unknown to our institutions. Before our Revolution all free persons born within the dominions of the King of Great Britain, whatever their color or complexion, were native-born British subjects—those born out of his allegiance were aliens. Slavery did not exist in England, but it did in the British colonies. Slaves were not, in legal parlance, persons, but property. The moment the incapacity, the disqualification of slavery was removed, they became persons, and were then either British subjects or not British subjects, according as they were or were not born within the allegiance of the British king. Upon the Revolution no other change took place in the laws of North Carolina than was consequent on the transition from a colony dependent on a European king to a free and sovereign State. Slaves remained slaves. British subjects in North Carolina became North Carolina freemen. Foreigners, until made members of the State, remained aliens. Slaves, manumitted here, became freemen; and, therefore, if born within North Carolina, are citizens of North Carolina; and all free persons born within the State are born citizens of the State. The Constitution extended the elective franchise to every freeman who had arrived at the age of twenty-one and paid a public tax; and it is a matter of universal notoriety that, under it, free persons, without regard to color, claimed and exercised the franchise until it was taken from free men of color a few years since by our amended Constitution."

Continuing his review of the Chief-Justice's assumptions, Justice Curtis said:

"It has been often asserted that the Constitution was made exclusively by and for the white race. It has already been shown that in five of the thirteen original States colored persons then possessed the elective franchise and were among those by whom the Constitution was ordained and established. If so, it is not true, in point of fact, that the Constitution was made exclusively *by* the white race. And that it was made exclusively *for* the white race is, in my opinion, not only an assumption not warranted by anything in the Constitution, but contradicted by its open declaration that it was ordained and established by the people of the United States for themselves and their posterity. And, as free colored persons were then citizens of at least five States, and so, in every sense, part of the people of the United States, they were among those for whom and whose posterity the Constitution was ordained and established.''

Justice Curtis was not content with refuting the logic of the Chief-Justice. He seized the weapons of his antagonist and turned them against him with decided effect. Witness the following:

''I do not deem it necesary to review at length the legislation of Congress having more or less bearing upon the citizenship of colored persons. It does not seem to me to have any considerable tendency to prove that it has been considered by the legislative department of the Government that no such persons are citizens of the United States. Undoubtedly they have been debarred from the exercise of particular rights or privileges extended to white persons, but, I believe, always in terms which, by implication, admit that they *may* be citizens. Thus the act of May 17, 1792, for the organization of the militia directs the enrollment of every 'free, able-bodied, white male citizen,' An assumption that none but white persons are citizens would be as inconsistent with the just import of this language as that all citizens are able-bodied or males.

''So the act of February 28, 1803 (2 *Stat. at Large,* 205), to prevent the importation of certain persons into States when, by the laws thereof, their admission is prohibited, in its first section forbids all masters of vessels to import or bring 'any negro, mulatto, or other person of color, not being a native, *a citizen,* or registered seaman of the United States,' etc., etc.

''The acts of March 3, 1813, Sec. 1 (2 *Stat. at Large,* 809), and March 1, 1817, Sec. 3 (3 *Stat. at Large,* 351), concerning seamen, certainly imply that there may be persons of color, natives of the United States, who are not citizens of the United States. This implication is undoubtedly in accordance with the fact. For not only slaves, but free persons of color, born in some of the States, are not citizens. But there is nothing in these laws inconsistent with the citizenship of persons of color in others of the States, nor with their being citizens of the United States.

''Whether much or little weight should be attached to the particular phraseology of these and other laws, which were not passed with any direct reference to the subject, I consider their tendency to be, as already indicated, to show that, in the apprehension of their framers, color was not a necessary qualification for citizenship. It would be strange if laws were found on our statute-book to that effect, when, by solemn treaties, large bodies of Mexican and North American Indians, as well as free colored persons of Louisiana, have been admitted to citizenship of the United States.''

Justice Curtis cited with effect the action of Congress in 1821 on the admission of Missouri, whereby that State was constrained to abandon and repudiate her attempt to prohibit the settlement of free negroes and mulattoes within her borders, whereof he said:

''It is true that neither this legislative declaration nor anything in the Constitution or laws of Missouri, could confer or take away any privilege or immunity granted by the Constitution. But it is also true that it expresses the then conviction of the legislative power of the United States that free negroes, as citizens of *some* of the States, might be entitled to the privileges and immunities of citizens in *all* the States.''

He summed up his conclusions as to the right of Dred Scott to bring this action, as follows:

''*First.* That the free, native-born citizens of each State are citizens of the United States.

''*Second.* That, as free colored persons born within some of the States are citizens of those States, such persons are also citizens of the United States.

''*Third.* That every such citizen residing in any State has a right to sue, and is liable to be sued, in the federal courts as a citizen of that State in which he resides.

''*Fourth.* That, as the plea to the jurisdiction in this case shows no facts except that the plaintiff was of African descent, and that his ancestors were sold as slaves, and, as these facts are not inconsistent with his citizenship of the United States and his residence in the State of Missouri, the plea to the jurisdiction was bad, and the judgment of the Circuit Court overruling it was correct.

''I dissent, therefore, from that part of the opinion of the majority of the court in which it is held that a person of African descent cannot be a citizen of the United States; and I regret I must go further and dissent both from what I deem their assumption of authority to examine the constitutionality of the act of Congress commonly called the Missouri compromise act, and the grounds and conclusions announced in their opinion.

"Having first decided that they were bound to consider the sufficiency of the plea to the jurisdiction of the Circuit Court, and, having decided that this plea showed that the Circuit Court had *not* jurisdiction, and, consequently, that this is a case to which the judicial power of the United States does not extend, they have gone on to examine the merits of the case as they appeared on the trial before the court and jury, on the issues joined on the pleas in bar, and so have reached the question of the power of Congress to pass the act of 1820. On so grave a subject as this, I feel obliged to say that, in my opinion, such an exertion of judicial power transcends the limits of the authority of the court, as described by its repeated decisions, and, as I understand, acknowledged in this opinion of the majority of the court."

Justice Curtis proceeded to confute at length and with decided ability the doctrines of the majority, affirming the invalidity of the Missouri restriction, and asserting the paramount right of each slaveholder to remove with his slaves into any territory of the United States and there retain and control them under the ægis of the Federal Constitution. He showed, further, that the majority erred in upholding a majority of the Supreme Court of Missouri in overruling their own Chief Justice and their own former decisions, whereby it had been established in accordance with kindred decisions in Louisiana as in other slave States that a slave taken by his master or removed with his assent to a Free State or to any country wherein slavery is prohibited becomes thereby a freeman and cannot be returned or reduced again to slavery. It is not, however, necessary to quote further on this head. He concluded:

"For these reasons I am of opinion that so much of the several acts of Congress as prohibited slavery and involuntary servitude within that part of the Territory of Missouri lying north of thirty-six degrees thirty minutes north latitude and west of the River Mississippi were constitutional and valid laws.

"In my opinion, the judgment of the Circuit Court should be reversed and the cause remanded for a new trial."

Thus the majority of the Justices composing the Supreme Court, after deciding that Dred Scott had no standing in that court and that the case was therefore entirely beyond or outside of its jurisdiction, proceeded to take and make jurisdiction for the purpose of ousting Congress and the people from all right or power to exclude slavery from the Federal Territories, organized or unorganized.

Senator Stephen A. Douglas [Ill.] accepted the Dred Scott decision, although it denied the principle of his doctrine of popular sovereignty (the right of the people of a Territory either to admit or debar slavery) by stating that slavery extended by force of the Constitution into the Territories.

On June 12, 1857, he delivered a speech at Springfield, Ill., in which he passed under the party yoke on this question. Two weeks later (June 26) Abraham Lincoln replied to him at the same place.

The Sacredness of Judicial Decisions

Abraham Lincoln

The Dred Scott decision declares two propositions—first, that a negro cannot sue in the United States courts; and, secondly, that Congress cannot prohibit slavery in the Territories. It was made by a divided court—dividing differently on the different points. Judge Douglas does not discuss the merits of the decision and, in that respect, I shall follow his example, believing I could no more improve on McLean and Curtis than he could on Taney.

He denounces all who question the correctness of that decision as offering violent resistance to it. But who resists it? Who has, in spite of the decision, declared Dred Scott free, and resisted the authority of his master over him?

Judicial decisions have two uses—first, to determine absolutely the case decided; and, secondly, to indicate to the public how other similar cases will be decided when they arise. For the latter use they are called "precedents" and "authorities."

We believe as much as Judge Douglas (perhaps more) in obedience to, and respect for, the judicial department of government. We think its decisions on constitutional questions, when fully settled, should control not only the particular cases decided, but the general policy of the country, subject to be disturbed only by amendments to the Constitution as provided in that instrument itself. More than this would be revolution. But we think the Dred Scott decision is erroneous. We know the court that made it has often overruled its own decisions, and we shall do what we can to have it to overrule this. We offer no resistance to it.

Judicial decisions are of greater or less authority as precedents according to circumstances. That this should be so accords both with common sense and the customary understanding of the legal profession.

If this important decision had been made by the unanimous concurrence of the judges, and without any apparent partisan bias, and in accordance with legal public expectation and with the steady practice of the departments throughout our history, and had been in no part based on assumed historical facts which are not really true; or, if wanting in some of these, it had been before the court more than once, and had there been affirmed and reaffirmed through a course of years, it then might be, perhaps would be, factious, nay, even revolutionary, not to acquiesce in it as a precedent.

But when, as is true, we find it wanting in all these claims to the public confidence, it is not resistance, it is not factious, it is not even disrespectful to treat it as not having yet quite established a settled doctrine for the country. But Judge Douglas considers this view awful. Hear him:

> The courts are the tribunals prescribed by the Constitution and created by the authority of the people to determine, expound, and enforce the law. Hence, whoever resists the final decision of the highest judicial tribunal aims a deadly blow at our whole republican system of government—a blow which, if successful, would place all our rights and liberties at the mercy of passion, anarchy, and violence. I repeat, therefore, that if resistance to the decisions of the Supreme Court of the United States, in a matter like the points decided in the Dred Scott case, clearly within their jurisdiction as defined by the Constitution, shall be forced upon the country as a political issue, it will become a distinct and naked issue between the friends and enemies of the Constitution—the friends and the enemies of the supremacy of the laws.

Why, this same Supreme Court once decided a national bank to be constitutional; but General Jackson, as President of the United States, disregarded the decision and vetoed a bill for a recharter,[1] partly on constitutional ground declaring that each

---

[1] See Volume XIII, Chapter iv.

public functionary must support the Constitution "as he understands it."

Again and again have I heard Judge Douglas denounce that bank decision and applaud General Jackson for disregarding it.

I have said, in substance, that the Dred Scott decision was, in part, based on assumed historical facts which were not really true, and I ought not to leave the subject without giving some reasons for saying this; I therefore give an instance or two which I think fully sustain me. Chief Justice Taney, in delivering the opinion of the majority of the court, insists at great length that negroes were no part of the people who made, or for whom was made, the Declaration of Independence, or the Constitution of the United States.

On the contrary, Judge Curtis, in his dissenting opinion, shows that in five of the then thirteen States—to wit, New Hampshire, Massachusetts, New York, New Jersey, and North Carolina—free negroes were voters, and, in proportion to their numbers, had the same part in making the Constitution that the white people had.

The Chief Justice does not directly assert, but plainly assumes, as a fact, that the public estimate of the black man is more favorable now than it was in the days of the Revolution. This assumption is a mistake. In some trifling particulars the condition of that race has been ameliorated; but, as a whole, in this country the change between then and now is decidedly the other way, and their ultimate destiny has never appeared so hopeless as in the last three or four years. In two of the five States—New Jersey and North Carolina—that then gave the free negro the right of voting, which right has since been taken away, and in a third—New York—it has been greatly abridged; while it has not been extended, so far as I know, to a single additional State, though the number of the States has more than doubled. In those days, as I understand, masters could, at their own pleasure, emancipate their slaves; but since then such legal restraints have been made upon emancipation as to amount almost to prohibition. In those days legislatures held the unquestioned power to abolish slavery in their respective States, but now it is becoming quite fashionable for State constitutions to withhold that power from the legislatures. In those days, by common consent, the spread of the black man's bondage to the new countries was prohibited, but now Congress decides that it will not continue the prohibition, and the Supreme Court decides that it could not if it would. In those days our Declaration of Independence was held sacred by all and thought to include all, but now, to aid in making the bondage of the negro universal and eternal, it is assailed and sneered at and construed, and hawked at and torn, till, if its framers could rise from their graves they could not at all recognize it. All the powers of earth seem rapidly combining against him. Mammon is after him, ambition follows, philosophy follows, and the theology of the day is fast joining the cry. They have him in his prison-house; they have searched his person, and left no prying instrument with him. One after another they have closed the heavy iron doors upon him; and now they have him, as it were, bolted in with a lock of a hundred keys, which can never be unlocked without the concurrence of every key—the keys in the hands of a hundred different men, and they scattered to a hundred different and distant places; and they stand musing as to what invention, in all the dominions of mind and matter, can be produced to make the impossibility of his escape more complete than it is.

There is a natural disgust in the minds of nearly all white people at the idea of an indiscriminate amalgamation of the white and black races; and Judge Douglas evidently is basing his chief hope upon the chances of his being able to appropriate the benefit of this disgust to himself. If he can, by much drumming and repeating, fasten the odium of that idea upon his adversaries, he thinks he can struggle through the storm. He therefore clings to this hope as a drowning man to the last plank. He makes an occasion for lugging it in from the opposition to the Dred Scott decision. He finds the Republicans insisting that the Declaration of Independence includes *all* men, black as well as white, and forthwith he boldly denies that it includes negroes at all, and proceeds to argue gravely that all who contend it does, do so only because they want to vote, and eat, and sleep, and marry with negroes! He will have it that they cannot be consistent else. Now I protest against the counterfeit logic which concludes that, because I do not want a black woman for a slave I must necessarily want her for a wife. I need not have her for either. I can just leave her alone. In some respects she certainly is not my equal; but in her natural right to eat the bread she earns with her own hands without asking leave of anyone else, she is my equal and the equal of all others.

Chief Justice Taney, in his opinion in the Dred Scott case, admits that the language of the Declaration is broad enough to include the whole human family, but he and Judge Douglas argue that the authors of that instrument did not intend to include negroes, by the fact that they did not at once actually place them on an equality with the whites. Now this grave argument comes to just nothing at all, by the other fact that they did not at once, or ever afterward, actually place all white people on an equality with one another. And this is the staple argument of both the Chief Justice and the Senator for doing this obvious violence to the plain, unmistakable language of the Declaration.

I think the authors of that notable instrument intended to include *all* men, but they did not intend to declare all men equal *in all respects.* They did not mean to say all were equal in color, size, intellect, moral development, or social capacity. They defined with tolerable distinctness in what respects they did consider all men created equal—equal with "certain inalienable rights, among which are life, liberty, and the pursuit of happiness." This they said, and this they meant. They did not mean to assert the obvious untruth that all were then actually enjoying that equality, nor yet that they were about to confer it immediately upon them. In fact, they had no power to confer such a boon. They meant simply to declare the right, so that enforcement of it might follow as fast as circumstances should permit.

They meant to set up a standard maxim for free society, which should be familiar to all and revered by all; constantly looked to, constantly labored for, and, even though never perfectly attained, constantly approximated and thereby constantly spreading and deepening its influence and augmenting the happiness and value of life to all people of all colors everywhere. The assertion that "all men are created equal" was of no practical use in effecting our separation from Great Britain; and it was placed in the Declaration not for that, but for future use. Its authors meant it to be—as, thank God, it is now proving itself—a stumbling-block to all those who, in after times, might seek to turn a free people back into the hateful paths of despotism. They knew the proneness of prosperity to breed tyrants, and they meant when such should reappear in this fair land and commence their vocation they should find left for them at least one hard nut to crack.

I have now briefly expressed my view of the meaning and object of that part of the Declaration of Independence which declares that "all men are created equal."

Now let us hear Judge Douglas's view of the same subject, as I find it in the printed report of his late speech. Here it is:

No man can vindicate the character, motives, and conduct of the signers of the Declaration of Independence, except upon the hypothesis that they referred to the white race alone, and not to the African, when they declared all men to have been created equal; that they were speaking of British subjects in this continent being equal to British subjects born and residing in Great Britain; that they were entitled to the same inalienable rights, and among them were enumerated life, liberty, and the pursuit of happiness. The Declaration was adopted for the purpose of justifying the colonists in the eyes of the civilized world in withdrawing their allegiance from the British Crown, and dissolving their connection with the mother country.

My good friends, read that carefully over some leisure hour, and ponder well upon it; see what a mere wreck—mangled ruin —it makes of our once glorious Declaration.

"They were speaking of British subjects on this continent being equal to British subjects born and residing in Great Britain!" Why, according to this not only negroes but white people outside of Great Britain and America were not spoken of in that instrument. The English, Irish, and Scotch, along with white Americans, were included, to be sure, but the French, Germans, and other white people of the world are all gone to pot along with the judge's inferior races!

I had thought that the Declaration promised something better than the condition of British subjects; but no, it only meant that we should be equal to them in their own oppressed and unequal condition. According to that it gave no promise that, having kicked off the king and lords of Great Britain, we should not at once be saddled with a king and lords of our own.

I had thought the Declaration contemplated the progressive improvement in the condition of all men everywhere; but no, it merely "was adopted for the purpose of justifying the colonists in the eyes of the civilized world in withdrawing their allegiance from the British Crown, and dissolving their connection with the mother country." Why, that object having been effected some eighty years ago, the Declaration is of no practical use now—mere rubbish—old wadding left to rot on the battlefield after the victory is won.

I understand you are preparing to celebrate the "Fourth" to-morrow week. What for? The doings of that day had no reference to the present; and quite half of you are not even descendants of those who were referred to at that day. But I suppose you will celebrate and will even go so far as to read the Declaration. Suppose, after you read it once in the old-fashioned way you read it once more with Judge Douglas's verion. It will then run thus: "We hold these truths to be self-evident, that all British subjects who were on this continent eighty-one years ago, were created equal to all British subjects born and then residing in Great Britain.''

And now I appeal to all—to Democrats as well as others— are you really willing that the Declaration shall thus be frittered away?—thus left no more, at most, than an interesting memorial of the dead past?—thus shorn of its vitality and practical value, and left without the germ or even the suggestion of the individual rights of man in it?

But Judge Douglas is especially horrified at the thought of the mixing of blood by the white and black races. Agreed for once—a thousand times agreed. There are white men enough to marry all the white women, and black men enough to marry all the black women; and so let them be married. On this point we fully agree with the judge, and, when he shall show that his policy is better adapted to prevent amalgamation than ours, we shall drop ours and adopt his. Let us see. In 1850 there were in the United States 405,751 mulattos. Very few of these are the offspring of whites and free blacks; nearly all have sprung from black slaves and white masters. A separation of the races is the only perfect preventive of amalgamation; but, as an immediate separation is impossible, the next best thing is to keep them apart where they are not already together. If white and black people never get together in Kansas, they will never mix blood in Kansas. That is at least one self-evident truth. A few free colored persons may get into the free States in any event; but their number is too insignificant to amount to much in the way of mixing blood. In 1850 there were in the free States 56,-649 mulattos; but for the most part they were not born there— they came from the slave States, ready made up. In the same year the slave States had 348,874 mulattos, all of home production. The proportion of free mulattos to free blacks—the only colored classes in the free States—is much greater in the slave than in the free States. It is worthy of note, too, that among the free States those which make the colored man the nearest equal to the white have proportionably the fewest mulattos, the least of amalgamation. In New Hampshire, the State which goes farthest toward equality between the races, there are just 184 mulattos, while there are in Virginia—how many do you think?—79,775, being 23,126 more than in all the free States together.

These statistics show that slavery is the greatest source of amalgamation, and, next to it, not the elevation, but the degradation of the free blacks. Yet Judge Douglas dreads the slightest estraints on the spread of slavery, and the slightest human recognition of the negro as tending horribly to amalgamation.

The very Dred Scott case affords a strong test as to which party most favors amalgamation, the Republicans or the dear Union-saving Democracy. Dred Scott, his wife, and two daughters were all involved in the suit. We desired the court to have held that they were citizens so far at least as to entitle them to a hearing as to whether they were free or not; and then, also, that they were in fact and in law really free. Could we have had our way the chances of these black girls ever mixing their blood with that of white people would have been diminished at least to the extent that it could not have been without their consent. But Judge Douglas is delighted to have them decided to be slaves, and not human enough to have a hearing, even if they were free, and thus left subject to the forced concubinage of their masters, and liable to become the mothers of mulattos in spite of themselves: the very state of case that produces nine-tenths of all the mulattos—all the mixing of blood in the nation.

Of course, I state this case as an illustration only, not meaning to say or intimate that the master of Dred Scott and his family, or any more than a percentage of masters generally, are inclined to exercise this particular power which they hold over their female slaves.

I have said that the separation of the races is the only perfect preventive of amalgamation. I have no right to say all the members of the Republican party are in favor of this, nor to say that as a party they are in favor of it. There is nothing in their platform directly on the subject. But I can say a very large proportion of its members are for it, and that the chief plank in their platform—opposition to the spread of slavery—is most favorable to that separation.

Such separation, if ever effected at all, must be effected by colonization; and no political party, as such, is now doing anything directly for colonization. Party operations at present only favor or retard colonization incidentally. The enterprise is a difficult one; but "where there is a will there is a way," and what colonization needs most is a hearty will. Will springs from the two elements of moral sense and self-interest. Let us be brought to believe it is morally right, and at the same time favorable to, or at least not against, our interest to transfer the African to his native clime, and we shall find a way to do it, however great the task may be. The children of Israel, to such numbers as to include four hundred thousand fighting men, went out of Egyptian bondage in a body.

How differently the respective courses of the Democratic and Republican parties incidentally bear on the question of forming a will—a public sentiment—for colonization, is easy to see. The Republicans inculcate, with whatever of ability they can, that the negro is a man, that his bondage is cruelly wrong, and that the field of his oppression ought not to be enlarged. The Democrats deny his manhood; deny, or dwarf to insignificance, the wrong of his bondage; so far as possible, crush all sympathy for him, and cultivate and excite hatred and disgust against him; compliment themselves as Union-savers for doing so; and call the indefinite outspreading of his bondage "a sacred right of self-government."

The plainest print cannot be read through a gold eagle; and it will be very hard to find many men who will send a slave to Liberia and pay his passage while they can send him to a new country—Kansas, for instance—and sell him for fifteen hundred dollars, and the rise.